SAGE was founded in 1965 by Sara Miller McCune to support the dissemination of usable knowledge by publishing innovative and high-quality research and teaching content. Today, we publish over 900 journals, including those of more than 400 learned societies, more than 800 new books per year, and a growing range of library products including archives, data, case studies, reports, and video. SAGE remains majority-owned by our founder, and after Sara's lifetime will become owned by a charitable trust that secures our continued independence.

Los Angeles | London | New Delhi | Singapore | Washington DC | Melbourne

Global Cities

Thank you for choosing a SAGE product!
If you have any comment, observation or feedback,
I would like to personally hear from you.

Please write to me at **contactceo@sagepub.in**

Vivek Mehra, Managing Director and CEO, SAGE India.

Bulk Sales

SAGE India offers special discounts
for purchase of books in bulk.
We also make available special imprints
and excerpts from our books on demand.

For orders and enquiries, write to us at

Marketing Department
SAGE Publications India Pvt Ltd
B1/I-1, Mohan Cooperative Industrial Area
Mathura Road, Post Bag 7
New Delhi 110044, India

E-mail us at **marketing@sagepub.in**

Subscribe to our mailing list
Write to **marketing@sagepub.in**

This book is also available as an e-book.

Global Cities

Past, Present and Future

ZHOU Zhenhua

Los Angeles | London | New Delhi
Singapore | Washington DC | Melbourne

Copyright © Truth and Wisdom Press, 2020

All rights reserved. No part of this book may be reproduced or utilized in any form or by any means, electronic or mechanical, including photocopying, recording, or by any information storage or retrieval system, without permission in writing from the publisher.

First published in 2020 by

SAGE Publications India Pvt Ltd
B1/I-1 Mohan Cooperative Industrial Area
Mathura Road, New Delhi 110 044, India
www.sagepub.in

SAGE Publications Inc
2455 Teller Road
Thousand Oaks, California 91320, USA

SAGE Publications Ltd
1 Oliver's Yard, 55 City Road
London EC1Y 1SP, United Kingdom

SAGE Publications Asia-Pacific Pte Ltd
18 Cross Street #10-10/11/12
China Square Central
Singapore 048423

Published by Vivek Mehra for SAGE Publications India Pvt Ltd and typeset in 10.5/13 pt Berkeley by AG Infographics, Delhi.

Library of Congress Cataloging-in-Publication Data

Names: Zhou, Zhenhua-author.
Title: Global cities: past, present and future/Zhou Zhenhua.
Description: New Delhi, India; Thousand Oaks, California: SAGE Publishing India, 2020. |
    Series: Sage China studies | Includes bibliographical references.
Identifiers: LCCN 2020013242 | ISBN 9789353882990 (hardback) | ISBN 9789353883003 (epub) |
    ISBN 9789353883010 (ebook)
Subjects: LCSH: Cities and towns. | Globalization. | Cities and towns–China–Shanghai. |
    Globalization–China–Shanghai.
Classification: LCC HT119.Z487 2020 | DDC 307.76–dc23
LC record available at https://lccn.loc.gov/2020013242

ISBN: 978-93-5388-299-0 (HB)

SAGE Team: Amrita Dutta, Satvinder Kaur and Madhurima Thapa

CONTENTS

List of Figures	vii
List of Tables	ix
Acknowledgements	xi

Introduction	1
Chapter 1 Literature Review	**16**
1.1. Global Cities Research	16
1.2. The Studies of Global Space	26
1.3. Studies on the World City Network	32
1.4. Dynamic Evolution Research	41
Chapter 2 Definition of Global Cities	**49**
2.1. Methodology of Conceptualization	49
2.2. Global City Paradigm	59
2.3. Clarification of Some Confusing Concepts	77
Chapter 3 Evolutionary Ontology and Its Core Category	**85**
3.1. Ontology of Global Cities	85
3.2. The Core Category	99
3.3. Connected Spaces	105
Chapter 4 Evolution Framework: World City Network	**112**
4.1. Complex Interlocking Network Model	112
4.2. Network Structure	133

Chapter 5 Evolutionary Dynamics	145
5.1. Framework of Dynamics	145
5.2. Influencing Factors	153
5.3. Evolutionary Process	169

Chapter 6 Evolutionary Model	180
6.1. Dominant Model of Evolution	180
6.2. Diversity in Evolution (Types)	194

Chapter 7 Evolutionary Tendencies of Global Cities	210
7.1. Evolutionary Tendencies Based on Network Intensification	210
7.2. Evolution Trend Based on the Isotropic World City Network	220

Chapter 8 The Evolution of Space	242
8.1. Space Expansion	242
8.2. Evolutionary Trend of Spatial Expansion Processes	255

Chapter 9 A Case Study of 'Shanghai 2050' Global City Vision (Part I)	271
9.1. Strategic Drive: Prospects of Globalization	271
9.2. Strategic Opportunities: Reshaping of World Pattern	291
9.3. The Rise of China as Strategic Support	306
9.4. Shanghai's Endogenous Foundation for Global Cities Evolution	321

Chapter 10 A Case Study of 'Shanghai 2050' Global City Vision (Part II)	331
10.1. Prospects of Shanghai's Evolution to a Global City	331
10.2. Shanghai's Vision of Becoming a Global City	346
10.3. Core Functions of Shanghai as a Global City	359

Bibliography	381
About the Author	425

LIST OF FIGURES

5.1	Relationship between Selection Unit and Selection Environment	152
6.1	The Evolution of Global Cities	185
6.2	The Common Process of the Evolution of a Global City	189
6.3	Types of Global Cities in Different Combinations	198
6.4	Types of Evolution Based on Connectivity	204
6.5	Two Types of Position in Correlated Network Structures	205
6.6	Types of Evolution Based on Correlated Structures	209
7.1	Vertical Hierarchical Organizational Network	223
7.2	Heterarchical 'Universal' Structure	226
9.1	The Share of New Economies in Global GDP and Consumption	294
9.2	Projection of China's Capital Deposit in the Next 30 Years (in Billions of RMB)	307
9.3	China's Employed Population Forecast for the Next 30 Years	311
9.4	Forecast of China's Potential Economic Growth Rate in the Next 30 Years (Unit: 10,000)	311
9.5	Regional Headquarters of Multinationals in Shanghai 2004–2015	329

LIST OF TABLES

2.1	Global Rankings of Eight Cities in Five Major Flows	71
4.1	Comparison between the Three Forms of Social Organization	138
7.1	Cities with the Highest CCI in 2006 and 2012	230
9.1	Groundbreaking Innovations Marking the Long Waves	276
9.2	Analyses and Predictions on World Economic Growth Based on the Long-Wave Theory	276
9.3	Projections for Asia Economic Growth and Its Share of the World's GDP in 2050	296
9.4	China's Total Population Forecast for the Next 30 Years (Unit: 10,000)	309
9.5	Forecast of China's Economic Growth Rate (%)	313
9.6	Changes of Population and City Area in Major Cities	318
10.1	Top 10 Country's GaWC Connectivity in 2008	334
10.2	Hinterworld Properties of Asia-Pacific Cities	336
10.3	A Comparison between Beijing and Shanghai's Connections	338
10.4	Sectors Where Shanghai Has Stronger Connectivity than Beijing	340
10.5	Sectors Where Beijing Has Stronger Connectivity than Shanghai	341

10.6	Top 20 City-Dyads That Include Chinese Cities	343
10.7	Top 20 City-Dyad Over-Connections That Include Chinese Cities	345
10.8	Relative Strengths of Shanghai and Beijing in City-Dyads with Other Top 50 GNC Cities	348
10.9	Strategic Network Connectivity	351
10.10	Residuals from Regressing Strategic Network Connectivity against GNC	351
10.11	Top 20 GNC Cities Ranked by Top 40 Dyad Memberships	353
10.12	Changes in City-Dyad Connectivity (2000–2010)	354
10.13	Assets under Management (2005–2010)	366
10.14	Size of the Middle Class (2009–2050; Millions of People and Global Share)	366

ACKNOWLEDGEMENTS

Special thanks to Dai Wenchao, Gong Rui, He Wenting, Wang Yuwei and Zhao Zhengting for translating this book into English. Thanks also go to Sheng Wei for providing literature research and bibliography proofreading support, and to the Shanghai International Studies University Summit-Plateau Advanced Interpreting and Translation Project (2017-22000412) for sponsoring the translation.

Introduction

The 21st century is a century of cities. As the forces of globalization and informatization continue to impact, an intertwined world city network (WCN) has been formed by rapidly developing city clusters and transnational connections. The pivotal nodes in this network are global cities, which serve as spatial carriers for the transnational flow and allocation of resources in a globalized world. Global cities have supreme strategic value in the areas of global economy, politics, science and technology, and culture and society. Therefore, global cities research has attracted worldwide interest and attention, becoming a focus in modern academic research, and is considered as one of the major development strategies by some countries.

I.1. RESEARCH BACKGROUND AND SIGNIFICANCE

The joint impact of globalization and informatization has brought significant changes in the modern world, one of which is the increasingly strong connectivity within global network. This connectivity beyond territorial boundaries leads to a reordering of the global political space, bringing geo-economics to the fore. And from the perspective of geo-economics, all countries will be committed to controlling the nodes in the global network as their source of national strength and influence. Against the new context, the strategy for global connectivity management will become a key determinant of whether a conflict will be resolved. As the pivotal nodes of global network, global cities are the faucet controlling the flow of global connectivity, including the connectivity of pipelines, channels, trade routes as well as Internet connectivity. Apparently, those who take control of global cities will have power over the flow of economic connectivity. In that sense, the role of the 'global cities' in formation could even be more important than that of the old nation states (Perulli 2012). For this reason, the rise and development of global cities has been of great significance worldwide.

Early in the 1970s, well-developed global cities were gradually formed in some developed countries, thanks to their national dominance in globalization and world economy, playing significant roles in global connectivity management. As globalization furthers, the world economy is shifting its centre of gravity. As emerging economies continue to grow vigorously in the course of their integration into globalization, a group of new global cities is on the rise, delivering great impacts on the flow of global connectivity. Looking forward to the next 30 years, we will be living in a fast-changing world, where new situations and problems will keep emerging and everything will upgrade, transform and evolve rapidly. These 30 years will be a period of extreme instability, uncertainty and complexity, with changes even faster and at much greater level. This will be an important period for major changes, readjustments and rearrangements of the world order. As a result, in order to adapt to the new changes of situations and achieve further development, global cities, whether well developed or emerging, call for strategic planning for future development.

Healey (2010) once argued that the idea of strategic planning for a city should be borne in mind by those related to the exercise of authority and those related to the allocation of resources. Such idea has material effects on people's living conditions and local environments and is critical to the competitiveness of cities in the global context (Newman and Thornley 2005). That is why some well-developed global cities have already been making prospective planning for the next 20–30 years, such as 'New York 2050', 'London 2030', 'Paris 2050', 'Chicago 2040', 'Seoul 2030' and so on. For new global cities from the emerging economies, it is even more critical to catch the wave of the changing global environment and seize the strategic opportunity brought by world development. By scientifically evaluating their powers in the world arena and their positions in the global economic pattern, and by leveraging strategic resources and social dynamics, they should pick their suitable pathways to become well-established global cities. As one of the main engines powering the growing world economy, China has become increasingly prominent in the global arena. The next 30 years will be a critical period for China to realize the 'Chinese Dream', namely the great rejuvenation of the Chinese nation. As the influence of global cities is on the rise, China will become a key player in global connectivity management. Shanghai, one of the rising global cities in China, plays an important role in realizing the 'Chinese Dream', and it needs far-sighted thinking and strategic insight to plan its future development. To this end, Shanghai has carried out a 2050-oriented development strategy study to work out approaches towards outstanding global city and a clear framework for sustainable development, so as to promote social consensus and cohesion, to put strategic thinking into practical action and to ensure the continuity and comprehensiveness of major initiatives and policy implementation.

The research towards city development strategy has its own research paradigm, its emphasis on trend forecasting, target research, scenario analysis, etc., and such paradigm should be built on a certain theoretical framework. Otherwise, the research could be no better than a series of illogical text and subjective arguments, with no scientific value to make any prediction. For research into development strategy of the well-established or emerging global cities, the global cities theory is an adequate theoretical framework. In this framework, methods for analysing characteristics and functions of global cities network, global city regions and network spaces can provide immediate support, the most important of which is the dynamic evolution theory of global cities. However, current researches applying this framework seldom include the theory of dynamic evolution, which diminishes the support provided by the framework. Specifically, these researches have the following problems:

1. Failure to factor in the mechanism of future development of global cities to figure out the overall development pattern due to a lack of ontological grasp of the dynamic evolution theory.
2. Failure to catch the core factor affecting the future development of global cities due to fragmented analysis on the development trends

caused by a lack of systematic grasp of the major variables of the dynamic evolution of global cities.
3. Failure to make sound judgements through historical and logical analysis due to highly subjective research goals caused by a lack of grasp of the dynamic nature of the evolution process of global cities.

More or less can these problems be spotted in the current strategic researches on global cities, and they may have become a prevalent issue. This, in turn, has highlighted the significance of the global cities' evolution theory. It is necessary to conduct in-depth research into this theory, so as to build a dynamic evolution framework for the strategic research of global cities and provide further researches with more theoretical guidance and support.

Meanwhile, as for the global cities theory per se, dynamic evolution research constitutes a crucial aspect of the in-depth study and improvement of the theory. It can be concluded from the research literature on global cities that early qualitative research usually rested on the summary and comparative analysis of observation, directly extracting simple connections among global cities against the background of globalization. This qualitative research method focused on establishing a research framework of the function and hierarchical structure of global cities and had led to many academic findings on explaining the role of global cities in economic globalization, and the mechanism behind their unique influence. Later, as the academic pendulum swung, researchers started to explore the network and flows of global cities from the perspective of transnational intercity relations and greeted a wave of correlation analysis challenging the global cities theory (Derudder 2008). Researches base on this new theory and its empirical insights view global cities as main nodes in flux in the global network, with a focus on the intercity network structure, and have produced some ranking of global cities by measuring the intercity links through empirical studies. Researches of this kind have boomed in quantity in recent years, developing various methods to depict from diverse aspects the strength and property of the connections among global cities, promoting the numbers and the diversity of the cities being analysed, and have deepened the academic understanding of global cities. During this period, some dynamic analyses have been put forward. For instance, both Jacobs (1969) and Castells (1996) stressed, at different times and on different theoretical bases, that a city should be viewed from a progressive perspective, thus laying the foundations for the dynamic analysis of global cities. But their argument was based on the understanding of 'how cities function', and, therefore, it only paid more attention to the major characteristics displayed by a city formed under an orderly mechanism. Although there were some other dynamic analyses, they were usually conducted in traditional methods and were limited to the historical perspective on how global cities came into being. For instance, Tilly (1992) explained the formation mechanism of cities and their systems from the perspectives of both capital accumulation and capital centralization, and by adopting this analytical framework he made some tentative analysis on the specific historical developmental pathways of global cities' systems. This research draws our attention to the city development's dependence on pathways and puts pathways as a key variable in the ensuing comparative studies. Some of the researches have also conducted comparative analysis on the change based on temporal sequence but failed to give sufficient explanation for the dominating variables that led to such change, or merely analysed these changing variables as irrelevant units rather than as a whole. Overall, current research on global cities is in nature based on a static comparative analysis framework, with a few dynamic analyses at most, but no evolutionary analyses. Some scholars have also realized the shortcomings of comparative static analysis and noted that global urbanization should not only focus on the uneven nature that (re)emerges in the contemporary globalization but also dissect this uneven process. Sadly, this is, to a large extent, absent (Short 2004). Robinson (2002) pointed out even more sharply that global cities should be studied from a position off their maps. Therefore, if we could further expand our research to include dynamic evolution and to construct a basic framework for the dynamic evolution of global cities, the whole picture of the evolutionary trajectory of the coming and going of global cities will be complete. This is of great significance to enrich the concept of global city as well as improve and deepen the global city theory.

I.2. RESEARCH FOCUS AND OUTLINE

This book attempts to explore the evolution of global cities, a dynamic process involving the formation, rise, development and tendency of global cities. Specifically, the ontology and background conditions of the evolution of global cities are discussed; the evolution of global cities is compared to that of species and is studied under the theory of evolutionary dynamics, based on which the evolutionary model and form of global cities are analysed. In the final part of this book, Shanghai is studied as a typical case for the evolution of global cities since Shanghai aims to build itself into a global city before 2050.

To develop a theoretical framework of the evolution of global cities, we need a simplified paradigm for the research of global cities. First of all, we need to figure out its ontological foundation so as to express more clearly the intension of global cities and to develop a deep understanding of some basic issues, such as what global cities are? How they come into being? What impetus is behind their development? And what their characteristics are? If the intension of global cities is not stated clear, it will be hard to identify variables affecting their evolution and study the interaction among variables. If the definition of the evolution of global cities at the ontological level is not clear, it will be impossible to reveal the nature of this dynamic process and develop a theoretical framework. Therefore, it is of great importance to propose theories of global cities based on definition and expression of their intension at the ontological level. Only by proposing theories down to the ontological level can we differentiate various epistemologies and research methods of global cities, thus avoiding futile debates over the basic concepts of global cities and maintaining the major theoretical framework of the global cities research even if there might be controversies over empirical data based on instrumentalism. As a matter of fact, discrepancies among different theories can be well settled through discussion at the ontological level because this is how evolvement or development of a theory comes from. After ontological theorization, this book sets out on a core category that can reflect the nature and characteristics of global cities—connections, laying a solid foundation for the development of a theoretical framework of the evolution of global cities and avoiding conceptualization of global cities. Based on connections, key concepts such as the existential space (shift from geographic space to space of flows) and the manifestation (global cities network) of global cities are introduced. These key concepts reflect the prerequisites needed for global cities to come into being, to develop and to function and, therefore, form the theoretical framework for the evolution of global cities. Finally, this book gives a definition of global cities and reveals its unique characteristics in this modern world.

In this book, a fundamental theoretical framework of global cities is developed to explain the change of variables over time and to provide a theoretical view to understand the dynamic process of the evolution of global cities. To this end, this book first identifies and chooses a group of major variables for the evolution, aiming to figure out what these variables are and how they interact to accelerate the formation and development of global cities. Second, this book emphasizes the importance of considering the evolution of global cities as differential and dynamic developmental pathways caused by various combinations of these major variables (Olds and Yeung 2004). In other words, these main variables have different combinations that can have an impact on a certain city, giving it a unique pathway to evolve. In order to carry out an in-depth study on the intension of global cities network as well as intercity network, the perspectives and motivations of socio-economic actors in the global city network are included for analysis. Finally, this book discusses how a global city, formed under an orderly mechanism model, should define its role in the future and create its own unique characteristics.

A case study on the 'Shanghai 2050' strategy is explored under the analytical framework of the evolution of global cities. The rationale behind the selection of this case goes as follows: on the one hand, although the theory, as an abstract summary of numerous practices, features universality and the case analysis of historical evolution, in particular, plays an essential role during the development process, the power of a theory lies in not only interpreting the past and the present but also predicting the future. Therefore, the theory of the evolution of global cities should also involve the case studies to future evolution so that the projected results can be utilized to verify and revise the theory in turn. Unlike the case analysis of historical evolution based on textual research, the future-oriented one in effect examines the predictive force of the theory via guiding and supporting the strategic studies on global cities. On the other hand, Shanghai is chosen to be researched as a case due to its typical significance. The US weekly *TIME* once commended Shanghai in a special coverage, 'Shanghai! Inside the World's Most Happening City', that Shanghai, 'the world's love child, a hybrid of history, is stepping out again, with not just Chinese but global aspirations'. 'No metropolis better captures the striving spirit of the times' and 'no place has the kind of energy that Shanghai does'. 'The civilization from which it draws strength is five millennia old'. 'But Shanghai, as a city, is only 150 years young, a patchwork of East and West the vitality and optimism of which embody the very essence of the future. Who can deny Shanghai's role as the 21st century's most happening city?' Of course, the remark focuses only on the city's unique characteristics. Had it been put against the backdrop of a rising China in the world family in the next 30 years, Shanghai's rise and its position in the WCN would be relevant to some significant historical changes, including the reconstructions of world economy and global cities network. The thrive of Shanghai represents not only the rise of global cities in emerging economies like China but also the shaping of a new type of global cities in the future that profoundly reflects the new changes and characteristics of the globalized space. Probing into the 'Shanghai 2050' strategy requires considering a variety of influencing variables, involving globalization, world pattern reshaping, China's rising, global cities development, Shanghai city genes and the vision and core functions of the evolved Shanghai. This study attempts to debunk the myth that individuals' subjective desires, namely 'what human beings expect to do' and 'what human beings want', bring the evolution of Shanghai as a global city in the future. Instead, such evolution depends on the strategic environment, strategic opportunities and the driving forces faced by Shanghai, as well as its ability to respond and innovate. Based on these premises, Shanghai needs to learn from its history of development, plan for the future and systematically factor in these interconnecting major variables to simulate a dynamic evolutionary process, making preliminary analysis on its short-term tasks to complete and long-term core functions to perform, thus calculating its possibility of becoming a global city.

I.3. RESEARCH METHOD

The theoretical research of the dynamic evolution of global cities studies the evolving pathways, evolving speed and evolving direction of global cities. Since the evolution of global cities is a complex phenomenon that demands theoretical explanation from different perspectives, generally a set of approaches are adopted.

1. **Structure–process approach:** The evolution of global cities brings about a 'new world' in which many phenomena change in an idiosyncratic way, both in time and in space, leading to the emergence of new business forms during the economic process, due to which new entities may come into being. Therefore, the evolution of global cities is in nature a temporal transition in structure rather than a quantitative expansion of urban areas, thus, the structure–process method is required to identify the relative importance of economic activities and their functions based on differences and diversity. Since their differences are diachronic and persistent instead of random, the structure–process method can be used to analyse an internal relationship, namely the casual relationship, formed by the evolution of global cities. To be specific, the structural causality is related to the way of organizing, namely how different sectors of global cities have coordinated into a whole, while process causality, an analysis method, is employed to understand the dynamics of diachronic changes of global cities.
2. **Population approach:** Since the regularity that dominates the behavioural diversity changes during the evolution of global cities can only be summarized by observing a group of cities, population approach is often adopted to analyse an actual group of cities instead of a single city. By collecting a set of research subjects for descriptive study, population approach is able to explore regularity from a group of cities rather than from any single city. Therefore, when we explore the rise and development of a single city, we should also take into account the study of the general evolutionary process of the group of cities that it belongs. The population approach is different from typological approach in that the former one holds that diversity, real and consequential, is a prerequisite

for changes, while an assumption of typological approach is that the diversity within a group of cities is relatively small, and all deviations from the ideotype are only contingencies. Population approach measures the influences of different statistical characters within a group of cities upon evolution, namely the changing rates of a certain behaviour within the observed group, thus reflecting the typical core characteristics of the evolution of global cities.

3. **Taxonomy approach:** The concept of global cities consists of many entities with emergent characteristics at the ontological level, so there are no standard measurements for global cities. For example, within the designated framework of external constraint, the adaptability varies in different cities, so there are no standard measurements. Moreover, since this constraint evolves through generation time and physical time, it reflects different environment pressures in different periods; in turn, it proves that this is not necessarily a unified world. Therefore, other than the descriptive study and case study for individual phenomenon, this research adopts another formal approach—taxonomy in understanding the evolution of global cities. In this approach, certain phenomena of global cities in the spatial and time dimension are classified into natural categories, as their behaviours conform to some (phenomenological) laws in the sense of empirical rules. The taxonomy approach emphasizes differences rather than similarities between cities, thereby avoiding the aggregation of all standards. In fact, the aggregation problem appears in the synchronic analysis of the global city phenomena, but the evolution of the global cities belongs to the diachronic dimension. As a result, it is necessary to use the taxonomy approach to sort out the differences between cities.

4. **Narrative approach:** As what was mentioned earlier, the understanding of the temporal evolution of global cities must rely on the analysis of its structure. However, it is impossible to measure and aggregate the structural elements with one unified standard, so this research also needs to apply the narrative approach to include the influence of time, and derive a historical way from the interaction of different time dimensions. Therefore, it is necessary to apply the narrative approach to analyse the evolution of global cities. This descriptive research connects the casual mechanism,

which studies the universal laws, with the description of distinctive features. It also combines various theoretical statements about a single mechanism under a network of ideas that are arranged in an informal and non-accidental way and keeps a balance between induction and deduction. As new phenomena keep emerging, it is necessary to apply the induction approach. If the emergence of such new phenomena is structuralized during the research, especially when the synchronic process was integrated into the diachronic analysis at the final stage, the mechanisms of structure selection can be analysed under the deductive model.

5. **Analogy approach:** Due to certain common elements and general characteristics, analogy method to some extent, in particular the adaptive evolution method, can be adopted during the study of the evolution of global cities. For example, global cities can be analogous to a biological organism, and features such as diversity, variation and selection mechanisms can be applied to the study of the evolution of global cities. This interpretation of the evolution of global cities by means of analogy is useful and relatively common, but limitations should be noted for the reason that human free will exists in the evolution of global cities which makes its adaptive evolution process different from that of a biological species. Moreover, the characteristics of the selection behaviour of the relevant actors, shaped by the memory (gene) of the prior selections and the predictions for the future in the selection process, must play a role in the evolution process. But such selection cannot be rational in the general sense, nor can it be that all actors play a role in the evolution process in the same way. In fact, different predictions made by different actors are the core of the process of evolutionary mutation, and innovation or innovative strategies made by these actors promote idiosyncratic predictions. Therefore, to decipher the evolution of global cities requires an approach not found in other applied disciplines. This approach is not like biological studies in nature, and analogical method of the latter can only be used partially or locally.

In addition, there are some theoretically appropriate evolutionary research methods, but putting them into practice can be very difficult.

Take, for example, the replicator-equation-based statistical method; this equation models the distributive trend of the position of global cities in the global network. The relative position of global cities depends on how their special selection characteristics are distributed around the current population average. All dynamic movements obey the principle of 'staying off the average value'. In this sense, global urban evolution could be described by theories from statistical theory (Horan 1995). However, since the evolution of global cities cannot be viewed as a process of something that converges towards a point of attraction, it cannot be described through the calculation probability. Rather such evolution should be viewed as a temporal evolvement of statistical 'moment' of the total distribution under the pressure of selection and development. In other words, the purpose of the replicator-equation method is to find explanation to the evolutionary transition based on the 'moments' of the population by using statistical distributive characteristics. However, due to difficulties like building large-scale database and so on, such statistics-based approach has always been a daunting and almost impracticable task in global cities research. Thus, this method has not been used in this study.

To conduct case study or strategic study on the evolution of global cities, one important step is to make prospective analysis based on diachronic transitions of and synchronic interactions among major variables affecting and regulating the evolution of global cities, as well as dynamic analysis based on the impact lag process of the evolution following adjustment of the major variables. Therefore, we also adopted approaches such as multi-view observation method based on multiple parallel reality, system integration method, eclectic method based on uncertainty of the research, historical–logical deduction method, macrohistoric level method and so on.

I.4. RESEARCH HIGHLIGHTS, INNOVATIONS AND LIMITATIONS

Since the evolution of global cities is a practice-based process, the evolutionary theory of global cities essentially stems from the growth of practical knowledge and its high-level abstraction. However, the growth of ideas (theory) doesn't only depend on the growth of practical knowledge; instead, ideas can achieve self-development based on the existing ones as an autocatalytic process in which ideas beget ideas. This is the so-called dynamics of idea creation. In this sense, the evolution of global cities is also driven by the growth of ideas (theory). However, production function for ideas shows that existing ideas have limitations, and what is worse is that the stock of ideas about the dynamic evolution of global city is not sufficient and thorough. Moreover, despite the non-rival property of information that an idea can be used any number of times, applying more research efforts to a given stock of ideas will eventually lead to diminishing returns (Machlup 1962), which is the main challenge we face in studying the evolution of global cities. To address it, we must make greater innovation and breakthroughs in theory.

In the research, the preliminary work is to review a large number of literatures on global cities, which means to grasp the development of previous theoretical research on global cities, categorize different theories and viewpoints, and to explore interrelations between various viewpoints. By doing so, we need to create a simple paradigm of global cities theory instead of simply applying the existing research results. We will:

1. Make a systematic combination of theories and viewpoints on global city, which means not only to combine the consistent and complementary ones but also to reconfigure the inconsistent ones.
2. Tentatively make an ontological definition of global cities and define its core category, regardless of their maturity or evolutionary stage. Such attempt is rarely seen in the existing literature.
3. Outline a simplified paradigm of global cities theory, providing new insights into the evolution of global cities.

The effort to establish a theoretical framework for the evolution of global cities requires creative and tentative exploration. In this book, efforts have been made to fully discover and elaborate on the mechanism of systematic selection, because the theory of the evolution of global cities is supposed to cover not only the random mutations or disturbances experienced by the variables or systems but also the mechanism by which the existing mutations are systematically screened. The evolution of some global cities is greatly driven by population selection, and the selective criteria of which is an extremely complicated mechanism to probe into. Only when these criteria are clearly identified can the theory of evolution generate sound explanations or, to some extent, predictions. Otherwise, its explanatory power will be limited. Besides, the major elements of the evolution of global cities research, namely the visions and predictions over new development, and the creation of theory and model of scalable activities, will be tested in practice, because the evolution of global cities is influenced by inseparable factors such as individual learning, organizational adaptation and environmental selection. It is, thus, crucial to find out how the global cities respond to a number of exogenous changes at national and global levels and what the endogenously generated initiatives dominated by the creation of new economic activities and functions are. As such, it requires a comprehensive research on the exogenous stimuli, an in-depth analysis of the new economic activities and its function creation, as well as the relationship between them. Attention must also be paid to the inertial impacts of evolution, as it gives the survivors from the evolution a lasting competitiveness. Furthermore, attempts have been made to clarify the interdependence between the three basic forces that propel the evolution of global cities, which cannot be reduced to merely the selection towards behavioural variations, microscopic diversity or functional transition patterns. Factors affecting their developmental process must be taken into consideration; otherwise, the evolutionary framework will be seriously flawed. And it is through such developmental process, a city can achieve its innovation in economic activities and functions. The relationship among the three forces depends on whether the 'better' approach to economic development can become more valued over time. This research also seeks to figure out the role the institutional framework plays in evolution of global cities and particularly its practical value for the development from a dynamic point of view, because these institutions and organizations have also undergone an evolutionary process of mutation, selection and development. Given this, the evolutionary framework should include both the evolution within the institutional structure and that of the structure itself.

After the theoretical framework of the evolution of global cities has taken its initial shape, we will attempt to apply the framework to the case study of the future evolution of Shanghai as a global city. Strategic researches set developmental vision or goals for a city by referencing to its history or to the traditional thoughts in historical studies that assume that the past and the future are symmetrical under an invariable law, or by comparing an external system such as cities with a relatively high frequency of being researched or by simply projecting subjective judgements. By following the key laws of evolution, the relatively certain variables out of uncertainty, and the main evolutionary trend out of two complex choices, this research answers questions like what Shanghai would possibly be like in the future, what strategic position it should take and what 'essential' work should be done to realize its goal.

Due to the limited understanding of the research subject and the challenges that come with the innovative approaches, the research is still a preliminary attempt, where the paradigm of the theory of global cities is only being incompletely and generally explained, and further in-depth insights and detailed illustration are required. The analytical framework of the evolution of global cities, though having generally covered the key points, is still not a complete theoretical system. These problems are left to be resolved by more in-depth studies on the evolution of global cities. After all, the research is too enormous and difficult to be carried out by individuals alone; the establishment of a complete evolutionary theory requires continuous research and joint efforts.

Literature Review

As a dominant aspect of global cities theory, the evolutionary study of global cities answers the questions of what a global city is on the ontological level, what the condition or background is for the selection, what drives a city to develop and how a city evolves with a certain mechanism. As evolutionary research of global cities isn't officially an independent academic sub-field, different theories and insights should be selected and summarized from subject-related publications in global cities studies. More importantly, global cities research itself is in the early stage of development, with ontological concepts of the global cities to be defined and theoretical problems on spatial structure to be addressed. For these reasons, the literature review part covers an extensive range of sources.

1.1. GLOBAL CITIES RESEARCH

Global cities research has been ongoing for decades since the 1970s, and the current literature provides various definitions for this concept and even uses different terms (e.g., global cities and world cities). Many researchers considered that these two terms meant the same thing, but some disagreed and advocated a clear distinction (e.g., Sassen 1991). I prefer to use the term 'global city' (the reasons will be explained in Chapter 4). But in the literature review section of this book with citations of other author's works, these two terms are considered as interchangeable. Over the past 40 years, global cities research has extended its reach and evolved into a new paradigm which uses various methods and combines quantitative and qualitative analysis, and is, thus, totally different from the traditional urban studies. In traditional urban studies, intercity relations are explored through analysing national urban systems. Usually, a hierarchical urban structure will be established based on NoSQL databases of national census and the size of a city's population, as such cities are examined through the perspective of a whole nation, and the exploration of intercity relations are limited within national territory. That's why traditional research failed to capture the development pattern of global cities such as London and New York under the backdrop of economic globalization.

1.1.1. Development of Global Cities Studies

The concept of global city was brought up before the 1970s. Drawing on the seminal work of Geddes (1915), Hall (1966) defined world cities as 'certain great cities in which a quite disproportionate part of the world's most important business is conducted'. He was mainly inspired by regional research in the realm of traditional urban studies, but didn't capture the essence of what we now call a global city. Global cities studies emerged in the 1970s under the following circumstances: first, the collapse of Bretton Woods system in 1971 drew researchers' attention to the global financial market and then big cities which served as international financial centres. Second, with the emergence of multinational corporations (MNCs) and new international division of labour (NIDL), researchers turned to explore cities' functions of control and centralized management and their roles as a hub of enterprise headquarters (HQs). Third, airlines operated more international flights that connect major cities all over the world. The aforementioned trends are part of globalization, and global cities serve as a window to understand these historic changes. That's why a wealth of vibrant research on global/world cities have been conducted.

Early research on global cities were 'economy oriented', and mainly focused on the exploration and establishment of the new world economic map (Frbel, Heinrichs and Kreye 1977). Hymer (1972) studied cities all over the world using the method of political economy and found that with the emergence of MNCs, high-level decision-making of companies tended to concentrate in a few major cities. He proposed the correspondence principle: the centralized control in multinational companies is consistent with that in the international economy. In this way, major cities of the world will become the centres of high-level strategic planning, and a new urban hierarchy will take shape, which means a few key cities in developed countries where high-level decision-making activities are concentrated will be surrounded by some regional-level secondary cities. Cohen (1981) took heed of companies' demands for advanced producer services (APS) and the connection between the emergence of these new demands and the rise of global cities. He, therefore, expanded Hymer's research interest on multinational companies, and viewed global cities not only as the centres of HQs but also as the hubs of international banking and strategic enterprise services. He advocated that only places with an extensive network of international business institutions could be called world cities. This is a new strategic role for global cities—the centre where multinational companies can control and coordinate the new international system. At the same time, Cohen described the global system and its internal hierarchical order by combining the organizational structure of MNCs and urban networks in his comparative empirical analysis. Heenan (1977), who was the first to put forward the term of global city, clearly stated that he 'pays attention to the emerging phenomenon of global cities', connected the rise of global cities with the world economy and believed that the globalization of multinational companies and regional organizations were generating the 'need to create global cities' and, therefore, the existence of global cities was an inevitable outcome. Likewise, Reed (1981) saw cities as international financial centres. These early exploration serves as the foundation of the current global cities studies.

In the 1980s, a theoretical framework for the study of global cities was put forward, and two important researchers, Friedmann (1986) and Sassen (1991), spearheaded this new round of development. Friedmann (1986) proposed the famous hypothesis of world cities on the basis of economic methods: (a) the integration of a city into the world economy is a decisive factor for the structural changes that take place within it; (b) world cities are 'basing points' in the spatial organization and articulation of production and market, and the location for the concentration for international capital. The resulting linkages make it possible to arrange world cities in a complex spatial hierarchy; (c) the global control functions of world cities are directly reflected in the structure and dynamics of their production sectors and employment; (d) world cities are major sites for the concentration and accumulation of international capital; (e) world cities are points of destination for large numbers of domestic and/or international migrants; (f) world city formation brings into focus the major contradictions of industrial capitalism—among them spatial and class polarization; (g) world city growth generates social costs at rates that tend to exceed the fiscal capacity of the state. Therefore, he narrowly defined the world cities as a limited number of interrelated control points needed by the increasing economic and geographical complexity of economic globalization through the power and control of MNCs. Friedmann's hypothesis of world cities quickly became the foundation of many studies on urban development in economic globalization. Sassen (1991) explored global cities from the perspective of the strategic function of APS, emphasizing that global cities acted as the access point for producers to enter the global economy, and geographically adjacent business service companies served complementary functions. At first, Sassen only listed London, New York and Tokyo as global cities, and later expanded the list to include a group of 20 cities, whose vital role in global economic development was explored (Sassen 2002b).

A large body of literature has emerged since the 1990s when global cities studies began to thrive. For example, Knox and Taylor (1995) and Massey (2007) attempted to establish and extend the theoretical framework of global cities studies. Short et al. (1996), Beaverstock et al. (2000) and others developed methods to measure the formation of world cities. Hill and Kim (2000) and other researchers examined some mainstream assumptions. Wang (2003) and Hamnett (2003) provided insightful views in their well-selected case study on world cities. In sum, a large number of perspectives, structural narratives and different methodologies were produced during this period.

On the other hand, global cities studies have received some criticism. Brenner (2004) argued that Friedmann and Sassen's perspectives mainly came from their attempt to understand contemporary economic development and were not developed from the study of cities per se. One of the main limitations of their study is a lack of a solid theoretical foundation. They only proposed a vague presumption on hierarchy, and their conviction of what cities are and how they relate to each other remain untested. In addition, Friedmann's 'World City Hierarchy' was identified as a mainstream structure, but the actual normative hierarchy is a 'materialized theory' with seven standard lists. Similarly, Sassen's (1991) definition of global cities is still based on the idea of hierarchy. This world city hierarchy uses the classic 'materialization theory' approach to evaluate the importance of a city, focusing on the concentration of the city's companies rather than the interrelations between different companies. Smith (2001) criticized that 'global city' was an inappropriately materialized social concept, providing little help to understand the increasingly urgent issues raised by the global cities themselves. In particular, he asserted that the economic bias found in this paradigm and its pursuit for a fixed urban hierarchy 'should be discarded', and 'the (global) flow is diversified and frequently contradictory, because debates on global cities will inevitably spur social polarization'.

1.1.2. Analysis of the Modern World System

The analysis of the modern world system serves, in a sense, as the theoretical premise of global urban studies. In fact, many proponents of global cities studies draw their knowledge, more or less, from Wallerstein's analysis of the modern world system.

Christaller (1933), a researcher on traditional urban theories, proposed the renowned 'central place theory', an urban location theory that purports to explain the interrelationships between sizes, functions and hierarchy of cities. He also developed a hexagonal model of the relations between the size and order of a city as the optimal distribution pattern of services within a system of central places. His theory focused on the economic development model confined to the linear, binary territory relationship between regions and nation states. In contrast, Wallerstein (1974), an American researcher, developed a theory of modern world systems on the basis of the dependency theory and studied social changes from the perspective of an overall world system encompassing all countries. He focused on the world economy instead of national economies, and analysed how core–periphery alteration in the process of capital accumulation had shaped the capitalist world system by looking at the dynamic imbalance in spatial development. He emphasized on cycles of expansion and contraction of world economy, specifically Kondratieff cycles (each spanning about 50 years), and the longer hegemonic cycles. In the latter, Wallerstein (1984) proposed an influential view that there existed three hegemonic or dominance cycles throughout the history of the modern world system: a Dutch cycle in the 17th century, a British cycle in the late 18th and 19th centuries and an American cycle in the 20th century. Geographically, such hegemonic cycles follows a core–periphery pattern: the core is closely related to high-tech, high-wage and high-profit economic input and output (e.g., the core role of a leading company in the management of a commodity chain), while the periphery is related to the opposite, that is, low-tech, low-wage and low-profit situation. These economic processes typically lead to geographical concentration and isolation, in step with the evolution of market forces, access barrier and chain governance mechanism. As such, the core areas dominate the economic expansion and the periphery areas experiences stagnation or contraction. In this core–periphery pattern, the core areas consist of a complex economic structure that can dominate and create simple peripheral economic structure to satisfy its greedy needs. Wallerstein (1979) argued that these structures were not stable and suggested that there is a semi-peripheral area where a relative balance is struck between the core-making and periphery-making process. Semi-peripheral development can explain the rise and fall of some regions and countries in the contemporary history of the world economy.

The modern world system theory is widely used in global cities research. For instance, Friedmann (1986) applied the method of world system analysis in his world city hierarchy theory, classifying cities into those located in core countries and those in semi-peripheral states. According to Friedmann (1986), 'core' cities especially referred to those located in 'core countries'. But in the views of some scholars, although modern world system theory has shifted its focus from national economy to global economy, it was merely a bold and unfounded idea stemming from central place theory, that is, transforming from a bottom-up rural market and a top-down centralized model of the 'national urban system' (Berry and Horton 1970) to a transnational model. Such transformation implied that the global economy was actually seen as a 'mosaic' of national economy with national territory serving as a 'power container'. The hierarchy theory was based on mechanisms such as 'feedback loops' and 'tendency to equilibrium', but it failed to capture the real intercity relationships. Moreover, seeing intercity relations as an integral system encouraged introspective thinking, but cities should not be deemed as a set of separate relations (Taylor 2013). Therefore, the world system analysis has been criticized as a simplistic dualism since it clearly borrowed its core concept from the central place theory, namely the peripheral paradigm. For example, Dicken et al. (2001) criticized that the global commodity chain approach 'is a clear reflection of the world-system ancestry'; Leslie and Reimer (1999) opposed the 'highly binary language', which led to a geographic location at the 'surface energy level'. However, some scholars believed that the earlier criticism might come from a subtle misunderstanding of the core–peripheral concept of the world system, which reflected the deep structure rather than the 'surface', and was far from being only a simplistic 'dual world'. The revised core–peripheral model involved two interwoven mechanism; thus, it was more complicated than the commonly defined geographic structure that used country as a parameter for spatial categorization (Daviron and Ponte 2005; Terlouw 1992). The key is to understand that the core–periphery model doesn't just describe a never-changing geographical territory, but a spatial structure that supports a very dynamic world system.

The core–peripheral model in the modern world system has exerted major impacts on the formation of global commodity chains and city networks, and is, to some extent, derived from the two mechanisms. One of the main reasons to use this model to analyse global commodity chains is that it can track the chains crossing core–peripheral boundaries, so as to find out how values are added and how profits are unfairly distributed during the process. When examining global city networks, core cities in the upper structure are usually defined as global cities and 'global urban area' dominated by the core process, while periphery cities in the lower structure are usually defined as cities and urban areas dominated by the peripheral process. Therefore, the core–peripheral model is crucial for the analysis of global commodity chains and city networks.

1.1.3. Studies on Transnationalism

According to Smith (2001), urban studies should be reformed in a transnational way, and the understanding on what an economic centre is should be changed, so as to respond to the real challenges of the 21st century. Therefore, he proposed the idea of 'transnational urbanism'. The term 'transnationalism' refers to multiple ties and interactions between regions maintained by different yet connected migrants, and, therefore, it is not a concept of binary opposition, for example, opposition between immigrants and stayers, between people inside and outside of the country, and between integration and family communities. Researchers including Vertovec (1999) described a new geography–transnational social space and emphasized simultaneity and multiple transnational social relations within and beyond nation states. This kind of transnational urban space in global–regional networks created by actors without a distinct national identity is being utilized based on new transnational organizational logics (e.g., market transparency). Overall speaking, there are two types of research approaches on transnationalism during the past decade.

The first approach focuses on the work and life of the transnational capitalist class (TCC), (primarily yet not exclusively) including MNC executives, professionals of producer service companies, and bureaucrats and politicians. According to Sklair (2001), these groups of people constitute 'the transnational capitalist class', both because they own and/or control major means of production, distribution and exchange, and because they 'function in the global capitalist system', rather than specific nation states. These groups of people rely on multiple and frequent cross-border connections, with their public status applicable to migrants in multiple nation state relations.

The second approach involves transnational urban life and consists of three research topics. The first is the study of transnational social relations. Smith (2001) saw cities as 'a transnational practice network site against the background of transnational network formation, a social structure setting for social interaction and a medium of power, which reflects the outcome of two-way transnational flow'. Transnational social relations act as an 'anchor' and, at the same time, transcend one or more nation states. The study of transnational urbanism underlines the socio-spatial processes by which social actors and their networks forge the translocal connections and create the translocalities that increasingly sustain new modes of being in the world. During these processes, transnational practices are important because they compel us to think about the location of moving objects. Transnational cities are viewed as 'spaces pregnant with these sorts of power relations, i.e. social relations of domination–accommodation–resistance' (Smith 2005). The second is the study of transnational relations in urban transformation (such as modernization, sanitation and housing reforms). Kenny (2009) held that transnationalism must be considered as

> the product of multiple linkages that connected western cities to one another through the many threads of an elaborate, multidirectional web. The case of urban sanitation and housing reform brought together specialists of different nationalities, revealing the interplay of both local and global frames of reference in this period, and demonstrating how the problems faced by individual cities like Montreal and Brussels, far from being unique, found resonance on a transnational scale.

Benmergui (2009) called for the dominance of 'transnational' thinking, but the idea of the city as an agent of transformation of the individual cannot be imposed on the local and central governments in Latin America. The idea was shared by major groups in Buenos Aires and Rio de Janeiro, which 'were transnationally built through the constitution of networks and the encounter of actors across national and international borders in conferences, entrepreneurial meetings or in multinational organizations like the Organization of American States or the United Nations'. The third is the transnational building. Sklair (2005) thought that the role of the TCC in architecture is that most globalizing cities have looked to iconic architecture 'as a prime strategy of urban intervention'. Presas (2005) also focused on the relationship between globalization and the recent reshaping of urban landscape.

'A new type of building has emerged—the transnational building'. More than just a local office building, the transnational building transcends the city's skyline, interconnecting urban spaces via diverse global flows, and defines the transnational characteristics of the main actors in the production and use of the particular urban space, as well as its function as a node between global flows and local infrastructure. Therefore, another significant characteristic of transnational urban spaces is that they are becoming globally homogenized, standardized and even McDonaldized, which means they are lifted out of the local context.

The earlier research saw cities not merely as a physical structure but as a social environment, not from the perspective of immigration, and from the perspective of social revolution. Wirth (1938) pointed out that 'As long as we identify urbanism with the physical entity of the city... we are not likely to arrive at any adequate conception of urbanism as a mode of life'. The influence of urban life extends far beyond the rural-to-urban migration: it defines contemporary lifestyles and social relations, and sets the metropolis as 'the initiating and controlling center of economic, political, and cultural life'. Therefore, it highly resembles what Massey (1993) described—the local 'natural relationship' arising from the intersection of physics and society. However, in his narration of the changing process of urban architecture and urban landscape, Sudjic (1992) powerfully reminded people that: do not forget the physical existence of the city, which is easily neglected in the academic debates on issues about locality, mobility, social relations and globalization. Another author King (1990) made a similar point from a more historical perspective, advocating that the physical elements of global cities should not be forgotten in academic abstraction, and one should take into account the physical nature of urban style as symbolic power. As described by Bourdieu (1989), this kind of power is a power of utterance built upon the vision of legitimate divisions in other academic disciplines. Therefore, social space is defined as an advantage in one's 'world-making' process when negotiating between typical individuals. To this extent, the physical nature of a city is socially reflected in a great deal of diplomatic activities, since it collects the symbolic images that construct a dialogue with the city and the (intra)city politics.

1.2. THE STUDIES OF GLOBAL SPACE

Globalization is the background of and driving force for the evolution of global cities. As such, the studies of global cities should first break from the shackle of the traditional ideas of national urban hierarchies and look at global cities in the global context, instead of from within national territory. Meanwhile, a structural shift from the study of 'space of places' to the study of 'space of flows' based on globalization is necessary. Hence, researchers on the global cities study showed greater interest in global space and there are a fair amount of studies addressing this topic.

1.2.1. Space of Places and Space of Flows

The complexity science of space emphasizes the need to look at space from different angles. But for a long time, people only focus on space of place. Even when they try to look at space from different angles, their perspectives were all based on space of place. For example, Lefevre (1991) proposed a triad spatial model: lived space, perceived space and conceived space. In his view, lived space forms the basis of our social relations; perceived space is the physical and materialistic environment; and conceived space is the conceptualized space produced by architects, politicians, scientists and any other designers and planners who deal with spatial contours and physical spaces. This model involves three spatial dimensions: distance, function and process. In fact, such space of place views were deeply rooted in the urban studies, in which cities were simply seen as entities with geographic spaces, as proved by the original urban studies in the 1930s by Jefferson (1939), all the way through Davis' (1959) study of megacities (with a population of over 1 million) in the 1950s, to a set of parameters (including the number of HQs, banks, financial institutes and non-governmental organizations [NGOs]) introduced in the second half of the 20th century by sociologists, economic geographers and economists to identify the most commercially, politically and culturally important cities in a region or worldwide. The earlier global cities studies were also largely built upon the monopolistic nature of space of place. The 1990s have seen the rise of new economic geography (NEG), a genre of research pioneered by Krugman (1991) and based on the increasing returns theory. NEG challenged the traditional practice of analysing economic realities on the assumption of constant returns to scale and perfect competition, and, in particular, overcome the limitations of economic spaces. Therefore, it managed to capture the dynamics of the agglomeration of economic activities in geographical spaces and the agglomeration of regional growth. Krugman (1991) proposed a systematically elaborated thinking on increasing returns and tried to develop a new NEG theory. However, in his view, increasing returns were in essence of regional and local nature. NEG has, by using the D-S model of increasing returns in its exploration on space, dug deep into the nature of and interaction among increasing returns, external economies, transport costs, the flow of factors and the relation of input to output, and, thus, played an important role in understanding production, trade and economic development in the context of globalization. Yet it was still based on the assumption of space of places, with no breakthroughs made in this respect.

Global cities, as an expression to indicate global spaces, must go beyond the single spatial dimension of location. In this regard, some scholars stressed the need to consider the spatial transformation related to the evolving regional development theories and use new spatial theories to depict the dynamics of geometrical and regional development. Castells (1996), in his seminal work, proposed to make use of a 'new spatial logic' when analysing the changing nature of contemporary society. He distinguishes the contiguous space of place and the space of flows that allow distant synchronous real-time interactions. The networked space of flows is the major material support for social practices, leading to the transformation from spaces of place to spaces of flows. Cities are defined as the nodes that manage global information and drive innovations for economic growth.

> Some places are exchangers, communication hubs playing a role of coordination for the smooth interaction of all the elements integrated into the network. Other places are the nodes of the networks; that is, the location of strategically important functions that build a series of locality-based activities and organizations around key functions in the network. (Castells 1989)

In such a network, power comes from the ability of controlling flows. Cities, as nodes in the global network, are crucial to the world economy, because they serve as the threshold and range for the free flow of money and ideas. Based on the theory of space of flows, Appadurai (1996) put forward the five scapes of major global flows: technoscapes, financescapes, ethnoscapes, mediascapes and ideoscapes. Technoscapes refer to the flows of technology, software and machinery from MNCs, international organizations and government agencies. Financescapes refer to the rapid flows of capital, currency and securities, and apparently it is achieved not only through the transfer and concentration by financial service providers but also the rapid change of geographical locations for investment and the recoupment of investment. Ethnoscapes refer to the flows of businessmen, clients, tourists, immigrants and refugees. Mediascapes refer to the flows of images and information from print press, television and cinemas. Ideoscapes refer to the flows of ideas and notions. Taylor, Hoyler and Verbruggen (2010) introduced central flow theory featuring non-local inter-urban relations to compliment the urban relational process, while central place theory describes local urban hinterland relations. This new structural concept defines the city as the spatial interaction of continuous network process and degrades its role of nodes in the network. It is very important for two reasons: first, there is no hierarchical structure for global cities. Second, in a network process, all cities will probably be included into the network. This means the focus of study has shifted from cities as physical existence with certain attribute (local characteristics) to cities as the making of a series of inter-urban relations.

However, some scholars found that the metaphor of flows is unsatisfactory, since there were two fatal flaws: first, space is known to be intransitive (Law 2000), while Castells' space of flows refers to the possibilities of connecting time-sharing social practices in different places through technologies and organizational methods, which disrupts the continuity of flows. This discontinuous flow becomes an abstract or material space, which is a self-evident contradiction. Second, the space of flows excludes the causal relationship of spatial structure. In addition, Deleuze and Guattari (1988) pointed out that the flow in Castells' theory is a tool of power rather than a damage to power, which not only counteracts the superficial power in countless flows as termed by Castells but also generates an exterior agency that exercises power in spaces of flows.

1.2.2. Flow Measurement of Space of Flows

Different from the traditional perspective of space of places that emphasizes the agglomeration function, the space of flows focuses more on external connectivity, which is measured by flow. Most researches on this topic saw cities merely as transportation centres. For example, Parnreiter (2002) studied the portal function of cities through examining the flows of major shipping lines and seaports, while Niedzielski and Malecki (2012) studied the flows of railway network. More scholars have sought to examine global air transport network flows (O' Connor and Townsend 2012; Taylor, Derudder and Witlox 2007; Zook and Brunn 2006), since air transport networks usually develop simultaneously with urban systems (Choi, Barnett and Chon 2006). Smith and Timberlake (2001) used multiple network analysis methods to analyse international air passenger flows in the whole year of 1997 and of six different time slots during that year. They found that although New York, Paris, London, Tokyo and some other major European and North American metropolitan cities were the major contributors to the flows, the roles of some other cities had also changed dramatically over the past 20 years. Using air traffic to measure flows and define intercity connectivity has since made it possible to conduct longitudinal studies of intercity flows. Nonetheless, these studies have limitations. First, they rely too much on geographical territory and cannot be applied to some cities where air transport is not the most frequently used means of transportation or even there was no airport at all. Second, the measuring method based only on air transport has excluded some other important flows which are also important to intercity connectivity, like product or information flows through electronic or non-electronic infrastructure networks and other movement of people not achieved by air transport. In addition, air traffic data cover all kinds of airline passengers, so it is not possible to distinguish between business flows and leisure flows, which differ a lot from each other in terms of their way of travel and communication (Limtanakool, Schwanen and Dijst 2007). Last but not least, the analysis of the highly airline-dependent city networks may be warped by some external factors like the location of the airport hub, since some cities might have busy air traffic, but they usually only serve as a transfer point. Therefore, estimation on the network-based flows of hub-and-spoke airports might be deviated. In sum, a more inclusive and refined approach should be developed to examine intercity flows and intercity connectivity when conducting research on city network based on infrastructure and flows. As such, different means of transportation such as planes, trains and automobiles (Batten and Thord 1995) should be combined together to analyse long-range and short-range relationships of different cities in the city network, and new methods should be adopted to distinguish business flows from holiday flows and passengers' destinations from their transfer points. These studies are of great value since they have examined in considerable detail the physical connection and flow measurement of different dimensions between cities in the world city system.

The space of flows exists not only on the physical level but also includes invisible flows of information and knowledge. Seemingly, the importance of information itself in an ICT-driven world is widely recognized in academia, but, still, the topic has attracted little attention from researchers in field of urban and sociological study. Only a few researches focused on intercity information flows in the information age. For instance, some analysed news sources or minutes of meeting on particular topics at a certain time as an alternative way to examine the external relations of a city (Derudder 2006; Pred 1980). As Hillis (1998) pointed out, the flow of information and knowledge was often invisible, but it could be observed by measuring the flow of people, products and objects. Therefore, it is important to promote the research on information infrastructure and its flow measurement. Michelson and Wheeler (1994), in their seminal work, proposed the idea to examine the exchange of information that occurs among and between American cities, in order to reveal how the ongoing process of globalization had affected the ranking of these cities in the system of information exchange. Malecki (2002) and Rutherford, Gillespie and Richardson (2004) established a network among 82 cities in 2002, using data of Internet backbone bandwidth and air passenger traffic. The network is utilized to measure the Internet connection between a pair of cities by the size of bandwidth in mbps. Devriendtl et al. (2011) use the World Wide Web (WWW), a vast and valuable information source, to monitor changes in urban relations, and to quantitatively identify and rank cities by financial criteria. Generally speaking, researchers tended to track the flow of information through infrastructures or media (books, magazines, letters, documents, etc.), rather than the information itself (Michelson and Wheeler 1994). For example, some use the cyberplace (CP) approach (a specific approach that locates physical infrastructure and investigates actual connections between physical points) to analyse the flow of bits (unit of digital data) between spaces. An analysis of how such information flows are networked reveals that the uneven political, economic geographical distribution of Internet-based assets (such as Internet service providers, servers and so on) underpins this virtual world (Dodge and Shiode 2000). The physical location of the Internet's infrastructure provides the basis for such flows, on which an exciting 'borderless world' is built (Ohmae 1990). Indeed, Kellerman (2002) and Bakis, Abler and Roche (1993) also realized that further knowledge of cities and their relative role in a globalized world in the information age would rely on research into tangible information infrastructure, related urban networks and how information flows in between (using the CP approach), together with a qualitative and quantitative analysis of the flow of information using the cyberspace (CS) approach. Network information is not only guided or transported between locations: it does not only neutrally represent a hidden corporeal reality, or an 'information cloud' floating above (de Vries 2006). The CS concept suggests that how information and space appear (either in maps, photos, numerical data, etc.) is related to complex local experiences. Brunn (2003) studied the connections (flow or its quantity) between the four Eurasian cities: Moscow, Istanbul, Tehran and Beijing by examining the number of hyperlinks. Williams and Brunn (2004) used maps to describe linkages between Asia's largest cities and categorize information on 197 cities obtained using the most powerful search engine. Devriendt, Derudder and Witlox (2008) adopted two approaches (CP and CS) to analyse the European intercity information networks.

But generally speaking, research into how traffic between spaces is measured is insufficient and lacking in existing empirical analyses. Alderson and Beckfield (2004) noted the exceeding scarcity of data on economic, political, social and cultural linkages between cities, which is essential in the ideal construction of a multi-relational network to explore and assess the statements of the world city hypothesis. Also, Derudder (2006) noted the prevalent challenges of prioritizing such information flows and linkages that transcend local (physical) attributes.

1.3. STUDIES ON THE WORLD CITY NETWORK

Unlike regular cities, global cities have evolved into nodes in an ever-expanding WCN. The dynamics of these nodes in the WCN shape the way global cities evolve. Therefore, it is important to study the WCN for a better understanding of how global cities rise.

1.3.1. Organizational Paradigm of Global Cities

While Friedmann (1986) and Sassen (1991) emphasized that global cities have risen in a 'city system' or 'city network', which implies how the WCN has come into being, they did not put forward any specifications of the WCN. As a result, most researchers in subsequent years just concentrated on global cities and their attributes. They predicted how much the world would be connected and defined city systems based on place-bound attribute indexes, such as companies' HQs, capital and market size. Also, they built a network hierarchy on the basis of rankings of global cities.

Yet some researchers started to think about a globalized network. Decades ago, Jacobs (1969) noted that a city cannot grow if it only trades with the rural hinterland. In fact, she pointed out that a city seems to always trade with a group of cities. Sheppard (2002) believed that the status of cities is defined by 'their position within transnational networks'. He acknowledged the importance of non-local relations in the formation of cities, because how conditions change in a place does not just depend on 'local initiative' but also on its 'direct interactions with distant places'. Taylor (1997) also found that the world city hierarchy can only be defined in a network. 'So the need for a precise specification of the world city network is obvious. Without it there can be no detailed study of its operation—its nodes, their connections, and how they constitute an integrated whole' (Taylor 2001a). Thus, Taylor et al. (2007) studied how the nodes and hybrids affect each other within the WCN rather than the nodes and hybrids themselves. They illustrated how the nodes are connected in the network to explain non-local relations. Considering the necessity of strategic control of decentralized economic activities and global reterritorialization, Taylor ([2003] 2004) insisted that participants in global cities have achieved strategic control through their network capacity. What matters more is not the cities themselves but intercity relations or the so-called 'global connectivity', especially the quality and strength of the connection. Therefore, researchers on the WCN have assumed that 'cities are situated in a "system," and some cities—as a result of the position that they occupy in this system—are better situated than others' (Alderson and Beckfield 2004).

Since the early 1990s, many researchers such as Camagni (1993) and Yates (1997) have studied intercity flows to better describe the WCN. Despite inadequate relational data and limited empirical studies on WCNs (Smith and Timberlake 1995a), existing research has touched on various aspects of the topic. Going beyond infrastructure and economic measurements, some scholars have been examining the WCN through the lens of participants or institutions, including Brown et al.'s (2010) global commodity chains, Meyer's (1986) international bank network research, Barba and Venables' (2004) cross-border M&As and FDI research (greenfield investment) and Yeaple's (2006) intra-firm trade. Three network models are particularly representative. In spite of their differences in hypothesis and research methodology, they all rely on 'city by firm' data sets to assess how cities are linked through corporate networks.

1. **Multinational firm ownership linkages model:** The model defines city networks by examining the network of ownership relations between the MNC HQs and their subsidiaries because 'a subsidiary owned by a multinational firm in a foreign country is interpreted as a direct interaction between the city where

the headquarters are located and the city where the subsidiary is owned' (Rozenblat and Pumain 2006). It is noteworthy that this model involves the study of corporate structure (Beckfiled and Alderson 2006) and the interlocking corporate directorates (Carroll 2007). Along this research pathway, 'city by firm' matrices built upon geographical positions of the largest multinational firms in the world have been produced, including Forbes Global 500 (Alderson, Beckfield and Sprague-Jones 2010), and the largest European firms (Rozenblat and Pumain 2007). The empirical rationale for this kind of city networks is very simple: it creates asymmetric (from the HQs to subsidiary locations) and values (the number of ownership linkages) intercity matrices. Alderson and Beckfiled (2004) explained that out-degree centrality represents the power of a city network, while in-degree centrality is regarded as the prestige of a city. Of course, there may be some more complicated network analysis tools that could be used, including tools that evaluate the geographic locations in a wholly linked system (Rozenblat and Melancon 2009). In addition, while the basic rationale seems easy to understand, it may become very complicated when it comes to hands-on analysis, because this general research method can be expanded in many aspects. For example, the nodal centralities and linkage structures of cities can be defined, respectively, when different levels of corporate ownership are considered (Wall, Burger and van der Knaap 2011).

In conclusion, the ownership linkage model holds that multinational enterprises (MNEs) are a central agent in the generation of the world city system (Alderson and Beckfield 2004), with a focus on the relationship between HQs versus subsidiaries in the corporate network. Moreover, this model explains the transition from a 'city by firm' relationship to a cross-border command and control one. However, the ownership linkage system, in most times, generates an incomplete and hierarchical city network, for it neglects the irregular distribution of different branches.

2. **Interlocking network model:** On the basis of Sassen's core concept, Taylor and his colleagues at the Globalization and World Cities (GaWC) developed an accurate and standard 'interlocking network' model and based their empirical study on it (Derudder

and Taylor 2005; Taylor 2001a), leading to an in-depth understanding of the WCN and its global–regional tensions. Noting that multinational service firms set up offices in different parts of the world to provide quality service for their consumers, Taylor argues that if a firm does business involving both city A and city B, it can be implicitly interpreted as the probability of the predicted connections being possible in the interactive model, that is, the service quality a client can expect when doing business in a given pair of cities. In this logic, an interlocking network is defined as the relations between a pair of cities in the network, meaning (a) that offices of a given firm are located in the two cities and (b) that these offices are functionally equivalent. The interlocking network model focuses on APS that are proven to represent the 'tip-top' economic activities in the world (Taylor [2003] 2004). This is because producer service firms have become a part of multinational firms in the process of building a basic 'interlocking' world office network and they can use the heterarchical structure when forming a 'smooth' intercity network on the basis of rich empirical analyses.

Certainly, it is only one of the perspectives and methods to examine the WCN. Taylor et al. (2008) also acknowledged that the way in which the GaWC looks at the WCN constitutes an informed, empirically sound evaluation of cities in globalization. However, only global capital services, one of the many factors driving the development of cities, are measured by the GaWC. Moreover, the network projection method the GaWC uses in the study 'expands' the network connections, making it hard to distinguish the 'actual' clusters that closely connect cities in the city network from those in projection functions. In addition, some scholars have had doubts about the interlocking WCN model. First, if cities (nodes) are mere containers independent of vacuum commercial service firms (i.e., they are unrelated/unconnected to one another), any attempt to rank them is inevitably bedevilled by a sorites paradox problem (Smith 2014). Second, the interlocking WCN model overemphasizes even intercity relations, which does little to help better understand uneven relations between the cities (where the offices of a given firm are located). The world system includes the core and peripheral areas, which complement each other (Hopkins and Wallerstein 1977). Furthermore, the connectivity value is based on the size of producer service firms' offices, but size cannot be translated straightforwardly into global importance or into power relations (Parnreiter 2014). Beaverstock (2011) believed that 'a reluctance of the key proponents of the model to focus their energy on researching agency in the networks' leads to 'the impasse in an advancement of theory accounting for the genesis of and nuances in the world city network'.

3. **Dual-mode network model:** Neal (2008) and Liu and Derudder (2012) believed that the city by firm matrices can be considered as a network, a so-called dual-mode network or dual network. A two-mode network consists of two disjoint sets of nodes (i.e., cities and firms). In the two-mode firm network, cities are connected by offices of a given firm, that is, the presence of firms in cities. The dual-mode network involves connections between cities and between firms, helping evaluate a city's position in the city network and a firm's position in the firm network at the same time. Similar to earlier models, the two-mode network model can be used to rank the connectivity of cities. The model can also be applied to capture interactions between cities and firms, and examine hypotheses about how the city network has come into being, which can help deepen our understanding of how specific cities and firms deal with local interactions and observe the world firm network. Dual-mode model doesn't lead to information loss as observed in the network projection model, and simultaneously analyses where companies and cities stand in the corporate network through the use of a complete city by firm database. However, this model has seen limited use by scholars because it often involves a complicated and calculation-intensive process, and seldom results in intuitive findings.

In addition, the most recent trend has been to study pairs of cities, especially the connectivity between them (Taylor, Hoyler et al. 2011). Of course, this is a building block for overall network connectivity evaluations. Some scholars argue that city-dyads constitute the entry point into global city network analyses rather than individual cities. Apart from NY-LON as an identifiable city-dyad, there has been mention of 'PAR-LON' (Halbert and Pain, 2010) for

Paris and London, and 'MIRO' for the Milan–Rome dyad, to name just a few. City-dyad analysis can be taken further using the concept of a city's hinterworld—the geography of a city's connections across the world (Taylor [2003] 2004). Though comprehensive studies on the city network are not many, several attempts have been made (Taylor [2003] 2004). Taylor (2005a) took an important first step in examining city connectivity by analysing four types of networks—economic, cultural, political and social.

1.3.2. City Network Makers

Unlike social networks, the WCN is made up of global cities and globalized cities, which are only physical nodes in themselves, rather than actors or participants to this network. Thus, this is an interlocking network, in which institutions or groups domiciled in these nodes are true actors. They interlock the city through their connections and movement, and, thus, are builders of the city network. Sklair (2001) broadly defined the 'transnational capitalist class' groups as city network builders, including transnational executives, producer service company professionals (primarily, but not absolutely), bureaucrats, politicians and immigrants. Their cross-border movements have created intercity linkages and a new world pattern where cross-locality is increasing being reinforced. Latour (2005) even specially put forward the 'actor–network' theory (ANT) that the WCN is built on combined actions and heterogeneous associations.

However, the mainstream view narrowly defines APS as city network builders, which interlock linkages between cities by mobilizing and connecting comprehensive factors of corporate networks. Initially, Pryke (1994) and Grabher (2001) focused their studies on why APS companies are located in city clusters in a break from the widely used accumulation and location approach in analysing cities' economic functions, markets and innovation. Bagchi-Sen and Sen (1997), building on Dunning and Norman's (1983) eclectic paradigm, analysed the location advantages of different APS in the city. The size and characteristics of markets, market regulation, personnel (skilled workers) and physical assets were defined as essential factors that dictate where international APS companies build their overseas outposts. Besides, they conducted comparative analyses in terms of accounting and advertising industries, and noted the significance of differential international strategies across sectors.

Cooke et al. (2007) further pointed out that APS firms play a special role in promoting interactions within and between the most knowledge-intensive regions around the world. As Pain and Hall (2008) mentioned, APS companies

> occupy a distinct position in the new global division of labour as centres for the generation of knowledge-intensive APS: clustered activities that play a key role in providing specialized services, embodying professional knowledge and processing highly complex information, to other businesses and to each other.

Therefore, they are central to regional innovation and economic development while connecting multiple participants, companies and economic sectors. Pain (2007) also mentioned that APS wholesale functions have a different locational logic from that of other 'hi-tech' and retail business services which have a more dispersed cluster geography. In studies of how APS companies can drive economic globalization, Yeung (2005) was further inspired by calls to open the black box used to represent firms and strategies, and sought to identify: (a) groups of firms that share common strategic objectives; and (b) the different roles of cities in fulfilling these objectives. An issue related to these studies is that it is possible to distinguish between what might be called the ubiquitous presence versus the strategic present approach. For one thing, the Big Four accountancy firms (Beaverstock 1996), major financial institutions (Wójcik 2011) and hybrid producer–consumer services such as temporary staffing agencies (Coe, Johns and Ward 2007) applied to the ubiquitous presence include maintaining a presence in as many cities as possible to achieve the maximum revenue by serving the needs of local clients. For another, advertising (Faulconbridge et al. 2011), architecture (McNeill 2008) and law firms (Faulconbridge 2008) that are more strategic presence-associated are driven by a desire to situate firm offices in the most strategically important locations, with strategic importance being defined by a place's (a) global influence, (b) connectivity to markets and (c) extent to which work in these places is cutting edge based on how it goes global through innovation. In their analysis of the location strategy of Japanese multinationals, Goerzen, Asmussen and Nielsen (2013) noticed a similar change to strategies, and that only certain enterprises prioritize strategically important global cities as their targeted locations.

It's worth noting that city network makers may be defined narrowly or broadly, but the key differentiating factor should be their role in the formation of the WCNs, and in making it different from what there ever was before. Castells (1996), Sassen (2001) and Taylor ([2003] 2004) regarded the WCN that has taken form thanks to APS firms as a combinatorial matrix of substitutable functionaries. Latour's ANT, through decomposition of structure, shows a disposition to locate it within the eventfulness of 'a momentary world... which must be acted into' rather than within the functionalism of 'a contemplative world' that can be controlled and commanded from a distance. Yet while so many writers have settled upon the notions of performance, practice and association as an entry point to research into world cities, they also believe that the illimitable associability of ANT risked annihilating all vestiges of the other. With this in mind, Badiou (2006) focuses on the subtractive approach to ontology (the non-binding force between events), emphasizing that for an event to occur, it must be subtracted from the stabilization of a fully deployed situation, because the place (or structure) itself only gives us repetition. As Badiou (2003) saw it, an event is linked to the notion of the undecidable. If it is possible to decide, its occurrence would be calculated within the situation. The so-called event is not an event, generating nothing other than dull repetition. Doel (2001) argued that global cities are neither commanded and controlled by structural powers nor practised and performed by actor–networks. They are multiplicities. Obviously, a multiplicity is not one. It is a multiple of multiples, whose composition and decomposition can be perpetually reworked. The WCN, therefore, remains in a state of undecidability against the force of domination and normalization, rather than a unity or constancy.

1.3.3. Major Research Directions and Analytical Tools and Methods

The WCN is being examined from different directions and various theories and practices have been developed and integrated. Some scholars have focused on intercity connectivity. For example, Taylor and Walker (2004) and Taylor, Derudder et al. (2011) put forward the notion of urban hinterworld—a targeted approach. Taylor, Catalano and Walker (2002) and Neal (2011) presented the measurement of power differentials. Taylor et al. (2004) and Hanssens et al. (2011) identified and compared different service sectors. Taylor et al. (2012) looked into the strategic network and defined local strategic places. A number of scholars also extended the research into institutions. For instance, Taylor (2005a, 2005b) and Lüthi, Thierstein and Goebel (2010) applied models to non-commercial organizations, another network maker in addition to major APS companies. Krätke (2011), Toly et al. (2012) and Bassens, Derudder and Witlox (2011) added cities as nodes in diplomatic, United Nations (UN) and NGO networks, or applied an adapted model to analyse other network makers. Several researchers expanded the scope of research. For example, Hoyler, Kloosterman and Sokol (2008), Thierstein et al. (2008) and Lüthi et al. (2010) focused on megacity regions (MCR). Taylor and Derudder (2004) and Schmitt and Smas (2012) expanded the research to the world regional level, while Rossi and Taylor (2007), Taylor et al. (2001) and Growe and Blotevogel (2011) focused their research on the country level. Some scholars made real-time comparisons of changes in the WCN. Taylor and Aranya (2008), Derudder et al. (2010) and Hanssens et al. (2011) captured connectivity changes in the WCN, while Pereira and Derudder (2010) identified and explained the determinants of dynamics.

A bunch of analytical tools and methods has been applied in WCN research such as principal component analysis (Taylor et al. 2002), multidimensional scaling (Taylor et al. 2001), discriminant analysis (Taylor [2003] 2004), fuzzy set analysis (Derudder et al. 2003), cluster analysis (Derudder and Taylor 2005) and city-dyad analysis (Taylor et al. 2010, 2012). Some models have been assessed and improved. For example, Liu and Taylor (2011) assessed the robustness of models;

Hennemann and Derudder (2013) adopted an alternative approach to the calculation of connectivity; Neal (2011) differentiated centrality and power, analysed the duality of world cities and firms (Neal 2008) and presented structural determinism in the interlocking WCN (Neal 2012); Rossi, Beaverstock and Taylor (2007) differentiated between 'decision cities' and 'service cities'; Pain and Hall (2006) and Parnreiter (2010) pointed out the need of a qualitative approach.

1.4. DYNAMIC EVOLUTION RESEARCH

A relatively less extensive literature is available on dynamic evolution, scattered in research papers on urban dynamics, evolutionary economics and the process of world city dynamics.

1.4.1. Research into Driving Forces of Urban Growth

Jacobs (1969) divided urban production activities into two types: 'old work' (what people have been doing for a long time and are still doing) and 'new work' (activities that lead to new kinds of goods and services). Instead of representing time—past, present or future, this classification implies the significance of division of labour. More old work means the same division of labour in cities as before, while new work leads to more complex division of labour. Jacobs believed that, given the same division of labour, the simple economic growth driven by repetitive old work cannot be regarded as economic expansion. Although the economy may grow, it essentially involves the same economic activities and structures, and is as simple as it used to be. In the context of more complex division of labour, innovative new work will create new division of labour and change economic activities, structures and complexity, thus promoting the economic growth and contributing to a real economic expansion.

Building on the aforementioned theory, Jacobs (1984) defined two kinds of cities: stagnate and dynamic. The former is a 'passive place' where goods are transported but few economic activities occur and no extra wealth is created, while the latter is the centre of innovation, directly connecting the local production with trade activities.

According to Jacobs (1984), not all cities are dynamic, and only when their economy expands through new work will they become dynamic. That means economic expansion may transform stagnate cities into dynamic ones through import replacement. Import replacement creates economic independence and competition and helps to build trade relations with other cities. Therefore, competitive cities are finally included in the network. Dynamic cities grow as a result of two drivers. One is the multiplier effect of exporting: new work creates new export markets (other cities); and the other is the multiplier effect of import replacement: new work is created in situ by copying to meet local demands (replacing suppliers from other cities), thus replacing imports. As noted by Jacobs (1969), compared with the stable economic expansion brought by the former, the latter brings explosive economic growth, huge progress or even formidable economic power.

Myrdal (1957a) used a region as an example to illustrate the 'circular cumulative causation' theory, namely that any form of causal or interactive circles are cumulative and non-equilibrial. He admitted that endogenous changes may exist and interact with upward or downward circles, but these interactions cannot help achieve an equilibrium in the economy, as 'equilibrium is not stable'. Normally, there is no such tendency towards automatic self-stabilization in the economy system. He stated:

> A change does not call forth countervailing changes but, instead, supporting changes, which move the system in the same direction as the first change but much further. Because of such circular causation as a social process tends to become cumulative and often gather speed at an accelerating rate.

This kind of interaction will change over time, causing chance occurrences to have an enormous, long-lasting impact. Afterwards, the growing internal and external economy in this region reinforces or maintains its economic development.

Dixit and Stiglitz (1977), in their monopolistic competition model, introduced the concept of increased returns and imperfect competition. They believed that the evolution of economic activities is not linear, dominated by non-linear dynamics. Any firm enjoying economies of scale will choose one location to provide their services for a whole country's market. In order to minimize transport costs, a firm will choose a location where there is sufficient demand. However, demand in a specific location depends on the number of firms choosing to do business there. Therefore, according to W. Brian Arthur's path dependence theory, in the absence of external disruptions, this will become a self-perpetuating cycle once an industrial cluster is formed. In a sense, industrial agglomeration was most likely as the product of a series of historical contingencies. If specialization and trade were driven by increasing returns rather than comparative advantages, then it would be highly uncertain which industries cluster in what locations; instead, it would be history dependent. But regardless of the reason, once the pattern of specialization and trade is established, it will remain locked up as benefits of trade build-up.

The NEG theory proposed by Krugman (1991) is based on non-equilibrium economics, and its basic model is non-linear with increasing returns as its theoretical basis. This increase of returns refers to the interconnection between industries or economic activities, which saves costs through spatial proximity or intangible assets in economies of scale. Therefore, Krugman considered spatial agglomeration as the external representation of increasing returns, which is the economic result of spatial concentration in several industries and economic activities. It is also the centripetal force that attracts economic activities to a certain region, thus explaining the dynamics of urban growth. People move to cities for higher salaries and more diverse goods, while factories move to find bigger markets. Therefore, spatial concentration is the basic factor leading to the formation and expansion of cities and regional development. Fujita, Krugman and Venables (1999) used historical methods to emphasize the persistence and accumulation of forces that influence agglomeration. In other words, the development of path-dependent, historical incidents reflects the basic workings of spatial economics evolution.

Krugman's 'core–periphery model' is based on a static framework in which there is no assumption of long-term growth. Baldwin and Forslid (2000) extended Krugman's model by introducing capital and product innovation and by setting long-term growth and selection of industrial sites as endogenous variables of the model. They also explained the effect of long-term growth on spatial distribution of economic activities and discussed integrating different types of economy and its effect on spatial distribution of economic activities. Currie and Kubin (2003) focused on the long-term stability of Krugman's model in continuous time periods, and they adopted discrete time assumptions to discuss its dynamic changes in the short-term framework.

1.4.2. Evolutionary Economics

The modern form of evolutionary economics which emerged in the 1980s is a new paradigm of economic science for studying the creation and transmission of new things in the economic system and the resultant structural changes in the system (Boland 1981; Witt 2001). Winter (1964) pointed out that evolutionary economics, as a theory about becoming instead of being, focuses on dynamic economic changes, studies on those 'changes' and analyses on how to reach equilibrium. Evolution is defined as observable systematic self-transformation (Witt 1993). Alchian (1950) applied non-linear dynamics theory to analyse economic development and Batten, Casti and Johnsson (1987) carried out an in-depth analysis of economic changes and technological changes.

With Darwinism as its theoretical underpinning, revolutionary economics establishes its basic analysis framework based on the three mechanisms of Darwin's theory of evolution, that is, inheritance, mutation and selection. Nelson and Winter (1982) suggested a new research agenda inspired by organizational genetics and created the evolutionary theory of economic change, focusing on the elements of selection and mutation. Hodgson (2002) proposed that research methods should be changed from analogy to ontology. Weibull (1995) and Vega-Redondo (1996) put forward the evolutionary game theory and identified that individuals by heredity demonstrate fixed patterns of strategic interaction in groups. These modes are shown by the relative frequency of interaction by each individual in a group, or by different individuals who have relatively different frequencies of interaction under the same strategy.

Revolutionary economics emphasizes the roles that routine, creativity and imitation play in economic changes, among which creativity is the core. Herrmann-Pillath (1993) proposed the human creativity principle and contended that lying at the heart of evolutionary economics are human creativity, invention and innovation—basic components of human learning for dealing with the real world. The fundamental idea is to prioritize the subjective initiative of humans. Individuals are neither slaves of desires nor screws in machines. Instead, they have human agency. Hodgson (1995) contended that novelties result from individuals' creativity and knowledge of socio-economic structures and their variability and specificity. Witt (1993) underlined that it is vital to evaluate the emergence of novelties as an appropriate concept of socio-economic evolution and their dissemination. Foss (1994) pointed out that revolutionary economics focuses on the emergence of novelties, possible proliferation and transformation of existing structures.

Evolutionary economics underlines the influence of contingency and uncertainty on economic changes and the importance of time and history to the evolution of economics. The existence of time means that economic change is an evolutionary process which not only contains uncertainties and inconsistencies in the future but also includes the constraints from the past on future development. Rosenberg (1982) contended that the uncertainties we mention refer to the unpredictable outcomes or the shortcut to reach goals. These uncertainties have a very important implication: actions cannot be planned. Arthur (1994) and David (1993) emphasized the importance of path dependence to the dynamic economic changes and argued that economic evolution is an irreversible, 'lock-in' process (Cowan 1991).

Evolutionary economics also adopts perspectives of dissipative structures and chaos theory, emphasizing self-organization in the process of evolution (Weise 1996).

1.4.3. Studies on the Dynamics of Global Cities

Early studies on the dynamics of global cities were mainly comparative research on the urban trends in Europe. Hall and Hay (1980) proposed a classic sequence model of urban growth and decline, which was in line with the mainstream literature in urban and economic geography, including access space trade-off models of residential location and related accounts of industrial decentralization. There were three main stages: 'urbanization' (spatial concentration of activity) followed by 'suburbanization' (decentralization and decline in the core) and ultimately 'desurbanization' (dispersal of economic activity scattered into satellite towns and rural areas).

Van den Berg et al. (1982) tested the model they established by analysing population changes in 189 cities in 14 Western and Eastern European countries over the period 1950–1975. They found considerable evidence to support the basic evolution from urbanization to suburbanization and then decentralization and decline. Different countries and cities varied in the timing of these phases of development, with Eastern and parts of Southern Europe lagging well behind the West. Urban decline is probably an inevitable process driven by relentless forces once cities reached a certain size and people achieved a certain level of income, partly because of their desire for homes with more space and gardens, enabled by higher car ownership and mobility.

This analysis was updated and extended by Cheshire and Hay's (1989) work on urban trends in Western Europe. It also had a problem focus, but was more comprehensive in scope, with stronger economic underpinnings. Data on demographic and employment variables were analysed for 229 cities over the period 1971–1984, complemented by a wider range of social, economic and environmental variables for a smaller sample of 53 cities. They confirmed the main conclusions of previous studies that urban systems were maturing in a broadly similar way in different places. Although decline was the dominant feature of cities in most developed economies, Cheshire and Hay also raised the prospect of an urban revival. They saw possibilities arising from two sources. First, the general shift in the industrial structure from manufacturing to services was important because the service sector was thought to have a stronger urban orientation. In addition, certain demographic trends tend to favour city locations.

Cheshire (1995) updated the earlier analysis using population data from 1990–1991 censuses across Europe. His main conclusion was that a more complex pattern of urban development was emerging with a wider range of experience across cities. In some cases, there was clear evidence that the rate of decentralization slowed down compared with the 1970s, indicating relative recentralization. This was particularly the case in selected Northern European cities, namely those that were medium-sized, with historic cores, old universities and a highly educated population. In other places, decentralization was continuing and the prospects of halting the process seemed slim, especially in old industrial cities. Champion (1995) analysed similar data and also concluded that the rate of decentralization seemed to slow down during the 1980s. However, he struggled to generalize because of the wide differences between countries. This diversity promoted him to suggest that there was no single evolutionary trajectory for European cities. He was also very cautious about the broad direction of change and the balance between concentration and deconcentration tendencies.

A European Commission report (2006) based on a larger 'urban audit' study examined changes across an assortment of 258 cities of very different sizes in 27 countries between 1996 and 2001. The principal conclusion was that contemporary population trends are extremely diverse, covering the full spectrum between rapid growth and steep decline. Furthermore, the disparities between cities are far greater than the differences between regions or countries. There was no attempt to categorize cities according to their different trajectories or to examine the factors behind their differences. There was also no assessment of whether the position of cities was improving or deteriorating.

From the mid-1990s, researchers started to discuss the possibilities of global cities emerging in developing countries and countries with transition economies. For instance, Olds (1995) analysed globalization and the production of new urban spaces in the Pacific Rim in the late 20th century. Lo and Yeung (1998) analysed the emerging world cities in the developing world. In addition, the United Nations University Programme on Mega-cities and Urban Development was initiated to examine the growth of megacities in Asia-Pacific, Latin America and Africa (Lo and Yeung 1996). In the last several decades of the 20th century, the rapid economic growth in Asia-Pacific also gave rise to the research on the development of global cities in this region. To name a few, Yeung (1996) gave a comprehensive overview of Asian global cities; Shin and Timberlake (2000) analysed the core and periphery of the world cities in Asia-Pacific and their connectedness; Chen (2005) examined the rising of global cities in Asia-Pacific from the perspective of transnational spaces and Hang Seng Bank (1999) described Hong Kong's road to becoming a world city.

Definition of Global Cities

2

Global cities as the units of selection in the process of urban evolution are supposed to possess selected characteristics that remain sufficiently stable over time, so that they could share identical definition. The basic definition of global cities is the prerequisite for analysis of urban evolution. Though the term 'global cities' is commonly seen in academic works and mass media and increasingly accepted by the public, its meaning is generally unclear and even ambiguous. It is, therefore, necessary to define and conceptualize global cities being the subject of this research and analyse related concepts in the first place.

2.1. METHODOLOGY OF CONCEPTUALIZATION

The methodology applied in conceptualization or defining a term constitutes its major tool. The fundamental reason there exist various understandings and definitions of the concept global cities is that different methods are applied in its conceptualization or definition. Discussing the definition of global cities without taking into account the methods of conceptualization will only lead to distraction by minor issues and conceptual confusion. In this sense, this study will above all address the methodology of conceptualization before any discussion and definition of global cities.

2.1.1. The Perspective of Globalization

Conceptualization is always based on a particular perspective or position, which directly defines the meanings and viewpoints underlying a concept. Likewise, to conceptualize global cities, a proper perspective or position needs to be adopted.

Almost all existing studies on global cities take on a global perspective, while previous studies rarely disagree or debate on this issue. However, there are, in fact, different interpretations on globalization, which reflect different perspectives as implied in the conceptual expressions of global cities. Some studies saw globalization as an activity on a specific geographical scale or an enlarged geographical scale to distinguish it from those on a 'nation state' scale or 'local' scale. This is actually based on the theory of central spatial distribution in traditional urban studies, but only raises the 'national urban system' onto a global scale. From this perspective, some scholars building upon the traditional notion 'space of places' consider global cities as 'central places' in global economy playing important roles such as trade centres, financial centres, industrial centres or ports. These include, for example, the nodes used by global capital for organization and coordination of manufacturing and markets, the major places where international capital floods in, the bases for provision of professional services, manufacturing of financial innovation products and production of market factors and the destinations for mass domestic and international migration. Although notions such as networks and nodes are mentioned in their conceptualization of global cities, these studies tend to focus on the urban qualities and functions based on the space of places, but only with a central space model on an enlarged global scale. Therefore, the issue here is not whether global cities should be studied against the backdrop of globalization, but how modern globalization should be interpreted, which will provide the basic perspective for the conceptualization of global cities.

Globalization, in the most basic sense, is indeed an activity on a specific geographical scale. As an activity on a specific geographical scale, globalization is not an entirely new phenomenon, and it has proceeded in a cyclical manner for centuries (Andrade, Mitchell and Stafford 2001; Bordo, Taylor and Williamson 2005). The global scale is often in contrast with the scale of a 'nation state' or, sometimes, a 'local' scale. However, globalization is not simply an 'upgraded' activity at the global scale; instead, it is essentially modernization of processes. The contemporary phenomenon of globalization, deeply rooted in the economic and technological restructuring in the 1970s, is a non-political transnational process, given the circumstances at that time. Although the fact that political changes are international in its nature, which entails countries extending relations between one another across the globe, was and is still undoubtedly critical, globalization as we understand it today, is not about international relations. The transnational process of contemporary globalization is not an action organized by countries, but rather a non-political action beyond national borders. The NIDL has resulted in a decisive shift in the proportion of the world's economic activity that is transnational in scope (Sassen 1997), which has expanded and accelerated global flows (Held et al. 1999). In the same way, the productive capacity and exported final goods have been dispersed to an expanding network of periphery countries and core countries (Dicken 2003a) to form a 'thick relationship' on multiple levels (Keohane and Nye 2000). Meanwhile, the characteristics and the organization of international economic activities have changed fundamentally. The flow of commodities, capital and information within and between MNCs is increasingly replacing traditional international trade. Currently, the production process of a commodity involves an unprecedented number of countries, while each country specializes in a certain task according to their comparative advantages (Gereffi 1994). This trend towards neo-Fordism requires a more sophisticated, internationalized financial and business services. This, in turn, has resulted in the renewed importance of major cities as sites not only for management and coordination but also for servicing, marketing, innovation, the raising and consolidation of investment capital and the formation of an international property market (Sassen 1999). The creation of the new mode of regulation is deeply connected with this trend, which features public–private cooperation, selective trade reforms, less restrictive labour laws and heavy subsidies for telematics, high-tech infrastructure, and science and technology with commercial potential. The ideology of competitiveness attached to this new mode of regulation has resulted in a distinctive geopolitics of 'techno-nationalism' (Petrella 1991). In addition, the proliferation of transnational, NGOs can be seen partly as a result of global geopolitics and partly in response to economic globalization.

Nowadays, globalization is regarded as a paradigm that can be universally applied in economic, social, cultural and political dimensions, and as 'the widening, deepening and speeding up worldwide interconnectedness' in all aspects of contemporary social life (Held et al. 1999: 2). Because of such interconnectedness, globalization can be defined as a state of the world involving networks of 'multiple relationships' among actors at a 'multicontinental distance' (Keohane and Nye 2000: 105). In this sense, globalization is a new kind of spatial organization. As is pointed out by Castells (1996), before the trend of globalization, the space of places was the main spatial form, for which the best known example was the world political structure based on international relations between countries. However, the new supporting technology industry combining communication and computing technologies in the 1970s brought more variability in the geometric structure of economic activities, faster economic rhythm as well as the compression of social environment and the world's space and time, leading to an increase in the flow of technology, population, capital, goods and ideas across borders (Appadurai 1996). As a result, the modern globalization that is set in a space of flows has some new advantages. It provides enterprises with simultaneous social interactions worldwide, which enables them to make truly global decisions. It also contributes to the formation of a more interdependent global economy with more functions by linking enterprises with countries (Hirst and Thompson 1996). In this space of flows, cities, especially global cities, serve as major vehicles for the non-political transnational flows, and linkages are (in other words, cities are) regarded as dynamic entities that dissipate and receive flows of multiple types at various levels. Thus, they have become a main organization in the space of flows rather than in the space of places. Following this logic, the space of modern globalization has severely undermined the basic role of nation states as managers of their national economies (e.g., Held et al. 1999), yet highlighted the central importance of global cities to the contemporary politics and economy. This is the key evidence that the world spatial order is no longer revolving around countries but 'interlocking' urban networks (Beaverstock et al. 2000). In this sense, the world urban network is the 'operational scaffolding' of the global economy (Sassen 2001) and also the connector between globalization and global cities. While the space of globalization is represented by networked connection, global cities are a consequence of the intra-firm networks of producer services and the intercity networks. As the main nodes in WCNs, global cities play the roles of channels and hubs for the flow of global resources and, thus, become the expression of the space of globalization.

From the basic perspective of the spatial representation of modern globalization, globalization and informatization may be set as a qualifying parameter, which describes the existence of a global city in global interpersonal relationships and the historical particularity and contingency of its role of both a 'product' and a 'producer' of globalization and informatization. Globalization has brought about a NIDL, which has changed the geographical distribution and composition of the global economy, causing economic activities that are organized in a spatially decentralized but globally integrated manner. Meanwhile, globalization has been accompanied by the transition from an industrial society to a new information society, that is, the rise of the 'global network society' (Castells 2009). The communicational revolution and informatization have fundamentally changed the relationship between time and space. Spatial organizations that previously had to be activated by people at the same time and in the same place now can be activated in different places of the world simultaneously without people coming together. In conclusion, the interaction between globalization and informatization has, on the basis of the existing 'space of places', introduced a key spatial dimension—the space of flows—as a feature of the contemporary world.

Nowadays, the interaction between the waves of globalization and informatization has enhanced the global connectedness and the structure of global integration. This exerts huge impacts on at least a certain percentage of the world's population who are substantially and closely connected with the global systems of production and exchange, and the global networks of communication and knowledge, redefining their roles as both producers and consumers, and rearranging the time and space of social life in a profound way. Nevertheless, many of these changes have been processed and communicated by the global cities, which serve as the nodes for various connections and linkages of the world economy. Therefore, global cities as a new urban form have arisen in response to the background of interactions between globalization and informatization. Of course, they should also be considered as the product resulting from an active reaction of the cities themselves to the advanced science and technology, the business strategies rolled out by MNCs, and the governing bodies on the regional, national and supranational scales. This is of great significance, because it means that global cities are not 'passively' created by 'external forces' but rather they are results of their own active responses to the interactions between globalization and informatization.

In a word, to interpret globalization as a process of modernization and place emphasis on the new space of modern globalization will offer a new basic perspective for the definition of global cities. From this perspective, global cities are specific to particular cases, neither a concept that is universally applicable to all cities nor a common urban theme under the background of a globalizing or globalized world. The concept of the global cities is merely a theoretical abstraction referring to the space of modern globalization.

2.1.2. Approaches to Conceptualization

The approaches to conceptualization are usually related to the basic perspectives adopted in its process, and different approaches lead to the theoretical abstraction of global cities with different meanings. Existing literature is found to contain a range of basic approaches to conceptualization that differ significantly from, or even stand in stark contrast with, one another. These can roughly be put into two categories as follows.

The first type is based on functionalism (and structuralism), that is, analysing the structure of a city to reveal the characteristics and functions of its internal organizational structures, thereby pinning down the unique characteristics of the city and its status. This type of basic approach was widely adopted in early studies, such as the theory of 'global' urban hierarchy proposed by Hymer (1972), Cohen's (1981) interpretation of global cities as centres of corporate control and coordination for the new international system, Heenan's (1977) statement that the global development of MNCs and the regional organizations are generating 'the need to create global cities', the well-known World City Hypothesis by Friedmann (1986) and the global city model proposed by Sassen (1991) based on the strategic functions of APS.

The other type is the basic approach of relationalism, which analyses global cities as entities of major relationships, with a focus on exploring how the meanings and functions of global cities result in the flows, processes and relationships. Considering that the approach is usually applied beyond the boundaries of traditional cities, global cities are the result of de-territorial flows. This approach focuses on the networking of external linkages of the cities, taking the major functions of global cities as an all-round flow that deals with an increasingly networked society. The cities, defined as nodes, play here only the role of leading the global mobility. As main nodes, global cities handle the most flows in terms of not only the number but also the types. For example, Castells (1996) clearly states that global cities are not defined by their internal characteristics, but by their strategic position in the global 'space of flows', or, to put it in a nutshell, global cities are 'the world's most direct influential nodes and network centers'. The GaWC reanalysed urban systems based on the intercity relations, replacing the hinterland research with the analysis of 'inland world' in the (world) urban area (Taylor [2003] 2004).

These two types of basic approaches are different in that they are grounded on different spaces: the functionalism (and structuralism) approach is based on the space of places, while the relationalism approach on the space of flows. What they have in common is that they completely separate and isolate the space of places from the space of flows. However, the conceptualization of global cities based on the separation of the two spaces is seriously defective. For the former approach, as pointed out earlier, the space of globalization is at a scale of non-territorialization, with which the space of places is completely inconsistent. Using this approach to conceptualizing global cities actually follows the traditional methods of urban theories, by treating global cities as material entities purely made of capital and other elements. For the latter, although the space of globalization is more characterized by the state that the space of flows dominates the space of places, the space of flows does not exist alone in isolation and the flows without 'places' are ineffective. In conclusion, this approach of conceptualization is incomplete.

The space of modern globalization is neither the space of places nor the space of flows but the space of both places and flows which are mutually constitutive. As a fundamental spatial organization of society, the space of flows indicates that the power of society now resides in the flows rather than in the physical places. However, this virtual world of flows needs to be connected to a 'specific place' (node), where its necessary coordination and control functions can be performed, and its innovation and development processes executed. In fact, the active interactions and flows between cities are not simply the flows of information, services and financial resources across the earth's space that are realized through information and communication technology (ICT) and people's physical movements. More often than not, global cities become the place where transnational and transcontinental trade between cities happen, because they are the clusters of global corporate HQs and their international workforce. It is the co-presence and interaction of these professional and experienced participants in global cities that enable the transnational flow of high-level functions. Such a situation is made possible through a mixture of formal and informal, face-to-face and virtual interactions in global cities. A large number of cross-border and global decisions and trade are happening in the same places of the global cities. In this sense, the constitutive relation between the space of flows and the space of places is created and maintained through the world cities as nodes, which are a special expression of the relation as such.

Thus, the spatial structure of the global city should be understood based on the logic that the dual spaces are constitutive of each other, which requires integration of the functionalism (and structuralism) approach and the relationalism approach in the conceptualization of global cities. By employing such 'functionalism–relationalism' method, more attention is put on the process itself, in which functions and relations of global cities should be unified. In other words, global cities are deemed as a process, which is physical (functionalism) and fluid (relationalism) at the same time. Through the process, central functions including the production and consumption of APS and the subordinate local society (entity) are connected to a global network, and, in turn, due to the complementarity of the intra-firm, intra-industry and intra-sector networks and the inter-firm, inter-industry and inter-sector networks, they serve the cities that are internally connected through economic relations. In the entire process, cities and regions play varied roles and have strategic functions (Taylor and Pain 2007). Given that global cities are acknowledged as a process, the characteristics of their internal organizational structure are highly consistent and inherently related to the networking of their external linkages. On the one hand, each element in the internal organizational structure of global cities has its own global or regional network, which facilitates extensive external connections of the cities. On the other hand, any strategic function of global cities in their external network linkages is supported by the constitutive elements of their internal organizational structure. This also indicates the interaction between internal clustering and external networking of global cities. The reason why global cities play a pivotal role in leading the economic growth is that the overlay of these two trajectories of economic externalities (the clustering externality and the networking externality) provides them with critical market strengths.

2.1.3. Types of Concepts

Concepts of theoretical abstraction are not solely limited to one type but can be descriptive, analytical or both. Different types of concepts are, in fact, concerned with the dimensions of a definition. A descriptive concept mainly deals with 'what are global cities and what are their features', and, hence, known as a concrete connotative definition, while an analytical concept offers explanations to 'what are global cities like, what are their implications and effects, and how they evolve', and, hence, known as a basic connotative definition. In the conceptualization of global cities, multiple concept types may be adopted to express connotations at different dimensions. However, one should not mix all types of concepts indiscriminately, which will cause chaos and confusion as well as ambiguity in the conceptualization of global cities. This is one of the reasons that it has long been difficult to reach a consensus on the definition of global cities. Therefore, in conceptualizing global cities, distinction should be made above all between different concept types, before settling on one type.

Taking a look back at the literature on global cities, we can find many descriptive concepts of global cities, which focus on describing their functions to limit the meaning and coverage, and enable better understanding of this term. However, a most problematic issue about descriptive concepts, because of their prescriptive nature, is that they will inevitably generate a lengthy, messy and confusing 'list of items'. To summarize the views of scholars such as Hall, Ullman, Friedmann, Sassen, Thrift and Taylor, the functions of global cities include: (a) centres of politics and power; (b) gateways to trade and business (e.g., ports, airports, railways, commercial routes); (c) places for information and cultural gathering and dissemination (e.g., internationally influential academic institutions, museums, web servers and Internet service providers, mass media); (d) venues of global (e.g., sports, cultural and political) events; (e) concentrated nodes of population; (f) hubs of global mobility and tourism; (g) magnets for human capital and academic specialists (scientists, artists, civil societies); (h) major religious sites (e.g., pilgrimage sites, spiritual places, 'HQs' of major religious groups); (i) HQs' locations of international organizations, NGOs and corporations; (j) places with iconic landmarks; (k) large-scale 'havens' for foreign residents; (l) world renowned metropolises and so on.

Even more items may be added onto the list as more dimensions will be included into research over time. Consequently, it is very difficult, if not impossible, to reach a consensus on all the items mentioned in this list. In practice, every scholar tends to describe only some of the functions, depending on their perspectives and research focus. In other words, the existing literature on the functions of global cities is partial and disconnected and, therefore, cannot give the whole picture. And for another thing, the relevance and order (relative importance) of these functions are not fixed, but changing dynamically in space and time, hence the difficulty to capture them timely. At present, researchers continue to lay emphasis on producing descriptive concepts of global cities, viewing the list of functions as a key indicator in the assessment of global cities and their positions, which is apparently more misleading.

In terms of the paradigm of global cities, we may agree with Sassen's (2006b) insightful statements: '"global city" is not a descriptive term.... It is an analytic construct that allows one to detect the global...' Such analytic conception of global cities provides a stable structure of meaning that does not change with time and applies throughout the process of global cities. In other words, the basic definition of this concept always remains true, no matter how global cities evolve and how their functions change, unless they are no longer global cities. Therefore, only an analytic concept of global cities rather than those descriptive ones can be adopted for the development of the global city paradigm.

With that said, it does not mean that the analytical concept of global cities can completely replace the descriptive ones. The descriptive concepts are still useful in some unique ways, only if applied on basis of the analytical concept and premised on the given time and space. That is to say, we should first propose the analytical concept of global cities to develop the global city paradigm, and then define global cities at different times and spaces using the descriptive concepts. Under this dual conceptual framework, the definition of global cities is not only stable but also dynamic, more suitable for the research on the evolution of global cities. Specifically, the analytical concept and the global city paradigm built upon it will reveal the fundamental driving force behind the evolution of global cities and its process, while the descriptive concepts and the variable definitions of global cities they provide will reflect every detail in the process of the evolution of global city.

2.2. GLOBAL CITY PARADIGM

There are already a lot of descriptive concepts in the existing literature on global cities, which provide variable definition of the term, while the analytical concept is rarely found, which plays an important role in the development of the global city paradigm. Therefore, this research tries to propose an analytical concept of global cities through theoretical abstraction to clarify the basic meaning and inherent characteristics of global cities.

2.2.1. Narrow and Broad Definitions

Before limiting the meaning of global cities, we should first distinguish the narrow definition from the broad definition of global cities. Such distinguishment is mainly based on two different perspectives on the spatial expression of modern globalization: one is the perspective of economic globalization and the other is the perspective of comprehensive globalization.

The narrow definition of global cities is circumscribed by theorists' prescription of economic globalization (economic determinism), which is explained by 'world/global city' hypothesis proposed by Friedmann and Sassen. The core of the hypothesis is that economic globalization has the impact of these cities going beyond the nation state, bring their control functions into play at the global level. In this sense, global cities are results of the NIDL, the financial internationalization and the global strategy of transnational corporations (TNCs). The global city concept is an economic geography approach towards grasping the new organizational structure of the world economy that has emerged with globalization processes (Parnreiter 2014). The concept presents, in its essence, an economic geography perspective on how globalization processes are organized and governed: 'A key purpose of the model is to conceive of economic globalization not just as capital flows, but as the work of coordinating, managing, and servicing these flows' (Sassen 2001). This narrow definition of global cities mainly describes their spatial economic nature and strategic position in world economic systems.

The broad definition of global cities derives itself from the prescription of comprehensive globalization (comprehensive determinism), which is represented by the Los Angeles School that applies post-modernism to the global city study. Soja (1996) believes that the contemporary urbanization is a fully social process of globalization, with urbanization and global social changes concomitant and globalization based, and that post-Fordist urbanization creates global cities such as Los Angles. Lefevre (1991) sees changes in the urban space as a kind of reflection of social, political and economic changes, emphasizing that it is necessary that spatial changes should be associated with capital circulation and economic and social change of different spatial scales, even global scale. Knox (2002) also believes that today's global city has become both the cause and consequence of economic, political and cultural globalization. Therefore, global cities are not only related to the operation of TNCs, international banks and financial institutions but also influenced by a surge of supranational politics and international organizations (international NGOs and intergovernmental organizations).

Academically speaking, the definition of 'global city' in a broad sense seems to be more complete and accurate. Urban economy is essentially a manifestation and result of social interactions, and the notion of social structure still proves to be significant in the studies of urban economy today. Urban sociologists of the Chicago School stressed the importance of social and political impacts on urban development. They examined the relationship between the economic and ecological aspects of a city, regarding the city as a laboratory for exploring social interaction. Lefevre (1991) also considers 'the production of urban space' (including the concepts of political organization and territory) in association with social practice. From this perspective, some major works on global city were criticized for basing its analysis mistakenly on economic theories only without enough support from social theories (cf. Pahl 1986).

However, the narrow definition of 'global city', as frequently adopted in major studies, seems to be reasonable in some sense. Although globalization may be an all-inclusive process, it starts from and remains most intensified in the economic domain. After years of development, economic globalization has reached a significant degree of expansion in spatial terms. In contrast, the social, political and cultural globalization process is still in its infancy spatially, restricted to a certain area. More importantly, it is still unclear whether the spatial expansion of social, political and cultural globalization is highly in sync with that of economic one. If there is a big difference between the two, then we have yet to figure out whether they can assume the same pattern of spatial expansion and how to make that happen. Therefore, in most cases, scholars chose to use the narrow definition of global city which focuses on economic globalization.

In this book, we primarily base our research on the narrow definition of global city, while taking into account, where necessary, its social, political and cultural dimensions. This approach is also suitable given the trend that economic, technological and cultural development of global cities is increasingly integrated. In future, as globalization continues to deepen and global cities manifest strong tendency of spatial expansion in the social, political and cultural fields, similar to that in the economic field, we will switch to the broad definition of global city.

2.2.2. Basic Meaning of 'Global City'

Though the narrow and broad definitions of 'global city' differ obviously in the specific aspects they touch upon, for example, the narrow definition concerns the economic sphere only, while the broad one considers much more; they nevertheless agree with each other on the basic meaning of the term in an abstract sense. In this section, the basic meaning of 'global city' will be elaborated from the following five aspects.

1. Global cities are embedded in the WCN, whose most essential feature is connectivity based on flows: Global cities are major nodes of the WCN, which is constituted by numerous interconnected cities. From this perspective, a city's external relation is not an optional 'addition'. As no city can operate on its own, its connection with the outside world is very important to its development. Global cities, embedded in the WCN, are both the result and source of flows. Their position in global economic activities depends on their connection with other nodes of the network. More specifically, cities exert their influence by establishing an interdependent and mutually supportive relationship with the network. In this sense, any discussion of global city is meaningless without reference to connection (Taylor [2003] 2004).

   Therefore, the key indicator of global city status is not whether a city has large-scale, impressive economic strength or a sizeable cluster of TNCs and global APS firms. The question is whether 'coordination and specialized servicing of global firms and markets is taking place' (Sassen 2001) or, in other words, whether the city has a strong capability of building connections in the network. This connectivity is demonstrated by the links between commodity chains at the local, regional, national and global scales provided by various functional institutions, whose networking activities cover a full range of localities—from farming villages to industrial or tourism cities, and then to global cities. On the one hand, global cities can be closely connected to other cities in different countries: for example, as conceived by Taylor (2001a), two global cities can be linked to the extent that they both contain branch locations of the same APS firms. On the other hand, global cities can also form strong internal (domestic) linkages. In terms of the intracity diagonal values (self-ties), New York, London, Paris and Tokyo dominate the upper echelons of the list (Wall and van der Knaap 2011), which shows a strong coherence between a city's global and local economic functions. Hence, an important trait of global cities is their ability to articulate among global, regional and local networks. Such connectivity also indicates opportunities for producers in one city to have direct access to markets in another. The more central a city is in the WCN, the more favourable it is as a location for producers seeking to exploit global markets. Therefore, the position of a global city in the network is not only a core concern of the global city paradigm but also a defining feature of a global city which differs it from a traditional international metropolis (the differences will be elaborated in the next section).

A diversity of explanations has been proposed for the connectivity of a global city. Friedmann (1995: 22) clarifies the concept by citing MNC HQs as an example, whose 'command and control' functions contribute to the city's connectivity, stressing that world cities are 'spatially organized socio-economic systems' that represent 'places and sites'. Sassen (2002a: 17) refers to producer service firms as corporate subsectors in each city that can be conceived as part of a network: being organized in a cross-border division of labour, their affiliates or other representative offices connect global cities across the globe. In this sense, there is no such entity as a single global city that is separate from others, just as there could be no single capital of an empire that is isolated from other cities. 'Global city' as a category only makes sense as a component of a global network of strategic sites. Castells (1996) proposes the 'space of flows', and interprets global cities as networked hubs and nodes in global spaces of flows, through which places (local) are being transcended in a new informational society. Undoubtedly, the earlier explanations provide irrefutable evidence of the connectivity of a global city. However, it is noteworthy that regarding 'global city' merely as 'spatially organized socio-economic systems', which represent *places* and *sites* rather than *actors*', implies an ontological hypothesis that views global cities as 'mechanical devices'. On the contrary, based on the ontological assumption of 'organic entity', a 'global city' should be described as a city that gains global connectivity through the development of urban entrepreneurship and a balanced urban order. The connectivity of a global city, in this sense, has a dual nature. As Acuto (2011: 2968) suggests, a global city can be characterized as a social (urban) entity that serves as an articulatory node of global flows; performs multiple and significant world city functions; contains central command roles within such functions; maintains balanced urban order at both local and global levels and projects such order towards the global through entrepreneurial activities.

2. Global cities are key or central nodes in the network of spatial organizations, marked by spatial duality (geographic space–flowing space) and process uniformity: In the WCN, global cities interact more widely and intensively with others, thus becoming significant central nodes, while other cities merely serve as ordinary nodes. Central nodes demonstrate obvious spatial duality, that is, global cities are both a 'geographic space' and 'flowing space'. From this perspective, a global city has the following specific features:

   - Expansion and centralization: As its connectivity grows, a global city will have broader and intensified intercity connections, while its global services will become clustered and centralized. As Rodrigue, Comtois and Slack (2006) observe, the centralization of services in global cities seemed to be coupled with production fragmentation.
   - Fluidity and reliance on physical facilities: On the one hand, global cities are seeking intangible (informational or virtual) channels to achieve mobility within the network, with a tendency of moving beyond geographic space. On the other hand, such movement increasingly relies on tangible infrastructure even if in the most digital industries, such as financial sectors. This reflects a 'structural conflict' between the two different spaces, namely the 'geographic space' and 'flowing space'.

- Network connectivity and 'territorial governance': Even though the WCN facilitates the circulation of APS around the world, forming synergic intercity relationship in many respects, cities in the network are independent of each other in terms of territorial governance.

These are the decisive factors that govern the dynamics of modern urban business activities.

Such spatial duality can also be regarded as a kind of process duality in which process can happen at the same time and same place. First, as the economic and political processes in contemporary countries become constantly decentralized, the significance of global and local actions increase. In addition, the globalization and localization processes are uniform in global cities. In other words, global cities provide vertical 'global–local' connection, and meanwhile link to each other horizontally—a typical form of glocalization, with local linkages being the foundation of coordinated global activities.

Second, global cities are a combination of static structures and dynamic processes. For example, taking the large number of skyscrapers in global cities. On the one hand, they are prominent landmarks forming the impressive skylines of the cities; on the other, the main function of these strong static structures is to serve as dynamic nodes, as offices in these buildings have extensive connections with the outside world, stimulating the flow of resources. Such flow in service economy is possible through, for example, an effective cross-border multimodal transport system.

Lastly, the development of global cities has two overlapped processes: inward clustering and outward networking. On the one hand, networking gains more momentum thanks to constant clustering of multinational organizations. On the other, it's the increasingly extensive network that attracts more such organizations to cluster. In short, both networking and clustering feature externalities and complement each other.

3. The key function of global cities: Linking economic activities at different geographical levels to the larger world economy to achieve the flow and rational allocation of resources at a global scale. As key nodes in the WCN, global cities promote the massive flow

and allocation of global resources by being control centres of the world economy that pool specialized services and resources, and providing entrance into the world economy for producers. In other words, by playing a governing role in cross-border economic activities, global cities manage and control the world economy. According to an argument in Ullman and Harris (1945) that 'the support of a city depends on the services it performs', a global city rises to prominence in the global economy through its allocation of resources in the global network.

Different explanations have been proposed as to what *produces* and leads in this key function of global cities. Friedmann and Wolff (1982) stress that world cities are '[t]ightly interconnected with each other through decision-making and finance', thus 'constitute a worldwide system of control over production and market expansion'. 'The global control functions of world cities' are reflected in the cluster of corporate HQs, international finance, infrastructures of transportation and communications that serve the global commerce, high-level business services and the production and dissemination of information and cultural artefacts (Friedmann 1986). Sassen (1988), however, argues that global cities are places 'from which the world economy is managed and serviced' and 'highly concentrated command points in the organization of the world economy' (Sassen 1991). In her view, producer services firms are the main actors in managing the world economy.

What pushes the spatial concentration of 'global resource distribution functions' in global cities is not only global commodity chains established by TNCs but also the interplay between business services companies and their transnational clients and, more importantly, the professional synergy among business services firms themselves. APS firms tend to value the benefits of proximity to other specialized companies: complexity and innovation often require highly specialized input across multiple service sectors (Moulaert and Djellal 1995).

HQs of TNCs tend to concentrate, forming an agglomeration that producer services industry follows. The reason why they are concentrated in a global city is that it has the intensive knowledge and specialized skills that can be found readily available in the milieu (Bourdeau-Lepage 2007). The community of these high-skilled, high-paid workers and the agglomeration of their activities, in turn, act as the main contributor to the global city's role of a Neo-Marshallian node in managing the global economy (Amin and Thrift 1992). In a broader sense, every functional institution, directly or indirectly participating in global activities, is performing the global city's key function of promoting the flow and rational distribution of global resources.

4. Global cities have multiple spatial power relations and play an important role in multidimensional connection: The power of a global city as a space is obtained through the flow in the WCN, during which it has gone through two processes. One is de-territorialization, facilitated by global financial institutions, multinationals and global producer service providers, as well as technological revolution in transportation and communication sectors. The emergence of global cities has broken the traditional relationship between cities and their hinterlands proposed by the central place theory and created a pattern of connections called 'hinterworld' across continents, with their influence transcending the territories of countries. The other is the impact of domestic national systems on the formation of global cities. It is generally believed that as MNCs can build factories anywhere around the world, geographic factors become insignificant (cf. Cairncross 1997). However, the world is not 'flat' (McCann 2008), and multinationals have to take into account the geographical features of a country when deciding where to locate their HQs and offices (Brakman and Van Marrewijk 2008). Therefore, global cities demonstrate power relations from two dimensions: first, they are geographic areas with territorial rights and a part of the countries to which they belong; and then, they are also nodes in the WCN.

Such relations enable global cities to play an important role in connecting economies at the local, national and global levels. On the one hand, the flow of financial and other resources across the world driven by functional institutions such as offices of MNCs in global cities, has pushed globalization to a new level; on the other, national economy also relies heavily on the connectivity of global cities in the network or, in other words, global cities have become an important gateway to the world economy for their countries. In fact, global cities have the ability to link regional and national markets to the world economy, allowing their surrounding cities in a wider area to benefit from globalization. In general, the relationship between global cities and other domestic and overseas cities is not a zero-sum game; by complementing each other in service provision and building synergy between them, they all benefit from the multidimensional connection.

5. The influence of global cities on international affairs changes with the level of their connectivity in the WCN: Global cities' network connectivity level signifies where they stand in the network when dealing with international affairs. Generally speaking, the wider and higher level a city's network connectivity is, the greater its influence becomes in global affairs. Yet the connectivity level does not remain the same all the time, but changes in two different ways. One is the change in absolute terms, namely rise or fall in the number, density and quality of the connections that the city has built in the network. The other is relative change—a city's connectivity level may be on a relative decrease compared with a sharp increase in other global cities connectivity level, even though the city's own connectivity level remains stable or even raises to some extent. Both of these two changes have an impact on a city's role in international affairs and its position in the global network.

In addition, the network connectivity of a global city is not balanced or equally powerful in all aspects, and may differ in terms of economic fields or industries. It may also have different ways of connecting to the WCN in terms of out-degree (the number of ties sent) and in-degree (the number of ties received). 'Out-degree' means the degree of ownership that companies in a particular city have over their relative companies in other cities, which can be interpreted as the city's control over the other cities. Accordingly, 'in-degree' shows how much companies in one city are owned by those in other cities, representing the attractiveness of the city. In this sense, structural changes, such as the change in the significance of economic fields and industries (especially those in which the city has considerable competitiveness) in the world economy, and the change in in-degree and out-degree, can affect the city's role in international affairs and its position in the global network as well.

The aforementioned five aspects constitute the global city paradigm, based on which we can now propose a definition of 'global city': global cities serve as 'key nodes' in the WCN that, based on their connectivity, spatial duality and process uniformity, have multidimensional spatial power relations, facilitate the flow and allocation of resources worldwide through their various forms of connections in the network, and demonstrate certain dynamics of changing role in international affairs depending on their connectivity level.

2.2.3. Attributes

Having summed up the basic meanings of global cities, we now move forward to analyse the essential attributes that distinguish global cities from other cities, which will help us gain a more comprehensive and accurate understanding of global cities. Different descriptions of the essential attributes of global cities are found in existing studies based on different methodologies. Early studies on global cities focus on functional attributes. For example, Friedmann (1995) thinks that 'the key indicator of global city status is whether a city contains the capabilities for servicing, managing, and financing the global operations of firms and markets'. Sassen (2010) insists that the global city is 'a space for the production of organizational commodities needed by firms and markets to operate globally and to shift national wealth to global circuits', and that this entails 'command functions that are distributed across those operations'. Later studies, on the other hand, focus more on relational attributes. In this section, we will elaborate on the attributes of global cities based on the paradigm proposed in the previous section.

1. Disproportionate flows: The most crucial factor in the broad connections of a global city as a key node in the network is not what it possesses, but what it exchanges with other cities. In other words, a global city depends on those flowing through it instead of those existing in it to gain and accumulate wealth, control and power.

What matters to it is not its fixed position in an inward and stable system, but rather the ways of inflows and outflows, and the speed of shrink and expansion. The primary aim of such inflows and outflows is not to facilitate the accumulation of wealth and capital within the city, but to boost the allocation of resources that serve the world economy. That's why the scale of resource flows through a global city often exceeds disproportionately what it demands for internal accumulation.

Driven by globalization, the global resource flow increases dramatically. The flow of goods, services and capital in 2012 reached $26 trillion, accounting for 36 per cent of the global GDP, which is nearly 1.5 times the global GDP in 1990. A majority of such flows happen thanks to the connections of global cities in the network. Therefore, compared to ordinary cities, global cities usually witness the greatest movement of goods, people, capital, services, information, technology, etc., in and out of them. In another sense, it is the development of global cities acting as facilitator of global flows that stimulate, in turn, the exponential swell of global flows. McKinsey Global Institute (MGI; 2014) estimates that with the wide application of digital technologies and the further development of emerging economies, the global flow will have increased three times by 2025, contributing $250–450 billion to the annual growth of the world's GDP, or representing 15–25 per cent of the world economic growth. Thus, the already disproportionate flows will continue to grow, and eventually become a fixed attribute of global cities.

Such disproportionate flows are different between global cities due to their different types. For example, some global cities whose connections with the outside world are mostly global in scale have a higher disproportion of flows than those featuring mainly regional ties. In addition, global cities with diversified strengths feature high-level comprehensive flows, while global cities with strengths in a few notable areas show high-level specialized flows. Nevertheless, global cities, regardless of their type, all have disproportionate flows, reflecting the significance of connectivity in the WCN.

Another thing is common for all global cities, that is, they do not have balanced or equal scale of flows in all fields. For example,

London and New York rank high in financial flow while lower in port goods flow. Los Angeles performs well in immigrant flow; flow of airport goods, services and people; and data and communication flow, while poorly in financial flow. Shanghai ranks first in port goods flow, but lags behind in other flows. Distinctions across these five flows are also apparent to Singapore, Hong Kong, San Francisco and Dubai (Table 2.1). Nevertheless, the key function of global cities—global resource allocation—is to allow the flows of different resources to interact with, instead of separate from, each other, thus ensuring global cities to have high-level comprehensive flows in general. The eight global cities in Table 2.1 are good examples, as they appear in the top 25 for these five types of major flows.

Flows in and out of global cities also experienced structural changes. In the past, global flows were dominated by that of port goods, and port global cities always boasted largest flow in this respect. Then with the rise of global investment and trade, financial flows began to gain share and global cities serving as financial centres had larger financial flows than others. Now, digitalization is transforming and enriching all flows, especially

Table 2.1 *Global Rankings of Eight Cities in Five Major Flows*

	Port Goods	Airport Goods, Services, People	Financial	Immigrants	Data and Communication (Internet Bandwidth)
New York	25	18	2	1	5
London		3	1	3	2
Hong Kong	4	10	3	3	
Singapore	2	16	4	10	10
Shanghai	1	19	21		23
Los Angeles	19	5		2	6
San Francisco		21	9	11	9
Dubai	9	6	16	15	

Source: McKinsey Global Institute (2016).

promoting the soaring of information and knowledge flows and making them the new dominance. In 2012, global flows have seen 11 per cent growth in goods, 10 per cent in services, 6 per cent in finance, 2 per cent in immigrants and 52 per cent in data and communication, an increasingly important part in global city flows (McKinsey Global Institute 2014). Today the knowledge-intensive flows account for half of global flows and are growing at 1.3 times the rate of capital- and labour-intensive flows, which indicates that global cities will carry more knowledge-intensive flows in the future.

2. Collaborative networked platforms: To facilitate disproportionate flows, global cities have a large number of collaborative networked platforms to serve as important infrastructure for global resource allocation. There is a wide array of platforms: specialized platforms focusing on a specific element (goods, people, information, capital, technology or services) and also comprehensive ones for a combination of elements; unitary platforms with a specific function and mixed ones with comprehensive functions; physical platforms and Internet-based virtual platforms and those with mixed forms. These networked platforms interact and coordinate with each other, and work together to promote the massive flow of global resources and their allocation. Therefore, they are highly internal agglomerated and, in turn, have agglomeration externalities. Also, these networked platforms are mainly for connecting with the external world, and thus have network externalities.

Despite all their different forms, each of the networked platforms is an organic whole, consisting of the following four basic functions:
- Fast and convenient exchange and integration of large amount of information: Such information exchange mainly happens via the Internet, powered by big data, cloud computing and other smart technologies, but it also includes wide and frequent face-to-face communication through platforms such as conventions and exhibitions, forums, clubs, associations and public spaces. Although ICTs have been intensively used in cross-border office networks, face-to-face communication is still an important way of dealing with high-valued APS trade

and production. That's why business trips and virtual communication increase at the same time.
- Efficient, transparent and well-managed product and resource trade facilitators, including all kinds of product, service and resource markets and exchanges, invisible markets and OTC trading platforms.
- Provision of a full range of professional services, including assessment, consulting, planning, advertising, accounting, legal affairs and HR training.
- Convenient and accessible transportation of products and resources by providing transportation and information infrastructures, especially transportation hubs, which play an increasingly important role. The main characteristic of infrastructure, in general, is that it is part of the overall capital stock which is important for the subsistence of general purpose technologies which are essential for the maintenance and growth of production (Biehl 1991). In a word, these networked platforms themselves have a collaboration-based functional structure.

However, this functional structure is also subject to change. Take the transportation of products and resources for example. The significance of different transportation means have changed over time. In the mercantilist era, since international trade could only happen by sea, port cities were most likely to become economic centres. As major transportation platforms, ports became nodes in the global network of goods flows, providing services for more regions on a broader scale and engaging more in global trade. Compared to inland cities, port cities were more able to attract flows of commodities including rice, coffee, petroleum, automobiles and textiles, and, thus, could develop more rapidly. In 1925, 60 per cent of the 25 largest cities in the world were port cites, and by 2000 the number increased to 80 per cent (Bosworth 1996). In conclusion, many global cities in the past were generally important port cities and international trade and shipping centres.

But in the service economy era when global cities are also service centres, marine transport becomes less important (Ducruet 2004) than air transport. Global cities such as London and New York, though located near the coasts, witnessed a decline in marine transport as opposed to dramatic increase in air transport. Besides, given that ICTs have increased complexity, volatility and 'wired' communications in high value added production and trade functions, more emphasis is put on saving time costs than transportation costs (Pain 2007), and transport (travel) time has been taken into special consideration. As a result, air transport becomes the top choice for passenger transport, and so even though freight continues to be transported mainly by sea because of the lower cost, the economic heart of the city has partly shifted from seaport to airport (Cartier 1999).

To some extent, port transportation infrastructure is no longer a necessary prerequisite for a global city. In future, the networks tend to be horizontal in order to intensify their functions of connecting scattered places. Hence, information infrastructure becomes more and more important with profound effect on creating comparative advantages (Hepworth 1989). As a general purpose terminal (GPT) with the most standardized applications such as e-mail, the Internet is essentially required to produce, distribute and exchange goods and services (Batty 1997). The Internet backbone networks as infrastructures can play a big role in influencing potential income, productivity and employment. In addition, the Internet transports the valuable weightless goods of the digital economy in the same way transportation networks transport the industrial goods over the past two centuries (O'Kelly and Grubesic 2002).

3. Highly agglomerated global functional institutions: Being major actors that manage and generate massive flows through networked platforms, global functional institutions located in global cities are a key force in allocating global resources, including global capital, information, business services, science and technology, and high-skilled talent. These institutions include not only HQs of TNCs that control the global commodity chain but also producer service institutions such as financial and professional service companies. They play a coordinative role and also exert certain degree of control while providing professional services for industrial and value chains. In addition, with the deepening of technological globalization and the development of global cities as scientific and

technological innovation centres, global research and development (R&D) centres, centres of excellence, high-tech firms and venture capital funds have gradually become global functional institutions that cluster in global cities, and play a bigger role in driving global economy.

Global cities have greatly enhanced their monocentricity by highly clustering these global organizations of different functions. First, these global organizations have the knowledge structure and ability to generate and disseminate ideas and collective beliefs related to economic strategy and business environment, and this is the source where their authority came from. Second, as key practitioners in global cities, these organizations can gain access to information, build and maintain alliances and monitor implicit contracts, bringing advantages to their social interactions. Furthermore, these global functional organizations have accumulated abundant expertise to identify market gaps, develop new applications of science and technology, and generate innovation; they also have the ability to mobilize a large number of people to participate in the early stage of innovation, as well as the ability to provide rapid response to market segments via social networks, thereby promoting their capabilities to innovate. More broadly, the control, coordination and leadership functions of global organizations, as well as their interdependence and interaction, have equipped global cities with unique functions in global resource allocation.

4. Dominated by a standard interaction model of the global village: Those global organizations gathered in clusters have made global cities a place dominated by a standard interaction model of 'global village'. This is an important part of the global urban 'soft power', and, to some extent, this is the primary goal of a city's development. Otherwise, global organizations of different function cannot successfully carry out transnational operations, which will, in turn, make it difficult for these organizations to form highly integrated clusters in global cities.

It is worth noting that, as part of the overall attributes of global cities, this standard interaction model does not refer to the general investment environment or business environment, but to the underlying patterns of the 'global village' interactions. As more and more participants in global cities exchange information in global affairs, their general knowledge is becoming more and more globalized through the increasing global discourses and communication based on universal motive and context, making their pattern of behaviour and networking of resources in a more standardized model. Most of their open interaction must follow the international common practice and deal with all kinds of affairs according to the standards of multilateral, bilateral or regional and cross-regional investment and trade agreements. The interaction model also makes the public participation into political consultation and governance more common, and the coordination of the relationship between social and economic activities within an institutionalized framework a necessity. Based on the interaction of sharing and win-win, we must give full play to the enthusiasm and potential of all kinds of participants, maximize social utility and meet the different needs of all kinds of participants. Propelled by various endogenous interests and needs shared by its participants, this 'global village' interaction model is becoming increasingly prevalent in global cities.

5. Global leading role in vigorous growth and innovation: Global cities achieve worldwide resource allocation within an interlocking network connecting the outside world. Economic activities remain robust and have profound interactions with culture and society in those cities. This, in turn, has made these cities the centres for producing and disseminating information, entertainment and other cultural products. Global cities, the current or potential 'dynamic cities' (Taylor [2003] 2004), provide an exciting environment with multifaceted concepts and great opportunities for the manufacturing of new service products integrating information, knowledge and creativity to create more jobs and increasing wealth. For this reason, a conclusion was drawn by Malecki (2002) that 'world cities are alive'. Furthermore, global cities can keep developing their innovative capacities during extensive communication with other cities to make revolutionary progress. Taking the advantage of comprehensive system integration, clusters and rapid diffusion of innovation can be formed in global cities, by which they will

become major cradles for innovative idea, creative behaviour and entrepreneurial mode that lead the world, for instance, workplaces for leading industries including innovative sectors. Therefore, full of vitality and innovation, global cities will be very influential leading the world development.

The aforementioned five attributes of global cities are not separated or exist in the form of a simple set of characteristics. Instead, they function as a whole with intrinsic connections. As key actors in global cities, global functional organizations could run well only by utilizing various network platforms and the standard interaction model of global village, promoting a disproportionate scale of global flows in global cities. This, in turn, gives these cities the leading roles globally featuring vitality and innovation. It indicates the relationship among five attributes, presenting as a 'core elements-prerequisites-outcome' model. In addition, they exist on the basis of each other. For instance, the value of the network platforms only exists when they are operated by relevant parties. The standard interaction model of global village is insignificant unless participants are involved. Without the supply offered by network platforms and the standard interaction model of global village, global functional organizations won't tend to agglomerate inside these global cities. In turn, without demand created by the agglomeration of global functional organizations, collaborative network platforms and the standard interaction model will not be developed.

2.3. CLARIFICATION OF SOME CONFUSING CONCEPTS

Global cities research is in the stage of conceptualization, during which scholars came up with numerous concepts and terms with different interpretations. In the practice of strategic planning research, different concepts were often put forward without giving explicit explanations, such as international metropolis, world cities, global cites, which are frequently used but sometimes mixed up. As far as we are concerned, these different concepts were brought up against particular context with specific meanings; thus, they can't be mixed or replaced arbitrarily. By comparing different concepts and clarifying their meanings, ambiguity and misusage can be avoided. More importantly, it will help deepen our knowledge and understanding of the connotation of global cities.

2.3.1. Global Cities and World Cities

The concepts of 'world cities' and 'global cities', proposed under the background of economic globalization for illustrating its spatial structure, are to some degree based on the same theory that the global economic activities take place in an uneven geographical distribution, making some of the activities concentrated, in certain cities. In other words, to ensure the global economic activities go smoothly, the function of strategic control must only be performed by certain cities. Because of the same theoretical basis, the two concepts are used as the same meaning or alternative in many documents. Some scholars only consider them different in terms of their meaning extension. As Taylor (2005a) suggests the use of 'global cities' as the top echelons of some 'world cities' with hierarchical patterns, in this sense, the term 'global cities' is used to describe one type of 'world cities', but 'world cities' does not necessarily refer to 'global cities'. It is believed that there are some connotative differences between the two terms, which can be distinguished by analysing the relevant institutions that perform the strategic functions of cities.

'World City Hypothesis' put forward by Friedmann was basically premised on the global decentralization of production of MNCs (especially manufacturing multinationals). The HQs of these multinationals were concentrated in a few large cities, exercising control and command (CAC) of production management. The spatial concentration of HQs of multinational companies in world cities is of central importance, thus centralizing the various strategic functions of CAC of the world economy. After that, the majority of works focus on the command and control function of the major cities of the global economy, which is often determined on the basis of location of the HQs of the leading multinational companies (Alderson and Beckfield 2004; Godfrey and Zhou 1999). Sassen's further research on global cities has demonstrated that as global firms outsource their functions overseas, they rely on increasingly complex HQs functions with greater demand for highly specialized services. More specifically, these outsourcing companies are a vast array of APS firms, that is, accountancy, advertising, banking/finance, insurance, law, management consultancy firms, needed to manage increasingly complex and uncertain cross-border transactions, especially for producers with global ambitions. To this end, Sassen (2001) puts forward the global urban theory on the basis of the fact that multinational professional service companies are concentrated in a few large cities—'my use of the notion of global city functions (is) to identify a particular case, that of a city which fulfilled a fairly limited and highly specialized set of functions in the management and servicing of the global economy' (Sassen 2001: 351). That is to say, Sassen uses the dominant and interdependent APS firms as the foundation of the global cities concept, emphasizing that the new dynamic 'aggregation' has prompted advanced business service firms to gather in a few places. In this way, the concept of global cities transcends the meaning of 'command centres', and becomes the 'global service centre' since the emergence of cities. Therefore, the concept of global cities marks a clear shift from Friedmann's emphasis on the concentration of corporate HQs in the world's urban space to a more comprehensive description of the meaning of global urban functions, namely not only the HQs of MNCs but also APS firms. It also plays a strategic control and coordination function for globally distributed economic activities. As Sassen's conceptualization of global cities takes into account variations in the nature of different cities, it, in turn, not only summarizes the nodes that Friedmann originally envisioned but also highlights its global position stemming from the special outputs of advanced production, mainly centred by APS. In fact, it surpassed Friedmann's 'World City Hypothesis'.

Therefore, the two concepts are constructed on very different basis, with its connotation defined differently. Although this is not some difference in nature, it does not mean that we can ignore their differences in connotation and use them simultaneously and alternatively. More importantly, the difference in meaning involves the question of whether the concept is more applicable. As economic globalization and informationization continue to develop across the world, the connotation of these two concepts has been tested in practice, and the 'balance' of its applicability seems to be gradually tilted towards the concept of 'global cities'.

First, the past decade has witnessed a trend among HQs of MNCs, especially those from the manufacturing sector, to outsource their service functions on a large scale and even decentralize themselves, to some extent, by moving from global cities to suitable general cities that are nearby. Lyons and Salmon (1995) noticed a new tendency that had been particularly obvious in the USA since the mid-1970s where large corporations tended to relocate their HQs to smaller cities with improving infrastructure and lower costs. Florida and Jonas (1991) also found out that it had become quite common in the USA for HQs to relocate from large cities to suburbs since the 1970s. Today, in more and more large cities, we can only find secondary HQs with highly specialized functions (Sassen 2006a). Godfrey and Zhou (1999) argued that as functions of MNC HQs became a poor measurement of the 'global urban hierarchy', more emphasis should be given to regional HQs to reflect strategic location decisions instead of simply where a company was founded. Alderson and Beckfield (2004) drew a conclusion from the perspective of command and control functions that some regional centres were better positioned than world cities in the urban hierarchy. And these regional centres may, dependent on the performance of their companies, eventually develop into focal points of the global economy in certain industry sectors (Taylor and Csomós 2012). Apparently, the changes in the actual operation of HQs of MNCs have partly weakened the world city concept based on corporate HQs. In contrast, a strong concentration trend is maintained in the APS functions in particular for global use, which are increasingly concentrated in global cities because the sharing of tacit knowledge for these professional services still largely relies on face-to-face communication despite the widespread application of information technologies. Sassen (2006a) noted that compared to the MNC HQs they served, the producer–services complexes—although strongly oriented towards the corporate sector—were more likely to remain concentrated in urban centres, which, in a sense, supported the world city concept based on APS instead.

Second, despite their common theoretical foundation underlying the WCN, the interlocking models or internal networks connecting the cities within these two concepts are different. MNCs mainly operate within an internal network between the parent company and its affiliates (manufacturing and processing establishments) located in non-core or general cities of other countries through which the two sides can exchange information on command and control of production activities as well as human resources. In contrast, APS firms involve an internal network that connects head offices and branch offices set in megacities or major cities worldwide, where diversified specialized service sectors can support and complement each other and, thus, benefit from the cluster effect. These firms capitalize on the network to interactively share information on service coordination and human resource exchange on a far more comprehensive and frequent manner. Such an internal network for APS firms excels the former one in terms of not only the distribution or scale of internal network but also the frequency and extensiveness concerning information and human resource sharing. To sum up, 'global cities' based on APS firms put higher emphasis on international interaction within a global network, which is in contrast with the concept of 'world cities' where power is 'seen as concentrated by those group who take advantage of command-and-control functions embedded in specific central places' (Allen 1999). The concept of global city better embodies the core ideas of the WCN.

Third, multinational organizations (corporations), against the backdrop of industrial integration and high-end management of global value chain (GVC), are embracing changes and reforms as well. A growing number of international companies in the manufacturing sector, in particular, are transforming into service-oriented corporations by increasing the share of services in their added value. Moreover, more and more MNCs are transforming themselves into global companies as the proportions of overseas employees, the share of overseas operations and the revenue generated by overseas branches increase steadily. The behavioural characteristics of these service-oriented MNCs and global companies are better in line with what the concept of global cities highlights, which, in turn, makes the concept more applicable to a certain degree.

To put all into a nutshell, the two concepts share similar theoretical foundation yet lay emphasis on different perspectives due to their distinction in underlying ideas. The concept of global cities is more applicable in relative terms, which explains why global cities are preferentially employed in this research. It is worth noticing that this research does not simply follow Sassen's definition of global cities. Instead, similar to the establishment of a more abstract paradigm (with defined fundamental connotations) for global cities in previous sections, efforts are made to enrich the connotations of global cities and to reconstruct its tacit ontological assumptions.

2.3.2. Global Cities and Globalizing Cities

Global cities are basic nodes of WCN, which also includes other cities as general nodes. Therefore, from the perspective of WCN, we should analyse the concept of global cities as the basic nodes and globalizing ordinary cities as the general nodes, as well as identify their relations and differences.

To talk about WCN, which is the product of globalization process, it is necessary to deal with the degree and scope of the influence of globalization upon cities. Some research showed that the processes of globalization essentially affects all cities (Marcuse and van Kempen 2000). It has been indicated that some 'medium cities' have just as much need to respond to globalization trends as their larger neighbours (Knox 1996), so as to achieve more options and improve adaptability in space utilization, and to establish a stable cooperative relationship with other cities through the flows of capital, labour, commodity, service and information. Therefore, the process cannot be construed as affecting just a few privileged cities. On the contrary, the process of globalization is organized and governed from multiple places. We are facing cities in remote inland areas that the transnational economic network stretched into, including more and more cities from the Global North and the Global South that are contained in the complicated WCN.

Previous literature that studies global cities also holds that global cities are basic nodes of WCN. However, the connections between global cities and ordinary cities are seldom dealt with, so 'millions of people and hundreds of cities are dropped off the map of much research in urban studies' (Robinson 2002), especially most cities in the 'South' are missing in the geographical map of world cities, resulting in a serious limitation in previous studies concerning global cities. A city is defined as a global city because of its widespread connectivity within WCN, which is more of connections with ordinary cities rather than other global cities. Therefore, when we study global cities, if we only focus on the limited numbers of interconnections among global cities and ignore the connections between global cities and myriad ordinary cities, our subject, namely the WCN will be reduced to a network among global cities, and the widespread connectivity, a necessary prerequisite for a global city, will no longer exist; thus, global cities can no longer be defined as basic nodes of WCN. In other words, if the connections between global cities and numerous ordinary cities are excluded, the space of contemporary globalization is incomplete and, as a result, global cities cannot be viewed as the spatial expression of contemporary globalization.

In fact, globalization is neither like the oil slick that covers the whole world nor entirely controlled by some 'super cities'. Quite the opposite, in the WCN enabled by globalization, there are not only global cities, but a large number of interconnected ordinary cities which are 'impacted' by globalization. It is due to the inclusion of these ordinary cities that globalization can be credibly viewed as a geographic phenomenon: WCN. Just as Taylor ([2003] 2004) has noted, although only a limited number of cities in the world can be defined as global cities, which make possible a highly centralized global service mechanism, many other cities are also intertwined in this global network of advanced, interconnected producer services. The emergence of global cities has enabled their producer service industry to conceptualize the management, and command and control of the world economy. Also, the significance of global cities is self-evident as they are able to connect an unlimited number of non-global cities to its mechanism, so as to establish a global network of cities. In other words, global cities not only constitute each other but also connect with 'ordinary cities' (Parnreiter 2010). These ordinary cities connected are still part of the global network of cities, involving in the production activities in the global market. Marcuse and van Kempen (2000) named these cities connected into the global network of cities under the impact of globalization as 'globalizing cities', while Taylor et al. (2006) named them 'cities in globalization'. In my book *The Global Cities on the Rise* (Zhou 2008), I am more in favour of the former term 'globalizing cities', which is differentiated from global cities. The key difference between global cities and globalizing cities is as follows: global cities are elementary or major nodes which lead the globalization, while globalizing cities are secondary or minor sub-nodes which are impacted by or connected with globalization. Expanding on various geographic scales, the WCN depends on the connection between global cities and countless globalizing cities. But the problem is, when putting theory into practice in differentiating and defining cities in reality, it is quite hard to measure these two types of cities by fixed standard. That is to say, globalizing cities are at the edge of entering into the list of global cities, thus difficult to set a dualistic boundary between the two. How to measure and define categorical standards for cities is exactly at the core of the research on global cities.

To differentiate between global cities and globalizing cities not only facilitates an in-depth understanding of the concept of global cities but also takes on much significance in the research on the evolution of global cities. If the differentiation between global cities and world cities only serves the purpose of making their definitions more accurate and expanding scenarios for the application of these concepts, and if the differentiation between global cities and international metropolises implies that the former are an upgraded version and replacement of the latter, then the differentiation between global cities and globalizing cities will carve out a new theoretical framework of the dynamic evolution of global cities, that is, as the positions of the nodes in the WCN change, some globalizing cities will likely evolve into global cities, while some global cities may return to globalizing cities.

Evolutionary Ontology and Its Core Category

3

The analysis of the evolution of global cities requires a conceptual framework that is quite different from other urban sciences, as they have very different approaches to deal with real entities. In order to establish a new evolutionary paradigm for the global cities theory, it is an essential prerequisite to assume an ontology for the evolution of global cities and elaborate on it. Moreover, a highly abstract core category is indispensable for developing an analysis framework for the evolution of global cities, and it must be able to fully cover the process of dynamic evolution.

3.1. ONTOLOGY OF GLOBAL CITIES

Ontology, though on a philosophical level, defines our basic view of global cities and is a prerequisite for studying how global cities come into being, develop and evolve. Moreover, most assumptions in studies on global cities are made based on ontology. Therefore, before starting a comprehensive analysis of the evolution of global cities, the ontology of global cities must be discussed and, therefore, basic views as well as methodological positions of global cities should be clearly stated.

3.1.1. Significance of Ontology

Most studies on global cities adopt a phenomenological approach—examining specific cities, such as London, New York, Tokyo and Paris, discovering their common characteristics different from other general cities, and then producing so-called world/global cities theories. These studies reveal the background, driving force and mechanism behind the global city formation and development, and describe the attributes and functions of global cities and their roles played in globalization, thus creating a basic theoretical framework for global cities research. Based on that, abundant studies have been carried out, including case studies on specific global cities, comparative studies on different global cities, multi-perspective studies on various functions of global cities and empirical studies on the hierarchy of global cities, thus complementing and enriching global cities theories. However, these studies do not explicitly propose ontological claims, but take an implicit methodological position. Or rather there is a lack of self-conscious reflection about the significance of specific methodologies that researchers themselves insist on. Why is this happening? This is mainly because most global cities studies are conducted from a perspective of methodological instrumentalism: theories are reduced to tools for observing and researching global cities phenomena, rather than as a description of reality. To make theory work for reality, many empirical analysing tools are used, such as an attribute analysis and a network analysis. The global cities theories guide specific empirical researches and, in turn, are verified through empirical evidence. However, this has brought a series of problems to studies on global cities.

First, most assumptions of global cities theory are made arbitrarily, which has two problems: on the one hand, the quantitative model based on empirical evidence and the theory for measurement are identical in their basic assumptions. In other words, in these empirical studies of global cities, the criteria chosen to determine, measure and analyse data are constrained by the theory that supports to test the econometric model, so we barely have an independent channel to understand the reality. On the other hand, as some common assumptions are not falsifiable, there are no contradictions among different theories of different empirical claims but adjustments between theories and the observed facts within a common conceptual framework. Consequently, the assumptions of global cities theory continue to be refined through the empirical verification, which will not cause any fundamental change to the structure of the theory. In fact, the empirical rule (phenomenological laws) of global cities is constrained by the theoretical framework, so that it cannot serve as an empirical basis for falsification (Lind 1993).

Second, as the empirical researches of global cities did not probe into any assumptions at the ontological level, they only intrigued superficial or even circular arguments, despite that they did form various opinions with many research methods or tools. Moreover, instrumentalism-based arguments over the empirical data did not change any opinions in global cities theory, for, in a general sense, the scientific methodology has its variations, but the internal dynamics of the development of any theory is more possibly to be driven by implicit methodological conflicts than empirical and theoretical issues. In fact, only researches at the ontology level can solve the disputes, and any theoretical substitutions or new theoretical development can only come from new theoretical assumptions.

Finally, from the realism perspective, we can conclude that any theory concerning the description of reality should start from basic ontological assumptions as to create a link between theory and reality. The essential task, then, of a practical ontology, that is, one that can play its role in theory construction, is to make the empirical status of ontology explicit and to discuss criteria of theoretical validity accordingly (Doppel 2004). It is known that the so-called 'physical world' is the objective reality in a world that we can feel, while the 'metaphysical world' exists in an abstract and imperceptible way. Ontology aims to discover the 'metaphysical reason' behind the existence of the 'physical world', or to discuss whether there is an abstract and independent basis behind all existences in this world, which is the fundamental nature of reality. The ontology of the evolution of global cities is to study what it is for global cities to develop and evolve, and what type of epistemological basis should be referred to. To some degree, the ontology of global cities represents our world views and basic methodologies on the changing development of global cities. The unification of global cities theory and empirical study is based on the ontological assumptions, and different ontological assumptions vary in world views and basic methodologies on the changing development of global cities.

3.1.2. 'Mechanical Device' Assumption

The literature of global cities includes both theories and empirical evidence about how the global cities have been formed and developed. The research follows, to a great extent, a traditional theory of the ontological assumption, though it has not clearly defined any methodology. The mainstream of traditional urban theories views city as some 'mechanical device' mainly controlled by the interaction between 'centripetal force' and 'centrifugal force'. In traditional urban economics, both the land models and the urban system models based on external economies focus on explaining what economic activities are and how they expand under the influence of the centrifugal force. In industrial location theory, central place theory concerning the size and the distribution model of global cities, the multiplier model analysing regional growth and the market potential introduced by Harris (1954), the distance-related joint effects created by the centripetal force and centrifugal force are taken into consideration. The joint effects are further elaborated by Krugman (1991), a representative of NEG, who proposed the 'core–periphery' pattern which is related to the Dixit–Stiglitz model talking about increasing returns and imperfect competition. On the basis of the ontological assumption of the 'mechanical device', researchers often have the following focus: (a) 'the size of the device' such as the city scale, spatial capacity, infrastructure and city functions; (b) 'the basic structure of the device' such as the division of labour, enterprises and organizations and spatial layout; (c) 'the operations processes of the device' such as the input and output of both the population and products, and (d) agglomeration and diffusion effects.

Although a new theoretical framework of global cities has been formed in research through the application of theories such as central flow theory and WCN, it follows to a large extent, the ontological assumption which compares the world city as a 'mechanical device', only to place this assumption in a completely different background, namely the global space. Both Friedmann and Sassen, pioneers in global cities research, have adopted functionalist (and structuralist) approach to reveal the internal organizational characteristics and functions of world cities, and thereby define their features and positions.

Therefore, in the research, the material possessions, and control and influence of global cities over the world are usually measured by their economic strength, market size and competitiveness, which are accumulated by their possessions (such as the unique location resource, facilities and economic strength). In the later research on global cities, more methods such as the space of flows and city network have been adopted, making the studies of their functions based on location space less important. In particular, theories of WCN proposed by Castells and Taylor based on the APS firms view the firms as a combinatorial matrix with alternative functions and the global cities as major (basic) nodes of the WCN. However, the basic methodology of the research still relies on structuralism and neo-structuralism according to which events are generated, commanded and controlled by an external agency. In other words, the distribution of centres, nodes and functions of command and control is determined by structural relationship. The occurrence of each event is only a repetition of this structural relationship. Although this process is dynamic, it depends on the relations instead of the event itself. During the process, the external agencies, the cornerstone of WCN (APS firms), function as relays that control global cities as major nodes, through 'a created world' which is commanded and controlled from a distance under functionalism. Why some cities are more connected is that such cities have followed a more structuralist–functionalist mechanism according to their special statuses.

Different from the WCN theory developed by observing the relations among advanced production services firms, Latour's (2005) ANT is based on deconstruction, aiming at restoring research interest in practice, function and implementation of global cities. Assume that out-thereness is an unstable potential which is overwhelming, diverse and dynamic, a flow that can't be ultimately determined (Law 2004). So global cities are more likely to be defined in the sense of 'what is framed as a faster and more uncertain world', one in which all 'must react to it more quickly' (Thrift 2000). Latour (2005) believes that the power of global cities comes from the internal effect of heterogeneous elements instead of external factors, leading to three aspects: contiguity, superficiality and translation. Hence, the three key injunctions of

ANT: 'don't jump', since the sequence of entrained associations cannot be skipped, least of all by shifting scales or adding dimensions; 'keep everything flat', since every conceivable qualification (e.g., weak and strong, small and large, near and far, low and high, and ephemeral and durable) is a local effect of association and disassociation; and 'don't fill in the blanks', since there is nothing that could be set apart from the full constellation of associations (Latour 2005: 190, 246). However, Latour (2005: 128) regards the institutions who created the network as transformers whose actions have made a difference. So 'Instead of simply transporting effects without transforming them, each of the points in the [network] may become a bifurcation, an event, or the origin of a new translation'. Based on the aforementioned conjunctions, the global city has been redefined as a mediator to fit in economic activities of a certain culture, connecting the heterogeneous elements with practice (Beaverstock et al. 2002). Therefore, although Latour breaks down the structure, stressing that the fact that some cities are more relative than others results from the mutual effect which tends to deepen the relevance, the key concept of 'mediator' indicates the basic assumption of 'mechanical device' ontology.

The ontological assumption of 'mechanical device' has become a huge inherent barrier to the development of the global cities theory. Based on this assumption, static analysis of global cities might still be possible, but the possibility to analyse the evolution of global cities has been ruled out. We can see that since the 'World City Hypothesis' was brought up by Friedmann, almost all of the related research has focused on the global cities that have already formed, and provided an extensive and detailed description of what role a global city played, what functions of a global city exercised and how the city operated. However, an important question has been forgotten or neglected––'how does a global city come into being?' (Douglass 1998). This question is critical to understand the evolution of cities against the backdrop of globalization. In fact, it's prescribed by the nature of the ontological assumption rather than by researchers' preference or subjective intention, because the assumption only leads to static and comparative research or an isolated and separated analysis of global cities that have already come into being, and can be hardly applied to analysing the evolution of global cities.

As 'mechanical devices' lack an intrinsic ability to change and develop, an external driving force is needed to kick-start the evolution of global cities, which means the construction and development of global cities are made possible through 'assembly' according to pre-designed blueprints, or through the implementation of detailed construction plans. 'Mechanical devices' lack reflective capability, which means that all the actions taken to drive the evolution of global cities are 'random'. The rise or fall of global cities, therefore, become random phenomenon, and cannot be analysed in other aspects except the change of city scale at a certain time. Also, the operation of 'mechanical devices' tends to enter into a state of equilibrium, indicating that the change and development of global cities based on the concept of equilibrium is an evolutionary process of general equilibrium movement, namely a process moving from a low-level equilibrium to another high-level equilibrium. Therefore, the research based on the ontological assumption of 'mechanical devices', though also dynamic, is a completely 'deterministic' interpretation of the evolvement of global cities. According to this physical–mechanical paradigm, the evolution of global cities reflects the law of global cities development, and the theoretical research of global cities aims to discover the universally applied law in space and time, which is assumed to be fixed.

3.1.3. Turning to a New Ontological Assumption

The earlier analysis shows that it is impossible to study the evolution of global cities by adopting the traditional ontological assumption; thus, we need make a new ontological assumption. Although most ontological assumptions cannot be tested empirically, we can choose an ontology theory through reasonable judgement. We built up our theories on the following judgement: cities, as a unique settlement at the centre of human civilization, are complex adaptive systems comprising multitudes of actors, firms and other organizations forming diverse relationships and evolving together. Frequent face-to-face contact and other cooperative and competitive interactions enabled by proximity help to increase people's knowledge and skills to improve their capacity to respond creatively to economic challenges and to develop new and improved products, processes and services. Other places cannot easily replicate these conditions (Turok 2009). In other words, the city is a dynamic economy that constantly diversifies its activities through creativity and, thus, scale up their population density and size. This does not mean that the city monopolizes creativity, but creativity is strongly reflected in the city, a place where creative activities are highly concentrated.

Therefore, our ontological assumption is that cities are living organism with reflective ability and intrinsic ability to develop. Obviously, this involves an analogy to living organisms in biological evolution. But, in fact, there are profound differences between cities and living organism. First, cities have no natural life circle and do not form a fixed size naturally. Second, cities are different from gene-centred phenotype (living organism)—they do not preserve norms and routine practices for a long time, but operate in a self-changing mechanism.

According to this ontological assumption, information and energy are the most fundamental concepts involved. In an abstract sense, cities as an organic existence are composed of information and energy. Though cities take the form of various physical existence including infrastructure, buildings, as well as intangible culture, custom and convention, in essence, they can be boiled down to a collection information, since orderly material is only a certain state for information storage. Of course, such information, always limited by choices on synchronic and diachronic dimensions, has internal feedback loop and restructuring ability. Since it does not indicate the simple relationship with the 'environment', it is different from the information of the 'outside world'. The life cycle of different kinds of information varies: some information lasts a long time, while some vanishes soon. It, therefore, decides the mutation and selectively preserved outcomes produced during the evolution of cities—some vanish over time, while some are preserved. Orderly material, as a certain state of information storage, is required to be diachronic and long lasting. Therefore, time is the key to the evolution of cities.

Relevantly, energy, as a primordial matter, is a prerequisite for preserving and maintaining information storage structures, that is, the ultimate standard to evaluate the value of information. As a living system, a city takes the form of a dissipative structure. If there are no external sources of energy supply, the free energy of the system will be dissipated to the environment, thus resulting in increase in entropy. Therefore, energy balance achieved through orderly free energy is the most fundamental constraint factor for the operation of a city. Without a sustained energy supply, the living system of a city will be susceptible to structural decay and loss of information, that is, energy, as an evolving collection of complicated constraints, is a prerequisite for orderly accumulation of information. As Bunge (1977: 123–140) pointed out, energy, as the most prevalent constraint factor on the production and preservation of information, became the ultimate conceptual building block. Since energy flows can achieve an endogenous order, it is safe to assume that non-referential knowledge about environmental conditions makes such an endogenous order possible (Barham 1990). This means that there is a direct and close relationship between information and energy.

The ontological assumption based on organism brings to light a structure that differs from the axiomatic approach in physicalism. Since a city is supposed to be a coordinated organism, it can also be conceived as an organism that contains structural information in each of its parts. Over time, the flow of information will change cities' knowledge base, which is defined as carriers' information structure, and is deemed as a prominent information structure adapted for both subjective existence and objective reality. Urban real objects is a phenomenon that can be observed distinctly by external observers, including the cities' physical appearance, sights and landscape, etc. They are the embodiment of rich historic cultural information, which is an integral part of cities' knowledge base. The subject of cities' participants takes the form of an urban mind with subjective agency, which is also an important part of cities' knowledge base. Certainly, it doesn't refer to the mind of individuals or some groups (governments, corporations or communities, etc.), but a collective mind of the whole cities' subjects, which is reflected in enterprises, markets, governments, families and other groups on different institutional levels. Actually, it is an interdependent process during which each element constantly exchanges information with others, endowing cities with reflective capability and intrinsic initiative and influencing the course of urban evolution. Hence, a city, as an organism, is considered as a dualistic ontology based on participants' urban mind (subjective agency) and urban entity (objective reality). There is a systematic causal interrelation and continuous interaction between the two. Especially, participants' urban mind is also a mirror image of cities, providing guidance for the participants' behaviour. That is to say, urban mind is an autonomous factor during the process of city evolution, the formation of which is of endogenous nature, and forms an integral part of urban evolutionary ontology. Therefore, it can't be separated from cities themselves. It is the simplest and bottommost ontological assumption for the study of subjects' behaviours.

Viewed from a static perspective, a city, as an organism, has reflective capability and intrinsic initiative to adapt to external changes, since its mind guides participants' behaviour. For example, against the backdrop of economic globalization and rapid development of information networks, every actor in a city, including enterprises, governments, institutions and families, had different responses to cope with external changes, since they have different levels of minds. They are forced to adapt to other subjects' rapid changes by adjusting and enriching their own behaviours. During this process, a stronger reflective capability of organizations and collective groups will be built. In terms of economic activities, it means a strong motivation to join in competitive learning. In terms of the society and consumption, it means dealing with the new changes brought by economic reflective capability in order to make other 'satisfied', that is, new risks brought to each company, family, individual and public institution. Reflective capability exists both in production and consumption, and depends on subjects' interrelations and various convention and custom formed in the cities; therefore, it varies in different cities.

Viewed from a dynamic perspective, the possible state of urban entity and the possible state of urban mind will interact with each other in the process of mutation and selection. The changes in the possible state of knowledge lead to the changes in the behaviour of the participants. Meanwhile, the changes of behaviour are selected according to the causal interdependence law as prescribed by the actual state of the city, which ultimately leads to changes in both the possible and actual state of the city. These physical changes may not be reflected in the new changes in the possible state of knowledge, but they will act as constraints in the evolution. Some initial changes may consist only of conceptual knowledge and are not included in the knowledge and information created in the subsequent evolution. However, such knowledge and information are stored in constantly changing constraint structures. Therefore, the sequence of state change is also a process of creating and accumulating information. Thus, we make the basic ontological assumption that the dual evolutionary ontology can be regarded as mutually connected information structures.

Accordingly, unlike the traditional literature that simplistically views global cities as 'locations and spots' formed by the 'external' force from globalization and informatization, we hold the view that global cities are geographical existence which take purposeful actions in the global system. A range of activities and entrepreneurship represent all the characteristics of global cities displaying in interpersonal relationship. Global cities are not only nodes in a network but also actors in the world system. As Latour (2005) put it, it is not 'an actor' (and its positive action) or 'a (passive) system', but a social entity of 'autonomous people' who are aware of the existence of life, material structure or institution.

On the basis of the ontological assumption that the city is an 'organism', we define the concept of plural ontology. First, the information structures of cities in the state of synchronic constraint are different, so they cannot be simply added up and there is no inherent ontological level. This means that the reflective power and intrinsic agency of different cities are different. There is no balance between the two, and they cannot be put in sequence in accordance with their structures. Even under the same external conditions, some cities can evolve into global cities, while others cannot. Second, the information of certain cities only refers to some part of the urban system because it contains a set of specific constraints of 'intentional knowledge'. Such cities cannot be reduced to a generalized type. Similarly, there is no universal measurement standard for cities with similar constraints. This means that there is no unified development model and measurement standard for urban evolution. Even though there are two cities which both tend to evolve into global cities, they have different pathways to take.

3.1.4. Ontological Assumption Based on 'Organism'

The ontological assumption based on 'organism' is not only dualist but also has a series of other structural features, which is completely different from traditional ontology. It provides a solid theoretical foundation for the study on the evolution of global cities.

In many articles, cities are often described as the realization of a series of possible states, and development and changes are viewed as a sequence of possible states that have been realized. This means that the evolution of cities can be expressed using state functions (Bunge 1977: 123–140). Yet in this case, cities are, in fact, viewed as a closed system. That is to say, the collection of the possible states of the evolution of cities is given and does not change over time. In contrast, in the ontological assumption based on organism, changes of city state are not viewed as a closed system, but an open system. This means that the collection of the possible states of the evolution of cities changes over time. In addition, the urban mind involving all city participants is also composed of a number of possible states, and learning and knowledge creation is an open process. This involves a presupposition: although there is a causal relationship and constant interaction between urban mind and urban reality, the collection of the possible states of the two are not exactly the same nor are they completely parallel. Otherwise, we would go back to a single model structure: either random generation of new states or a certain creative activity outside the city must be introduced in order to study cities evolvement. This is mainly because the urban mind involving all city participants is not a direct mirror of the urban reality, and it is impossible to achieve an optimal state since possible knowledge state is influenced by urban reality. This result can be explained by the human knowledge impossibility theorem, which reveals that people are born to misunderstand or develop biases. Therefore, the dualistic ontology based on 'organism' cannot build and formalize a unique concept system, thus unable to rule out theoretical monism and universalism.

From the perspective of evolution, changes of possible states of the urban mind involving all city participants are crucial driving forces that change the possible states of global cities, since warped or erroneous perception in urban mind is the only possible source of new knowledge (radical fallibilism; Levinson 1988). It is the warped or erroneous perception that leads to a clash with the reality, which ultimately leads to the generation of new knowledge or readjustment of existing knowledge by selection or retaining certain practices. In this sense, human knowledge will not inevitably evolve into a certain unique and real global landscape. It is an evolution of fallibilism. During the evolution of global cities, changes in the knowledge state lead to changes in behaviour (i.e., creativity), which, in turn, changes the collection of the possible states of global cities, and finally transforms the urban mind. The collection of possible states of unreal mind is much larger than that of the possible states of global cities; therefore, human creativity is infinite.

Meanwhile, due to the dual structure of reality, this infinitely large collection of possible states of unreal mind is not simply determined by the realized state of global cities and causal interdependence in itself. Therefore, the states of mind are a chance event, related to the real causal interdependence which is not fully or correctly reflected in human beings' knowledge. However, they are not random deviation from the rational expectation caused by fallacy. Since the states of mind are interdependent in the state of knowledge, they are not caused incidentally by certain dynamics in the thoughts of human beings. In this sense, the chance of altering the state of mind relies on a somewhat 'peculiar' change in the state of knowledge, which is also a major driving force for changes in the collection of possible states of cities. Such 'peculiar' changes in the state of knowledge lead to constantly emerging creativity of a city. By this logic, creativity also becomes a chance event. The continuously changing state of knowledge arises from the constant emergence of new possible states of the world, and peculiar events are the key determinant of a city's real changes. In this era, the important factors in the evolution of global cities are the formation of new preferences, technological and institutional innovations and the creation of new resources. In other words, the key factor in a city's evolution lies in the creation of new things. As to such a changeable creation process, we don't have to understand it in an essentialist way in the same way as we deal with other general terms, nor do we have to take a nominalist attitude. But it can be addressed by a dynamic view of mutation and selection, that is, of the selective retention of genetic features, that is, peculiar phenomena (as mutation of a chance phenomenon) become individual characteristics, and if they are expanded in an individual group by inheritance and selection, they will be named as a category of general term. Though the peculiar phenomenon cannot be theorized, we can theorize the whole process of mutation and selection.

One of the important features of the peculiar changes in the state of knowledge is its irreversibility. As time is taken into account in evolution as a fundamental dimension, evolution is conceived as a series of sequenced mutations and selection events, in which each mutation survives through selection and becomes a feature of an individual group that consists of many individuals, and meanwhile becomes a constraint condition for new features that may be generated in the future. Therefore, the irreversibility of the peculiar changes in the state of knowledge is not a nature of certain specific process, but is an issue of general ontology. Surely, the time introduced here is not 'physical' time, or simply 'historical' time, but 'Eigen-time' of the process. 'Eigen-time' of the process is a determinant of the evolutionary form of interaction between different processes, which produces what we call 'history' and, thus, becomes a necessary condition. Certainly, in the framework of dual ontology, we can also distinguish between the 'Eigen-time' and the 'observer time'. The former is the time for the evolution process of cities as objects, which is irreversible, while the latter is about the psychological time of urban minds, which is based on reflections, meaning that events in the past and future are conceived as what happens at present and vice versa. Therefore, from the perspective of the psychological time, there is no one-way causal direction like a fixed arrow of time. The different assumptions of these two types of time all play a role in the evolution of global cities. Therefore, time is a complex category containing the temporary order of different types of interaction processes in evolutionary changes.

In conclusion, the study of the evolution of global city based on 'living organism' assumption is essentially different from the 'determinism'-based urban change theories mentioned earlier. In fact, these two are incompatible with each other. Also, based on the 'organism' paradigm, the theory of the evolution of global city is a kind of 'changeable law'. Natural law is a result of and a factor imposing influence on evolution; therefore, it is only temporarily effective as an explanation to changes. In this sense, the study of evolution of global city is not universally effective and will change over time.

3.2. THE CORE CATEGORY

Now that we have decided to use the 'living organism' ontology of global cities, the next step is to identify the core category and apply it throughout the whole process of our study, so as to achieve a certain level of formalization.

3.2.1. Connection

In the ontological assumption of 'living organism', information and energy are basic elements in the urban system. And the key of information flow and energy exchange and their systematic causal relationship lies in connection, that is, interlinkage and interaction. Connection is the most basic requirement for the existence and evolution of 'urban organism'. The urban reality as reflected in its shape, appearance and landscapes are specific physical connections, and the urban mind as reflected in culture, social system, technology, governance, organizational structure, entrepreneurial activities, cognitive habits and financial systems are also specific connections. The constant interaction between the physical reality and the urban mind constitutes a commonly seen mechanism of connection.

Certainly, connections also exist in the ontological assumption of 'mechanical device', since without connections machines cannot operate. But they are mechanical connections largely based on internal relations. The change of such connections is not a developmental or evolutionary process, but a dynamic one. According to the 'mechanical device' assumption, it consists of the changes of stocks of capital, material wealth and their functions and qualities, and is reflected in the changes of these elements and their nature. Thus, scholars tended to describe this process with physical changes in the city itself, including physical attributes such as city scale, economic power, stocks in capital and the accumulation of wealth. Various indicators are also adopted to measure these changes, such as population, urban spatial scale, GDP, investment in the fixed assets, the number of infrastructures and enterprises, profits and taxes. Jacobs (1984) dismissed such thinking as merely 'a collection of things for producing', which is not a process of development, for these 'things' will not generate development without being part of a process that constructively incorporates the non-local. As a process, development should not be measured by accumulation of signifiers of development (machinery, tractors, industrial plants, factories, offices, dams, etc.). She later designated it as a fallacious 'Thing Theory' of development (Jacobs 2000).

Global cities are a specific urban form in the context of globalization, and are in the middle of a dynamic developmental process, rather than in a static state. However, we should not be easily satisfied with this superficial understanding and should go deeper to understand what the dynamic process is, or in what way it is formed and displayed. I appreciate Jacobs' critique of the fallacious 'Thing Theory' of development and her views on understanding dynamic processes of cities by the use of the expansion of flows. This aligns with the ontological assumption of 'living organism'—the intrinsic order is derived from energy flow. It is based on the fact that the city is a node in the network that allows all types of flows (though they are temporal and constantly changing) and people flow in different ways and on various scales, which have profound effects on the economic and social life. To conceptualize flow, Clark (2005) used the mercury rather than water as a metaphor for flows. In this sense, the city is not a pre-existing entity that flows are attracted to. Rather the existence of cities will not be noticed if there are no flows. That is to say, what is crucial is not to understand cities as a physical entity (which means using a fixed definition of a research object), but to understand the process of continuous transformation of its composition and functions brought about by flows. Therefore, a city is more like a 'meeting ground', a specific intersection of social relations, all of which is 'built on a larger scale than what we now define as the place' (Urry 2000). In Latour and Hermant's (1998) view, a city is an open theatre or stage where many visible and invisible actors play constantly shifting leading or walking-on roles. An empirical study by Wall and van der Knaap (2011) also showed that in terms of diagonal centrality, only 16 per cent of interactions proved to be intra-urban (self-ties), supporting the view that important cities derive their status from what flows between them rather than what remains fixed within them (Allen 1999). In today's world, accelerated flows and deepening intra-urban connections can be considered as the characteristics of globalization. Flows are not just one element of social organization; they are the expression of the processes dominating our economic, political and symbolic life (Castells 1996).

On the basis of the urban flows, we can further define the concept of connection. In an abstract sense, it refers to the interactions among physical entities featuring continuous connections and relative stability. It has three meanings: first, the connection of a city lies in the flow rather the physical entity of the city itself. Second, it is a continuous connection, which is different from the occasional and discontinuous connections. Since the connections brought about by international exhibitions (including World Expo), art festivals, major sport events (like the Olympic Games) and international aids for natural and man-made disasters are temporal and discontinuous, they are not what we call connections here. Lastly, the connection of a city is characterized by stable interactions. In the real world, intercity interactions are complicated since there are different interactions including some random, highly dissociative and transient ones. Although these interactions are objective and of great importance sometimes, they are not part of intercity connections. Hence, intercity connection can be defined as a flow with continuous and relatively stable interactions among cities.

So far, we see dynamic processes of cities as changing intercity connections based on urban flows, which are expressed in changing characteristics of internal and external interactions. As a dynamic process, economic characteristics, economic expansion and niche specialization based on dynamic division can only be formed on the basis of intercity connections. In all researches about ordinary dynamic cities, connection is a core concept, let alone in studies of global cities. Connections among ordinary cities based on urban flows are usually formed by trade activities (Jacobs 1984), and are, thus, less complicated than connections among global cities based on urban flows, which are usually conducted through investment, trade, commodity chain and supply chain, etc. Moreover, the connection mode of ordinary cities is relatively simple, such as point-to-point or plane-to-plane connections based on trade and investment, while network connections are more common in global cities, which are interlocked by the internal network of global functional institutions. In addition, the reach of the connection of ordinary cities is relatively limited, which mainly covers some surrounding hinterland, adjacent areas or domestic territory. In comparison, the connections of global cities at a global scale far exceed these areas. Global connection relationship is of fundamental importance to global cities and is a key to their existence. For ordinary cities, the non-expansion or reduction of connections only means that the city's economic expansion process is hindered, and it becomes a static city with slow economic growth. And for a global city, it will definitely disappear without a connection relationship at a global scale. Therefore, multi-scale connection is the essential attribute of global cities and, thus, becomes a basic core conception in the evolution of global cities.

3.2.2. Duality of Intercity Connection

According to the dual ontology of cities as living organisms, the connections of global cities also have dual nature: on the one hand, there are physical flows of connections and, on the other, there are the flows of urban mind such as information and knowledge. These two are inherently compatible with each other. For global cities, the connections of physical flows take the forms of the frequent movement of energy, raw material, intermediate goods, services, capital, technology and workers, which are tangible. These flows enable global cities to establish continuous and relatively stable interactions with others.

However, these flows have explicit purposes, their direction of movement is under control and their scale is manipulated; thus, at some point, they are relatively stable. This means that there is a power of dominance, control and guidance behind the flows, as reflected in a large number of strategic planning, project planning, order contracts, instructions, task assignment, communication coordination, consulting services, settlement and liquidation, etc., which are all based on information and knowledge. While these activities boost the flows of goods, services and resources, they themselves are also a kind of flows, thus forming an intercity connection based on the flows of urban mind. In the past, people tend to pay more attention to the physical flows of global cities, focusing on the scale of trade, capital and manpower while ignoring global cities' functions based on information and knowledge flows.

In fact, the core of the connections of global cities is the flows of urban mind, which manifest as the functional linkages. The tangible flows of trade, capital and workers are merely the medium and external expression of the flows of urban mind among or within global cities. Therefore, without the flows of urban mind, the tangible flows will stop running; without the tangible flows serving as the medium, the flows of urban mind mean nothing.

What will the inherent unity of the duality of the global cities connections ultimately lead to? Naturally it will come to our mind that the unity of the duality of global cities connections should lie in the cities themselves. But, in fact, this is not true. Global cities are only the spatial medium of the global flows. It is not the global cities but the various functional organizations that serve as the driving force of the global flows. Therefore, the unity lies in the latter. In a broad sense, this includes all kinds of functional organizations, such as enterprises, trade associations, schools and research institutes, cultural institutions and religious groups, governmental organizations and NGOs. However, since the current global flows are mainly economy related, this concept in a narrow sense mainly refers to TNCs and professional services companies, global operation centres and global R&D centres, etc. It is these organizations that unify the physical flows and flows of urban mind and form the connections of global cities with the help of infrastructure of transportation and communication, etc.

In addition, from the perspective of the external and internal, connections based on flows are also of dual nature, that is, the internal and external relations of the global cities. The internal connections mean the connections between various elements inside the city, and the external connections mean the connections between cities. In a dynamical process, various elements inside the global cities flow between each other, and are continuously connected to and steadily interact with each other. These kinds of internal connections are reflected in the division of labour in the cities and their structures. The complexity of the division of labour inside the cities is a result of centralization of departments and institutions. However, it is not the common preference of these organizations that results in the clustering of these organizations, but the proximity of many companies in different economic sectors due to economic expansion. Cities are knowledge-intensive clusters, the division of labour is knowledge-related, and inside cities, new jobs are created through innovation and imitation (Fujita and Thisse 2002). However, the vitality of global cities depends not only on the growing complexity of internal relations based on departmental division of labour, but on the flows of knowledge, bulk commodities and workers, which makes the cities spaces of flows. Therefore, the cities' external relations are as important as the internal relations. This kind of intercity relation expansion is the mechanism of urban dynamic expansion.

In fact, the intra and interconnections of global cities interact. To a large extent, stronger intercity connections can lead to more expansive intracity connections through the agglomeration of functional organizations, such as enterprises and industries. Such expanded connections, in turn, fuel the further agglomeration of industries and businesses, increasing the sophistication of division of labour among sectors inside the cities. Interactions between intra and intercity connections promote dynamic development of cities and lead to stronger connections in terms of (a) the number of connected cities, depth of connection, cities' functionality as gateways and their influence over other cities; and (b) greater development potential, including market expansion, capital accumulation, technological progress, employment growth and higher mobility. In a word, cities grow through interactions between intra and interconnections, or, to put it in another way, are formed as a result of continuously executed processes, events, behaviours and practices (Thrift 2008). Therefore, it can be concluded that global city connections are the results of both intra and intercity relations.

3.3. CONNECTED SPACES

City connections do not appear out of thin air, but happen in a certain space, based on a certain scale. Therefore, it is necessary to discuss the concept of connected spaces for a better understanding of the connections. Also, an investigation of meanings, motivations and fundamentals behind the flows and connections may help clarify what the global city network is and how it has developed (Lai 2012).

3.3.1. Types of Connected Spaces

To study connected spaces, the first thing to look at should be the spatial scale at which connections happen, either national, regional or global. Intuitively, these spatial scales represent how far the connections reach, which is easy to identify. However, lying at the heart of connected spaces is not spatial scales, but the types of space attributes. From the perspective of global city research, the key issue in the connected space study is not the spatial scale itself but its types and attributes of spaces, without which spatial scales are no different from sizes. In other words, connected spaces at a national, regional or global scale are simply different in the size of their sprawl. If so, research into global cities will go astray.

Most traditional urban theories are confined to territorial spatial scales (space of place). According to these theories, cities are like containers of resources and their relative importance are weighed based on their economic, social and cultural capital. The national urban system is a network of individual cities 'installing' at different spots or locations, one that may have many dimensions but that always has a hub. Viewed through this lens, global cities are just more expansive in special scale than regular ones. However, the connected space of a global city, as spatial representation of modern globalization, is in essence a globalized space that extends far beyond national borders (physical space). Different from a region or a nation, this space is non-territorial (space of flows). According to Castells (1996), the 'space of flows' represents the material arrangements that allow for simultaneity of social practices without territorial contiguity. The content of this space of flows can be described as three layers of material support for time-sharing: a circuit of electronic exchanges, nodes and hubs, and spatial organization of the dominant elites. Among the three layers, hubs and nodes are most important because they are where communication and coordination happen (Taylor [2003] 2004). Therefore, the 'space of flows' is actually a sea change, not an upgrading in the WCN.

In this globalized world, as inter-regional resource transfers lead to non-territorialization, cities are risking losing their traditional status as space hubs, and their structures are constantly being changed in space production. According to Brenner (2004), the development of cities is a constantly evolving process that has multiple layers and geopolitical strategic implications, rather than a territorial concept. But even during the transformation process, cities are still defined in various ways because there is no uniform model that defines all cities. Therefore, new city models are constantly developed, created and reinvented through technological, economic and political changes. But in the globalized world, city models have some common new reticular features: open, scattered, growing in the periphery, rather than the centre. In other words, cities are transformed from 'space of places' to 'space of flows', which demonstrates the importance of regional networking. In the first mechanism 'space of places', places matter because activities happen right there. In the second mechanism 'space of flows', flows are important because activities happen right there, serving as the channel that coordinates other activities. In this regard, it is a new city model that emerges in the globalized world.

Taylor (2007) further distinguishes between local and non-local spatial scales. He also uses this theory to divide the city development process into 'town-ness' and 'city-ness'. While the words 'city' and 'town' are used interchangeably in practice, they are both defined as a 'large town' in the dictionary. But Taylor does not use the two terms in its dictionary meaning, neither does he use the terms in a much formal administrative sense. In China, urbanization and rural urbanization are defined on the basis of administrative mechanisms. Rural urbanization refers to the transfers of surplus labour force in rural areas to city centres, while urbanization is used in a much broader sense, including transfers of surplus labour force in rural areas to city towns, village towns and market towns. Therefore, Taylor's interpretation of town-ness and city-ness is different from what we Chinese understand. Town-ness and city-ness are interpreted as a dual process in which city expands its external relations under different spatial scales. 'Town-ness' is a localized process that links the urban community to its centre area, turning the city and its centre areas into a consistent economic unit. An interactive functional area that has a static, hierarchical and stable relationship between the periphery and the centre is created. In contrast, 'city-ness' is regarded as a non-localized city networking process, where cities themselves are the consistent economic units. These cities have networking features that are unbounded, dynamic, complex and interdependent. Taylor takes urban development into consideration in order to establish more specific classifications of connected spaces, which essentially has expanded the scale of Castells' 'spaces of places' and 'spaces of flows' notions. According to Taylor, global cities are simply a result of 'city-ness' and a clear distinction is made between global cities and cities based on 'town-ness', even megacities. In this context, such a classification method makes a difference.

3.3.2. Constitutive Relations between Connected Spaces

According to the analyses earlier, it is crucial to distinguish between the diverse attributes of connected spaces, especially in global city studies. However, confusion remains about the best approaches to do so. It appears difficult and crucial for a traditional conceptualization of cities which have immediate hinterlands within territorial boundaries to incorporate into the intensive, global circuits of transmission and exchange (Taylor [2003] 2004), because many factors behind the cities' development as centres and agglomerations of economic activities require the constant importance of their physical, territorial and, in many cases, historical advantages (Beauregard and Haila 2000). Therefore, it seems that many urban development studies are fundamentally involved in a kind of conceptual spectrum and focus on the spaces of places at one extreme or spaces of flows at the other, which results in an opposition between the two concepts.

For example, as mentioned earlier, Taylor distinguishes between 'town-ness' and 'city-ness' on the basis of local or non-local spaces, which, to some extent, represents a contrast between definitions of both concepts. Virtually, a central place is able to develop external relations by economic interactions with a surrounding area (regardless of its size). In this case, although the area is a local hinterland within boundaries, two-way flows of factors can be brought about. In addition, as long as such flows are sufficient, labour divisions will become more complex, contributing to the expansion of the city's economic life. Jacobs (1984) uses this scale to identify five 'great forces' that are derived from dynamic city economies: (a) enlarged city markets (size and variety); (b) more and varied jobs (new work); (c) increased transplants of city work (old work); (d) new uses of technology and (e) growth of city capital. In the city region, the five forces work together to promote balanced growth: markets impulse new production; technology helps develop new labour divisions in the central place, causing outsourcing (old work) in this region as transplanted work; and all of these provide opportunities for city capital. As a result, it is critical that these forces strengthen one another in a positive way so as to develop a vibrant regional economy integrated with the core city economy. Taylor believes that city hinterland relations are relatively stable, but it is true only under comparatively closed conditions. Otherwise, due to strong external impacts (such as substantial foreign investment and trade activities), such relations will become unstable and give rise to rapid economic changes. A good example is that Shanghai has experienced changes of relations with surrounding areas as well as rapid development since the launch of China's reform and opening-up policy in 1978. Moreover, Taylor (2001a) also has an idea of modelling extended global city/state relations, which is called the globally two-stage stratified spatial economic model. This global spatial economy is composed of two types of interactive spaces: spaces of flows that are concentrated in global cities (whose drivers include tariff rates and labour policies made by governments), and spaces of places comprising state economic jurisdiction (whose drivers include agglomeration of businesses). However, this model has failed to include city/state relations.

In our opinion, the two extremes of the connected space spectrum should be viewed as consistent interaction process. In the connection space, we do not see a space of places diametrically opposed to a space of flows, but more a mutually constitutive logic.

Indeed, as flows always have a start and an end point, they are meaningful only if and when they become '(re)territorialized' (in cities) at their end points. For example, information or capital can only be used once it reaches its destination. Places are only ever constructed through processes of 'fixing' flows, while flows are only ever produced (and 'consumed') from more or less 'fixed' bases/places. The paradox of the network society is that its main focus (flows) proves to be useless whilst in transit and always requires place-based fixity for utility. From this perspective, and contra some recent strands of urban studies, one could argue that there is essentially nothing in between cities. In turn, however, places are never self-bounded entities but are open social and material constructions (Latham and McCormack 2004). They are always constituted by networks of flows. Globalization and digitization processes contribute to a vectorization of places, that is, to their increasing engagement in a geography of exchanges and distant links.

Thus, global and local connected spaces of flows and places should neither be viewed as distinct objects facing each other nor mechanistic assemblages, articulations or combinations, but as one mutually constitutive, cogredient process in which flows and places are co-produced, continually defining and reinforcing one another. Cities are outcomes of multiple and diverse processes of commutation through which flows and places are always being interconnected. First, urban commutation of flows and places occurs primarily through a series of everyday practices, constructed by actors in relation to the tools, instruments, norms, regulations and technologies that they use in their actions. Commutation of flows and places in cities always relies on and works through the tools and instruments that these actors have at their disposal and that they use on an everyday basis, which many scholars have failed to realize (Guillaume 1999).

Second, the spatial continuum of flows and places inherently involves and (re)produces the complex and dynamic systems of power relations between sets of actors with more or less diverging or conflictual objectives. The presence of powerful and less powerful actors throughout the flow-place commutation process ensures that urban development is shaped within a constantly unstable context of tensions and harmonies between different actors. Therefore, it is crucial to explore how actors situate themselves and their actions in relation to others, and to what extent their use of particular tools and instruments materializes relations of power and influence in urban development (Moulaert, Rodriguez and Swyngedouw 2003). Last, urban commutation of flows and places inherently involves a transcalar, systemic set of processes and practices from multiple scales, thus requiring a conceptual shift beyond scalar fixity to view space more as a soft continuum of communications between the here and the distant (Massey 2007). In other words, the spatial arena of flow-place commutation always extends well beyond any political or functional city boundaries. Flow-place commutation is, thus, believed to be inherently transcalar, invoking (continually changing) links and connections between socio-technical practices and processes on a priori differing geographical levels. From this perspective, the commutation of flows and places is seen as mixing multiple scales into a soft continuity (though not necessarily without rupture) of spaces. For this reason, Harvey (1996) identified the importance of 'cogredience' in urban life and propounded a focus on 'the way in which multiple processes flow together to construct a single, consistent, coherent though multi-faceted time–space system', underlining the continuing need of mobile flows for (temporary) territorial fixity. That is to say, cities are dynamic and unstable flow-places, in which the respective qualities of flows and places cannot be meaningfully disarticulated. Therefore, to separate out how flows shape places from how places shape flows would lead in this case to potentially misleading and simplified conclusions.

Of course, this dual process is uneven at different stages of urban development. At the early stage, expanding local relations remain the dominant driver of urban growth for a protracted period in many cities; as cities grow, more and more non-local relations are formed and start to gain momentum, becoming a new driving force for urban development. However, urban development is more like a dynamic balancing process between these two kinds of relations. We are witnessing a profound rescaling as cities are impacted by, on the one hand, 'global forces' and, on the other, 'national systems of regulation', as Short (2006) argued, 'we need to conceptualize the city at the multiple and interacting scales of global, national and local'. Indeed, Short is certain that 'scalar processes' exist. 'Global, national and urban processes are affecting individual cities around the world, while globalizing cities are the site and platform for shifts in national and global articulations'.

When it comes to global cities, more attention is being paid to their non-local relations and the connection among the spaces of flows, because these characteristics are their essential attributes. Although a city accumulates and retains wealth and power because what flows through and is embedded in it—which invites attention to its inner linkages as well as connections with other cities—it should be noted that this is a kind of 'grounded' flow. Global cities are places influenced by a set of historical, political, social and cultural factors. What's the significance of regarding them as places? First, it recognizes the different roles that global cities play in a global city network and connects them in a meaningful way. This point of view helps better identify the historical context and background against which a city becomes a part of the WCN, thus contributing to the development of global cities. Second, it recognizes the fact that global cities are inhabited by residents and communities with a social, political and economic life, who, in turn, are affected by how the global cities are formed.

Evolution Framework
World City Network

Traditional research on urban dynamics often focuses on city scale changes and uses the 'core–periphery' evolution model of the world city system to examine the way cities connect, such as star configuration, bilateral and multilateral circles and other dynamic changes. Global cities reach beyond national borders and connect through networks. Its significance lies in the recognition of transformation of spatial relations, and a challenge to the traditional dualistic geopolitical narrative; its dynamic evolution occurs inside the WCN and is mirrored by the status of other networks. Therefore, the research on the dynamic change of global cities should be measured by how nodes in the network change and be based on the evolution framework of the WCN.

4.1. COMPLEX INTERLOCKING NETWORK MODEL

In the field of global city research, the mainstream is the interlocking network model developed by Taylor and his colleagues on the basis of the APS firms. Although this model is useful for understanding the attributes and characteristics of global cities, it is insufficient to explain how global cities evolve due to its underlying implied 'mechanistic' ontological assumptions. Therefore, the model needs to be upgraded and further developed to build one that fully explains the evolution trajectories of global cities, taking into consideration cities' intellectual attributes.

4.1.1. Taylor's Interlocking Network Model

In fact, the modern model of intercity relations represents how cities connect with each other. The ties between global cities have two distinctive features: connectivity occurs on a global scale and is based on spaces of places and spaces of flows. Therefore, the WCN model shows the interconnectivity of modern intercity relations. On the surface, this network is one of interconnected cities with different formations, and dynamics, which ensure that they expand in different manners and on different scales, but essentially it is formed through patterns of association and interaction that bind people together in the pursuit of certain ends. The most effective networked practices are those which blend different forms of organizational reach. In this sense, it is a social network in which the nodes are social actors and ties are social. Given the globalized interactive intercity relations, the city, where trade (production and consumption) happens, should be used as the spatial unit of analysis to build a 'global spatial economy'. But the city itself is only a spatial unit, rather than a social actor. As for a spatial unit, a city is a joint (network node) for resources and factors to flow globally. Global flows of material and human resources enabled by the connection of cities is completed by actors (agents). For these agents, they can achieve the far-flung goals of increasing spatial coverage by creating an extended and dense network with the blending of authoritative and diffuse techniques. Therefore, it is required that agents as actors be involved in linking city spaces of flows (networks and chains), which automatically fit with the theoretical formation process of an interlocking network.

Unlike any other network, Taylor's WCN is a unique, interlocking one, in which linkages are established by diverse network-making agents. This network consists of three layers: the net level of the global economy, the node level of cities and the sub-nodal level of agents (actors). Taylor ([2003] 2004) argued that under globalization, city spaces take the form of a WCN wherein the nodes (cities) are connected through the activities of trans-nodal agents. In this sense, world cities are not independent of the firms that create them (Beckfield and Alderson 2006). In the interlocking network model, agents based in cities that operate across the globe are the WCN makers. As well as the role of cities in the formation of the WCN, network makers, or actors, need further research.

Generally, any agent (actor) that facilitates global flows of money, workers, information and commodities constitutes as a network maker. A variety of agents fit with the diverse processes of globalization, including TNCs, APS firms or even international NGOs. These global agents set up subsidiaries around the world which enable them to connect with many more cities. As Krätke and Taylor (2004) put it, this diversity of globalized activities leads to multiple globalizations within WCN formation. Since agents vary in the way they are distributed worldwide and organized structurally, they lead to different types of intercity relations, or interlocking networks.

In mapping out the world city interlocking model, Taylor identifies APS firms as major network makers, who, as the key economic agents, create intercity economic connections at different scales. This idea aligns with Sassen's (2001) argument that APS firms are major participants in the world economy, as well as complements Jacobs' contention (1984, 2000) that vigorous cities are constantly expanding the economic life with diverse economic processes, contributing to more complex intercity relations. APS firms not only themselves create global flows for the service sector as they operate across their office network worldwide but they also serve the major producers of global flows, assisting transnational companies to exchange information and services across their global offices, if not completely. Jacobs also suggests that sophisticated APS firms are a key index of city vitality. In other words, where there is the agglomeration of APS firms, there is a significant economic expansion.

On the basis of his observation of APS firms connecting producers with global markets in different cities, Taylor (2001a) explained how global cities expand the WCN. When a producer located in a city wants to enter a global market elsewhere, it can work most efficiently if the APS firm that supports its operations has branches in other cities. In order to adapt to changes in demand, APS firms must use the internal network between their branches that are located in different cities to provide seamless service to their customers. Supporting global professional service means that APS firms can provide their service products in different cities around the world. The branch network of an APS firm is the result of its regional strategy which connects cities as a global service centre. This shows that the scope of an APS firms' branch network defines the scope of access through which their customers can enter the global market directly, or at least effectively. An APS firms' branch network creates an economic link between producer A and markets B and C, or it forms a more abstract economic link between city A and cities B and C. In other words, the strength of intercity connection depends on APS firms' structure in the city and the extent of them overlapping. Therefore, the concentration of APS firms and their globalized internal networks indicate an intercity economic network, even if their internal network is interlocked with the intercity network. The contact created by these APS firms between branches in different cities creates an interlocking global city network. APS firms are essential for global cities as they create a network between them which is a key characteristic of global cities.

Since APS firms are widely distributed around the world, their internal network is complex and interlocking intercity connections are more comprehensive. Not only do they interlock the connections between global cities but they also create a connection between global cities and globalized cities. The WCN that is based on APS firms' activities includes hundreds of cities around the world, among which are global cities that are considered as basic or primary nodes of the network, and globalized cities that are considered as general nodes. The extensive coverage of the WCN is actually the overall spatial problem of globalization. This reflects the fact that economic globalization is an all-inclusive process leaving no cities 'non-globalized'. Cities are just in different forms and stages in the globalization process, depending on its historical timeline and current position (Taylor et al. 2014). Therefore, cities covered by the empirical analysis of its model are larger in scale compared to those in the WCN based in a company's HQs. For example, about half of the revenues of the Fortune Global 500 companies are created by corporations headquartered in just 20 cities. The GaWC's list of the 'Alpha World Cities', known as 'very important world cities that link major economic regions and states into the world economy', comprised of 47 cities.

From this difference in the network size and from the assumption that producer service firms exercise command functions for global commodity chain, WCN follows a more decentralized geography of economic governance. A third of these best connected global cities are located in middle-income countries, with Asia being particularly well linked. Considering the complete list of alpha, beta and gamma world cities, all 'Third-World' megacities (except Dhaka) are included. Apparently, this finding reflects the profile of WCN pretty well. More importantly, the WCN provides the basis and fundamental framework for understanding the evolution of global cities, because only in the spatial integration of globalization can we observe how some global cities develop into primary nodes while others degrade into sub-nodes.

As any theoretical model has its limitations, Taylor's world city interlocking network model has inevitable flaws. Up till now, criticism is concentrated on three aspects.

First, the one-sidedness of the interlocking network. The model merely discusses in detail economic forces driving the formation of global cities with a focus on the economic aspect of social relations, particularly intercity relations that operate to geographically structure the world economy. However, economic forces, in fact, are never the only factor that determines global city development. Globalization or world city formation is a three-dimensional process driven by political, economic and cultural forces. The three aspects are interlocked and it is unfair to casually evaluate their importance in isolation. Moreover, their roles in the formation of global cities vary with different perspectives. If the APS firms' network model is used, global economy is more important, but if the perspective is the multinational organizations network, it will be a quite different story.

Second, the notion that WCN is mainly formed by the transnational corporate HQs somewhat dismisses the role of cities as unique places and other participants' social practices in city network formation and development. Although this view helps to clarify the multifaceted ways in which flows shape places, the focus is very rarely, if at all, on the complex ways in which places (through their contingent mixes of social actors and institutions) may or do shape flows (Storper 1997). Obviously, these global flows are neither limited to the APS industry nor within corporate departments. In addition, some in-house services (e.g., design) are not necessarily outsourced, and some services (maintenance) barely have physical added value. Therefore, using this model to trace network flows has limitations.

Moreover, considering the nature of their services, not all major APS firms are primarily worldwide in the scope of their service provision. Many, especially in financial services, continue to operate through concentrations of offices in their region/country of origin with other offices in the remainder of the world limited in number and importance. This means the location strategies of APS firms are different (Taylor 2011a) by diverse measurements. A principal component analysis reveals that the advertising, legal and business service sectors are using locational strategies that are global in scope and are largely concentrated in global cities. These locational strategies help a city to integrate into the WCN, for example, the 'Advertising Services Locational Strategy' articulated through New York, the 'Legal Services Locational Strategy' articulated through New York, Washington, DC, and London, and the 'Business Services Locational Strategy' articulated though London and US cities, notably Boston. However, most strategies are not global in scope; instead, they are largely concentrated in just one major world region. For example, the 'Financial Services Asia-Pacific Strategy' is made up of Asia-Pacific cities. All the cities in 'Legal Services Pan-European Strategy' are European (two from Eastern Europe), including Frankfurt, London, Paris and Brussels. The 'Financial Services United States Strategy' consists of US cities but not including New York. There are minor regional service strategies that are based on a single country such as 'Financial Services Canadian Strategy' and 'Financial Services Australian Strategy'. These really look like 'national strategies' with the cities in each strategy roughly ranked in terms of their importance in their respective countries.

Despite their reasonableness and inspirational merits, the earlier criticism cannot shake the foundations of Taylor's interlocking WCN model. From the social network perspective, the development of WCN is not only an economic process but also a political and cultural one. Given that political and cultural aspects are constrained more by nation states, it is acceptable that Taylor and others' approach to the WCN mainly from the economic aspect. Global mobility is not limited within the APS sector or inside the businesses in the sector, and not all APS firms offer services in global terms. However, APS firms are the prime actor in the formation of WCN, because no other substitute could be more appropriate. Indeed, to study some more complex WCN, the roles played by other sectors in the economic connections among cities may also be referred to as a useful complement or compared with that of the APS sector.

We hold the view that the fundamental limitation of Taylor's interlocking network model lies not in technical dimensions, such as its focus on the economics of globalization and social relations, the identification and selection of APS firms, and alike and rather in its underlying ontological assumption that cities are regarded as mechanical devices. As it is mentioned in Chapter 3, the methodology applied in the present model of WCN is based on structuralism and neo-structuralism where events are generated, commanded and controlled by an external agency. Being the creators of the WCN, APS firms only function as 'power relays' and, thus, the occurrence of each event is merely repeating the structural relations. Therefore, in practice, Taylor's interlocking network model can be used in static and dynamic analysis on global cities, that is, to determine the positions and changes of global cities in the world network by analysing the clustering of APS firms and their extended network relations. Nonetheless, such a model can hardly be used to analyse the evolution of global cities, for it cannot explain why APS firms cluster in certain urban locations, how the supplier–customer relationship is established and how the endogenous relationship is extended. In conclusion, an evolution-based interlocking network model needs to be built on the basis of the existing one through some upgrading and transformation.

4.1.2. Building an Evolution-Based Interlocking Network Model: Step One

Although Taylor's interlocking network model explains the overall spatiality of globalization well, it is deficient in justifying its theoretical generalization. According to Taylor, the presence (or lack) of connectivity between cities in the WCN indicates opportunities (or obstacles) for producers to enter the global market directly and effectively or, more precisely, a degree of opportunity. In fact, this is based on the presumption that APS firms already have offices all over the world, or there already exist internal networks in APS firms. And here comes the question: why would APS firms establish offices in cities around the world, or what are the main factors leading to the formation and presence of the internal networks in APS firms? A widely accepted explanation is that APS firms usually 'follow in the steps' of MNCs in terms of their deployment of globalization, which means that economic connections have already existed between cities before APS firms establish their offices, and that the offices of as well as the internal networks in the firms are the consequences of these connections. Taylor's interlocking network, however, without any clarification on these connections, cannot reveal actual flows of information, knowledge and capital on the nodal and sub-nodal level—it rather detects the 'channel system' and the nodal intersections of potential flows. Saey (1996) has, therefore, questioned whether the apparent spatial correlation between world city formation and core processes is in and by itself sufficient to speak of a systematic relation between both structures, for the existence of a massive globalized producer service industry alone does not necessarily tell whether a certain city is the administration and governance centre of transborder economy activities. That is to say, it is not sufficient for a comprehensive evaluation of the formation of global cities. This actually demonstrates different focuses on the issue of agglomerative economies: global city studies focus on the functions of producer service clusters in global cities, rather than explanations for such clustering of the industry. Therefore, we propose to understand the fundamental conditions for the formation of internal networks in APS firms and interpret the interlocking effects of APS firms on cities at various scales, by combining the global commodity chain network of MNCs with Taylor's interlocking network model, in order to fully elucidate the generalization mechanism for the WCN.

Hopkins and Wallerstein (1986) define commodity chains as a 'network of labor and production processes, whose end result is a finished commodity', with an emphasis on seeking capital through the process from material inputs, to manufacturing, and to consumption in the end. Gereffi and Korzeniewicz (1994) propose a relatively coherent paradigm, the 'global commodity chain' approach henceforth focused on value creation, its distribution and control within transnational networks, which extend in a chain of nodes from raw material exploitation primary processing, through different stages of trade, services and manufacturing processes to final consumption and waste management. Taken as a whole, the global commodity chain may link up different organizational models of production, trade and service providing processes, and can even include the generation of externalities and inter-market spillovers (Gereffi and Kaplinsky 2001). As a consequence, this approach is better geared to reveal the spatial ordering of social relations that are being continually reproduced through everyday practices of production, distribution and consumption in a globalized economy. By modelling the commodity chain, we can draw attention to not only global cities that are based on value control and distribution but also intercity relations beyond global cities, because the commodity chain reveals how the small settlements are connected to the WCN through various flows of capital, labour, goods, services, etc. Global commodity chains do explicitly include the stages of primary production, which are located in rural areas and related to city-based transformation and trade processes (Jacobs 1969). Such an examination may, thus, help to develop a more spatially refined analysis of the WCN, depicting also the specific roles of those cities seemingly at the margins of the WCN. More importantly, it explains the premise of the formation of internal networks in APS firms, which means that the layout of the worldwide office network of APS firms is determined by the intercity economic connections shaped by the global commodity chains of MNCs. Meanwhile, the services provided by advanced producers are naturally translated into their participation in the management and control of the commodity chains.

Although there is usually a symbiotic relationship between HQs of MNCs and APS firms, and a certain correlation between the manufacturing sector network (the global commodity chain network) and the service sector network, such relationship is only strong at the top of the system, but generally weak in the entire system. That's because the networks based on the global commodity chain and based on the global service chain are different in terms of the following relationships:

1. Investment relationship: The global commodity chain network is closely connected and involves large-scale investment and usually holding companies, while the global commodity chain network with relatively loose connections and small-scale investment

involves HQs, regional HQs and branches, which are not necessarily complete holding companies in the strict sense.
2. Operational relationship: The former is completely subordinate to the superior command, while the latter is relatively independent with greater autonomy.
3. Hierarchical relationship: The former features a hierarchical structure, while the latter a metamorphic one.
4. Geographical distribution: The former is vertically distributed with limited extensions and partially concentrated in cities or in the outer suburbs or areas adjacent to cities. In contrast, the latter is horizontally distributed and easy to extend, especially as the advancement of computing and communication technologies enables the extended geographical distribution of service firms, which always cluster in cities to provide professional business services.

Therefore, while the producer service sector takes the lead in blending the city into a global network, the manufacturing sector is likely to use the global commodity chain to construct other forms of network connectivity among cities. Rather than conceptualizing the global economy through a series of exclusively market-oriented containers, the global commodity chain approach allows us to focus on system-wide networks of labour and production processes.

Of course, the analysis of the global commodity chain network has some limitations

> because the focus of the approach is upon the spaces of flows involved in the production of particular commodities, commodity chain research has been less successful in specifying how chains contribute towards the complex dynamics of the broader economic system in which they are located. (Bair 2003)

In addition, more 'Global Commodity Chain research also lacks a comprehensive treatment of the spatiality of commodity chains' (Leslie and Reimer 1999). 'Despite the theoretical insight that a Global Commodity Chain connects inputs from different parts of the world, pulls them together in specific sites and provides output to different locations, the study of the actual geographies of these commodity chains has remained relatively underdeveloped' (Brown et al. 2010)

What's more, 'Although a number of writings have focused on the role of Global Commodity Chains in regional development and the potentials of localities (e.g., Schmitz 2000)…overarching spatial conceptualization remains an unfulfilled task' (Brown et al. 2010). That is to say, it is urgent for us to track the commodity chain at spatial level as a contact of destination between different regions. It still remains preoccupied with the nation state as geographical scale of analysis (Coe et al. 2004) for purpose of 'improving the position of firms or nations in international trade networks' (Gereffi 1999: 39). 'Another more specific limitation in Global Commodity Chain research is that the empirical scope of analysis has been somewhat limited, with the majority of studies focusing on a number of primary commodities and industrial sectors'.

> Services, in particular, despite an early call for exploring the 'service sector nexus' (Rabach and Kim 1994), have not been analysed particularly effectively in commodity chain research, either in industries where the service constitutes a commodity in its own right or where it is used to facilitate the production of other more tangible commodities.

'It is perhaps above all the lack of attention that has been paid to understanding the crucial role of producer services in setting up and sustaining global networks of production that has been the most crucial omission in this literature' (Daniels and Bryson 2002). Finally, the new node of the commodity chain (such as a new plant in the commodity chain) is a non-networked extension that is merely the result of cumulative effect (Shy 2001). But in an actual networked economy, every new node joining the network has a potential flowing exponential growth effect, which reflects the essential difference between the increase in the entity of node in commodity chains and the development of the relationship among the nodes in a networked economy.

The work we are going to do is not simply replacing the interlocking network based on APS firms with the network of global commodity chain, but integrating the two by leveraging their common foundation and internal relationship.

First, both of them originate in world systems analysis (Brown et al. 2010) and share a general concept of similar economic spaces, or the relationship between discontinuous regions in the global network. Thus, 'they both depict fundamental spatial models of flows: a chain of production nodes connected by commodity flows and a network of city nodes connected by information flows' (Brown et al. 2010).

Second, global cities are at the intersection of these two networks, or the connection between the two networked spaces of flows come from very reasonable existence of global cities, which reflects that economic activities at different geographic scales have joined in the world economy (Derudder and Witlox 2010). Basically, all global commodity flows in the world economy run through global cities. This is why a global commodity chain is difficult to start and sustain without global cities, no matter how it is distributed geographically. The formation of the global commodity chains needs the control from these global cities. Similarly, the formation and operation of interlocking networks depend on the connectivity of these global cities to a large extent.

Third, provision of producer services is essential for the production and consumption that are connected and scattered along commodity chains (Parnreiter 2010). It's because these companies, which are supposed to be most competent in serving, managing and controlling their global operations, provide key inputs to the global commodity chains, from production through financing from bank loans in the beginning to promote consumption through services by advertising companies in the end. In particular, it is incomprehensive for the analysis of commodity chains to regard services as separate chains, because it may isolate producer services, rather than enable their necessary service provision to support the development and proliferation of commodity chains. In addition, it is worth restating that these are all producer services, whose intellectual goods as an intermediate product need to be inserted into the global commodity chains, so as to realize capital gains. Therefore, the provision of producer services in cities is vital for the connections between scattered production and consumption sites, thereby ensuring the successful operation of commodity chains. Of course, the primary prerequisite here should be the demand for producer services by MNCs in their global business (or commodity chains). In order to operate in this increasingly complex and globalized world economy, the commodity chains of MNCs must be transmitted through city networks based on APS, which constitutes a strong demand for producer services. As a result, there comes the trade of producer services, implying the creation of data on relations assumed to be functional linkages of global cities.

So what is the point in the integration of these two networks?

First of all, it can better show the overall spatiality of globalization. In the context of economic globalization, all cities are inevitably integrated into global commodity chains, even though in secondary roles, because only by flowing in such spaces can they sustain and develop in the world economy. Thus, the question that how cities are connected to the WCN is solved, and so is the question why the WCN covers a large number of globalized cities in addition to global cities. This overall spatiality of globalization will help us to understand how global cities are associated with globalized cities.

Second, the overall centrality of global cities in world networks can be more fully explained. If world urbanization is understood as a process (providing APS to make global production feasible), it must reflect the various connections between enterprises engaged in economic activities in the world market and service providers in a particular city. That is to say, MNEs as customers of producer services and producer service firms as service providers both gather in global cities. The relationship between producer service providers and their customers is crucial, and they serve as dynamic 'shaker and mover' in the WCN (Beaverstock 2007). Since all global commodity chains 'operate' through global cities, global cities are seen as key nodes in the commodity chains; and precisely because their APS are inserted into the production process, global cities are also service nodes for countless commodity chains, which gives global cities their overall centrality.

Finally, the position and role of global cities in global resource allocation can be more clearly demonstrated. In terms of the service provision by APS providers, the interlocking network based on the APS sector emphasizes the coordination function of global cities; while in terms of the value creation and distribution under the control of multinational companies, the network of global commodity chains focuses on the command and control functions of global cities.

As the integration of the interlocking WCN and the network of global commodity chains has demonstrated how producer service firms in global cities interact with enterprises in global commodity chains, the forward linkages of producer service firms and the backward linkages of enterprises in commodity chains can be mapped out to provide deeper understanding of where the actual control over production comes from, how and where value is created and where it is distributed. Specifically, the value creation and (unequal) distribution in commodity chains are jointly organized and managed by multinational companies and producer service firms in global cities, while the capability and power of value creation and distribution are the potential driving forces for the formation of global cities. Therefore, the control and coordination functions of global cities in global resource allocation are integrated and internalized.

4.1.3. Building an Evolution-Based Interlocking Network: Step Two

Following the first step, we should further confirm that the WCN is built upon ramifications of operations across different scales through macro-regional and national to local (Parnreiter 2003). Precisely, WCN is a scale-free network, which breaks the spatial scale limitations of the evolution of global city and brings internal impetus for the evolution.

Traditional global city studies used to be conducted at different scales such as macroscopic and microscopic, and global and local scales. Taylor's interlocking network approach also failed to transcend his primary scale of interest, the global, and became a one-scale analysis of a few leading cities. Although other scholars' attempts to analyse the city network in greater geographical detail (Derudder et al. 2003) have extended our understanding beyond a limited number of leading cities, they fail to explain the connection to other scales. That is to say, these analyses are the end result of ever-larger data sets that depart from the logic of considering only the nodes at the global scale, but they are weak at revealing the way in which urban networks at national and regional scales are connected to the wider WCN (Hall and Pain 2006). In fact, these research methods have further limited global city studies at the global scale, leading to a natural opposition between 'global' and 'local' development processes or arbitrary distinctions between 'cities' and 'super cities' and, thus, resulting in man-made differences between endogenous (internal) dynamics and exogenous (external) dynamics, and between the hierarchical scales and their opposite scales. Moreover, such issues should not be neglected by thinking from a reversed perspective but be solved by blurring the boundaries of spatial scales, for example, through 'global localization'. The aim of doing so is to show an established state, a foundation and a given and undoubted framework, and then we can explain what is happening in the given situation. Therefore, the 'scale' here should be understood as a post-structuralist approach.

We should take a comprehensive approach to integrate different scales, global or local, into the nodes in the WCN.

> That is the idea that the local is a structure that in itself contains elements of global. In other terms that the local is not a small-scale structure, but it is something that in itself already contains the global scale. The global is a modeled terrain where tangles, hybrids will form. The local structure in reality has also been pre-formed by other things, sites, times, actors. (Perulli 2012)

Adopting this approach, we, rather than starting off from the place, start off from the circulation between places. As Perulli (2012) pointed out that

> we are not starting from the place, from this place, but we start from the fact that this place has been made possible because it has been pre-formed by a number of other places, sites, actors, moments that have formed it: what we see is not so much the place itself in its definition, but the systems of movement between places that have made each of these places possible.

From this perspective, 'cities are intersections of multiple networks of social relations at various geographical scales, to which transnational actors are materially connected through employment, political mobilization and cultural practices, or through the means of communication and travel, which they use for their transnational lives' (Smith 2001). Therefore, global cities are places where transnational economic, social, cultural and political flows are located, and where local economic, social, cultural and political practices become transnationalized. In this sense, the macro- or micro-scale, a larger and a smaller scale, no longer exist in the WCN (Latour 2005). Cities, as network nodes, are both local and global, or we can say they are neither local nor global, but are part of both. Likewise, cities are a continuum of both 'spaces of flows' and 'spaces of places'. Each city is a both 'physical and social environment', or an 'urban form' as well as an 'urban process' (Soja 2000).

Therefore, we should incorporate the ANT into the interlocking network model based on evolution, in order to integrate different scales, especially the relationship between 'space of places' and 'space of flows', into the WCN, and to refine the theory of WCN makers.

The ANT helps us to observe cities from a socio-technical perspective, explicating in theoretical terms how short-term and long-term networks are made up by human and non-human actors and how they function as the foundation of urban production processes—constantly creating, maintaining and reshaping urban spaces (Smith 2003). More importantly, the ANT opposes confining cities to fixed geographical spaces or hierarchical tiers. The local is not in any sense more tangible than the global, and networks are by nature neither local nor global but are more or less long and more or less connected (Latour 1993). From this perspective, globalization does not result in changes of scales or multi-scalar dimensions for activities of any sorts. Smith (2008) proposes on the basis of the ANT more scale-bending factors, such as the long- or short-range network and the remote or close relationship. This suggests that it is fundamentally impossible for city actors to integrate or reorganize what were not separated from the start, since neither space of flows nor space of places can perform any function or exert any influence on their own in the first place. On the contrary, the ANT focuses on how space of flows and space of places are synergistically generated in cities through the socio-technical converting process. Such conversions between space of flows and space of places constitute a process of interaction, in which the relationship between two or more than two systematic entities is (temporarily) established, maintained, adjusted and/or interrupted (Guillaume 1999). The conversions always occur in the centre of urban production and reproduction. Slightly different from Crague's (2004) view that cities can be regarded as commutators that attract and pool various types of flows in its territory, the ANT by definition places more emphasis on the conversions between space of flows and space of places. Such conversions do not (just) take place between different types of flows, but are achieved through multiple, and sometimes contradicting, methods that city actors have taken while using tools, devices and techniques. During this process, city actors may find environments with the specific spatial duality that go well with their own dynamic situations, rather than simply operate in the gaps of networks to connect flows. In almost the same way as the telephone exchange system connects users based at different locations (though with an increasing mobility) to the operational network, what many city actors do can be considered as conversions involving only flows and places. In this sense, global cities are both nodes in the network and a result of these varying socio-technical conversions.

Apparently, the integration of the ANT into the evolution-based interlocking network model can bring advantages in three aspects. First, by stressing non-mechanical methods, ANT makes the point clear that cities, as entities with spatial duality, are established through the actions and strategies of multiple actors, hence a better fit for the analysis on the evolution of global cities. Meanwhile, it complements the interlocking network that stresses the role of single actors (APS firms). Second, the ANT emphasizes that the conversions between space of flows and space of places in cities constitute a socio-technical process, as the process is not only initiated, managed, resisted and experienced by different social actors but also relies on the tools and devices used by the social actors in dealing with their routine tasks. This urban production–technology dimension makes an important part of the dynamic evolution and should not be taken as only some conceptualization of urban theories. Third, ANT emphasizes that the range and connectivity of networks do not necessarily correspond to their scales, and that only one continuous association exists in a variable-range network. It has, to a large extent, complemented the sole global scale in the interlocking network or the commodity chains network or, in other words, resolved the incompatibility between different scale measurements, making it possible for continuous associations inside the networks to be represented at different spatial scales.

4.1.4. Building an Evolution-Based Interlocking Network: Step Three

The previous two steps aim to extend the interlocking network, endowing it with wide coverage and scale-freeness, while step three represents a fundamental change to the interlocking network, introducing city minds as the mandate of the WCN.

As we all know, a network is built on a series of interactive flows, of which the basic elements or physical forms are resources. The most essential resources that form global flows are labour, capital, ideas and world-applied solutions (expertise, technologies and intellectual products). The global flows of these resources constitute an internal force shaping the WCN. Thus, WCN, as a whole, is based on both physical and non-physical relations. The former refers to networks of transportation and telecommunication infrastructures, physical assets and resources. The latter includes social networks of trade, communication and organization. Obviously, the former plays an important and necessary role in supporting the WCN, which is nevertheless subject to the functions of the latter. From this perspective, the external linkages and interactive flows of cities as nodes in the WCN, whether they are global cities or globalizing cities, are integrations of both physical and non-physical relations. According to the ontological hypothesis of the urban organism, the physical relations are represented by substantive relations in cities while non-physical relations by those of the urban mind.

The agglomeration of global functional institutions like APS firms in certain cities results from, other than external driving forces such as globalization and shift of world economic focus, the internal factors of these cities. But when analysing these factors, most analyses centre on locations, transport and other infrastructures, physical assets and even political influences, seldom factoring in the urban mind. Actually, for cities with the same external factors such as globalization and shift of world economic focus, the urban mind will be the core factor in attracting global functional institutions like APS firms. This is because the business environment, which largely depends on the urban mind, is a primary concern of APS firms in their development of location strategies. For instance, as indicated in an comparative analysis on the competition between London and Frankfurt to be the global financial centre, Frankfurt, despite its advantageous conditions of location, infrastructures and physical assets, and not to say its unique competitiveness as the location of the EU Central Bank HQs, eventually lost the battle as London had developed a more mature urban mind. London, though with disadvantageous urban infrastructures, had attracted an influx of talents and professionals, and thus held a strong appeal to all financial institutions, thanks to its unique city character, cultural diversity, financial networks, and formal and informal institutional environments.

More importantly, the agglomeration of global functional institutions like APS firms in some cities enables these cities to enhance their urban minds in a self-driven way. Such self-driven enhancement is made possible through internal and external networks of those global functional institutions. As previously mentioned, Taylor's interlocking network model emphasizes that APS firms identify intercity relations through their internal branch networks, and interlock the city network. Meanwhile, the internal branch networks of these global functional institutions mainly deal with massive flows of intellectual products, such as information, ideas, decisions, management strategies and solutions. Even labour flows in the form of face-to-face interaction are mostly communication of tacit knowledge. Therefore, such flows of intellectual products within global functional institutions introduce a lot of information, new ideas and insights, as well as explicit and tacit knowledge to cities where the institutions are based and thereby enhance their urban minds. The larger cluster of global functional institutions like APS firms in a city, the more input channels of external minds, and the more opportunities for interaction between external and internal minds.

In addition, when the offices of different companies are located in the same city, they are connected to each other through the resources, industry norms and social environment they share and, thus, form the inter-firm network (external business network) among global functional institutions like APS firms. This is the concept of global dual networks proposed by Neal (2008)—one among cities, and the other among companies. For customers, companies with good inter-firm networks have more merits than those without. For example, 'firms organized in networks have higher survival chances than do firms which maintain arm's-length market relationships' (Uzzi 1996), which means that they are capable of providing more stable services to their customers. These companies can also harness technological innovations more effectively (Barley, Freeman and Hybels 1992), which means that they are capable of providing more advanced services to their customers. To what extent the inter-firm networking can benefit a company is affected by the number of companies in the city, but much more by the shared environment of the city in which the company is located, so the city is the key organizational unit and the source for the company to gain advantages. For the customers of service producers, where (in which city) they buy services is more important than from whom (from which company) they buy them. This is because cities can offer advantages through a larger range of differentiating capabilities, while the differentiation between companies is relatively smaller. This largely reflects the significant impact of the city environment that is based on the urban mind on the formation of inter-firm networks. At the same time, the flows and exchanges of information and knowledge in the inter-firm networks also continuously reinforce the urban mind.

When the HQs or subsidiaries of different firms are located in the same city, they share at least two major resources—labour and customers. In terms of labour, as they all recruit managers and professionals from the same local labour pool, it is possible for employees with professional know-how to switch from one firm to another. For instance, experienced employees of accounting firm A may be the major candidates coveted by the nearby accounting firm B, if such employees can bring the latter some advantages or needed knowledge. Even if an employee does not change jobs, he or she may still know and interact with people of the same profession and share information with them in private, due to the homophily in social networks (McPherson,

Smith-Lovin and Cook 2001). In addition, as the knowledge of APS workers becomes increasingly specialized, inter-organizational network platforms and other new models for expertise sharing soon become popular. Therefore, through recruitment, employees' social interaction and network platforms, information can be shared immediately among the subsidiaries of APS firms located in the same city.

On the other hand, sharing the same pool of potential local customers can contribute to the indirect information exchange among APS firms. In case of competing for customers, firms may seek to obtain information on the core technologies and strategies of others, in order to stand out and gain a competitive edge. In case of cooperation, they may work to form a strategic alliance to provide customers with service packages. Both strategies bring opportunities for information exchange.

Basing in a common operating environment also means sharing its uncertainty and complexity. When the environment creates uncertainty, APS firms may model themselves on their counterparts in the same city (DiMaggio and Powell 1983), a mimetic process that signifies indirect transfer of information on operational practices, conscious or unconscious, from one organization to another. In response to resource scarcity, these firms will seek collaboration to form economies of scale with complimentary resources (Pfeffer 1982). When the unstable supply of resources raises transaction costs—to the extent that a market-based solution no longer suffices, yet a vertical integration is not necessary—the same set of firms, however, will enter alliances, partnerships and networks (Powell 1990). In other words, as Gulati and Garguilo (1990: 1443) have discovered, 'organizations enter ties with other organizations in response to the challenges posed by the interdependencies that shape their common environment'.

Therefore, the inter-organizational network ties indicate opportunities for information sharing. The more global institutes with different functions are in one city and the more deeply they operate in the shared environment, the more opportunities they will have to exchange information and personnel with each other and, thus, the more it is possible for urban mind to strengthen itself.

Now, as illustrated, whether the entrance of a firm (organization) into a city, or the flows within intra-organizational networks or between inter-organizational networks in the same city—all demonstrate certain defining features of urban mind. Thus, the interaction between cities is, in essence, the interaction between their minds. The physical flows and institutions that form the sub-nodes of the WCN are vehicles that make mental interactions possible. In this sense, it is the interaction between minds of cities that make the networks interlocked with each other. To be more specific, the interlocking network based on evolution is constituted by the wide-ranging, scale-free mental interactions between cities which take place as a result of diversified actors' flowing and changing of locations.

4.2. NETWORK STRUCTURE

The WCN covers all the cities that are integrated into this system. Measured by centrality (an indicator of the nodes' position in the network as demonstrated by their connectivity), these cities can be divided into key nodes and non-key nodes or, in other words, global cities and non-global cities. The two types of nodes form a hybrid network structure, which is neither hierarchical nor purely horizontal, allowing each node to further evolve and fuelling competition between them.

4.2.1. Nodes

Networks usually consist of two layers: the net level and the node level. Although the world city interlocking network has three layers, the net, node and sub-node levels, the sub-nodes only serve to interlock nodes, and it's the connection between nodes that form the network as such nodes—cities that are integrated into the network—are more important.

Cities as nodes show various degrees of centrality. In the context of economic globalization, the centrality can be described as a city's ability to control economic exchange, particularly the advantage it can offer to producers in the global economy. In other words, the more central a city's position is in the network, the more advantages it can offer to its producers in the global economy. Network centrality is measured by three indexes, namely degree, closeness and betweenness

(Freeman [1978] 1979), representing three possible structural advantages a city can bring to its producers, which, in turn, define the differences between cities as nodes.

Degree centrality, defined as the number of outward links a node has, is used to demonstrate how important a node is in the network or, in other words, how many opportunities a city can offer to its producers to have 'direct access' to global market, indicating the city's ability to enable its producers to be directly involved in the global economy. In fact, to grant producers direct access to markets in many different places is probably the simplest way for a city to take advantage in the global economy. If a city is home to multiple branches of global APS firms, its high connectivity (e.g., Chicago has direct links with 55% of cities in the WCN) can allow its producers to enter many markets in a direct and effective way. By contrast, if a city has only a few such branches, its low connectivity (e.g., Saint Louis connects with merely 2% of cities) can only enable its producers to have direct access to very limited markets. Obviously, cities of the former type can provide more opportunities than those of the latter type for producers to enter markets and make intercity transactions. Accordingly, nodes with more links are considered as more influential, as they have more partners and resources. However, since 'degree centrality…is defined as the total number of edges that are adjacent to a node', it only roughly indicates a node's position relative to the centre of the network without offering any information about whether the node is a 'smaller component' of a disconnected cluster or large fractionated network and, thus, may sometimes give misleading impression of a node's real influence (Liu et al. 2005).

Closeness centrality, defined as the number of markets that a city can enter indirectly via its APS firms serving as intermediate agents (or the number of indirect links it has in the WCN), measures a city's ability to grant its producers 'indirect access' to markets, thus revealing its ability to allow its producers to be indirectly involved in the global economy. Some cities provide only a few chances for its producers to enter foreign markets directly, but this is not the whole picture. For example, let's assume that, in an extreme case, a city has only one branch of a global APS firm and, thus, seems to be able to offer its producers only marginal opportunities to participate in the global economy. However, if the HQ of this firm happens to be located in New York, the city may form more partnerships through its indirect relationship with New York and, thus, provide more global business opportunities for its producers.

Betweenness centrality is an indicator of a node's importance by measuring the potential of its relations. If a node is an intermediary between other nodes, acting as the broker or messenger for others' access into markets, it has higher potential because of its favourable location. As Lyons and Salmon (1995: 106) note, 'the function of the global city may be to "broker" or mediate the global links or corporations located in cities throughout the nation', and they 'perform a "brokering" role' in the flow of resources within the network. This kind of centrality, measured by the number of times a city serves as a broker in intercity connections (or the number of links it builds as an agent in the word city network), reflects the city's ability to help producers enter global markets and its position in the network as an intersection. Although horizontal connection has been proven to be central to globalization, intermediary position still plays a critical role, and remains so even when we look at the bigger picture. That's why, in addition to their horizontal connections, major global cities still act as portals in their countries and the wider global landscape.

The position of each node in the WCN is determined by its degree centrality, closeness centrality and betweenness centrality. Due to their differences in the network centrality, that is, different degrees of connectivity in the network, cities form a spectrum of nodes ranging from weak to strong in terms of linkages they provide. Usually, in the WCN, only a few cities have sufficient critical mass and endowment of territorial capital (understood as a set of tangible and intangible assets) to maintain global relations or develop extensive networks. Serving as key or major nodes of the network, they are, hence, known as global cities. By contrast, most cities in the network are ordinary or secondary nodes, though they are also important components of the network. While major nodes can connect to ordinary nodes, the latter can also relate to the former in the same way, exchanging resources with them on a more limited scale.

The foregoing notion of considering cities as nodes with varying degrees of connectivity across a spectrum is important to explain the evolution of global cities. In the global city system, there are two possibilities in the way cities develop: ordinary cities may progressively evolve into global cities as their connections with other cities increase and intensify and, likewise, global cities may degrade into globalizing cities when the intensity of their connections decrease. In addition, even global cities themselves differ from one another in terms of their connectivity and, hence, have different positions on the spectrum, and the same is true for globalizing cities.

4.2.2. Node Relations

The relations among cities have been a key issue in global city studies, which involves the question of whether cities as forms of social organization have a hierarchical structure.

In early research on global cities, it was generally believed that cities had a hierarchy. For example, Friedmann (1986) points out that the extent of a city's integration into the world economy depends on the functions to which it was assigned. Key cities across the world are used by global capital as 'basing points' in the spatial organization and articulation of production and markets. The resulting linkages make it possible to arrange world cities into a complex, unbalanced spatial hierarchy. Accordingly, Friedmann (1995) proposes a hierarchy in which world cities (countries) are arranged in accord with the economic power they command: cities that top the ranking list of connectivity are 'the command and control centers of the global economy', and those in the secondary echelon are cities that articulate national economies into the global economy. The criterion is whether cities house MNC HQs with command and control functions. As such, global cities where MNC HQs are highly agglomerated are the command and control centres of the global economy.

However, Friedmann (1995: 23) also admits that

> [E]stablishing such a hierarchy once and for all may, in any event, be a futile undertaking. The world economy is too volatile to allow us to fix

a stable hierarchy for any but relatively short stretches of time. Assigning hierarchical rank may therefore be a less compelling exercise than recognizing the existence of differences in rank without further specification and, based on this rough notion, investigating the articulations of particular world cities with each other.

In the argument of Sassen (1991), by contrast, it is APS firms rather than MNC HQs that are identified and used to explicate the global city hierarchy, which are regarded to fulfil critical 'top-level management and control functions'. In this sense, global cities with a high concentration of APS firms exercise strategic control functions, based on which they can be hierarchically ranked.

Following these early studies, the hierarchical structure has been further discussed in many empirical studies by mainstream researchers of global cities, such as those by the GaWC Research Network that analysed the network of global APS firms (Taylor [2003] 2004), the relationship among multinationals on the Fortune Global 500 list (Alderson and Beckfield 2004), the worldwide inter-corporate directorships (Carroll 2007) and three scales of worldwide corporate shareholds (Wall, Burger and van der Knaap 2008). These studies show that the hierarchy formed by MNCs has been stable, with no evidence found indicating a new geography of centrality or marginality. Therefore, it is still the few countries where HQs cluster that are inclined to dominate in the global arena. In the power structure of global firms, most shareholders still strictly keep their activities within the boundaries of developed countries which remain the commanding heights of world economy. As a result, the corporate elite network across cities have strengthened, instead of undermining, the dominant position of core developed capitalist countries, as illustrated by the fact that cities located in these core countries are more powerful and famous than those in non-core ones. Therefore, cities where a high connectivity is shared among multinationals and which are closely tied with their own countries are deeply connected with each other. According to Carroll (2007), this 'uneven network' is shaped by several factors such as transnational political–economic structures, nationally specific legal frameworks and business systems, linguistic/cultural affinities, the structure of political space and the structure of geographic space. The path dependencies of this network, to a large extent, are determined by long-standing social and physical infrastructure which does not change frequently (Harvey 1982), which further explains why the dominance of core countries is not undermined by the power structure of global firms. In this regard, the operations that generate this network 'have to do with the management and control of corporations and the exercise of strategic and allocative power within particular contexts' (Scott 1997).

However, according to the theory of Powell (1990), market, hierarchy and network are three forms of social organization. Thompson (2003) further points out that each of these forms has its key feature: mutual relation is at the core of all networks; bureaucratic mechanism plays a role in stabilizing hierarchy and price mechanism promotes market activities. Therefore, the formation of a network is based on the trust of its actors; hierarchy, on norms and rules; and market, on legally binding contracts. These practices, in turn, label the aforementioned organizational forms with three different social relations: network is associated with cooperation, hierarchy with unfair competition and market with free competition (as shown in Table 4.1). Concluded from earlier text, the global city network is incompatible

Table 4.1 *Comparison between the Three Forms of Social Organization*

Key Features	Market	Hierarchy	Network
Types of organizational structure	Dispersive and decentralized	Pyramid shaped and vertical	Horizontal
Institutions	Independent	Dependent	Interdependent
Behaviour of agents	Contract and law based	Norm and regulation driven	Reciprocity and trust seeking
Social relations	Free competition	Unfair competition	Cooperation
Mechanisms of organization	Price mechanism	Bureaucratic administration	Mutual relationship
Opposite	Monopoly	Anarchy	Atomization
Areas of activities	Economy	Politics	Society

Source: Powell (1990); Thompson (2003).

with hierarchy or, in other words, the global city network cannot and should not be hierarchical.

The debate over whether there is a hierarchy in the WCN actually implies different views of whether the relationship between different cities in the network is characterized by cooperation or competition. When it comes to changes in the WCN, merely considering (emphasizing) city's rise or fall in the rankings based on a hierarchy suggests an approach focusing on competitive analysis.

For example, as Friedmann (1995: 23) proposes, world cities are 'driven by relentless competition, struggling to capture ever more command and control functions that comprise their very essence', and, to some extent, 'competitive angst is built into world city politics'. Sassen illustrates her global city model by APS firms. Though she also considers cooperative relations (as within the intra-firm networks) in addition to competitive ones, she still emphasizes the latter by regarding the management and coordination of APS firms as strategic control.

However, in the GaWC's researches, firms rather than cities are agents of change, which means that the essence of intercity relations is cooperation between offices of global service firms in different cities, rather than the natural competition in terms of capital, resources, knowledge, etc., between cities (Beaverstock et al. 2001). This does not mean that there is no competition between cities (Begg 1999). Instead, cooperative processes are prioritized, because they require the basic reproduction of intercity relations: cities exist within city networks, and city networks exist through complementary relations between cities (Taylor et al. 2014). This conclusion conforms to general organizational theories in which competition and hierarchy are thought different from network and cooperation. However, in a pure network theory, there are only cooperative relations and no competitive relations.

From our perspective, the hierarchy of WCNs proposed by Friedmann follows, to some extent, the same approach adopted in theories such as 'national urban system' and 'core–periphery model', as it highlights the cities' power-seeking functions such as 'command and control' and 'strategic control' and their efforts in improving their own competitiveness. Obviously, this approach is at odds with the essence of WCN.

Moreover, there is

> a profound construct–validity problem at the heart of the global-city/world-city network paradigm advanced by Sassen and Taylor: 'strategic control' cannot be squared with 'corporate service centres', 'inter-city/intra-firm office networks', or any such envisioning of the world economy as a totality that is structured from a distance. (Smith and Doel 2010: 25)

> One cannot infer interaction, coordination, command, control, domination and subordination from the mere existence of office networks, nor can one assume that office networks express a distribution of strategic control functions across cities. Similarly, the conceptual and empirical specification by both Sassen and Taylor of strategic control is inadequate. They have conflated strategic control with the 'servicing', 'management', 'co-ordination' and 'financing' of the global economy, and even routine business-service activities have been regarded as critically important 'top-level management and control functions' (a.k.a. global-city functions). The capacity for business-service firms to accomplish truly strategic control of the global economy is not a self-evident outcome of corporate service complexes (i.e., spatial agglomeration) or inter-city/intra-firm office networks (i.e., the world-city network). (Smith and Doel 2010: 27)

In fact, this problem

> so far has not been addressed properly. First, a producer service firm's size does not determine the share of its cross-border clients. A sizeable national accountancy firm which operates for a couple of years in a global network might nevertheless have more business cases stemming from its long local tradition than a smaller advertising firm specialised in global clients. Second, the IWCNM does not distinguish between the sub-sectors of the producer service economy. For example, a minor local office of a global law firm might have more bearing on the economic decision-making of its client than a midsized office of an accountancy firm in the same city. Third, even within one sector of producer services, the importance of an office might change from case to case. In accountancy, for example, the firm–intern hierarchy depends on the city from whence the client comes. Moreover, within each producer service firm, some tasks are more relevant to governance function than others. Lawyers specialised in intellectual property or tax laws are likely to exert a stronger influence on the client's position in a global commodity chain than those engaged in compliance issues. (Parnreiter 2010)

Therefore, the 'world urban hierarchy' is not a suitable approach to observe cities in globalization, because simply focusing on cities' rankings and their competition goes against the very nature of network.

Of course, we cannot simply use the classification of social organizations proposed by Powell (1990) and Thompson (2003) to define the relationships among nodes in the WCN. In fact, most social network analyses are designed to deal with incomplete graphs; therefore, the number of links among nodes is of key importance. At the same time, 'networks can only operate on the basis of mutuality among nodes' (Thompson 2003). The nodes include not only global cities (key nodes) but also globalizing cities (sub-nodes or ordinary nodes), which have different number of links, respectively, and thus play different roles in the network.

The earlier analysis has showed that WCN is composed of nodes that are in different positions (which means they play different roles and have varying degrees of importance). Such different positions or roles allow cities to offer different kinds of structural advantages to local producers. These advantages are not evenly distributed in the network, suggesting a structure of different layers, which can facilitate various global business activities. Therefore, although we do not advocate the approach of stressing hierarchy, it does not mean a denial of differentiation in the development process of global cities. In fact, the WCN is not a single network organization, but a hybrid one and, thus, the clear-cut system of classifications cannot be applied to its analysis.

We believe that this hybrid network has two features. On the one hand, the nodes of the network, regardless of their different degrees of importance and sizes, are interdependent and equal, which is totally different from the traditional *dominance–subordination* hierarchy, as 'all hierarchies involve asymmetric power relations between members at different levels; those above impose their will on those below' (Taylor 2010). On the other hand, the nodes can be divided into different layers according to their positions in the WCN. It should be noted that this is a special process. Cooley (2005) suggests two kinds of hierarchy for international relations. One is unitary hierarchy, 'whereby the lower layers are closely controlled from the centre. An alternative organization, multidivisional hierarchy, provides for more autonomy away from the centre' (cf. Taylor 2010). The structure of the WCN is more like the latter, described by Frank (1969) as metropole–satellite relations, which 'is an autonomy within an extreme asymmetric relation: power is held at the centre without the need for overt domination' (cf. Taylor 2010). This structure is obviously different from the pure horizontal network; and though having different layers, nodes of the network tend to have more complicated mutual relation than that featured by zero-sum game between cities and regions within the same hierarchy.

The two aspects of the hybrid network are of asymmetric importance. More specifically, cities are by nature networked, while the layered structure is conditional, only applicable when the importance of cities' locations is concerned. It means that 'competition exists alongside cooperative relations' (Begg 1999; Sassen 1999). 'Cities need each other and all contribute to the wellbeing of the network' (Taylor [2003] 2004); and networks, in turn, 'can only operate on the basis of mutuality amongst nodes' (Thompson 2003). In sum, the cooperative processes between cities are much more complex than the competitive processes.

It is true that all cities are networked, 'but under certain circumstances there are hierarchical tendencies that create competition between select cities' (Taylor 2010). As Taylor (2010) proposes, 'there are three specific situations where competition between cities is created'.

1. *'Process: political over economic.* The interlocking network model is an economic process, but we live in a world of political economy. This means that in some circumstances, political process can dominate the generic mutuality of cities to produce powerful hierarchical tendencies'. For instance, in the globalization era

    cities are encompassed in 'international relations' thinking with city mayors taking on the traditional competitive role of state presidents/prime ministers. A new political purpose is given to city governments: to devise plans to make their city a successful world or global city at the expense of rival cities. (Taylor 2010)

2. *Place: Gateway battles.* Within a specific and restricted area, only one major city can serve as a gateway that links a region to the rest of the world, a position for which all local cities are in competition (Andersson and Andersson 2000). Such position is 'traditionally related to transport hubs' (Pain 2008a). But over time, new meanings and other conditions may be added to the gateway position; thus, cities will start to compete again, resulting in a new winner of the position.
3. *'Time: cyclical effects.* In good times, cooperation between cities is considered beneficial as the economy produces a win–win scenario, while the downturn prospects may generate a more competitive relation between cities' (Taylor 2010).

'These three circumstances induce a competitive process that creates strong hierarchical tendencies within city networks' (Taylor 2010). However, these are not 'inevitable tendencies'. Because 'in the interlocking network model, it is private agencies that are the "interlockers" of cities. They do this through carrying out their everyday commercial business' (Taylor 2010), which are mostly cooperative activities between cities. Therefore, even though competition between cities might be produced under some specific situations, cooperative processes are central and dominant.

Considering the WCN as a complex multifarious network is an appropriate perspective for our analysis of the evolution of global cities. In the major research carried out by Friedmann et al., since the WCN is viewed as a hierarchical structure featuring uneven power relations, it follows that cities under control barely have any opportunities to develop independently and further evolve, which is a relatively static interpretation of intercity relations. In reality, however, relations between the nodes of the WCN change frequently and rapidly, where cities may witness sharp increase or dramatic drop in their global connectivity in a short time. Such changes indicate that the argument about uneven power relations is invalid. On the other hand, in a pure horizontal network, as nodes do not need to compete for power, they consequently have no motivation to further evolve. De Filippis (2001) reckons that networks encompass hierarchies of power; otherwise, they would not be networks in the first place, as 'there would be no incentive for the more powerful members to remain in the network if they didn't disproportionately gain the benefits of network participation' (Christopherson and Clark 2007). Therefore, it is the hybrid structure of the WCN that offers the nodes incentives to compete with each other and, thus, further develop themselves.

Evolutionary Dynamics

Global cities are composed of multiple agents (institutions) interacting across the globe in a multiplicity of connected ways and subjected to a great deal of noises—precisely the conditions for complex, adaptive and evolutionary patterns of change. More specifically, as the change of cities demonstrate multiple dimensions of complexity, which involve dispersed interaction, the interlinking of hierarchies at different levels, perpetual novelty, continual adaption, self-organization and out-of-equilibrium dynamics, the study of the evolutionary dynamics of global cities needs to take into consideration the dynamics arguments that cover all the related subjects, such as contingency, stochastic drift, adaptive selection, self-organizing and non-linear processes.

5.1. FRAMEWORK OF DYNAMICS

Global cities, whose evolution is based on the ontological supposition of the 'organism', can be regarded as a unit of selection with inner agency and reflective ability. Meanwhile, there is a selection environment independent of entities. In other words, as a unit of selection with both inner energy and physical entities, global cities can adapt to the changing environment and evolve through interactions. As such, the unit of selection and the selection environment constitute the fundamental framework of evolutionary dynamics.

5.1.1. Selection Environment

The selection environment, as an important constraint condition and a strong driving force for the evolution of global cities, seems to be a straightforward concept. However, this is not the case: the selection environment is not the external, natural environment in the general sense. Based on the ontological assumption of regarding global cities as 'organic entities', the latter is merely a part of the former. Suppose it were equal to the external environment, then the selection environment will become only an exogenous variable of the evolution of global cities, which means that the response of global cities (the unit of selection) to the changes of environment is just a passive and mechanical selection and that the evolution is essentially driven by external forces. This is again a conclusion drawn from the ontological hypothesis that views global cities as 'mechanical devices', which has been proven wrong.

According to the ontological assumption of 'organic entity', the selection environment has a dual nature: it is external and a natural given (exogeneity) and it is internal and has inner agency (endogeneity) at the same time.

On the one hand, exogenous environments involve globalization, urbanization, informatization, business cycle and changes in global economic landscape at the global level; a country's geopolitics and economic power, degree of openness, structure of national economy, spatial layout, culture and language at the national level and the degree of regional integration at the regional level. It can be said that these external environments are the constraint conditions for the evolution of global cities.

On the other hand, endogenous environments are constructed by the actors within them, to some extent, and are the outcomes of transforming selective characteristics in the past evolution of global cites into selective advantage. That is to say, endogenous environments are selection environments in real time caused by the past selection outcomes of the actors. In addition, endogenous environments can also be regulated by external actors. For example, when a country gives strategic importance and preferential treatment to a city or a large amount of foreign investment is attracted to a city because of its foreign policy to open wider to the world, the city can convert the selection environments into selection advantages and, thus, the outcomes of them will become selection environments in real time. Furthermore, in some particular cases, the units of selection may not treat the selection as a parametric given but may instead devote considerable effort to shape the selection environments. For example, they can construct a selection environment in an advantageous way with the help of the spontaneous evolution of rules of conduct and the interaction between cities, various institutions relevant to global cities and the network of them, and political activities. This kind of construction of selection environments, in a way, can be treated as a 'higher evolutionary' process.

In conclusion, the selection environment of the evolution of global cities is a result of the interaction between endogenous environments and exogenous environments.

It is stressed that selection environment is not only an exogenous variable but also an endogenous one and shouldn't be equated with external environment in a general sense, since it provides a fundamental framework to analyse various entities within it. The selection environment constructed by actors involved is the outcome of past long-term evolution of global cites during which selective characteristics are transformed into selective advantage, resulting in differences between big cities and small cities, central cities and edge cites, and cities with high quality of life and cities with lower quality of life. Big cities tend to get more prone to improvement than smaller ones because they boast larger economics of scale and more social opportunities, equipped with better cultural facilities and universities with more efficient information spillover effect, international connections as well as available assets in flow of talent and companies. As the centre of economic development and politics, central cities have experienced sharper growth than edge cities with business wealth and technology innovation gathered. Cities with higher quality of life (good climate and liveable environment, etc.) may be more resilient in economy. Therefore, even though they are under same external conditions in real time, different cities (the unit of selection) are faced with different actual range, space and possibilities of selection. That is to say, the selection environments differ in diverse conditions formed during the long-term evolution or due to the endogeneity of selection environment itself. It can well explain why some cities rise to be global cities while others don't even though they have experienced globalization simultaneously. Apart from cities' mindset, the reason lies in different endogenous environments, which refers to different selection environments.

Formally, selection environment can be analogous to the concept of 'gene'. Information about the environment an organism lives in is stored in its genes, which consists of an endogenous constraint on its evolution. Of course, what we talk about is the genes of a city, which can be conceived as social routines connecting cognitive subjects in cities. They differ greatly from the biological genes, which we've discussed in the ontological definition of global cities. Depending on the relative success in their (changing) environment, those routines may replicate differentially (Nelson and Winter 1982), so that cognitive individuals starting with various routines may systematically change appearance by changing the composition of routines. Those social routines are embodied in the following three aspects

1. Standard operating procedure (SOP) that determines how the cities run with designated stock and other constraints on its behaviours;
2. Routines of investment behaviour of cities, which dominate the growth and decline of cities and
3. Processes that involve searching for better practice, which will help improve search abilities and, in turn, enhance the ability to adopt new routines.

Therefore, any state of global cities at present can be traced back to a sequence of variation and selective retention in the past, which has led to nested heterarchies of constraints transmitting information. And any kind of conscious decision-making of cognitive objects takes place under a complex system of constraints. Knowledge accumulated from the past can be a constraint on its selections and, combined with actual constraints, will constitute the 'internal opportunity set' of a decision-maker in real time. Obviously, it doesn't imply that actual behaviour (selections) is explained as being genetically determined but suggests that certain constraints on other perfectly flexible behaviour are genetically fixed.

Of course, it does not mean we can ignore or exclude the general external environment, because the changes happened in the external environment are very important, sometimes they are even decisive during the evolution of global cities. The city per se is an open system that constantly makes the energy exchange with the external environment and, therefore, is constrained by it. For example, a 'genetic variation' is often induced by significant changes of external conditions during the evolution of global cities. Imaging a world without any major change such as globalization, these cities may continue to evolve into higher forms, but will never 'metamorphose' into global cities. That's why we believe global cities are the product of globalization, and globalization is the main driving force for the evolution of global cities. As an external factor that influences or even decides the evolution of global cities, these changes are comprehensive and complex, that is, there are many external factors interacting with each other. These factors exist at different levels, whether at the world level, the national level or the regional level, and they are exerting different impacts on the evolution of global cities.

In fact, the selective characteristics of urban practitioners are transformed into selective advantages, which are always influenced by changes in external environment. Urban practitioners often make new choices under the changing conditions of external environment and turn them into selective advantages and, as a result, they internalize into immediate endogenous selective environment. Therefore, the evolution of global cities is the outcome of the transformation of selection characteristics into selection advantages in the interaction between endogenous and exogenous environments.

5.1.2. Selective Unit

During the dynamic evolution, the city itself is a dynamic selective unit as well. Because the city's ontological structure is composed of 'city' (object) and 'citizen' (person), the city as a selective unit in evolution is based on the dualistic assumption of 'organism' ontology, which can be defined as the carrier of knowledge and information in an abstract sense. But the knowledge carriers and information carriers we discussed belong to different categories, for the former is a category of mindset based on urban cognitive subject, and the latter is a material category based on the physical form of cities. This is a vital distinction in the research methodology towards the evolution of global cities.

The reason why cities are viewed as carriers of knowledge is that there are a large number of cognitive agents in cities that participate in various activities, who are also known as city participants (actors), playing the roles of both the container and incubator of knowledge. Apparently, these cognitive agents store and create different kinds of knowledge, including expertise in various fields, but they share some kind of 'general knowledge' that indicates their cognition level and also represents a city's intelligence level. Put it another way: suppose these cognitive agents are 'people of reason', then their 'general knowledge' represents 'the reason of a city'. More importantly, as these cognitive agents are city participants (actors) themselves, the knowledge that depends on them can, in a sense, be viewed as a kind of action. In other words, this knowledge is in itself the 'general knowledge' that represents the city's mindset. Apart from its theoretical framework, this knowledge originates from people's practice and experience as well. This viewpoint takes on great practical significance in analysing the dynamic evolution of global cities, because only this practical knowledge, instead of purely theoretical one, is closely related to the inspiration of innovative and novel actions, directly shaking old orders and shaping new ones.

On the other hand, as carriers of information, cities can still exist without any cognitive agent. For example, information can be stored directly in a city's physical forms (including the infrastructure, buildings, cultural heritage, etc.). Since a city's physical forms (geographical conditions excluded) are not its innate characteristic but the diachronic product of generations of human beings, these man-made materials, despite their independence from present cognitive agents, carry a huge quantity of authentic (or nearly authentic) information about the development of a city, which has the following features. First, such information embodies distinctive messages. For instance, landmarks such as the Empire State Building and the Statue of Liberty in New York, the Tower Bridge and the British Museum in London, and Notre-Dame, the Eiffel Tower and the Arc de Triomphe in Paris, with their own distinctive significance, all reflect the unique development along history. Second, such information is diversified in that it doesn't integrate into a unitary system. To be specific, the information covers a wide range of fields, including economy, social studies, religion and culture; it also extends beyond the dimension of time, conveying messages from both the ancient and modern times. Lastly, as a component of the main structure of a city, such information lays a material foundation for present cognitive agents to engage in various activities.

However, in the ontological structure of cities, the role as knowledge carriers and the role as information carriers are inseparable. The integration and interaction of these two roles of cities guarantees the reflective power and the endogenously generated initiative, thus making it possible for cities to respond accordingly to the selection environment. It also should be noted that these two roles of cities function differently in the evolution of global cities. The information a city carries represents how well equipped this city is in the material level and yet, despite fewer limitations to some extent, does not provide the potentials for evolution, not to mention solely determining the city development. But the accumulated information is indeed what the evolution of global cities is based on. Differently, the knowledge a city carries refers to the 'general knowledge' part of its mindset and only knowledge creation brings potentials for the evolution of global cities. In this sense, knowledge creation counts more than accumulated information in the evolution of global cities as a city is a dynamic selection unit. This is because the knowledge accumulated in the pursuit of innovation will change the conditions of the temporary order, thus bringing about novel reactions and eventually forming a new temporary order. Obviously, the result caused by cumulative changes is closely tied to the creation and development of knowledge. In fact, the constant knowledge creation and development influences the result in two aspects. On the one hand, an individual city tends to make changes to adapt to the selection environment, and the cumulative knowledge constantly creates new selection environments. On the other hand, this process may also be repeated out of old systems as a result of cumulative knowledge creation and make a difference across the evolutionary systems. In this sense, the process of the evolution of global cities is one where we can clearly observe cumulative knowledge creation, which happens spontaneously. We can find no particular reason triggering the novel creation process. However, knowledge referred to here cannot be accumulated without certain contexts and time spans. A large amount of knowledge is accumulated along with the city development, so knowledge creation is based on material resources and material bases. To some degree, the level of material resources and material bases influences and even determines the extent to which knowledge creation is achieved.

It is apparent that the amount of knowledge and information that each individual city carries varies (sometimes greatly), due to differences in historical inheritance and accumulation, in present capacity and scale, as well as in dynamic factors like a city's mindset. In other words, considerable level of variation exists among cities, which means that they have different development bases and potentials. Therefore, under the same external environmental conditions, it is the difference in the amount of knowledge and information that helps some cities to be better integrated into the WCN, become pivotal nodes and evolve into global cities. Other cities may be separated from the WCN, and even if they are integrated into it, they only serve as general nodes and evolve into globalizing cities.

5.1.3. The Isomorphic Relation between Selection Environment and Selection Unit

As indicated by prior elaborations, the selection environment proves to be an objective constraint for the evolution of global cities, while the selection unit, cities per se, actively facilitates the evolution process via responding and adapting to the selection environment. The two concepts combine the unit and environment elements in the evolution of cities. Yet as the selection environment involves the endogenous environment created by the cities in advance (Figure 5.1), the two in effect form a unique isomorphic relation rather than a simple unity of opposites. The key to such a relationship shown in Figure 5.1 lies in

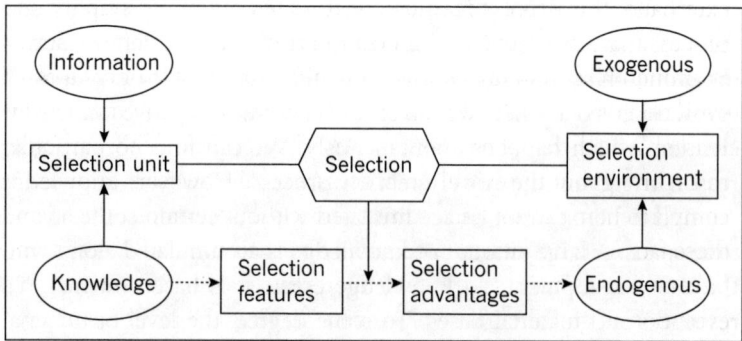

Figure 5.1 *Relationship between Selection Unit and Selection Environment*

Source: Compiled by author.

the iterative nature of knowledge creation by urban actors. It is a looping process of accumulating feedback for knowledge renewal, where the output of the previous iteration is reused as the initial value for the next iteration. As universally acknowledged, urban actors in the unit of selection consist of a multitude of cognitive agents such as governments, enterprises and social organizations, all serving as knowledge carriers. These agents, in adaptation to diversified selection environments, create organizations and corresponding networks (both internal and external). Facing the competitive selection environments, all the urban actors will purposefully improve or even renovate these organizations and networks, namely having them transformed through knowledge creation. However, had they survived and thrived under such circumstances, their features as organizations and networks might develop into restrictive and boundary conditions for potential participants as a result of responding to and managing pressures. These conditions, with both explicit and implicit influences, give rise to an endogenous selection environment that poses restrictions for urban actors to promote the evolution of future cities. In summary, the knowledge creation by cognitive agents and environment information of the past is connected with those at present, and such connection is expressed in the form of the path dependence of the evolution of global cities.

5.2. INFLUENCING FACTORS

The evolution of global cities is a complex process, with numerous external and internal influencing factors. And how to simplify such process turns out to be a significant part of social sciences research. Prominent factors, as the basic elements and components of the evolution of global cities, are expressly highlighted for further study. It is observed that these factors play disproportionately important roles throughout the evolution process, exerting decisive, supporting, complementary, direct and indirect impacts. Furthermore, the effect of these factors is not determined simply by their weights. Instead, they tend to work 'progressively and interactively' over the course of the evolution of global cities, where some serve as the main factor while others minor. In addition, changes in research perspectives could lead to differences in their roles. For instance, in terms of the holistic evolution of global cities, influencing factors at the global level are deemed to be the most prominent and paramount among others. But when it comes to individual city's evolution, influencing factors at the national level are more likely to directly exert crucial influence, regardless of the fact that it is the factors at the global level that constitute the basic environmental background. All in all, these major influencing factors play varying roles, including constituting the background, providing momentum and functioning as the basic conditions.

5.2.1. Influencing Factors at the Global Level

Global cities, cities that function across the world, are bound to be limited by global level influencing factors first and foremost.

5.2.1.1. Globalization

The foreign investment raised by economic globalization, especially the rise of MNCs, shaped GVC, which brought a large amount of intra-industry and intra-firm trade, leading to NIDL. Therefore, an elementary proposition of our study is that before the emergence of MNCs, there are no global cities, only traditional metropolis. The emergence of MNCs brought about global decentralization of production and centralization of control and management, thus creating global cities that based on centralized control. Following the globalization of APS firms of MNCs, global cities have added global coordination capabilities based on centralized control. These functional developments based on external network associations often involve enlarging potential agglomeration effects and network effects, as well as establishing integrated service functions. As a result, cities that focus on these structures—functional improvements will benefit from them, while other cities will be at a disadvantage.

The evolutionary model of MNCs that based on globalization resulted in the special evolutionary model of global cities. In an early stage of development, the WCN of global cities was loosely connected and their functions tended to be weak because MNCs are unstable and located randomly, so it was relatively easy for a general city to become a global city. With the deepening of globalization, MNCs have increased in number; they have become highly concentrated and have made progress in developing specialized functions. Under the basic aggregation of control and coordination functions, learning becomes cumulative, and existing institutions have advantages for potential candidates of global cities. Through the market mechanism, global cities are steadily composed of a number of giant established global functional institutions. Furthermore, globalized production and consumption that based on global commodity chain and value chain affect all relevant cities (Robinson 2006). From this follows that each global city constitutes a node for numerous commodity chains, while all commodity chains run through global cities seeking core labour processes such as producer services (Brown et al. 2010). Global cities are the main paradigm of the new geography of the world economy emerging in the process of globalization, and the increasingly deepened globalization process of urban centre activities, both at present and in the future, will be a change of trend, due to which 'globalization' has become a critical term in discussing the economic and social changes taking place in contemporary cities.

As globalization furthers in a dynamic process, it certainly involves different aspects. The relationship between trade and investment is going complex with intertwined bilateral and multilateral forms, during which the relationship may be strengthened or weakened alternately. The increasingly higher standards and demands also deepen the relationship, thus changing the overall pattern of global trade and investment. Besides, TNCs constantly adjust their layout of global industrial chains, which not only alters the organizational forms but also redraws a new world map of TNCs. Meanwhile, TNCs also keep transforming themselves. More and more transnational manufacturing corporations have an increasing and dominant share of services in their value added products, which transform them to service corporations, and the rapidly growing overseas business and profits also turn them into global corporations. Therefore, the dynamic process of globalization will definitely influence the evolution of global cities.

5.2.1.2. Informatization

The ICT modes for cities and regions is clearly of crucial importance. ICTs, including the Internet and its backbone networks, seem to play a more critical role in the era of 'new economy', making the process of production, distribution and exchange increasingly dependent on them. More importantly, the ICT configuration of urban systems even gives rise to spatial and hierarchical differentiation. Not only have these developments led to an intensification of virtual cross-border flows and an 'informational economy' but other economic sectors are increasingly dependent on specialized knowledge-based advanced services to add value to production and trade. Thus, primary and secondary as well as tertiary markets and their production networks increasingly involve cities (Pain 2008c). The Internet generates a double-edged effect on the development of cities, which simultaneously stimulates both centrifugal and centripetal forces. ICTs do not result in the decentralization of economic activity (Richardson and Gillespie 2000), but they generate both centralizing and decentralizing effects, contrary to the early 'death of distance' conceptualizations, which focused only on their decentralizing potential (Malecki and Gorman 2001). ICTs and the Internet backbone networks tend to cluster in major cities. Although ICTs have managed to remove some of the geographical barriers faced by remote locations, this evolution has not weakened people's and economic activities' tendency to cluster together in urban areas (Moss and Townsend 2000). Contrary to these early arguments, population and economic activities tend more and more to agglomerate in core metropolitan regions.

Serving as one of the driving forces behind the evolution of global cities, among which the relations are usually invisible, informatization plays an important role in global exchanges of ideas, information, knowledge, plans, commands and suggestions on business. The Internet was created partly for the purpose of interconnecting widely distributed computer networks. Benefiting from advanced telecommunications networks and related services, global cities have come into being and developed with unique functions. Global cities are born out of interconnections between distant manufacturing centres driven by technologies, as an example of which international capital markets transactions rely greatly on telecommunications technologies. In this case, how to gain access to the information world and to control the major nodes of the information network is the key to eventually winning the competition in global capital accumulation and evolving into global cities.

5.2.1.3. Long-Term Economic Cycles and Economic Changes

Long-term economic cycles and economic changes influence the globalization process and, thus, have an impact on the evolution of global cities as a sub-factor in the hierarchy. In modern world economy, generally, the periods of the expansion and peak of a long-term economic cycle contribute to furthering globalization, as a dynamic economy encourages global investment and trade. Accordingly, the periods of contraction or trough may slow the globalization process as economic recession leads to protectionism and discourages global investment. Economic changes taking place in the long-term economic cycles directly affect urban development such as the evolution of urban spaces, especially in the era of globalization. For example, the rising importance of the service economy and knowledge economy has further given cities the key role as nodes in the network of sharing tacit knowledge globally. Dicken (1998) concluded that the economic cycles driven by radical innovations would influence a hierarchical urban structure. The functions of a city in the WCN could be strengthened or weakened, depending on the economic environment.

5.2.1.4. Changes in the World Economic Landscape

The shift of the world's economic centre of gravity is an important factor for the evolution of individual global city or global cities as an individual group. In the modern society, the world's economic centre of gravity is almost synonymous with the centre of globalization. The regions of the world's economic centre of gravity account for not only a large percentage of global GDP but also a large share of international investment and trade, thus making them the centre of globalization. Obviously, these regions will see the rise of global cities as an individual group or become relatively dense in the distribution of global cities. Therefore, the shift of the world's economic centre of gravity means the shift of the centre of globalization, which brings about decline in global cities as an individual group in some regions, and prosperity in others.

Of course, the shift of the world's economic centre of gravity is affected by the intermediate variable, namely the foreign direct investment (FDI). Although FDI only accounts for a small or even a reduced share of global capital flows, it has a major strategic impact on global economic restructuring (Dunning 1993). FDI, driven by strategy and long-term intentions, is defined as an investment involving a long-term relationship and reflecting a lasting interest and control (UNCTAD 2001), which is different from indirect investment featuring high volatility and temporary investment. Such investment with a view to achieve 'strategic control' means that investors are willing to start business to establish and maintain its long-term economic relationship in a country, and then to affect the management. Therefore, FDI is not only 'the tool of economic globalization' (Wu and Radbone 2005) but it also represents the spatial behaviour of MNCs.

5.2.1.5. Global Urbanization

As a supporting factor, global urbanization plays a role in the evolution of global cities mainly by providing substantial foundations for the expansion of the WCN, which means that urbanization itself does not have a direct impact on the evolution of global cities, but the changes of urban attributes resulted from urbanization have an indirect impact on the evolution of global cities. In today's global urbanization, cities are separated from local geography and serve as an important spatial carrier for the global economy under the background of economic globalization and gradual breakthrough and penetration of national borders. Empirical research shows that 84 per cent of transnational networks occurs between cities and not within them, and that approximately 70 per cent of European and North American ties extend beyond their respective supra-regions (Wall and van der Knaap 2011), so the their positions in worldwide networks have grown. Now, it does not make sense if cities are not studied in a new type of global distributed system. In this sense, global urbanization will promote the expansion of the WCN and, thus, affect the evolution of global cities.

5.2.2. Influencing Factors at National Level

Although globalization and informatization alternately interact with cities to integrate them into WCN, any city always belongs to a certain country and region, even a city state like Singapore is no exception.

Therefore, national factors still play an important role in and have a direct impact on the evolution of global cities of the individual city or of cities as an individual group.

It is worth pointing out that considerable disagreement arises over what role do nations play in the evolution of global cities or whether nations are influencing factors or not, which is caused by the different understandings of the relationship between globalization and nations. In early global cities studies, some scholars regarded territorial nation states as a specific role in the formation of global cities. 'World cities lie at the junction between the world economy and the territorial nation state', and Friedmann and Wolff (1982) believed that 'the cluster of government services' and financial capacity of national states play a vital part in the function of global cities. In the subsequent global cities studies, however, the 'de-territorialization' theory began to gain momentum, and nations were no longer considered as explanatory factors for the formation of global cities. Some scholars believe that against the background of a rising global financial system and globally integrated production networks of MNEs, since 'the demise of territoriality is caused by the incongruence of the container-state and the global economy' (Taylor 1995), the global de-territorialization process is understood as the dissolution of the general mutual benefit for cities and territorial states, according to which the first is detached from the latter. Therefore, the territorial state lost its explanatory value for the dynamics of a globalized economy, which required new theories to overcome the 'territorial trap' (Angew 1994). In short, these views go beyond the concepts of the state and its territory, emphasizing the perspective of international relations and excluding the interpretation of states territories or welfare systems on the globalization process, especially at the city scale. However, in recent years, some scholars have questioned whether or not it is 'to throw the baby out with the bathwater'. Brenner (2004) emphasizes the role of national, political institutions and territorial arrangements in the formation of global cities through the term 'glocalization'. Different types of welfare state regimes, often the product of 'welfare-state characteristics', essentially remain in their historical arrangements (Esping-Andersen 1990), thus affecting the formation of global cities.

In our view, it is unreasonable to attribute the evolution of global cities solely to nation-related variables, or to ignore or deny their influences on the evolution of global cities, because modern nations are territorial political entities which can regulate the economic resources within its territory, control and intervene the flow of economic resources by its territorial borders and balance the impacts of economic activities in and out of its territory by budget management. This can be seen as the political effect of defining what 'local' and 'non-local' areas are; that is to say, it decides whether the 'imagined communities' consisting of local (within a nation) and non-local (outside a nation) areas are effectively established and how much the 'imagined communities' would achieve (Anderson 1983). Besides, it is related to the changed roles of governments. In the past, nations were empty territorial containers with limited governing authority produced and converted for the need of regulation (Brenner 2004). Today, we have witnessed the role of nations changing from a regulator for domestic economic development to a more active participant in global competition. Nations are able to constantly apply one city's experience in development to another and change anything that is directly related to cities' development by redefining their territorial boundaries in the new world system and narrowing the developmental gaps among cities in its territory. As such, the role of nations should be seen from a dynamic point of view rather than a static one that regards a nation as a closed and isolated space.

Even at the micro level, in contradiction to the changes associated with knowledge production—flexible organization and dynamic cross-border flows—government regulation is identified by firms as a structuring factor in network strategy. It is described by a major global management consultancy as creating 'market imperfections' which can shape the geography of cross-border relationships and production linkages from project development through to service delivery, implementation and operations support. Thus, national and trade bloc differences matter. Employment and migration legislation, education and training, taxation and infrastructure, structure skills supply, labour flexibility and operating costs differentiate across global locations. Government political stability, sensitivities and culture mould the location of functions, especially when government bodies are APS clients. Network relations are, therefore, not simply a product of cost and distance, but the outcome determined by comprehensive factors. Hence, both firm and state are interlocked in a struggle to capture global market shares, where the nation state remains an equally important institution of capitalism (Gertler 1992). Where firms prove to be more porous, nations differentiate themselves by artificially erected territorial boundaries, so as to distinguish and formalize their spatiality. These geographic units contain different forms of power and legitimacy with which to organize people and institutions spatially.

In short, a country might not constitute economic entities, but it does exercise significant economic power and, thus, wield a significant impact on economic activities and processes. In this sense, the rise and fall of cities are the result of national actions. Therefore, when examining the impact of globalization on global cities, we cannot ignore the background, environment and culture of the country behind them (Dieleman and Hamnett 1994), and need to examine the significant impact of the readjustment of a country's position and the continuation of historical arrangements and systems on the evolution of global cities. In this sense, countries are covariates of the evolution and development of global cities.

5.2.2.1. The Role of Global Cities in Global Economy

The birth and rise of any global city are closely related with the important role of its country in the world system. The evolution of a city is determined by its country's position in the global economy (Alderson and Beckfield 2007). For example, if the USA were not a globally dominant player, New York would not be the global city New York. The status of a country in the global economy directly determines whether its cities will develop into global cities.

The position of a country in the global economy, or geopolitical power, is also known as national competitiveness, a term that has multiple meanings. According to the hypothesis of the classical theory of international trade, comparative advantage is reflected by the developing factors of a country, including land, natural resources, labour force and local population size (Andersen and Van Wincoop

2004). Porter's (1990) theory of competitive advantage deepens the concept of comparative advantage, showing that the success of enterprises and countries today also depends on the development of unique skills, technologies and knowledge of specific industries, as well as the specific connection between internationally successful enterprises and other urban areas of this country. In addition, national competitiveness also depends on the relative centrality of a country, the specialization and differentiation mode of its activities and the division of its functions. The competitiveness of a country has a highly positive and significant impact on the number of a city's outbound and inbound connections, especially on the former (Wall et al. 2008), because only countries with natural endowment and strategic ability can create competitive advantages to attract FDI (Guisinger 1985).

Hence, the position or geopolitical power of a country in the global economy is a comprehensive impact factor, among which some elements are defined as pertinent explanatory variables, including national capital (economic strength), market size, military spending and soft power like culture and diplomacy. Especially, there's a positive relationship between the size of the national economies and the distribution of the formation of global cities (Taylor 2000b). Market potential as measured by the growth rate of GDP can be used to explain the rise of global cities in emerging economies.

5.2.2.2. Degree of Openness

In the contemporary world, countries define 'the space of economic regulation', which is crucial to expand urban economic activities. Whether it has a business-friendly domestic policy or a trade-friendly foreign policy directly determines when and how a country's cities will be integrated into economic globalization. Thus, we can assume that if a country is characterized by a high degree of openness, its cities will attract more APS companies adapting to globalization and become more closely integrated into the globalization process. The 'economic openness' of a country is an important factor in attracting global service companies to their major cities. Empirical studies by Pereira and Derudder (2010) showed that the normalized beta coefficient of this variable was the largest of all six variables and, thus, the largest independent variable to affect the dependent variable.

A country's degree of openness involves the openness of domestic industrial sectors, the extent of participation in multilateral, bilateral and regional investment and trade agreements, pre-establishment national treatment, post-establishment national treatment, positive and negative lists, competition neutrality, trade facilitation and the free flow in current and capital accounts. Generally, the following indicators will be used as explanatory variables: trade/gross national product, domestic direct investment and FDI, service trade and technology trade, trade and investment facilitation.

5.2.2.3. Macroeconomic Control

Obviously, difference exists in the type of economies between developed and developing countries. But even developed countries themselves have different type of economies and, thus, give birth to different forms of capitalism (Hall and Soskice 2001). It has a significant impact on the evolution of global cities. As the empirical analysis by Ma and Timberlake (2012) showed, the different forms and approaches of urban integration into global or national urban systems depend on the type of economies. Under the same conditions, macroeconomic control with higher level of economic liberalization and social labour productivity, together with a weaker social welfare and a larger social gap (measured by the Gini coefficient), may be more conducive to promote a country into global urbanization and vice versa. Therefore, different ways of macroeconomic control and types of economies can help explain the evolution of a city's integration into the global city network.

5.2.2.4. Institution-based Spatial Pattern in a Country

In a country engaged in urban development, the state itself plays an important role in the territorial organization and the structure of the urban system, typically leading to regional disparities and an uneven spatial pattern of urbanization. This process is, of course, influenced by historical factors. As noted by Flora (2000), the uneven spatial pattern of urban development extends far beyond the period when territorial statehood takes shape, and even throughout the process of state-building. The spatial disparities in urbanization already present today can be traced back to the influence of historical state institutions. For example, the heterogeneous mosaic of spatial territorial organization is originated from different degrees of federalism (the right of sub-national entities to enact laws and taxes) and decentralism (decision-making autonomy on public expenditure at the sub-national level) among states (Kaiser and Ehlert 2006). Hohenberg and Lees (1995) distinguished three spatial patterns of urbanization in Europe, namely the 'Rhenish model' in densely urbanized core regions, the 'Parisian model' in areas strongly organized by a dominant city and the 'Peripheral model' in loosely urbanized regions.

Other things being equal, such uneven spatial pattern will impact the formation and development of global cities. Surprisingly, studies showed that the evolution of global cities was facilitated by large cities in decentralized states with lower regional disparities and concentration degree in the urban system while hindered by those in federalist states. For example, France features centrally organized and spatially unbalanced urbanization which is dominated by only one global city (i.e., Paris), while Germany experiences decentralized and spatially balanced urban development led by five global cities, which indicates a higher gross network connectivity in Germany. Therefore, territorial states display very uneven distribution of global cities in varied spatial patterns. With several forms of combination available for the two dimensions of spatial territorial organization (federalism and decentralism), their impact on the formation of global cities seems not to be linear. However, it shall be assumed here that the territorial structure and the fiscal system for the spatial redistribution mechanism usually influence this process with a historical logic centred on territorial structures rather than a globalized economy.

5.2.2.5. National Preferential Support

The evolution of global cities will not proceed without policy support from national government—whether conscious or not—in various forms. Even in the states operating under laissez-faire capitalism, the 'visible hand' of government is commonly used to shape global cities.

For instance, London developed into a world city thanks to constant efforts of various national administrations—both conservative and liberal. The early liberalization policies in the 1980s powered the rise of London's financial sector (Big Bang in 1986) as well as the creation of new public institutions (Docklands Authority), development zones and new governance structures (Greater London Authority) to channel foreign investments into London's real estate market. It is fair to say that national support wields strong influence on the evolution of global cities, especially for those individual cities whose countries experience resource shortage resources, since the government may choose to give priority to certain promising cities through preferential measures and policies in resource allocation.

5.2.2.6. Culture and Language

A country's culture exerts a subtle influence on how its people think and behave, which is also reflected in its informal conventions including customs, norms and unspoken rules. Therefore, it is easier for people from cities with similar cultural background to communicate and reach consensus with one another. In contrast, people from cities with different cultures feel more distant from one another and find it harder to communicate ideas without having misunderstanding or contradiction. As a result, all other things being equal, MNCs and globalized APS firms are more willing to set up offices in cities sharing similar cultural background, making it easier to build a network of connections. Locating branches in foreign cities with completely different cultural background, by contrast, will generate greater frictional costs and require a rather long period to fit into that culture. Similarly, different language systems can create communication barriers, adding to transaction costs. This means that all else being equal, it is easier for cities using the same language to do networking and vice versa. Nevertheless, such elements as culture and language at the national level have a limited impact on the evolution of global cities compared with others, because it is (usually) possible for MNCs and globalized APS companies to adopt a localization strategy to reduce this impact when expanding their presence in cities of different cultural backgrounds and language systems.

5.2.3. Internal Influence Factors

From the perspective of evolution, the knowledge and information a city carries with it serve as an internal driving force for and herald the potential of its evolution.

5.2.3.1. Size of a City

In traditional urban studies, the size of a city is usually synonymous with the size of its population. However, the evolution of global cities has less to do with its population size than with its capability of exercising globalized control and providing globalized service, or the number of MNCs and globalized APS firms. The latter two are not significantly relevant to population size. According to Short (2004), a city's population size doesn't say very much about its role in the WCN in terms of its capability of exercising globalized control and providing globalized service. Here are two extreme examples. Less densely populated cities, such as London and New York, enjoy high global connectivity in the WCN, while cities such as Dhaka and Khartoum with a large population are actually 'black holes' and it is difficult for them to interact with other cities. Therefore, the size of a city in this context has more to do with industrial density than with population alone. Large cities in this sense are generally more likely to attract APS companies, which explains why an increasing number of globalized service companies are located in megacities around the world (Pereira and Derudder 2010).

5.2.3.2. Comprehensive Power of a City

From the perspective of wealth creation and accumulation, it is a city's GDP and its growth rate that reflect to what extent a city's economic activities have expanded, and thus decide whether the city can attract companies to exercise transnational control and provide global service there. However, during the evolution of global cities, the variable of GDP tends to exert weaker influence over time, while the comprehensive power of city is increasingly reflected by how large its economic flows are, such as the flow of cargo, capital, human capital, and information and knowledge. These flows can not only reflect a city's capacity of allocating resources globally but also serve as a direct indicator of global networks. Therefore, this variable can be used to measure whether the comprehensive power of a city has any impact on the growth of its networks.

In addition, the comprehensive power of a city is not simply about physical capital, but it is also increasingly embodied in its human capital, which is a fundamental factor for a city to attract global control and service as well. Cities with strong human capital are more attractive to global APS. Therefore, the variable of human capital is directly related to the evolution of global cities. A city's human capital is determined by the factors including its citizens' overall educational attainment, the quality of its vocational education and higher education, as well as the average quality and skills of the workers in that city, and can be measured by the specific indicators such as the average educational attainment of its citizens, student-to-faculty ratio, the number of top universities and the ratio of them to all the higher education institutions in the city and the percentage of high-calibre professionals and technicians.

5.2.3.3. Infrastructure

A city's infrastructure serves as an important means for connection with the outside world. In particular, transportation infrastructure carries heavy urban traffic and, thus, plays an important role in a city's connection with other places. As such, it has a great impact on the location choice of APS companies, since cities with well-developed infrastructure can often attract more (major) APS companies. Therefore, infrastructure becomes the most important variable that influences the service intensity of global cities (Taaffe 1962).

Today, 'great demand still exists for face-to-face relationships, despite the global telecommunications revolution' (Denstadli 2004). Therefore, air transport is now the preferred mode of travel for tourists, international migrants and the TCC across cities (Bowen 2002). Compared to transport by sea, rail and road, 'airline linkages offer the best illustration of transport's role in the world city system' (Keeling 1995). Neal (2010) longitudinally analysed the causal relationship between air transport and the importance of APS, pointing out that changes in airline linkages can often explain why the importance of APS in the labour market will change, and not the other way around. Changes in airline linkages influence employment growth in business services (Irwin and Kasarda 1991). Later, Brueckner (2003) and Debbage and Delk (2001) achieved similar results from their research and, therefore, researchers were further convinced that the level of airline linkages can be used to explain the current existence of major APS companies. In the empirical study by Taylor et al. (2007), it was found that a city's global service connectivity accounted for 53 per cent of the variability in its passenger number across cities. Therefore, 'air networks and their associated infrastructure are the most visible manifestations of world city interactions' (Smith and Timberlake 2001).

In addition, intelligent buildings, teleports, optical fibres and other key technologies have been parts of the infrastructure of emerging informational cities. The new urban-based telecommunications infrastructure is, in concert with the internationalization of services and the deregulation of financial markets, reinforcing the economic position of the major cities (Moss 1987). Pereira and Derudder (2010) used the cost of international phone calls to measure the overall development of telecommunication technology in a country. Using a linear regression model, they found that this indicator was a significant factor influencing the location choice of global APS companies: the lower the cost of international phone calls is, the more well-developed service network the city has.

5.2.3.4. The DNA of Cities

As a carrier of certain information and knowledge, the DNA of cities is unique and diverse. Different city genes have different responses and adaptability to changes to the external environment and always play a strong role in urban evolution.

Geographical location, as a city DNA carrying information, can be passed down from generation to generation. Some cities at special locations have become portals and passages throughout the region, attracting almost all the global APS companies. Thus, they will develop into major sites equipped with higher global service intensity than that in other standard models. Certainly, both economic changes and major development of transportation may alter a city's location advantages. Some cities may play weakening roles as portals, and some may become new portals and passages.

Different from the objective existence of geographical location, historical tradition is a result of long-term accumulation and inheritance of a city's minds (knowledge). Thus, it is a DNA carrying knowledge deeply rooted in the city, so it is hard to be changed in a short period, and will be constantly manifested through people's activities under new conditions. Therefore, cities with open, innovative and inclusive historical traditions tend to establish more external linkages and get involved in the global city network, while cities with conservative, stable and relatively closed historical traditions tend to be consciously or unconsciously unmotivated, passive or even refuse to develop external linkages.

5.2.3.5. Urban Primacy

The position of a city within its region has a huge impact on attracting MNCs and globalizing APS firms. Sassen (2001) hypothesized that a primate city of a country tended to attract companies with centralized transnational command and control. Taylor and Aranya (2008) proposed the 'political hypothesis', that is, capital cities were more likely to experience positive change in global connectivity. We have seen that globalized control and coordination activities are increasingly concentrated in major cities of high urban primacy, which leads to a high level of global service intensity in these cities. They attract more offices in the network of globalizing APS firms than people could have expected when considering their population size and number of passengers. Of course, since the location dynamics of APS firms is a complex and multifaceted phenomenon, urban primacy is not an obvious and important variable. Therefore, we can use urban primacy as a dummy variable to test whether major cities also have a disproportionate (oversized) number of globalizing APS firms.

5.3. EVOLUTIONARY PROCESS

The evolution of global cities is a variation and selection process of interaction between unit of selection and selection environment. The key lies in how the flow of matter and energy is organized in the order of knowledge, and one of the important links is the changing state space, which results from the evolutionary process of variation and selection in the dissipative structure.

5.3.1. The Creation of Novel Behaviours

From the perspective of evolution, cities observed at a certain time and place must be interpreted as a transformation in a continuous evolutionary process, or the product of rapid changes to varying degrees. This evolutionary process has two basic characteristics: one is its historical nature. Evolution means that urban novelty will emerge over time, which is immutable. Therefore, time is important. Even if the evolutionary process is likely be periodic, the process itself will not repeat exactly in the same way but will create urban novelty over time. The second characteristic is that the process of change is endless. Because urban systems have a dissipative structure, they have the ability to change themselves as they consume free energy (though they are also subject to external forces). In this sense, the continuous urban changes do not start from external driving force, but from the endogenous force within the urban system. The assumption that continuous urban changes start from external driving force results from the 'mechanism' ontology, which will inevitably lead to a decay during the process of change.

A solid historical and realistic foundation is obviously necessary for the urban system to realize diachronic self-transformation, especially to realize the evolution into a global city, because cities with this condition are more likely to respond promptly to and better adapt to a changing external environment. However, this is not a sufficient condition for evolution. The creation of novel behaviours based on knowledge (urban mind) is a sufficient condition for the evolution of global cities.

The emergence of uncertainties enables people to anticipate the possibilities of improvements in the situation, thus triggering the emergence of novelty. But generally, it can be expected to take place at a basic rate independent of the specific time and place but to increase significantly beyond this rate in situations of challenge and crisis.

As we know, when people have to deal with the uncertainties that emerge in a changing environment, they tend to identify and find out the reasons for them. In this case, they will enter into a 'question state' and, thus, kick-start the problem-solving process (the emergence of novelty). Since the process is constrained by the epistemology of the 'bonds of unknowledge', the meaning and explanation of it cannot be anticipated in advance. Meanwhile, as the number of novelty that is likely to happen in reality tends to be infinite, it is impossible to predict what novelty will come out in the future. This shows that the possibilities of novelty are constrained naturally, and the process of novel creation is determined by many constraining characteristics. These natural constraints are not only synchronic (energy and resources constraints) but also diachronic (institutional and traditional constraints), which are rooted in institutions such as norms that manifest as historical heritage and knowledge-based beliefs, and passed through the socialization of the younger generations. In this regard, the constraint itself is the result of evolution, that is, given the pressure of certain environmental choices, it is the result of variation and selective retention. Undoubtedly, institutions not only exert influence and function as constraints but also leave considerable scope for changes in the organization of society in its own way. Moreover, these constraints are not definite, but vary with the selective pressure from the environment. In particular, it is based on the knowledge accumulation or the 'knowledge track'. As Dosi (1997) pointed out, knowledge does not accumulate randomly. Rather it is guided by the rules of variation, together with a strong constraint on the search for any technological opportunities. What I emphasize here is that in dynamic evolution, creativity constraints and motivations coexist and weigh the same: endogenous creativity works within given constraints. In fact, this is not only used for the explanation of the stage of novel creation but also applies to the logical explanation in the evolution (selection and development) process demonstrated further and even in the global urban transformation. In this regard, there is no real causal determinism between environmental and selective changes, thus avoiding the historical determinism of global urban evolution.

When motivations and constraints coexist and interact, novelty creation is characterized by universality at multiple levels and diversity of content, that is, there are novelty creations both at the individual level and social level, and novelty creation tends to be increasingly diverse. At the individual group level, for example, in an industry and its enterprises, or a social organization, the synchronic individual decision of its members can be understood as the process in which the relative frequency of novel behaviours plays a role in the individuals. At any point in time, this process potentially interacts with endogenous novelty creation. As a result, novelty creation tends to be diversified, which is called the diversification of novelty creation. Novelty creation at the individual level is the basis and a mirror of the novelty creation at the social level to a certain extent. However, this does not mean that the sum of individual novelty creation is simply equivalent to the novelty creation of the whole society. The individual-level novelty creation is completely divergent while there is a certain degree of convergent directivity in novelty creation at the social level. Therefore, at a social or organizational level, selective reinforcement in the one or other direction channels innovativeness and may foster, or impede, the individuals' creation of novelty (Witt 1987). The convergence of these two directions will make things better and vice versa. Therefore, novelty creation at the social level has different attributes from novelty creation at the individual level. They are opposite to each other, yet dependent on each other.

Of course, the novelty creation of individuals, apart from leading to diversity, may also be disseminated later. They can be diffused through the system itself, certain components of the system or imitation. Especially when it is consistent with the selective directions of novelty creation at the social level, the possibility of conducting this new idea will be widely accepted, and the consequent behaviour is innovation. Therefore, the variation function is of great significance to the creation and diffusion of the novelty behaviour induced by the uncertainty of environmental changes. This is the reason why the urban system will never be in stationary equilibrium and will, thus, become a powerful driving force for the endless evolution process.

5.3.2. Selection and Development Process

Facing the uncertainty of environmental changes, persistent novelty creation destabilizes the stationary equilibrium of the urban system and becomes a prerequisite for dynamic evolution. However, the interaction of endogenous novelty creation tends to increase diversity and divergence. It is meaningless to dynamic evolution because it cannot guide the direction of the city's evolution. Therefore, from the perspective of evolution, it is meaningful only when novelty emergence is selectively retained. This selection process is a convergence process interacting with the divergent novelty emergence and will hinder or even erode the growth of novelty diversity, thus preserving some novelty creation as the seed of urban evolution. From this perspective, the selection process is an important part of the evolution of global cities.

To unfold this process, first there must be adequately diversified novelty actions to be selected, which means there must be a sufficient number of heterogeneous samples; otherwise, the possibility of selection will be rather low. At the same time, there must be a strong selection pressure to show different positions of different novel behaviours. Under this precondition, the selection process occurs through the interaction of a selection effect that exists simultaneously among different groups of individuals in the society. We know there is always some implicit value function in different types of novelty behaviours. However, the selection process is a trade-off decision, rather than an equilibrium optimization, which inevitably affects the different value functions of novelty behaviours and may lead to conflicts among these value functions. Therefore, although different groups of individuals have their own purposes or preferences when selecting novelties, their purposes are offset against each other by exerting influence mutually, and consequently they become aimless collective choice. Of course, in the process of selection, the influences of different groups of individuals may vary, which depends on their advantages or abilities. As a special group of individuals, the government plays a guiding role, and exerts big influence on this process. Some interest groups may also have big influence. However, most of the influences exerted by different groups of individuals in the selection process are offset against each other, including the influence exerted by the government. Hence, the government does not play a dominant role in this process. In this regard, the continuous adaptation of novelties is a result of natural selection of the society, rather than imposed by the upper level.

Undoubtedly, in this aimless process of collective selection, competition is an influencing factor. Competition puts pressure on the process which eliminates variations and reduces the diversity of novelties created by individual groups. Under such pressure, only when a novelty is developing faster than the average, it would be considered as something of greater importance or at higher relative status, and thus of higher possibility to be selected. Relative status is an important criterion for the selection of novelties. We all know that in this selection process, novelties are selected according to its adaptability, which makes it impossible to establish a measurement. In an environment full of diversified information and knowledge, it is impossible to measure novelties by simply calculating the opportunity costs of them. Only by comparing the relative status of novelties can we decide which one is better. In addition, relative status is a value criterion, which depends on how you feel about the novelty, and is not an objective criterion such as effectiveness. When comparing the relative status of different novelties, there is no single way of ranking, since novelties are categorized subjectively instead. Nevertheless, according to phylogenetic theory, the rise of relative status may be positively correlated with the success of different reproductions. Therefore, the relative status of novelties is actually a reflection of the optimization principle in the overall process, which will significantly influence the average quality of novelties. In this regard, the selection process is the prioritization of diversified novelties.

However, in the selection process, as the competition is about creating a better development model, instead of outperforming each other under the same development model, there might be cases where heterogeneous novelties coexist and develop even better than on their own. That is to say, though under selective pressure, novelties are not exclusive of each other and do not necessarily lead to cut-throat competition. They can coexist in the selection process or among balanced individual groups (polymorphism), and there may be multiple development patterns existing at the same time. Obviously, such polymorphic selection will increase the growth rate of all the novelties, hence higher average adaptability of novelties.

Also, in the selection process, interactions happen between different novelties based on the correlation of individual agents. When individual population members have correlated reactions on the creation of novelties, these novelties will interact with each other (usually purposelessly). To put it more accurately, individuals' selection of novelties is largely affected by how frequently they emerge in the population, known as the 'frequency-dependent effect'. In this sense, a novelty (variety) is selected depending on other varieties in the contest of selection the viability or survival of each novelty (variation) is dependent on other competing variants. Also, as Metcalfe (1998) noted, 'the population averages for each selective characteristic change over time in a way which depends on the distribution of each and of the other characteristics in the current population'. In other words, the selected ones tend to be the average ones. This dynamic frequency-dependent effect has regular influences on the individual population, only when there is enough time for novelties to react to the pressure of selection. Only in a broad timeline can novelties be systematically and varyingly expanded through the selection process, and the frequency-dependent effect based on the correlation of individual adjustments can, therefore, work. Otherwise, novelties will soon turn into innovative activities, which will disturb the influences of the selection process. If that happens, it is difficult to adaptively preserve novelties for urban evolution.

The selection process tends to end up with the adaptive preservation of diverse novelties. The dynamics of the selection process are not caused by the deviation of the attractor but the revealing of novelties' relative status and frequency-dependent effect. So there can be no multiple equilibrium dynamics, or circumstances where equilibrium changes before adaptation does.

However, any selection process destroys the initial variety of the existence on which it depends, which means that urban evolution consumes its own fuel. If this variety is not replenished over time, evolution will grind to a halt. To prevent this from happening, it is necessary to keep a dynamic balance between the pressure of selections (the impact of competition) that reduces the diversity of novelties and innovative activities that increase it. To this end, the process of selection should be correlated to the process of development for the continuous creation of novelty. Therefore, how this correlation works out in the evolution of global city depends on the way that the development and selection processes have been instituted and a complete evolutionary account would explain these instituted characteristics, in terms of those higher order processes of variation, selection and development.

The process of development and the process of selection interact in the evolution of global cities. In the process of development, novelties are nurtured and, of course, selected. This encourages novelties with relatively high status (relatively high value) to develop in a proper way. In this process, selective characteristics of the generation of novelty evolve into selective advantages that will be distributed (reallocated) around entities in the population.

In this sense, the process of development is not only the result of selection but also the start of a new round of selection. The interactive process between development and selection can happen on many levels, including micro (organizational), medium (regional or departmental) and macro levels.

In a given scenario, the result of the interaction of selection and development depends on how they are connected. Generally speaking, their connection is autocatalytic, based on the fact that knowledge generates knowledge. Since all knowledge is provisional, we adhere to what we know until something demonstrably better comes along. In addition, the accumulation of knowledge is an unfolding process in which the realization of possibilities makes possible the specification of new possibilities (Popper 1985).

Therefore, the production and application of information is autocatalytic and endless. Likewise, the process of cities moving away from equilibrium is endless. Development and selection processes are linked together in an autocatalytic way so as to create a positive feedback loop. In this way, cities are being transformed from one practice towards another. Of course, this transformation is not necessarily in line with the motives and beliefs of all individuals. There is bound to be approval, support, opposition and resistance. It can be assumed that some recurring factors systematically shape the transformation, though other factors are at play as well and show through frequency-dependent effects how many individuals in a group are transformed.

Frequency-dependent effects not only play a positive role in strategic interaction but also come as a result of non-strategic interdependency made in decision-making preference and expectation. In a word, in the positive feedback loop between development and selection, some novelties are retained and even further developed, creating new orders.

5.3.3. Self-Organization and Evolutionary Pathway

As shown in the previous analysis, innovation based on novelties plays an important role in the evolution of global cities. However, this innovation only works under constraint, and the degree to which it works depends on the level of synchronic and diachronic constraints. Therefore, while people have dispositive power over the global urban evolution (mainly in the form of agent), there tends to be a random element at work, and the evolution is highly self-organized.

As global cities evolve, the interaction of endogenous knowledge generation and organizational uses revolves around networks. Whether it is an internal or an external network, the mutual interest relationship within it results in various kinds of coordination, forming a collaborative mechanism. Self-organizing coordination dominates the evolution of global cities. It can occur at different levels: intracity coordination, regional coordination and intercity coordination. Self-organizing coordination can only maintain a temporary order instead of equilibrium. Therefore, the connecting forms of coordination in self-organization at different levels and random environmental interference are not only decisive in dictating the speed and direction of novelty creation, shaping its process of transformation, but they themselves are a process of institutionalizing a new order that helps draw an evolutionary landscape. In this sense, self-organization is a pathway to unconscious or partial design.

When all global cities are seen as organizations, their significant adaptation to environmental changes in the course of evolution does not mean that old forms of organization learn and master new methods but signals the death of the old and the birth of the new. In a city where a unique industrial structure and functions are developed based on its distinctive resource endowments or other competitive advantages, if a set of internally consistent, and sometimes inflexible practices related to learning and innovation are established to achieve efficiency, any improvement they bring at any time will be comparatively limited. In this context, the city's ability to learn something new is also limited. It is difficult for a city to effectively replicate the success of other cities because many different practices will have to be adopted at the same time. In this sense, according to the ontology of city organism, cities cannot change their patterns of behaviour, meaning that their ability to adapt to changes always depends on organizational diversity or the birth of a new form of organization at any time. It seems like 'competence-destroying technological advance' (Tushman and Anderson 1986) which is so fundamentally different from previously dominant technologies that the skills and knowledge base required to operate the core technology shift. Barriers to entry are lowered, and new firms enter the markets by exploiting the new technology. Likewise, global cities may deal with most factors of creative destruction and be reborn from the ashes of old organizations to significantly adapt to major environmental changes in the course of evolution. In other words, the evolution of global cities follows a pattern of 'discontinuous balance'. New 'species' emerge due to dramatic changes once in a while, which then gradually become stable, and replace old 'species' under certain conditions. As a result, a more complicated, diversified and intensive structure will fall into place, making global cities increasingly complex and sophisticated.

Lastly, it is worth exploring what selective preferences would imply for the evolutionary direction of global cities. If a special type of novelty creation in new knowledge flows is selected based on preferences, which can be accumulated in the course of evolution, the evolutionary trend may represent changes in one direction. However, the problem is whether selective preferences lead to general tendencies in the evolution. This builds on specific hypotheses as to what the content of preferences is.

The first is the selective preference that improves the innovator's situation. The opportunity cost that underlies the translation of novelty into innovative activities is often taken into consideration, and it can be expected to improve the innovator's situation if such translation does happen. There exists directional adaptation, and a firm's existing know-how is transferable in the process of innovation, but as a sort of unilateral action, innovation more likely means a future prospect destroyed or even a fortune lost for other people. Such negative external effects of innovations may be destructive to the environment. Therefore, thanks to such choice preference, evolution comes as a non-directional development towards 'higher' forms, which may be said to imply a tendency—though not a non-contingent one—towards 'higher' societal states. This can be viewed as a sort of progress, but evolution cannot be described in the notion of 'progress'. Although there are universal criteria that can be used to evaluate progress, in synchronous environments with their inevitable time constraints, the evolutionary nature of change and choice prevents their use. When it comes to evaluating the 'adaptability' of evolutionary choices, there is no unique standard. This is because, in one way or another, the evolutionary clocks differ from each other, and no uniform criteria may suffice.

Second, city actors share some basic, genetically determined preferences which are directed to the physical needs for survival and preservation of species. Meanwhile, a more or less long chain of culturally formed associations is learned, which leads from those few innate preferences to the huge variety of idiosyncratic, acquired tastes revealed in current choices. This is in itself a result of a city's evolution. These choices do not necessarily increase genetic fitness, yet actors' decisions are related in a complex subjective fashion to basic preferences that once had adaptive value. It may, therefore, by conjectured that the common genetic elements in actors' preferences which dictate some average tendencies in the actors' endeavours produce some direction in the path of evolution. This explains why we attach much importance to urban genes in the revolution of global cities. That is to say, urban genes determine the direction in which global cities evolve.

Evolutionary Model

On the basis of the evolutionary dynamics of global cities, we attempt to analyse how global cities evolve, namely how global cities demonstrate dynamics and diversity in the interaction of choices of locations and choices of the environment. First of all, a dominant model of evolution is constructed based on the evolutionary pathways of all global cities. Then, evolutionary diversity is elaborated based on the experiences of individual global cities.

6.1. DOMINANT MODEL OF EVOLUTION

To explain the formation and development of global cities in a general sense, it is essential to develop a basic theory based on a general review of the history of global cities. The next step is to examine the overall evolutionary process and characteristics.

6.1.1. A Basic Evolutionary Theory

Our theory on the revolution of global cities, which is more like an abstract generalization, is based on an overall review of the history of the world's global cities. In Chapter 5, five main factors influencing the evolution of global cities are presented. In this section, an attempt is made to analyse the specific roles that these factors play in the evolution of global cities.

Globalization is arguably the most determining factor in the evolution of global cities, providing a favourable environment for global cities to emerge and a major driving force for their growth. The wave of informatization, which leads to the time–space conversion, has direct impact on the dynamic changes of global cities, but, more importantly, it plays a significant role in the evolution of global cities through interaction with the wave of globalization. Obviously, economic globalization and informatization are increasingly mutually reinforcing. Advances in information technology have brought about unprecedented prosperity to transportation, international trade, investment and production led by multinational or global companies, as well as the global economic, political and cultural exchanges (except for some African countries) promoted by the finance-driven economic integration. In return, global flows of resources and factors have contributed to the widespread application and popularity of modern information technology. Therefore, although these two drivers play a different role in the evolution of global cities, we suggest that the study of the evolution of global city should be placed in the context of interactions of globalization and informatization, which may contribute to a better understanding.

It is known that globalization is originated in regional economic expansion and, thus, economic globalization geographically generates a complex duality: high degree of geographical isolation and high degree of global integration in economic activity. In the process of informatization, information flows driven by modern information technology and the Internet also have complex dualism geographically: high degrees of decentralization in the process of information to be understood 'instantly' and high degrees of centralization in the generation and spread of information. As the world enters the Services Age from the Industrial Age, the aforementioned two kinds of dualism continue to integrate, thus leading to the heightened levels of interaction of globalization and informatization. In fact, in the process of interaction, the importance of cities (especially big cities) increasingly highlights this scenario. This is not accidental but has inherent logic. For one thing, the interaction has made for a great deal of economic decentralization and wide dissemination of information, and strengthened economic, cultural and political ties between different regions across the world, thus shaping integrated global production and service networks based on information flows. For another thing, this has led to a need to control and manage highly decentralized economic activities. The phenomenon of globalization seems to be particularly obvious in the assembly points of regional economy—the city, which becomes the spatial carrier of global production and service networks and shows an important role in the global economy.

Cities, especially big cities with unique location advantages, are undoubtedly the best spatial nodes to implement such control and management. As a result, global cities become the basic node of the world network. World cities are not so much an exception to this decentralization as they are a consequence and shaper of it. As Amin and Thrift (1992) pointed out, centeredness is essential within a globalized world economy. In the process of interaction of globalization and informatization, those globalizing cities evolve into global cities, and the function, organization and architecture of these increasingly globalized cities will also undergo dramatic changes. For example, the services sector taking the place of manufacturing becomes a pillar industry that drives cities' development, and the level of innovation becomes a decisive factor of urban development, making the city a base of innovation. At the same time, the cities also become the centres of consumption and product sales.

Indeed, interactions of globalization and informatization development have to take place within the confines of time and space or, more specifically, different long-term economic cycles and conditions. How and at which stage of a long economic cycle is the economy changing will have a bearing on the pace of globalization and informatization, and the extent to which they interact with each other. It should be noted that these two factors are not independent variables in the shaping of globalizing cities, but are playing an indirect role. But economic changes have historically been viewed to have a direct impact on urban development. Europe, for example, experienced its highest emergence of new cities back in the 13th century, when technological inventions in the agricultural sector and a flourishing trade economy stimulated growth. Industrialization created the demand for a citywide spatial segregation of urban functions. Ebenezer Howard developed the garden city as a segregated place for living with low density (Howard 1902). However, low density in certain city spaces created disadvantages such as increased commuting traffic and loss of city enlivenment around the clock, which later on led to the postulation of traditional city spaces with a high degree of functional intermixture and density by Jacobs (1993).

However, as the evolution framework of world cities has gone through radical changes, economic changes in a certain long economic cycle cannot be simply identified as a dependent variable in the development of global cities either, given that they have less explanatory power for the evolution of global cities, without the interaction of globalization and informatization as a medium. Therefore, it is more like a covariate in the evolution of global cities.

Similarly, world urbanization is not directly related to the evolution of global cities. But as a special spatial existence, global cities have evolved from regular cities, not completely different from or independent of today's urban systems. The truth is that the process of world urbanization has promoted not only the development of the cities themselves but also that of the world urban system on a larger scale. From this perspective, world urbanization has certain impacts on the evolution of global cities. Indeed, the impact occurs only when the spatial function of cities shifts from being 'spaces of flows' to 'spaces of flows and places'—bringing about radical changes in the 'core–periphery' structure of the traditional world urban system. That is to say, as an independent variable, world urbanization can promote the development of new city networks and indirectly impact the evolution of global cities through the interaction of globalization and information as a medium.

However, it is not the case for changes in the world economic pattern. As a special variable largely different from the aforementioned four factors that focus mostly on how global cities come into being at the broader world level, it is designed to predict which parts of the world are more likely to witness the formation of global cities. In fact, it is directly related to a state's position in the global economy and is, thus, more essential for analysing the evolutionary pathway of individual global cities.

From the earlier analysis of the logical relationship among the influential determinants at the world level, we can see that global cities, as products of a certain historical stage, are formed and developed in the context of the interaction of globalization and informationization, and are thus given a specific connotation. Without such a background, there would have been no global cities. However, we are unable to jump to the conclusion that global cities have emerged as a direct result of these two factors, as Friedmann and Sassen did. Indeed, global cities have emerged as a result of the WCN, through which these two determinant factors interact. In other words, despite globalization and informationization being an endogenous driving force, the WCN is a vital intermediary for the evolution of global city. This clarification gives significance to a relational theory of flows of spaces and information, instead of a 'materialized' one, in capturing the essential characteristics of global cities.

Rather than functioning as a centre, cities serve as nodes in the WCN, whose value is recognized as its connectivity with different nodes. A node's connections not only represent its city functions and values but also determine its position in the network. Some cities, with the increasingly comprehensive and strong network connectivity of core city functions, have become major or basic nodes, namely global cities. In this sense, global cities are major higher tier nodes in a WCN. Their position and value as primary nodes are represented through their extensive network connectivity, while their important roles and functions through the WCN. From a dynamic perspective, the WCN is increasingly extended with the further deepening of globalization and information, during which more global cities emerge. As the nodal functions and positions change, some global cities are likely to lose steam, while others might ascend to global status in their stead. Therefore, it is inappropriate to approach global cities without examining the important part that they play in the dynamics of the WCN.

The earlier sections have gone to great lengths to answer the basic question of how global cities evolve (see the upper half of Figure 6.1). Specifically, when examining how individual cities evolve into global cities, we should also take into consideration factors at the national level and the variables in individual cities. Only in this way can we explain why global cities emerge in some countries and not the others, or why some cities have evolved into global cities while some have not, in the same context of globalization and informationization within the same

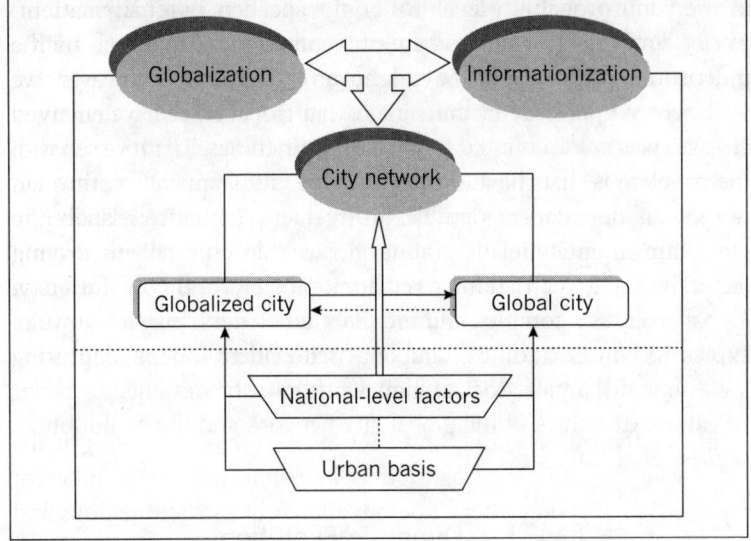

Figure 6.1 *The Evolution of Global Cities*

Source: Compiled by author.

period of time. Indeed, a fundamental law applies to the evolution of all global cities within a country or individual global cities. For one thing, factors at the national level affect the extent to which a country leads or fits into globalization and informationization, and, in turn, have an influence on the evolution of global cities in the country. For another thing, endogenous variables represent the conditions of a city underpinning its response and adaptation to the globalization and informationization process, and how well these conditions support a city to evolve into a global city. Both factors must be examined in alignment with the independent variables of globalization and informationization.

Otherwise, country-level impact factors and urban-level endogenous variables will be of little or no help for explaining global urban evolution. For example, Taylor and Aranya (2008) used a network model to assess changing global intercity relations from 2000 to 2004. Their connectivity model is based on a city's capability to generate strategic corporate information and knowledge flows through the presence of globalized APS firms. But 'regression' is statistically significant at a very low probability level, with only 6 per cent (after adjustment) of city connectivity changes being accounted for (explained) by the independent variables. In the end, however, the authors concede that well over 90 per cent of the variation in the observed connectivity changes was not accounted for by their hypotheses. The root cause of the problem is that the authors only used cities' appeal to organizations as an independent variable, rather than systematically analysing the shifting intercity relations at the global scale, especially the overall factors causing such shifting relations. Therefore, the evolution of global cities, as a complex and multifaceted process, may not be fully explained by just adding a couple of self-evident independent variables. Instead, a more logical framework must be designed to better reveal the dynamics of the global city network and the evolutionary process of global cities.

6.1.2. Dynamic Evolution

According to the earlier discussion, the global city is a spatial expression of contemporary globalization. Generally, it reflects the way in which social and economic activities are organized in a certain space (city). Based on the function of the city as a space, the global city is an urban functional space. This spatial change in urban function is the main indicator of the evolution of global cities. As mentioned earlier, Castells (1996) identified two contrasting ways in which social and economic activity is organized: a 'space of places' and a 'space of flows'. Urban functions actually exist in the local-flow complex space, rather than in separate spaces. However, for the purpose of modelling, we theoretically divided the spatiality of urban functions into two types based on flows (networks) and location (scale). Using them as two coordinates, we constructed a simple theoretical model to illustrate how global cities evolve.

A city as a functional space means that urban functions are organized hierarchically by their centrality or prominence in a network comprising spaces of 'places' or 'flows'. Although the levels of dependence of functional spaces on 'places' and 'flows' vary, their internal unity indicates that large deviation is unlikely. Therefore, we can assume that there exists a 45° isogonal line in between the x and y axes for spaces of places and flows. By that, we mean that the evolutionary trajectory of global cities is not from spaces of places to spaces of flows, or reversely, but evolves on the back of places-flows interplay.

As global cities are places that bring together place-bound resources with firm-bound specializations to serve as sites of global economic control, and as points to access the global economy for producers located within them, the network centrality of a city is assumed as its capability to provide services, coordination and opportunities for direct, effective access to the global marketplace. The presence (or absence) of connections between cities in the WCN reflects producers' opportunities for (and barriers to) direct, effective access to global markets. The hypothesis is based on the fact that except for a few large producers who internalize even the most complex specialized service functions, and meanwhile maintain multiple global locations, thereby have direct access to foreign markets, most mega-producers still rely on APS firms for access to the global marketplace, and they are impacted by the advantages (and disadvantages) conferred by cities and firms. What's more, during the process of globalization, not major multinational firms, but smaller producers have participated in the global economy. These smaller producers are vast in number and frequently interact with the larger ones, but they cannot participate in the global economy without external support. These smaller producers have to rely on APS firms to access the global market and are strongly impacted by the world city hierarchy.

Of course, the opportunities a city offers its producers for access to global markets are not simply either present or absent, but rather are a matter of degree. Intercity linkages are stronger or weaker depending on the extent of overlap in the composition of cities' entire APS firm complexes. This recognizes that when two cities contain branch offices of many of the same APS firms, they offer proportionately greater opportunities for producers to conduct seamless, direct and effective economic changes between them and vice versa. Therefore, a city's position within the WCN structure defines the extent to which it offers producers the advantage of direct or indirect access to the global economy. Such differential structural advantages, deriving from cities' different positions in the network, result in a world city hierarchy in which some places are better sites for producers than others. This means that urban functional spatiality is positively correlated with the scale of opportunities or the size of advantages the city offers producers located in it to access the global market. The larger the urban functional spatiality, the greater the opportunities it allows for producers to enter the global market and vice versa.

For global cities, the extension of urban functional spatiality is placed in the changing structure of WCN and, thus, the urban functional spatiality might be regarded as a function of the city's position in the city network structure. It is hypothesized that in any given decade, the difference in two cities' positions in the urban hierarchy is positively associated with the dissimilarity of their functional spatialities, that is, cities with similar ranks in the urban hierarchy are expected to have similar functional spatialities, while cities with different ranks in the urban hierarchy are expected to have dissimilar functional spatialities. For example, Ross (1987) found that US cities' centrality in a command and control network of HQs–subsidiary linkages predicted the presence of higher order functions, while others found US cities' relationships between urban functional differentiation and US cities' positions in networks of trade, banking, information diffusion and transportation.

The evolution of WCN is not stable over time, so that it must be seen more as a process than a static system. As mentioned earlier, the basic observation underlying the interlocking WCN model is that cities are connected through the internal networks of MNCs, ASP firms, government agencies and NGOs. Through the linkages generated by affiliated offices, vital strategic information/knowledge, capital and personnel flow between cities. Therefore, the connectivity between cities is defined by all the linkages between these entities and organizations, while global cities are the location choice result of these entities and organizations.

If this connectivity change is used as the dependent variable, and the functional agencies in the interlocking network are used as independent variables, the urban functional spatiality can be changed by the following three factors: (a) the migration decisions of functional institutions located in a certain city and their own changes, which include the possible changes in connectivity brought by the changing importance or size of their local offices. These determine the changes in terms of amount and size of functional institutions in the city. The conjecture behind conceiving this elemental interlock link as a surrogate for actual flows of inter-firm information and knowledge between cities is that the more important the office, the more connections there will be with other offices in a firm's network (Derudder and Taylor 2005); (b) the changing presence in other cities of functional institutions located in a certain city. For example, a given functional institution, by setting up more offices in other cities and gaining linkages with other parts of the world, increase the connectivity in the city it is located; (c) the merging of a functional institution in a certain city with the other functional institution located in other cities, which will connect the otherwise separated cities through the internal network of the institutions. For example, mergers and acquisitions (M&As) can lead to a permanent reconfiguration of global firm networks, bringing cities closer in the network.

Therefore, the common process of the evolution of global city can be seen as the functional spatiality evolution of cities. In general, the process appears to be a constant evolution of functional spatiality from a lower position (A) to higher positions (B and C) (Figure 6.2). Meanwhile, in particular cases, some global cities may experience a reversed evolution, or an evolution towards the decline, where the functional spatiality lowers from high to low positions.

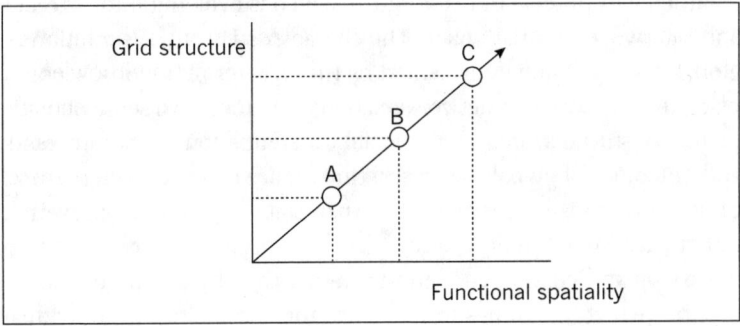

Figure 6.2 *The Common Process of the Evolution of a Global City*

Source: Compiled by author.

However, detailed analysis of the evolution process is still needed for individual cases beside the analysis based on common processes. This is because of the path dependence that comes with the evolution process of an individual global city, that is, the strong connection between the city's position as a node in today's network and its functional spatiality from the past; and also because of the diversity in evolution processes, that is, the varying evolutions in cities of various types, under the interactive influences of market, specialized organizations and political processes.

6.1.3. Characteristics of Evolution

Some 'general' characteristics, in contrast to those distinctive characteristics, can be observed in the common process of the evolution of global city, which are not only strong and explicit but also constant and non-sporadic. These characteristics imply an underlying regular pattern, which we will analyse from different perspectives to reveal the nature and the trend of the evolution of global city.

6.1.3.1. Extended Global Network Relations

In their evolution process, global cities generally scale up in terms of physical size (population, wealth, volume and capacity), though this cannot be regarded as the signature characteristic of evolution. According to Taylor ([2003] 2004), the development of cities can be regarded as a process of networking, which is evolving into different and interwoven spatial scales. The characteristics of the evolution of global city are mainly represented by the changes of 'a global sense of place' that are based on network relations. Such 'a global sense of place' might constitute a progressive social differentiation of the processes and outcomes of globalization and time–space compression. A vision of place which is processual rather than static, open and extroverted rather than enclosed and introverted, constituted by a constellation of varying and conflictual identities rather than by one unique identity, but which continues to recognize the specificities of individual places (Massey 1994). This extension of global network relations is the everydayness of spatially stretched and distant connections of the city. Spatial propinquity is no longer the defining feature of the city. Cities are 'assemblages of more or less distanciated economic relations which will have different intensities at different locations' or 'sites in near–far networks' (Amin and Thrift 2002). Therefore, porosity of the global city exposes it to all manner of more 'distanciated' rhythms, imaginaries and potentialities.

Furthermore, the extension of global network relations not only depends on the increase in quantity and strength of its external networks but notably on that of external networks of cities which the global city connects with. As Neal (2011) noted, whether a city's status rises or falls over time depends not on its own internal features, nor on its own network, but on the structure of the entire WCN. Therefore, as the major nodes in the WCN, global cities evolve, not in an isolated and independent way, together with the extension of WCN.

6.1.3.2. Expanded Integrated Functions Based on Multiple Networks

The evolution of global city is characterized by its unique role in driving the updates of the allocation function for global resource networks, and the creation of new functions, which do not simply replace existing functions, but rather expand and complement them within multiple networks. In this way, it has increasingly developed into a more powerful engine for the effective allocation of global resources.

At the early stage, global cities performed their function as production centres that are derived from the MNC-based global commodity chains, or the command and control function as defined by Friedmann. After that, following in the steps of MNCs, APS firms have increasingly become multinational firms in their own right as they look for a foreign presence in an international market to service existing clients and find new ones (Harrington and Daniels 2006). In order to provide their clients with seamless services and protect their brand integrity across the globe, APS firms have opened offices in numerous cities around the world and carried out all work within their office networks. The intercity relations are constituted by the information, instruction, specialized knowledge, design, planning, strategy, ideas, teleconferencing and face-to-face meetings that flow between city offices when implementing servicing projects for clients. The service flows between offices of such city are part of what Thrift (1999) calls the blizzard, that is, the global space of flows. Therefore, global cities have 'a particular component in their economic base', which gives them 'a specific role in the current phase of the world economy', as they have obtained a new function, the coordination function or the function of being centres for the organization of global capital, building on the APS global service chains. Though the global commodity chains network is different from the global service chains network, as we have elaborated in Chapter 4, the two networks can inherently complement each other. Then the evolution of global city based on the dual networks further incorporates the control and coordination functions in the allocation of global resources.

What's more, global cities will develop more integrated functions in the future. With the development of knowledge economy and, especially, the help of modern ICTs, the Internet and big data, all kinds of social and economic activities rely more heavily on knowledge creation and application, which increasingly demonstrates the accelerated self-driven shift of the urban economic foundation from commercial and business services to knowledge industries. At the same time, as the globalization of knowledge has sped up, there will be more frequent international academic exchanges and cooperation, an increasing number of international technological cooperation projects and the emergence of many global knowledge institutions, such as global R&D centres and global innovation alliances, which will develop into a global knowledge or innovation network. Therefore, global cities will again have a new 'particular component in their economic base' and a new function, the leading function or the function of being centres for scientific and technological innovation, which is derived from the network of global knowledge chains. Obviously, the network of global knowledge chains is again different from the previously mentioned two networks, but all of the three networks can inherently complement each other. In conclusion, based on multiple networks, global cities in the future may obtain integrated functions of control, coordination and leading in allocating global resources.

6.1.3.3. Enhanced Internalized Minds

In the evolution process of global cities, we can always note the changes in their positions, which means that the general contraction of space and the increasing fluidity of products and production factors have the effect of bringing about various forms of intercity and inter-regional division of labour (McKenzie 1933). It is noted that this urban division of labour is based on larger roles in an interdependent urban system, wherein occupations and industries are more advanced and globalized in line with their roles. Thus, it requires not only that new actors should continue to be involved to update and reorganize various groups of actors but also that a standard interaction model among various actors should be in place. Updating and reorganizing various groups of actors provide the foundation for a standard interaction model and, in turn, the formation of a standard interaction model facilitates the renewal and reorganization of various groups of actors. In conclusion, behind the changes in the positions of global cities are the emerging standard interaction models among various actors in the global cities.

As carriers of the 'generic knowledge', various actors in global cities have interactions with one another. Such interactions on the whole, on the one hand, can be represented as connections between 'generic ideas' and, on the other hand, as connections between knowledge carriers. The connection of ideas represents the 'imagined' interaction model design while the latter, the actual interaction model, embedded in the mind of it. And a composite of all connections represents an interaction model. Since we have conceived a real interaction as a composite of coordinated actors, it can also be conceived as a composite of structured information which is exchanged between the actors. Knowledge, thus, appears as an interdependent process of continuously exchanged information. The actual interaction model constitutes itself a physical actualization of generic knowledge. If the actual interaction model can be regarded as resource connections between various actors, then the resource connections can be viewed as representing the surface structure, and the generic knowledge connections the deep structure of the interaction model. Over time (as global cities evolve), the flow of information between various actors leads to a change in the knowledge base and generates a new connotation of the connections of knowledge (ideas), causing changes in the resource connections between the actors. Therefore, the interaction model is a reflection on and a response to the knowledge and information in question. It can be considered that it is the knowledge which is understood as self-referential and related to environmental conditions (as it relates not only to the mode of structure and emergence but also to an authority, who has the capability to know) that makes it possible for the standard interaction model to be a stable endogenous order.

Therefore, the evolution of global cities is not only represented by the changes in the cities' positions as nodes for resource connections, but it also involves changes in its deep structure including the enhanced mind and the upgraded connections of generic knowledge, thereby facilitating the evolution of the standard interaction model among various actors. Of course, given the non-linearity of the evolution process and the uniqueness of the constantly changing endogenous order, this process cannot be categorized as a phenomenon that follows empirical rules. In this sense, the aforementioned changes only occur at a specific time and place in the evolution of global cities: they are unique in the history of global cities and exclude other types of physical actualization.

6.2. DIVERSITY IN EVOLUTION (TYPES)

We have analysed earlier the overall trends in the evolution of global cities and the features of its common process. And yet the evolution of global cities shows (type) diversity under the different constraints by country-level impact factors and by endogenous variables of the cities themselves, which also constitutes an endogenous feature of evolution. Of course, to date, there is no fixed model for the categorization of global cities, and existing classifications mostly depend on the research purpose and research subjects, such as multidimensional classifications of cities that have focused on combinations of city attributes (Boschken 2008), or classifications focusing on the actual relations of cities and using them as tools to describe cities' position or status in the networks (Choi et al. 2006). In fact, the main problem is that no classification model based on one single perspective can reflect the diversity in the evolution of global cities. Therefore, we need to elaborate the (type) diversity in the evolution of global cities from different perspectives.

6.2.1. Evolution Types Based on Nodes' Characteristics

As key nodes in the WCN, global cities themselves have multiple characteristics, among which their sizes and types are fundamental characteristics. When cities are regarded as physical entities, their sizes refer to population, area and economic strength and their types entail resources, locations and functions. In contrast, when cities are regarded as nodes in networks, their sizes refer to network coverage reflected by network connectivity, and their types entail main channels of network connections including institutions, platforms and flows. Thus, to classify the evolution of global cities according to the types of nodes, we may look at two dimensions: spatial scale and categorical scale.

Spatial scale is used to measure the coverage of city network connectivity. Different from the geospatial scope, it mainly reflects the spatial size of connected cities, in addition to the length and quantity of connections. It, thus, works with the measures of degree centrality and eigenvector centrality. From this perspective, although global cities are the main nodes of the WCN, not all global cities are considered 'global' in the same way, because they are embedded in different flows of the world network, with different main scopes of connectivity coverage. Of course, the network connectivity coverage of a global city may be a hybrid combination, which comprises long-, medium- and short-range connections. However, we can still determine whether the main coverage of a global city is considered 'global' or 'regional' according to the weight of its different connections. Network connections of some global cities show a globalist orientation in that they have higher degree centrality and eigenvector centrality. That is to say, they have more connections to those core nodes or higher level nodes, which indicates that these cities control and coordinate global resources at the global scale. In contrast, network connections of other global cities show a regional orientation in that they have higher degree centrality but lower eigenvector centrality. That is to say, most connected nodes are general nodes or lower level nodes, which indicates that these cities control and coordinate global resources at the regional scale.

A categorical scale is used to measure the amount of types for city connectivity networks. Different from the general urban typology, it is not used to identify which type (such as industrial cities, resource-based cities, inland cities, coastal cities and so on) a city belongs to and instead it is used to identify the characteristics of city connection categories, that is, single or multiple connections. Therefore, this scale reflects the number of fields or types the city connections belong to. According to categorical scale, though global cities may be viewed as a complex with network connections that integrate multiple functions and cover numerous fields, not all of them are considered 'comprehensive' for the same model. This is because global cities are in different categories of global networks, such as economic networks, technology networks, cultural networks, diplomatic networks and informal organizational networks. Different types of global networks may have different levels of connectivity. A global city may have strong connectivity in one network, but weaker or even no connectivity in another. Therefore, we can generally identify the basic characteristics of connectivity categories, that is, field-specific or comprehensive connectivity. Some global cities show a higher level of external connectivity in networks of different fields or types, which means that they control and coordinate global resource in a comprehensive manner, while other global cities show a higher level of external connectivity only in networks of a certain field or type, which means that they control and coordinate global resources in a specialized manner.

The distinguishment between comprehensive and specialized global cities can be viewed from two perspectives. From a broad perspective, functionally comprehensive global cities show strong network connectivity in both economic and non-economic fields, while functionally specialized global cities show connectivity in either the economic field or the non-economic field. From a narrow perspective, whereas comprehensiveness is measured solely in the economic field (which equals specialization from the broad perspective), specialization is measured solely for a single economic function; while functionally comprehensive global cities display strong network connectivity with multiple economic functions, functionally specialized global cities display strong network connectivity with a single economic function. Since economic globalization has outpaced other spheres of globalization and the WCN is mainly based on economic connections, most studies have adopted the narrow perspective in distinguishing between comprehensive and specialized global cities. For example, Csomós (2013) distinguishes functionally comprehensive global cities from specialized ones using command and control index (CCI) based on the Global Industry Classification Standard (GICS). Functionally comprehensive global cities have a complex industrial sector structure. The command and control functions of these cities are determined by several (at least four) sectors, none of which are especially dominant regarding their CCI. Specialized global cities whose profile is determined by several (at least four) industrial sectors, with one of these sectors being dominant, contributing more than 50 per cent of the city's CCI. It is estimated that New York is a typical functionally comprehensive global city, given that the CCIs of all its sectors occupy one of the first ten positions in the rankings. And it is the only command and control centre of the USA that contains all 10 GICS sectors, with its financial sector providing 55.55 per cent of the city's CCI, the consumer staples sector and the healthcare sector ranking first in the USA, and the finance and healthcare sectors also being ranked first globally. Functionally specialized cities includes San Jose (information technology CCI: 93.86%), Washington (finance CCI: 79.46%), Dallas (energy CCI: 62.07%), Houston (energy CCI: 86.05%), Seattle (information technology CCI: 56.20%), Charlotte (finance CCI: 83.60%), Bridgeport (industrial sector CCI: 84.65%) and Cincinnati (consumer staples CCI: 71.54%).

On the basis of the characteristics of global cities as nodes in the network, or specifically the spatial scale and the categorical, we can identify four groups of global cities in theory: global comprehensive cities, global specialized cities, regional comprehensive cities and regional specialized cities (Figure 6.3). Taylor (2005a) has identified four similar types of global cities. First, at the global level, there are functionally comprehensive global cities such as London, New York

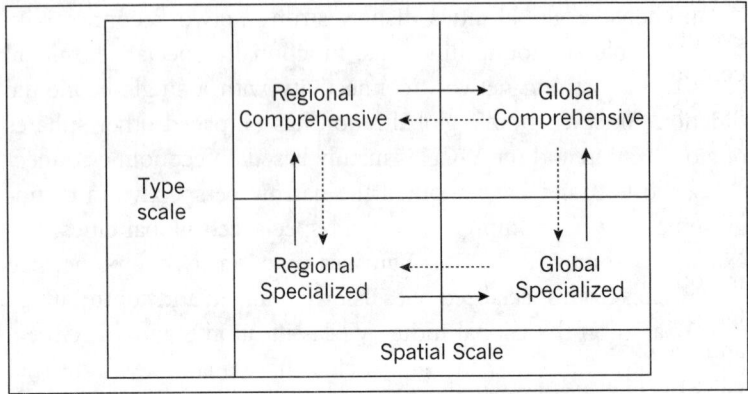

Figure 6.3 *Types of Global Cities in Different Combinations*

Source: Compiled by author.

and Paris; and so-called global niche cities with specialized global contributions, such as Hong Kong and Tokyo. Then, at the lower regional level, there are sub-net articulator cities (that are functionally comprehensive) and cities with worldwide contributions in particular spheres of activity. Each global city can find its place in these four groups based on its level of development, the main scope of its connectivity coverage and the type of its network connections. This may be a result of the 'natural division of labour' in the evolution of global cities. It also demonstrates that, during the evolution of global cities, the (type) diversity inherently determines that some cities play a certain role, while others act in another, providing a stable structure through such role allocation. Though structural changes may occur in terms of proportional relations, they have a relatively slow impact on the evolution of global cities. Of course, individual global cities may change their roles during the process, but these changes are actually of little significance and they seldom occur.

If some global cities change their roles in this (type) diversity structure, specifically from one quadrant to another as is shown in Figure 6.3, the change is always a linear movement in a certain dimension. For example, a regional specialized city can evolve into either a regional comprehensive city on the type scale, or a global specialized city on the spatial scale. If possible, the city can further develop into a global comprehensive city on the basis of the first-stage evolution. However, it is difficult for a specialized city to become a comprehensive one, which needs a longer period to accumulate the key elements for development. Likewise, it is rarely possible for a city to enhance its level of connections from regional to global because it depends mostly on the shift of globalizing centres rather than the city's own development. In reality, concurrent movements in two dimensions may exist, but a reach of synchronicity and equilibrium in both dimensions is so rare that it, if any, can only be an exception. Of course, due to the changing background of global urban evolution and the changing channels and routes of globalization, some global cities might also change their roles in a reverse direction, degenerating from a global comprehensive city to a regional comprehensive city or a global specialized city, or from a regional comprehensive city or a global specialized city to a regional specialized city, as indicated by the dotted arrows in Figure 6.3.

6.2.2. Evolution Types Based on Connectivity Functions

Despite various forms of functions of global cities, such as agglomeration and radiation, integrated services, hub and gateway, etc., their primary or essential function has to be the connectivity function in the global network, which is based on both the space of places and the space of flows. Though the two measures in themselves are an inseparable unity, they express different connectivity functions. Thus, we can use these two spatial dimensions—scale of places and scale of flows—to conceptualize the evolution types of global cities based on their connectivity functions.

The scale of places usually measures geographical positions. However, in the global network connections, it is a particular expression of positions within the network. Sheppard (2002: 324) points out that 'Defining the status of such cities by their position within transnational networks, one can see that the role and trajectory of such cities is bound up with their positionality'. We know that the positions of global cities result from the locations selected by a series of globalizing functional institutions. Only when these functional institutions choose specific urban spaces as a component of their strategic functions in support of market development and prioritization of innovation, the city will be seen as a strategic location. In this sense, globalizing functional institutions (firms) are a 'market' of the city, and the formation of high-level 'new products' in the market (exchange) is a unique process of strategic localization. These cities are the location of strategically important functions that build a series of locality-based activities and organizations around a key function in the network, because of their roles as significant nodes for globalizing functional firms to deploy and improve their core competencies (Castells 1996). Therefore, we can use this scale of places to measure the strategicness of urban connectivity functions.

Strategic cities are those that develop a reciprocal relationship between globally significant agglomeration and localization economies and HQs of TNCs and APS firms (Cook et al. 2007). What is strategic has to be treated from two directions. From the perspective of cities, there are key firms that operate as strategic networks, which cities need to be part of; but equally, from the perspective of firms there are key cities that are strategic places, where firms have to be. They are not definitive strategic places but rather specific strategic places relating to one economic sector. Of course, there will be other strategic places for global commodity chains defined by other criteria (Goerzen et al. 2013). In a word, these strategic places appear to have various combinations of command capacity and generation of innovations with APS firms that develop strategic presence internationalization policies choosing to operate in these, but not other, cities to access such qualities. This mutual relationship is at the heart of agglomeration and localization processes that define the cluster-like economies of world cities (Bathelt, Malmberg and Maskell 2004).

Although all nodes in networks are equal, some are more equal (strategic) than others. This same mutuality, which is the essence of network building, can lead the 'unequal power relations' that also inhabit networks. The power of position strategicness is mainly about the control of functional organizations, such as the MNCs' HQs' 'CAC' functions to their branch offices around the world or the governing and management functions to the GVCs. In fact, though at first glance it seems that the networks of producer service firms are rather flat, their organizational model implies that there is the chain of command. Some 'big' strategies are made by the lead partners (Parnreiter 2010). The monopoly created by service innovation has control functions, so their offices in global cities have similar strategic position of HQs of MNCs.

A city's global network connectivity (GNC) is an aggregate measure that tells us nothing about the specific intercity connections that constitute it, and neither does it mean that the city is a global city in a complete and rich 'strategic network site' as proposed by Sassen (1991). So we are now in a position to identify which cities are strategic places within the WCN by ranking their strategic network connectivity. It should be clear that not all multinational organizations have the same strategic significance. Corporate HQs and regional HQs are of high strategicness, while other offices have less strategicness. Similarly, not all APS firms have the same significance of strategicness. The ubiquitous presence strategy means that sectors, such as accounting and finance, have less strategicness, while firms in other sectors such as law, management consulting and advertising firms have more strategicness. Besides, while a firm may have tens or hundreds of offices, not all of these offices share an equal level of strategic importance. Variations in strategicness may be reflected in the organizational form used to manage presence but also in other characteristics such as size and staffing. Therefore, we need to define which functional organizations are of higher strategic significance and then find strategic places where there are more strategic firms or offices. As a result, we will find that some global cities with the strategic presence of more multinational HQs and of APS firms' innovation services have a location of higher strategic significance, while others with the presence of more branch offices and of APS firms' normal services have a location of lower strategic significance.

The flow scale, as a specific indicator of network connectivity in the context of globalization, measures the fluidity of the global cities' connectivity, which is associated with the role of globalized functional institutions (companies) as producers in the cities. Some functional institutions specializing in providing products (services) for local markets (especially in terms of marketing and logistics, and R&D) tend to be distributed regionally, while APS firms that provide general services adopt the location strategy of 'ubiquitous presence', that is, maintaining a presence in as many cities as possible or establishing an intra-organizational network across the world, thus developing a general network process.

The fluidity of connectivity is usually assessed by three indicators of centrality (i.e., out-degree, closeness and betweenness). When chosen as the nodes of regional network formed by functional institutions in multinationals' value chains or the nodes connecting APS firms with local markets, some cities can coordinate effectively the interactions between all the elements that are integrated into these networks, thus demonstrating a rather high level of network fluidity. These cities not only witness large flows within themselves but also serve as intermediaries that facilitate the flow of resources between other cities in the network. By contrast, some cities have only low fluidity of network connectivity, and hence a low level of centrality.

Cities with different network fluidity tend to have different power in the network. Such power mainly arise from the large number of external linkages that the cities provide for globalized functional institutions. As these institutions tend to provide global services based on their internal network, some cities in the network become places of choice for them, or places in which they 'must maintain a presence' due to their favourable locations, markets and other factors. These cities, thus, occupy central positions in the network, and as such possess certain power with a significant impact on and control over flows in the network. The power can be strong or weak depending on the centrality of the cities in the network. More specifically, global cities with high centrality has strong power and vice versa.

Based on these two parameters, we can divide global cities into four major categories, featuring, respectively: high strategic importance and high centrality; high strategic importance and low centrality; low strategic importance and high centrality; low strategic importance and low centrality. Obviously, cities of the first category have the highest energy, that of the second and third come next, and that of the fourth have the lowest energy. New York and London are typical first-category global cities, as they enjoy high strategic importance and high centrality in the network.

Generally speaking, Tokyo also belongs to the first category, but it displays the distinctive features of the second category as well. According to the 2010 Forbes Global 2000 list, Tokyo is home to far more HQs than its closest competitors—Paris, New York and London, with total revenue exceeding that of New York and London added together. Therefore, Tokyo is a city of great strategic importance. However, the global connectivity of its service companies is far below that of its HQs.

Hong Kong is a typical global city of the third category. Although it does not have a large number of HQs and, thus, has far less 'command and control' power than Tokyo, it surpasses the latter in global connectivity. A major gateway to the fast-growing Chinese market, it has strong network power, which compensates for its deficiency in the 'command and control' power.

Dubai is a classic example of the fourth category. It is home to offices of many financial services companies, which form a well-connected cluster of APS. The most 'controlled' investments into Dubai are those in real estate markets and large infrastructure projects. As a result, Dubai can be called a 'global gateway city', but is merely a gateway to itself.

Based on its fluidity and strategic importance, every global city can find itself fall into one of the aforementioned four categories and, thus, display evolution of certain type. The overall structure formed by the different roles of all these global cities putting together is usually stable. Nevertheless, the roles of individual global cities may change in the course of its dynamic evolution, though such cases are relatively rare. If making positive change in its role, a global city will eventually transform towards the first category to possess high strategic importance and high centrality. It may follow two paths towards this ultimate goal, that is, by becoming the second- or third-category city first (Figure 6.4). However, it is also possible that as multinationals and APS companies change their location strategy for establishing

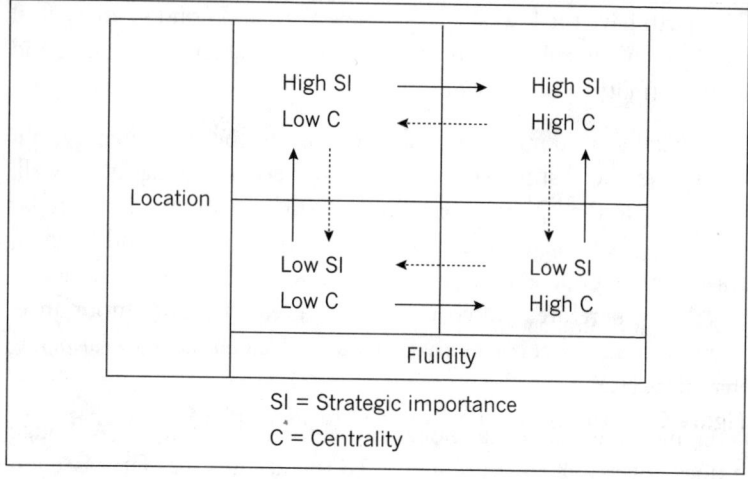

Figure 6.4 *Types of Evolution Based on Connectivity*
Source: Compiled by author.

connections, some global cities may undergo a reverse role change (as shown by dashed arrows in Figure 6.4).

6.2.3. Types of Evolution Based on Correlation

Global cities do not simply form linear and layered structures in the network. Instead, they are always part of correlated structures and have multiple dimensions (i.e., playing different roles) in the WCN. Based on the types of correlation, global cities have two dimensions: centrality and power.

In general, most scholars regard central position as equal to dominant position, or they think that at least there is causal relation between the two: power comes from centrality in a network, that is, the more central a city is in the WCN, the stronger it is and the more it can control or influence the flow of resources. For example, Allen (1999: 181–218) argues that powerful cities are at the intersection of all the important aspects of the global economy. Therefore, when the city's linking power reaches a certain level, it will become the core of several aggregated resource flows. Similarly, Boschken (2008: 8) describes centrality as 'based in part on the city's role as a node of power and

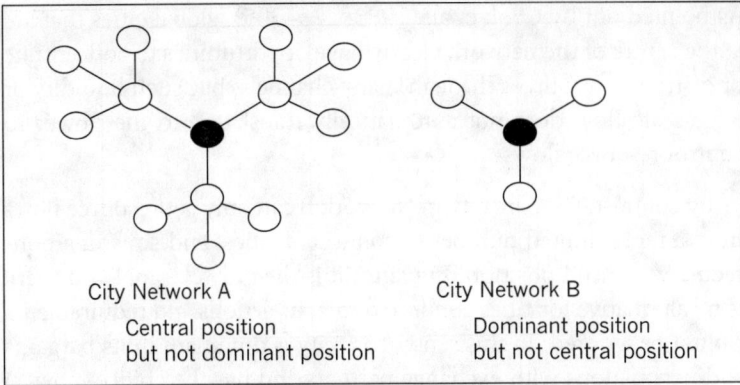

Figure 6.5 *Two Types of Position in Correlated Network Structures*
Source: Compiled by author.

connectivity'. However, from the perspective of correlated structure, centrality is not the same as dominant position, and the two lead to different results.

We can assume that there are two possible city networks, A and B (as shown in Figure 6.5), where circles represent cities and lines represent resource flows (connections) between cities. Obviously, these two networks have very different correlated structures, and the positions of core cities marked by the black circles are different in the two structures. In Network A, the core city not only builds links but also links to other connections, which helps to enhance its centrality and provide opportunities for capital accumulation or innovation diffusion. Since this kind of centrality depends not only on the connectivity of a city itself but also on the centrality of other cities connected to it, it is called recursive centrality.

Normally, such centrality provides core cities with a dual structural advantage, making them places where capital and resources can concentrate and from which innovation and reputation can also quickly and widely spread throughout the network. However, in this correlated structure, many cities are directly and indirectly connected to others, which gives them more alternatives, so that they can ignore the core cities' actions or requirements. In this sense, core cities lack control over its partner cities or the ability to affect resource flows.

As pointed out by Cook et al. (1983: 275–305), global cities that are at the centre of the network clearly have opportunities to concentrate or distribute resources through many channels, but such liquidity or large-scale flow does not automatically translate into the power to control resource flows.

By contrast, the core city in Network B can only get resource flows from a more limited number of connected cities, and so is in a non-recursive central position. But since it is the only channel and there is no alternative for cities connected to it, its actions and requirements cannot be ignored. In this sense, core city is dominant in its bargains and negotiations with exchange partners and has the ability (power) to control resource flows between cities. Power here is regarded as a capacity (Allen 1997: 59–70), which means that core cities influence the flow of resources in the WCNs more than any other cities. Since this capacity depends not only on the city's own connections but also on the connections (or, in fact, lack of connections) of cities linked to it, it is called recursive power, referring that the city's dominant position depends on its connection to cities without centrality. Allen (1999: 192) discusses about the advantages of cities being on such dominant position, pointing out that the importance of New York and Tokyo, and their like 'stems from the fact that the world of banking and the finance systems seems to have little choice other than go through the financial districts of those cities'.

The difference between the positions of core cities in different cor-related network structures cannot be measured by centrality, as in the aforementioned two cases, the core cities represented by black circles show no difference in degree centrality (both have the same number of links: 3). Similarly, when measured by closeness centrality and betweenness centrality, both of the core cities stand in the very centre of the networks. Such results imply that centrality can only be used to measure whether cities in the networks have connections but cannot determine if some of them have much stronger connections. The difference in city positions in various correlated network structures can be demonstrated by the distinction between hubs and gateway cities.

Traditional hubs and gateway cities differ greatly in their spatial organizations and functions. 'Hubs' have a relatively central position within a geographic region and a radial hinterland with a hub-and-spoke distribution of transportation corridors, promoting the movement of commodities and people, while gateways have a distinct spatial form and function which reflects their location on a regional boundary and their 'gatekeeper' role in controlling accessibility. Gateway city functions as an 'entrance' (and necessarily an exit out of some area) which tends to be narrow and will probably be used by anyone wishing to enter or leave the tributary area 'behind'. Thus, the city is in charge of the connections between the tributary area and the outside world. Traditional gateway cities commonly remain associated with their historical siting at so-called 'natural' gateways, harbours, fording points of rivers, etc., and the ability this has afforded them control over movement in and out of their regional hinterland markets. Hence, they are defined as cities that 'develop in positions which possess the potentiality of controlling the flows of goods and people' (Burghardt 1971).

Technological developments would transform the concept of gateway as 'terrain constraints', reducing the importance of physical barriers and prioritizing the 'spacio-economic connections' of cities. Moreover, flows of service economy and technology trade that develop increasingly rapidly may have different routes and geographies to those of material transportation corridors, leapfrogging coasts, mountain ranges, etc. Drennan (1992) states an important connection between the global 'exports' of such producer services and the changing role of traditional US gateway cities. Similarly, Pred's subsequent observations on the rise of the 'new' economy suggest the emergence of a change in the role of traditional gateway cities (Pred 1997). In short, new gateway cities can function as 'hubs' to some extent.

In the research of European Spatial Development Perspective (ESDP), 'gateway cities' are described as 'large seaports, international airports, trade fair and exhibition cities and cultural centers' which provide access to the EU territory and also to peripheral 'metropolitan regions', with advantages such as low labour costs or links with economic centres outside the EU. Elsewhere, 'global gateways' are described as transportation hubs, specifically seaports and airports, which are to be well distributed, and links with their hinterlands increased to provide more balanced access to intercontinental transport and service levels. As globalization develops, information of all kinds is now transported globally through electronic networks. In such environment, hubs keep reaching far beyond their hinterlands, extending to worldwide connections. The increasing importance of the border-hopping external relations of cities in globalization implies a role for regional hubs as new informational nodes and gateways. Therefore, globally speaking, hubs have some similar functions to gateway cities. Both traditional hubs and gateway cities tend to act as nodes for informational flows and exchanges associated with new modes of production in global APS networks (Castells [1996] 2001, 2000). However, there are still distinctions between hubs and gateway cities because of their different positions in the correlated structures. The former is the node for massive resources to concentrate and disperse, while the latter is the node with great influence where resources have to pass through.

Neal (2011: 2743) notes that 'centrality and power are distinct characteristics of cities' network positions', and they are subject to 'different structural patterns of linkages' (Neal 2011: 2745). 'Some cities may have structural opportunities to become sites of large concentrations of resources or efficiently to diffuse resources throughout the rest of the network, but little ability to control their flow' (Neal 2011: 2739). That is to say, these nodes enjoy sizeable flow of resources, though they cannot make big influence over the flow (they are central but not powerful). 'In contrast, others may have structural opportunities to control the flow of resources, but a limited capacity to accumulate or disseminate them' (Neal 2011). In this context, these cities serve as a 'minor site of flow concentration but a major site of flow influence' (Neal 2011: 2742) (they are powerful but not central). That means 'the positional status in the WCN is a multidimensional phenomenon' (Neal 2011: 2745), rather than a unidimensional one featuring a hierarchy of cities—from highly central and powerful global cities to non-central and unpowerful low-level cities. Centrality and power are distinct, and different combination of the two elements leads to different types of global cities.

Based on the two dimensions, global cities can be divided into four different types (Figure 6.6): cities in the upper right quadrant enjoy

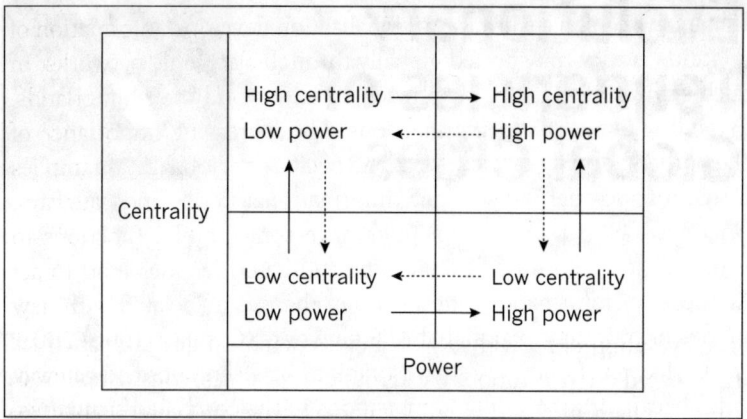

Figure 6.6 *Types of Evolution Based on Correlated Structures*
Source: Compiled by author.

high recursive centrality and high power, 'serving as the principal outposts of economic, political and social globalization' (Neal 2011: 2745). And in the upper left quadrant are 'hub world cities' which 'occupy positions of centrality but not power, and serve as sites for resource concentration and diffusion where innovation and investment activities are supported' (Neal 2011). The third type of cities is shown in the lower right quadrant, marked by low recursive centrality but high power. As 'gateway world cities', they 'serve as gatekeepers that gain influence through their ability to broker and mediate other cities' access to the rest of the network' (Neal 2011). And, of course, those global cities which fail to occupy positions of both centrality and power, as were reflected in the lower left quadrant, stand at the lowest rung on the ladder.

Observations of networks from the perspective of the flow of different resources (e.g., FDI and migration) might reveal that a single city can play multiple roles against different backgrounds. For example, a city can act as gateway world cities in some areas, but hub world cities in other areas. To conclude, a city's feature and position in the global stage are decided by its level of centrality and power in different networks.

Evolutionary Tendencies of Global Cities

The evolution of individual global cities demonstrates diversified features based on their various backgrounds, resources, constraints, 'DNA' (unique characters) and so on. But if we observe the evolution of global cities in different groups, we could discover certain patterns—spatial organizations from certain perspectives, which constitute an important part of the evolution of global cities. The study of the evolutionary tendencies of global cities reveals the development trends and features of the evolution of global cities.

7.1. EVOLUTIONARY TENDENCIES BASED ON NETWORK INTENSIFICATION

With the expansion of the WCN, the connections between the nodes become more intensive and closer, which means that the density of the network increases. During this process of network intensification, global cities also show dynamic tendencies of forming city networks, city pairings and smaller relational groups.

7.1.1. Development of Network Cities

As the WCN becomes more intensive, the density of nodes increases and the connectivity between cities becomes closer and more frequent, which allows more and more cities to gain benefits from the network instead of depending on their economies of scale and regional advantages. Thus, it will not only enhance the global cities' function as basic nodes of the network but also give opportunities for more globalizing cities to become emerging global cities.

When economies of scale represent the major engine of growth, cities can only enhance their positions by expanding their scale, which, over time, will lead to a basic city pattern with big cities occupying core positions and small- and medium-sized ones only peripheral positions. But when network connectivity becomes the key factor that drives cities' development, cities are no longer limited by their locations or scales, but can gain power by increasing their connectivity with other cities. That is to say, the introduction of networks into the urban equation complicated what was initially little more than an attempt to calculate the stock of resources at a city's disposal. Once networks entered the picture, a different kind of stocktaking evolved; one concerned to chart the network of connections, ties and flows which seemingly underpin a city's power and leverage (Taylor et al. 2002; Thompson 2003). 'Seemingly, because, where power is located in city networks is altogether more uncertain than simply pointing to such urban assets as the stock of professional service firms, corporate HQs, cultural capital, or strategic decision makers inside a city's boundaries' (Allen 2010).

During this transition, the functions of global cities will be more reflected by their focus on dealing with the complex network, which can reveal how they maintain, strengthen or lose their influence on and control over their surrounding cities (Carroll 2007). Another prominent change is that more small- and medium-sized cities that did not play an important role in previous world urban system now serve as nodes of the network which help enhance the network connectivity. Since good interactions enabled by positive network externalities can satisfy basic material needs, which were previously met by cities' scale in absolute sense (Capello 2000), small- and medium-sized cities are able to take full advantage of network effect by leveraging a variety of factors, including size, scale and location. Therefore, against the background of network intensification, cities that are near and also complementary to each other can jointly utilize their resources through infrastructure and trading networks, thereby forming 'network cities' (Batten 1995) or 'polycentric metropolises' (Hall and Pain 2006). The strong connection between these cities boosts their cooperation and information exchange, not only due to their spatial contiguity but also because they all serve as innovative and creative centres. Such connection allows the functions of the region to reach certain complexity, transcending the position of an isolated city in the urban hierarchy.

In the development of network cities, due to the spatial separation of management, production and consumption, spaces that mainly focus on satisfying supply and demand are less constrained, while urban market spaces have the opportunities to expand, which further weaken the global control potential of cities in the (old) hierarchy (Lyons and Salmon 1995). On the other hand, small- and medium-sized cities that benefit from network-triggered space compression can expand and transcend their economic centres, and gain influential positions by connecting with the key nodes of the network to which other separate parts of the network are linked, which can, in turn, create stronger economic linkages and even become the key nodes in the network of APS firms. This has two major impacts on the evolution of global cities.

First, it enables the spatial expansion of global cities. The evolution of global cities is indeed a process of transcending local relations and expanding non-local ones, which is particularly true for earliest global cities such as London and New York. During that period when economic globalization had not yet reached far and wide, as most of their neighbouring cities or regions only maintained local and domestic relations, these global cities experienced dramatic rise with their non-local relations appearing far stronger than local ones—a phenomenon resembling 'darkness under the lamp'. In the current context of network cities, however, local relations in its traditional sense have changed; for example, production has become less locally focused than before and is, in fact, trans-boundary. Influenced by cross-boundary dynamics of globalization, network cities, though still have administrative boundaries, witness different types of flows from various directions going across and through them. Such changes have led to the formation of multi-nodal urban agglomerations that include a series of core cities and dense groups of small- and medium-sized cities. Therefore, at present, local and non-local relations are no longer a clear-cut binary opposition but are intertwined and can coexist in the same place and at the same time.

Thanks to these changes, the evolution of global cities has broken previous space limits. While seeking to expand their global network connections, they also become increasingly embedded in their local relations by interacting with neighbouring regions and cities and, at the same time, integrate such relations into the global network to form a so-called 'global city region' or even MCR. Today, global cities such as London and New York have formed interactive relations with their surrounding cities in a global city region or MCR. In the south-eastern part of England, for instance, the agglomeration of APS firms has provided London with high connectivity to the extent that many distant, smaller urban centres are linking with each other and, thus, forming a network that spans 29,000 sq. km—an area that can be regarded as an internally connected global MCR. In this sense, the evolution of global cities is a process of achieving a dynamic equilibrium between global network connections and local ones. Although global cities such as London and New York focused on expanding non-local relations which far outweighed their local ones in an earlier period, they ultimately restore the balance between the two processes. This is what we call a dynamic equilibrium. If otherwise we neglect the changes in local relations of network cities or regional interactions of global cities, we may find it very difficult to properly characterize the evolution of today's global cities. We will elaborate on the spatial expansion of global cities in Chapter 8.

Second, it paves the way for the integration of small- and medium-sized cities into the global network as globalizing cities or even as emerging global cities. To explore the development of network cities is not simply to specify what kind of connectivity small- and medium-sized cities should have and how strong the connectivity should be upon their initial entry into the network, but to probe into these cities' potential for enhancing network connectivity in a dynamic process. In reality, although small- and medium-sized cities usually have only weak or indirect connections with other cities, it is such weak or indirect connections that 'may hold more potential for constructing new network relationships or for making links between existing networks than strong established ties which have been in place over decades or longer' (Burt 1992). This means that these cities can not only enter the network without being constrained by their sizes, but may have more potential for establishing new network relationships. As such, they have the possibility to experience explosive growth thanks to their intercity connections, some of which may even emerge as new global cities with key positions in the network, and further evolve into major nodes. In this sense, by offering new and more opportunities for evolving into global cities, this evolution path will become increasingly important.

7.1.2. Development of City-Dyads

The nodes in the WCN can be tightly or loosely connected. In one case, it may take many steps to go from one end of the network to the other, while in another, this can be accomplished only in a few steps. This indicates that the connections between nodes in this network vary according to average distance and overall centralization. These nodes may exist in the form of tightly connected nucleus or a number of loose or disconnected components. The former form typically manifests itself in the development of city-dyads.

The development of a city-dyad is underpinned by the fact that the two cities in the dyad have almost the same high level of network connectivity, and that there are complementarities between diversified intercity relations. Consequently, the two cities are inclined to form a close connection or exist in the form of tightly connected nucleus. If the diameter of a network is defined as the 'largest geodesic distance' (Hannemann and Riddle 2005), that is, the maximum number of steps between two edges of the network, then partners connected at shorter distances have better established and stronger ties than those connected at longer distances. In terms of the geodesic distance of a city-dyad, it is the shortest available path between two nodes in the network and is, therefore, the most 'efficient' link.

Among existing studies on global cities, only the dyad of New York–London has been widely discussed (Wójcik 2013), which even has its own name—NY-LON (Smith 2012). According to the 2008 data, these two cities are very close in terms of their network connectivity, with London scoring 98.96 and New York 100, which can be deemed equal. But statistics show that they play different roles in the global city network, as well as in various network connections. For example, New York has a higher level of connectivity (ranking 1st) than London in financial services (banking, finance and insurance), but beyond the financial sectors London performs better. Yet when it comes to non-financial services, New York still plays a leading role in advertising and consultancy (with New York ranking 1st and London 2nd). It is this complementarity in service provision that makes the NY-LON dyad possible. In fact, in Europe, there is also a city process like NY-LON, which is the growing connection between Paris and London. In the euro area, Paris has been proved in 2008 to have stronger global connections than Frankfurt (ranking 32nd) for its comprehensive clusters of business services. However, the connectivity of London is not lowered down even for the fact that Paris has taken part in the EU Economic and Monetary Union and has been better connected than before in the global city network. From 2000 to 2008, the network connectivity level of Paris and London tended to get close, which enhanced the image of PAR-LON as a new city space. Paris and London, both as major service nodes in Europe, have a lot in common (Halbert and Pain 2009), but they have established a relationship that is essentially non-competitive, and they are complementary in terms of their roles and functions in the global city network. While Paris has a lower connectivity level in finance (with Paris ranking 8th and London 3rd) and accountancy (with Paris ranking 9th and London 1st), it serves as the third largest service provider in advertising, law and consultancy around the globe. Therefore, compared with NY-LON, the PAR-LON dyad has been more well rounded with its first-class non-financial services in the global network.

The development of city-dyads is a process where the gap in global connectivity level between cities is narrowing, and more and more urban agglomerations are taking shape in the WCN, forming new city spaces. As globalization deepens, more cities will find their network connectivity get improved and closer to each other and, thus, as they play different roles in the network, they will form more city-dyads and even triads, contributing to the intensification of the WCN. In this denser network, geodesic distances between pairs of cities are relatively small, signifying greater continuity and connectivity between ties of cities. This can improve the cohesion and vitality of the network, making it less susceptible to interruptions.

As multi-polarization in global economy and the eastward shift of world economic centre continue, a new type of multi-connected city will take shape, which may change the existing city pairing pattern that only covers developed countries and regions (such as NY-LON-PAR). It is predictable that when Asia becomes the future economic centre, there will emerge a global city with distinctive Asian features which enjoys a high level of connectivity, and it will form a new dyad or triad with its counterparts in European and American regions.

However, in the WCN, small-sized urban agglomerations are more common, which means that more multi-connected cities will appear at regional level. As TNCs start to deploy their global supply chains 'nearshore', there will emerge a great number of regionally interconnected city pairs which are close in network connectivity and are complementary in terms of their functions, especially in core regions where sub-networks are intensive.

The global cities connectivity, of course, is not unilateral. Cities are interlinked with multilateral connections on account of the multifarious structure and complexity of WCN. For instance, London does not only perform as part of the NY-LON dyad as mentioned earlier, it also performs as part of London–Paris dyad, and the London–Hong Kong–Singapore triad. In the same way, Singapore and Hong Kong play such roles in other connections, one of which is the Tokyo–Zürich dyad system that includes Singapore. Therefore, it points to the complex and multifarious tendencies in dynamic global cities relations.

7.1.3. The Development of Cliquishness of World Cities

With a worldwide diffusion of globalization processes, nodes in the ever-expanding WCN are more generally distributed with increasing nodes density. However, spatial coverage of globalization is non-uniform, which leads to the non-uniform geographical distribution of network nodes. Within the WCN, some nodes may constitute an integrated whole while others are geographically dispersed, presenting as interlinked node sub-networks. These nodes integrated to be cliques are cohesively interrelated to each other, while dispersed nodes are relatively less connected. The world city cliques articulate an important regional dimension in the networked structure of cities around the world (Derudder and Taylor 2005).

Viewed from a dynamic perspective, the significant realignment or changes of global factors flow will result in a structural change within WCN in the wake of world economic shifting its centre of gravity. Some formerly crucial nodes will easily lose their importance or even be marginalized. Meanwhile, emerging nodes rising or formed are to play different roles in new rounds of factors flow, probably becoming main channels or control management centres in the course of enduring transformation. It is important to note that during this process, it is cities as cohesive groups that will be affected or changed, not a single city. It means that a group of global cities is expected to emerge in the course of global factors flow with a trend of growing and the evolution of city clusters.

Taylor's (2011) empirical research indicated how well a city is integrated into the WCN, particularly regional city arenas. The data show that Western Europe, North America and Asia-Pacific are the most integrated areas. According to the ranking of overall network connectivity in 2008, the following findings can be derived from Taylor's report:

- Asia-Pacific has 5 cities in the top 10, and 9 in the top 25.
- Western European cities are well-represented: 3 in the top 10 with London at number 1 and Paris at number 4, and 9 in the top 25.
- In contrast, for US cities listed in the top 50, New York is alone in the top 10, ranking number 2. Chicago is the second US city and ranks 19th, with Los Angeles ranking only 39th. Washington, Atlanta and San Francisco also appear in ranking, but all are in the bottom 10.

Beyond Asia-Pacific, there are numerous 'Third-World' cities represented as economic gateways to their respective countries in the top 50: Moscow 12th, Buenos Aires 16th, Mumbai 17th, São Paulo 21st,

Mexico City 24th, Caracas 38th, Santiago 41st, Johannesburg 44th, Manila 48th and Bogotá 49th is an impressive list clearly showing the global dimension of the WCN.

In summary, although an 'archipelago economy' appears to exist, it certainly is not uniform, but instead is comprised of three major archipelagos—connected almost entirely to each other. In contrast, the cities and regions in the Southern Hemisphere are less integrated into the WCN. This exclusion is related to the fact that these regions have very different state labour configurations, which arguably influence how these regions are articulated into global production networks (Coe et al. 2004).

The connectivity in the WCN is shifting all the time. A range of changes came out in intercity relations at the global scale in the period 2000–2008. The most notable changes are: the general rise of connectivity in the WCN; the loss of global connectivity of US and sub-Saharan African cities (Los Angeles, San Francisco and Miami in particular) and the gain in global connectivity of South Asian, Chinese and Eastern European cities (Shanghai, Beijing and Moscow in particular). This obviously points to an overarching 'world regional' trend, as the 20 most connected cities in 2000 included five North American cities and five Asian cities, whereas in 2008 only three North American cities (New York, Toronto and Chicago) made it in the top 20 as opposed to 9 Asian cities. Although New York and London change positions, the most notable feature is the stability at the apex of the WCN: London, New York and Hong Kong remain the most connected cities; and Paris, Singapore and Tokyo follow, albeit with different rankings. Below the top 6, there have been some major changes with 8 cities entering the 14 positions between 6 and 20: cities such as Chicago, Los Angeles and Amsterdam lose out in favour of the likes of Shanghai, Beijing and Seoul in an 'East–West swap'. It has frequently been suggested that the world system is in the midst of a major geographical transformation from 'West' to 'East' (Arrighi 2007) and these changes—even just before the current financial crisis got underway—suggest that this shift is indeed unfolding in terms of urban connectivity.

Meanwhile, another change is that MNCs are making major adjustments in the nearshore layout for their global supply chains.

As manufacturers around the world have turned to increasingly manufacturing intermediate goods that used to be mostly imported from foreign countries, they begin to relocate factories to places closer to their own countries or to muster them in a larger market. As a result, the deciding factors for MNCs' site selection in their global production layout have shifted accordingly from explicit ones, such as cost advantage and easy acquisition of production factors, to implicit ones, such as the potential market scale, better business environment and more competitive industrial supporting capacity. Having shortened the global supply chain, this type of nearshore layout for production chain has yielded relevant effects: the global consumption volume of many manufactured products (e.g., automobile and pharmaceuticals) has exceeded their trade growth, while the global trade growth of many intermediate goods (e.g., fabric and electronic parts) are losing momentum. More importantly, this kind of layout will further enhance the roles and functions of regional node cities, boosting the development of regional global cities and their interconnectivity. In other words, it will help form a network subset connecting a large number of surrounding globalizing cities, with global cities on the control end of the regional supply chain as its core and regional global cities as its framework. In this way, the current supra-regional network subset will probably be changed. Currently, the supra-regional East/West triad (Carroll 2007) between North America, Europe and Asia-Pacific is clearly evident. For example, the interlocking rate between Europe and other parts of the world has reached 70 per cent, while the number between regions within Europe is only 30 per cent; and in North America, 65 per cent of its interlocks are globalized. These data have convincingly proven that the global production network does feature strong coupling: about 30 per cent of the localized economic interlock originates from the mutual dependence of geographic concentration obtained by territorial embeddedness; on the contrary, about 70 per cent of the remote operating interlock reflects strong local and regional embeddedness. However, with adjustments in the global production network, more regional global supply chains have come into being, which will weaken the inter-urban interlocks in the network subset and strengthen the connectivity in the region, further underlining the role of regional global cities in the global production network. Besides, in terms of spatial distribution, greater development in the network subset should be expected, which will be more evenly distributed, not only in core regions such as North America, Western Europe and Asia-Pacific area but also in emerging regions. Particularly, a bunch of new global cities will rise along with the development of the emerging economies and constitute a small group of global cities of their own.

7.2. EVOLUTION TREND BASED ON THE ISOTROPIC WORLD CITY NETWORK

The economic relations between global cities are generally understood as an expression of a hierarchical world economy. 'The nature of these interrelations (e.g., frequency, strength, importance, dominance/subdominance) undergirds the structure of the world system, reproducing its hierarchy, and powerfully shaping social life in particular regions' (Smith and Timberlake 1995b). In the dynamic process of the evolution of global cities, the global urban hierarchy is constantly changing and ends up forming a purified WCN instead of destroying current hierarchy. On this basis, the evolution of global cities, especially that of their functions, will present new characteristics.

7.2.1. Fundamental Changes of the World City Network

As previously mentioned, the WCN is an interlocking network created by global functional organizations whose internal network characteristics have a direct effect on and even determine the global urban hierarchy. In other words, the hierarchy in MNCs can be reflected through the global urban hierarchy (Hymer 1972). In order to take advantage of and even create themselves spatial economies and market-making opportunities (Faulconbridge, Hall and Beaverstock 2008), MNCs function in three organizational forms: (a) the wholly owned firm, managed by either an executive board or a partnership, with all offices using the same brand name; (b) the networked firm, composed of several independent firms in a strategic alliance and (c) the hybrid firm, part of a formalized global alliance bringing initially independent firms together to trade under one corporate name. Once changes happen to the structure of these global functional organizations, so does the global urban hierarchy. Therefore, it is of great importance to research the fundamental changes of the structure of MNCs if we want to study the changes of the global urban hierarchy.

Given the growing uncertainty in the technical, commercial and regulatory environment, the big firms of international professional services offer their clients strategic knowledge and experience that they do not possess or cannot exploit without support (Wood 2002). These firms, as categorized by the organizational architectures, are usually networked and hybrid ones, which are more likely to adopt behavioural patterns without scale or hierarchy. Global professional service firms (PSFs), both domestic and foreign, are highly concerned with achieving collective advantages through collaboration and integration, and having the right network that can be built to enhance their capacity to both attract/access clients and service those clients seamlessly. They do not organize their operations according to a 'scalar logic' and do not have a 'scalar view of globalization'. For them, global cities are not operational command centres or hubs but are organized in the form of a network serving to lengthen and strengthen their network services. Consequently, their internal networks are also not organized as a nested 'hierarchy of scales'—with 'global', 'national', 'regional' or 'local' offices (hubs)—where power and knowledge flow from top to bottom. Based on the sizes of offices in APS firms, the GaWC Research Network measures the global connectivity of different cities and conjectures that the larger the office, the more connections there will be with other offices in a firm's network. Yet, in effect, the existing differences in the offices' size stem from the size of the market in a given city or country and do not reflect any command systems, weights and even less hierarchies. The relationships between their firm's offices are described as flat and functional. While all offices provide a broad portfolio of more or less standardized services, specialized fields of knowledge are offered through thematical groups which are represented in fewer cities. Such service specializations have emerged historically. Neither a hierarchy between the service specializations nor a general authoritative hierarchy is seen in the sense that a professional in the office of a certain city could command colleagues in another. Professionals of offices in other places fulfil 'management functions' for their clients' global operations, explaining why the city is a critical node in many global commodity chains. The firms' networks operate at the 'ground level' (flat, horizontal), which are only held together by relational forces. And the formation and lengthening of these firms' networks is the product of a number of actors coming together in joint action and a work of 'heterogeneous engineering' rather than a consequence of intersecting 'scalar processes'; there is no 'production of geographical scale' here.

Therefore, the new management system and organizational model developed by giant global PSFs make them easier to turn to global corporations. Deloitte Touche Tohmatsu, for example, one of the 'Big Four' accounting organizations, is by definition a firm without a national centre, each member firm of which provides services in particular geographic areas and is subject to the laws and professional regulations of the particular country or countries in which it operates. As a typical hybrid company, Deloitte and each Deloitte member firm are legally separate and independent entities, which cannot obligate each other. Deloitte does not provide services to clients but only help to coordinate the activities of its member firms. Deloitte is, as the self-profiling at the website states, a 'brand under which tens of thousands of dedicated professionals in independent firms throughout the world collaborate'. This very structure of the firm implies that there is no global HQ in the stricter sense of the word, nor a clear-cut hierarchy between the offices operating under the brand of Deloitte Touche Tohmatsu. Certainly, some cities may have more department leaders than other cities, but that's just because those cities have more vibrant economy and more global corporations, and department leaders always come from cities that have large numbers of clients.

On the contrary, multinational manufacturing companies, especially multinational manufacturing companies in early days, are always wholly owned multinational companies which feature interdependencies, multidimensions and decentralized organizational structures, carrying out value added process across the world. This is a 'distributed' (cross-national borders), while professional and complicated, configuration of property and capabilities that integrates dispersed resources and builds cooperation through strong interdependencies among different units of the multinational manufacturing company (Bartlett and

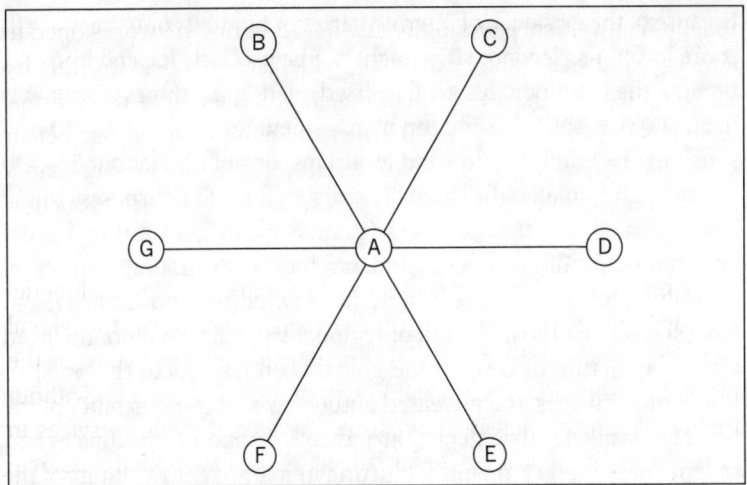

Figure 7.1 *Vertical Hierarchical Organizational Network*

Source: Compiled by author.

Ghoshal 2002), forming a hierarchical organizational structure within the company to ensure that specific functions including command, control and coordination are well performed by different departments. Hanneman and Riddle (2005) noted that the topology of a hierarchical, vertically organized network would resemble the star-shaped structure (Figure 7.1). Certainly, the architecture of today's firm is far more complex than this (Dicken and Malmberg 2001); it is important to move beyond simplistic projection.

However, the organizational structure of multinational companies is not invariable because the 'ownership, location and internalization paradigm' (the advantage theory of FDIs), which evolves with strategies and vectors of internationalization including organic growth, M&As activity, alliances and networks, may change over time and space (Faulconbridge et al. 2008). Since the early 1990s, except for greenfield investments, foreign portfolio investments and M&As undertaken by private equity funds have become a dominating form of FDIs, and about 80 per cent of all FDI flows are devoted to M&As (Küblböck 1999). The significant change arising hereof is that the origin of FDIs does not necessarily coincide with the location of their HQs; first, because of the existence of intermediaries or holding companies in off-shore locations. Second, HQs might not be precisely located in space, because their components are dispersed. Hence, the three components of an HQ (i.e., the CEO and top management team [about 10–20 persons]; the HQ staff function and group responsibilities [about 50–500 persons] and, finally, the domicile registered for tax purposes) might all be located at different places (Braunerhjelm 2004), thus having changed the traditional vertical hierarchical organizational structure of multinational companies. In addition, Godfrey and Zhou (1999) have shown that the inclusion of regional HQ paints a more nuanced empirical picture of CAC in the global economy. As to the possible horizontal linkages, the increased autonomy and responsibility of the branches facilitates the interaction and collaboration with affiliates and independent local companies, blurring in many cases the limits of the organizational space of TNCs (Nachum 2000).

Significant shifts have occurred as the capacity to produce and export manufactured goods has been dispersed to an expanding network of nations (Dicken 2003b). In manufacturing TNCs, the number of overseas staff, value of output, profits and added value will surpass those in their home countries. Some corporations even move their HQs out of the home countries. Then they will choose the place with business-friendly regulations, abundant resources and advanced communication technology as a perfect location to open bank accounts and build new plants, administration buildings and living apartment for staff. Sectors or administrative staff in charge of company registration, business management and financial assets management will be dispersed to different countries, and they tend to cooperate with each other through the Cloud platforms. In this way, they will become supranational corporations that are free from the geographical restrictions through online cooperation. These growing 'global' corporations go beyond the simple expansion of the geographical territorial units in which production, sales or consumption occur, meaning that emerging forms of connectivity and spatiality (Amin 2002) are fundamentally characterized by the space of flows of information networks, which is less affected by the social environment in the original location (Castells 1989). Hence, intra-corporate competition between various units of the firm serves as a vital mechanism by which to redefine spatial divisions of labour and time–space configurations, encapsulating the complex interrelations between 'flow economies' and 'territorial economies' (Yeung 1998). Consequently, it gives birth to a complex and integrated company network with disintegrated, interdependent and specialized configuration of assets and capabilities, which integrates global business through the coordination among different subsidiaries, featuring the knowledge developed jointly and shared worldwide, and simultaneous management of multiple innovation processes.

Besides, manufacturing TNCs are likely to transform into service-oriented corporations. In the new phase of capitalism development (globalization of economic systems, advance of ICTs or the increase in importance of intangible factors), the rising complexity of the client companies organization (as a result of internationalization strategies, manufacturing outsourcing processes or the introduction of ICTs) as well as the informational nature of this type of activities (Jones 2005), manufacturing TNCs are rapidly expanding both ends of the value chain (R&D design and marketing), resulting in rising value added of services while lowering the value added of production and manufacturing. TNCs are, thus, driven to construct new information systems, new format of knowledge management, work practices and the so-called 'internal and external organizational space' as to attain global competitiveness, flexibility and worldwide learning capabilities (Bartlett and Ghoshal 1989), which will further lead to a shift in the working practices outside and inside the boundary of large-scale companies and interpersonal interaction among staff (Jones 2007), because the key mechanism for knowledge transfer is through 'face-to-face' contact with work colleagues, clients, competitors and other actors in society, whether in the workplace or other spaces (Beaverstock 2004). Therefore, from this perspective, the network of offices becomes the mechanism which, through interaction–socialization process, allows firms to transfer the tacit knowledge within the organization, by means of local personnel or the 'expatriated' (Jones 2005). Therefore, manufacturing TNCs will evolve into an organizational structure similar to that of transnational PSFs.

Regardless of the shifting trend, the MNC has evolved from a comparatively simple set of unidimensionally and vertically controlled processes into a complex system of vertical and lateral intra- and inter-firm relationships (Maskell 2001). In this case, space and locations should not be viewed as a passive source of organizational resources 'out there' to be exploited by business organizations. Instead, organizational space should be conceived as an active and integral element in structuring the formation, management and performance of business organizations (Yeung 2005). This new organizational space configuration of economic efficiency and organizational benefits can be obtained through spatial economics leading to the disintegration of the dominant vertical business organizations (Taylor and Asheim 2001), and the creation of heterarchic 'universal' structure (Hedlund 1986; Figure 7.2). Three aspects distinguish heterarchic from hierarchical models of corporate organization. First, resources and managerial capabilities are dispersed throughout the organization, instead of being located only at the top. Second, lateral relationships exist between subsidiaries in terms of products, people and knowledge flows. Third, activities are coordinated along multiple dimensions, typically geography, products and functions (Hedlund 1994). In this heterarchical

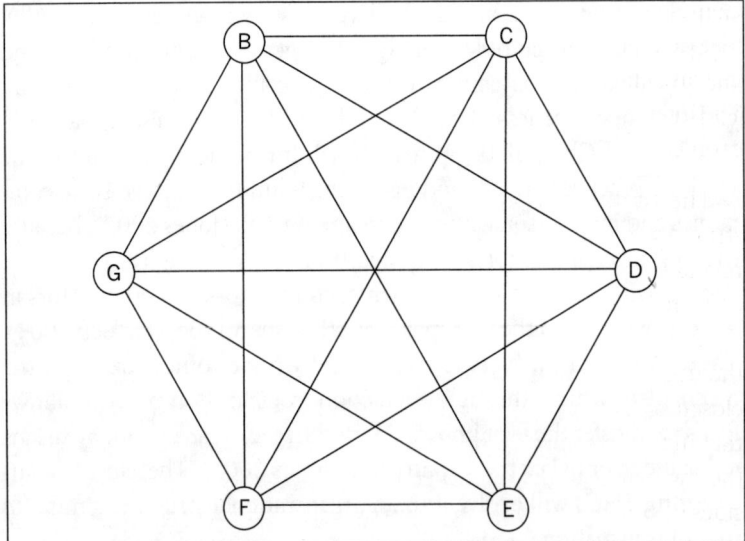

Figure 7.2 *Heterarchical 'Universal' Structure*

Source: Compiled by author.

system, firms become enmeshed in loosely coupled networks of interdependence, reciprocity and unequal power relations (Grabher 2006), in which all actors are mutually connected (Todeva 2006).

It may be true that a transformation of the aforementioned manufacturing multinationals towards a more integrated network is taking place, instead of a simple replacement of the vertical organizational structure and the primacy of the vertical, hierarchical dimension should not be neglected. It is, therefore, arguable that distinct categories of network structure do not exist in this network, but instead overlap and interpenetrate each other, with networks forming complex combinations of overlapping, juxtaposed and nested governance mechanisms (Grabher and Powell 2004). In this sense, they are intricate networks in which hierarchy and heterarchy coexist, and vertical and horizontal connections intertwine (Wall 2009), which confirms the coexistence of these different organizational principles.

7.2.2. Isotropic Trend of Network Structure

Consistent with the transition of MNCs to a more integrated network hierarchy, the WCN no longer takes on a hierarchical 'tree' structure; instead, cities at all levels interact with each other more horizontally. The interaction between cities cannot be simplistically defined as vertical hierarchy or heterarchy, but a mixture of the two.

The traditional WCN takes on a relatively 'steep' hierarchical structure because it is mainly based on the command and control relationship of MNCs, and the higher economic activities are highly concentrated in a limited number of cities. The research by Neal (2008) shows that within the city network, the level of inequality in the degree centrality hierarchy is significantly greater than that in the closeness hierarchy ($z = 16.60, p < 0.01$) and significantly smaller than that in the betweenness hierarchy ($z = -9.98, p < 0.01$). That is to say, the inequality in the degree centrality hierarchy is centred, on both sides of which is a fairly equal closeness hierarchy and a highly unequal betweenness hierarchy. Viewed from the perspective of the betweenness hierarchy with the largest inequality, New York, Paris, Tokyo and London have a strategic position, which are the main medium or broker for the global corporate ownership relations. Moreover, the degree centrality hierarchy varies with corporate ownership orientations (in-degree and out-degree). The empirical research by Wall and van der Knaap (2011), based on the data of 2,259 cities, shows that a rich variety of cities from both developed and developing nations have in-degree scores for all industrial sectors and for APS. The finding indicates that the city network has a relatively equal hierarchical structure. However, only 17 per cent of the cities have out-degree scores for all industrial sectors, and all are from developed countries. New York, Paris, Tokyo and London together hold 25 per cent of the corporate ownership of out-degree relationships. This is also the case for APS, where all the highest-ranking cities come from developed countries. Moreover, a strong correlation coefficient (0.84) is shown between the out-degree centrality scores for all industrial sectors and for APS. This finding indicates that cities that harbour HQs for all industrial sectors also have high counts of APS HQs. Obviously, the city network hierarchy based on the out-degree relationships is very 'steep'.

With contemporary globalization, especially the transformation of the organizational structure of MNCs, such fragmented pressure towards multiple hierarchies are lessened. Cities in the world network are increasingly strengthening their service and coordination functions as well as diluting their CAC functions, and increasingly associated with synergistic relationships. According to the concept of power hierarchy, there will be a 'homogenization effect' because service flow is not the performance of a limited number of cities. Such network of power relationships, related to the development of the global service network, has moved towards a new kind of relationships between world cities featuring higher heterarchy. Of course, this does not mean that the current WCN is devoid of hierarchical tendencies—London and New York clearly dominate (Taylor [2003] 2004).

Currently, cities in developed countries still play a vital role in performing their command and control functions over global economy, but, at the same time, a new tendency has emerged: the leading economies—the USA, Japan and the countries of Western Europe—tend to lose their global command and control functions to the emerging economies, especially Brazil, Russia, India and China, also known as BRIC countries (Bianconi, Yoshino and de Sousa 2013). From 2006 to 2012, other than Australia and South Korea that showed a considerable rise in their CCI,[1] developed countries witnessed a dramatic decrease in CCI, with the number of company HQs in the USA falling to 162 and its CCI dropping averagely. Comparatively, major cities in developing countries, especially in China, attracted more and more global leading companies, among which Brazil, India and Russia showed a significant increase in their CCI, albeit much less than that of China (Csomós 2013; Table 7.1). This is also true in different sectors. For example, in the auto industry, some global companies in European countries, the USA and Japan had a high 'out-degree' score, showing their leading position and their powerful control over the global capital flow, but it is worth noting that cities in the 'Global South' ranked relatively high in top 60 list, with Mumbai and Pune (India) ranking 12th and 25th, respectively, Shanghai (China) at 23rd and São Paulo (Brazil) at 25th. Similarly, the top 60 cities in the technical hardware and equipment industry also included many cities in the 'Global South', such as Shenzhen (24th), Bangalore (26th), Hong Kong (26th), Beijing (28th), Mexico City (29th) and São Paulo (31st; Krätke, Wildner and Lanz [2010] 2012). These facts clearly show that the 'emerging markets' are gradually integrating into the global production network. It is predictable that with the rise of multinational companies from developing countries, cities with company HQs tend to be widely distributed and the WCNs will be featured with more horizontal connection over time.

[1] CCI shows the level of command and control. $CCI_{x,y}$ of a given city x in a given year y is calculated as follows:

$$CCI_{x,y} = \sum_{i=1}^{n_{x,y}} \frac{R_{i,x,y} + A_{i,x,y} + P_{i,x,y} + MV_{i,x,y}}{4}$$

where

$R_{i,x,y}$ = the proportion of revenues in the total data set;
$A_{i,x,y}$ = the proportion of assets in the total data set;
$P_{i,x,y}$ = the proportion of profit in the total data set;
$MV_{i,x,y}$ = the proportion of market value in the total data set;
i = the number of the company headquartered in city in a given year ($i = 1,..., n_{x,y}$);
n = the total number of companies headquartered in city x in year y.

Table 7.1 Cities with the Highest CCI in 2006 and 2012

	2006					2012		
Rank	City	Country	Number of HQs	CCI	Rank	City	Country	Number of HQs	CCI
1	New York	USA	98	8.8206	1	Tokyo	Japan	154	6.8797
2	Tokyo	Japan	189	7.7271	2	New York	USA	82	6.5162
3	London	United Kingdom	89	6.2725	3	London	United Kingdom	68	5.5968
4	Paris	France	65	5.6447	4	Beijing	China	45	5.4434
5	Dallas	USA	28	2.1870	5	Paris	France	60	5.0274
6	Zurich	Switzerland	12	1.7997	6	Seoul	South Korea	60	2.1755
7	Seoul	South Korea	44	1.6590	7	San Jose	USA	25	2.1376
8	San Francisco	USA	24	1.6351	8	San Francisco	USA	17	1.9214
9	Chicago	USA	39	1.5981	9	Moscow	Russia	20	1.7560
10	Amsterdam	The Netherlands	13	1.5583	10	Hong Kong	China	48	1.7127
11	Washington, DC	USA	25	1.5480	11	Dallas	USA	21	1.6883
12	San Jose	USA	28	1.4947	12	Washington, DC	USA	18	1.6056
13	Houston	USA	30	1.3671	13	Zurich	Switzerland	16	1.5518
14	Charlotte	USA	8	1.3562	14	Chicago	USA	31	1.4084

15	Munich	Germany	9	1.3453	15	Toronto	Canada	23	1.4039
16	Toronto	Canada	21	1.3040	16	Houston	USA	27	1.3033
17	Beijing	China	15	1.2443	17	Madrid	Spain	18	1.1041
18	Osaka	Japan	34	1.1964	18	Sydney	Australia	21	0.9901
19	Atlanta	USA	17	1.1519	19	Munich	Germany	9	0.9806
20	The Hague	The Netherlands	3	1.1454	20	The Hague	The Netherlands	3	0.9671
21	Hong Kong	China	36	1.0836	21	Stockholm	Sweden	20	0.9489
22	Stockholm	Sweden	23	1.0701	22	Mumbai	India	26	0.9427
23	Bridgeport	USA	11	1.0652	23	Minneapolis	USA	14	0.9311
24	Minneapolis	USA	19	1.0434	24	Frankfurt	Germany	6	0.9172
25	Edinburgh	United Kingdom	3	1.0289	25	Rio de Janeiro	Brazil	7	0.9079

Source: Csomós (2013).

If we differentiate, in out-degree relations, between higher level decision-making and command functions and production-oriented functions downstream, we can observe that there are three levels of ownership: HQs to first-order subsidiaries, first subsidiary to second subsidiary holdings and the remaining linkages. This is a hybrid structure between hierarchical and heterarchical interdependence containing star-shaped structures, in which central cities exercise corporate governance over others clearly exemplify hierarchical, vertically organized interaction and triangulated structures connecting cities represent heterarchical interactions between cities. It is evident that the strongest evidence of 'horizontalization' is found between the top ranked cities and that this is most prolific at the top level of corporate ownership, gradually declining in importance as we drop down to lower levels. And below the third-tier subsidiaries level remain separated hierarchical structures. Since most of the individual ties are neither reciprocated nor triangulated, the system is still considered hierarchic in terms of the 'variety of connections'. Though most of the connections between cities are rather weak, the connections between a small number of cities in an interchangeable or triangle structure are surprisingly strong, which proves the system to be heterarchical in terms of the strength of the connections. We can see that as MNCs in developing countries continue to grow, more cities will be chosen to locate the HQs with increasingly frequent interactions through the interchangeable and triangle structures, which strengthens the connections, driving the WCN to be essentially more heterarchical.

Besides, the use of a considerable proportion of manufacturing and service industries in cities has also changed. For example, the initial 'internationalization' of the advertising service industry was known as the empire model, with its HQs concentrated at the Madison Avenue in New York City, which served as a major hub throughout the 20th century. HQs of advertising companies in New York were the base camp for all of the most sophisticated business, ranging from planning to creative design and financial organization, offering advertising services for customers around the world. Offices in other parts of the world (and sometimes dubbed 'post-box' office) sold the New York products directly to the local television stations, only making slight adjustments to fit in the local culture and language. As New York's advertising business spread to and was consumed by the rest of the world, it became the 'world centre' that spearheaded the design and demonstration of global economic activities. However, this highly hierarchical framework was only a temporary phase during the development of global network and did not survive. As the target audiences 'become more sensitive' to identify the changing needs reflected in subtler messages, it shifted to a more collaborative model between different offices and, therefore, between different cities. Offices around the world are understood to be made up of different sets of skills and must be connected to the customers. New advertising ideas usually came from offices outside New York with different cultural backgrounds. New York was no longer the leading office, but 'reduced to' part of the leadership of a project team. Finally, global advertising services become an industry that leverages multi-node networks from both internal and external assets around the world.

In short, compared with the 'sharpness' in the past, the global city network hierarchy tends to be purified. Of course, this does not mean that the hierarchy is already 'flat'.

7.2.3. The Functional Evolvement of Facilitative Power

In line with the changing trend of the purification of the global city network, major global cities, as the basic nodes of the global city network, will also undergo significant changes, especially the transformation of global city function from instrument-based power to facilitative power. The power mentioned here is obviously not administrative power, but power of domination, control and influence, which is related to the functions of cities.

From the historical perspective of urban development, most of a city's functions in the traditional urban hierarchy can be manifested as exercising control over others, that is, the ability to influence or dominate the will of others. In the early concept of the global cities based on the ownership relationship of MNEs, its 'command and control' function was more often manifested as instrumental power, since the ownership relationship between the MNE parent company and its subsidiary is equal to a command and control relationship. The global commodity chain constructed by this relationship is a value system created by employees of companies and other institutions, and the connection between different units of the chain is a chain connection of imperfect market sequences that reflects the asymmetry of market power, which leads to the inequality of value distribution. The dynamics of any particular chain is determined by the input–output structure of the node or chain fragment, geographic location, institutional and sociopolitical framework, and its governance and control structure, which also has command and control relationship. Therefore, the global cities that gather a large number of MNE HQs are the control end of the global commodity chain (product R&D, marketing), and have unique resource and ability to wield urban power and influence. It is through the realization of its most important mobility and allocation capacity that the power of the city is enhanced, so it enjoys a dominant position over more subordinate cities. Just as Friedmann (1986) pointed out, the importance of the world cities, which have been conceptualized as the 'meeting points of global capital', is a consequence of their ability to exercise global control functions. Unlike the power over of this ownership relationship, Sassen (1991) paid more attention to the centre of global professional services companies and the ability to enter the global market, emphasizing power to power, not the power itself. Instead, it provided the ability to manipulate the global commodity chain through the provision of service with expertise. She said its authority and power do not come from the new space of digital technology compression, but more from its ability to position itself in the global network to practice its own professional financial expertise. Hence, global cities reflect their comparative advantage through their accumulated expertise and, thus, form their unique ability to force or, more precisely, compel others to do business through them. It is the ability that makes it a key node in the WCN. Although Sassen's control power is not very straightforward, it is essentially a command and control function.

Therefore, cities such as New York, London and Tokyo that are frequently mentioned in the literature on global cities are able to leverage their dominant power in the WCN, since they have instrument of domination and a capacity of some resource mix. As a result, the others at the lower rank of the world city hierarchy have less power, influence and advantage (Neal 2008). When it comes to individuals, the dominant positions in cities are taken by traditional elites, such as company directors and CEOs who stand at the apex of the urban hierarchy (Savage and Williams 2008). Apparently, global cities make their presence felt at a distance with their instrumental power, other cities that are less endowed in economic, political and cultural terms accordingly, have little or no choice, given their restricted economic possibilities in a sense, to network with the global cities, or to go through them in other words. Even among global cities, competition exists for advantage over such instrumental domination and authority, leading to a zero-sum game over such power.

In fact, in a context where cities are continuously networked, the frequently shifting pattern of relationships in the dynamic networks, along with the varied reach of their coverage, has made it difficult to identify the city-ness of power as a phenomenon. The answer is seldom definitive or straightforward regarding the question whether cities 'run' the networks by virtue of their concentrated resources or networks themselves 'generate' cities as sites of power, which seems to lie in the spatial ambiguity of power in city networks. In the increasingly complex, dispersed global economy, the application of informational resources and market expertise is bringing people together to manage and manipulate interactions at a distance, and it becomes more possible to purchase more know-how and expertise in an open, detached network. The openness of networks is an integral part of such interaction, where the relations that they often rest on and the ability to handle daily complex transactions between cities of different countries have called attention to the mediation function of the networks. To a large extent, it has departed from the 'command and control' structure. Indeed, as business networks become more extensive and dispersed, a more complicated mix of interests involved will emerge along with a stronger will to negotiate, making it less possible for corporate HQs to make arrangements directly. In his study on 'global management' in transnational service firms, especially investment banks and management consultancies, Jones (2002) pointed out that diffused authority was of vital importance in networked organizations. The alignment of 'local' business transactions of a firm with its 'global' objectives requires mediation performed by managers and partners across transnational networks, and places a premium on the importance attached to business intermediaries (Morgan and Quack 2005). When the ties grow stronger, there is a tendency for business networks to build up existing behaviour patterns and emphasize more diversity of contacts and connections than the number as such, which will enrich the mix of relations that provide participants access to various resources and information.

The purification of hierarchical WCNs has brought great changes to the functions of global cities, that is, the focus has moved from pre-existing ties and connections to the construction of the net itself, and to the mediated forms of interaction which effectively bridge, broker and connect people together in some provisionally stable pattern of relationships, thus underlining the role of mediating élites in 'running' the networks. Burt (1976, 1992) refers to the weak connections as the 'structural holes' between networks, those spaces which in a dispersed economy open up access to new resources when brokered. Such an analysis points to the significance of the mediating élites who broker or bridge the 'holes' in the networks. Key mediators 'work' the net while not directly connected in their business dealings, nor does the 'work' span city networks and reproduce them through space and time. They are keen to exploit weak ties to gain advantage by bridging what was previously separate and unconnected people and practices in a network, so as to build a more innovative and resourceful network, and take a vital position of connecting and 'bridging'. As mediators, these professional élites exercise their power with rather than over others. They do not actually 'hold' power; rather they produce it through forms of association established at a distance over time and space. By exercising their power with rather than over others, such mediating élites are in a position to draw upon organizational resources to negotiate and persuade other actors—to some of whom they are only indirectly connected—to pursue certain goals (Folkman et al. 2007). Power here, in this context, is itself an effect generated by the relationships mediated through the actions of the financial and business élites. Such mediating élites do not compel others (organizations, institutions) to enrol in such networked ventures; rather they attract others into such a network reproduced over time and space by organizing trading activities that connect resources in global cities such as commodities, finance and real estate. This effect, when successful, is to stabilize a pattern of relationships which enable certain city networks to exert their leverage through collaboration rather than simply domination, which is the power to hold financial and business associations together for a given outcome, the promise of positive-sum gains (Savage and Williams 2008). The ability of such groups to 'fix' an overall orientation or direction to a networked arrangement combines both rewarding and disciplinary styles of exchange and amounts to a form of networked power that owes much to recent topological shifts in the architecture of globalization (Allen 2008).

For a global city that is a main node of the networks, this change is embodied in its greater functions and operations in connecting the networks in position, and the increasingly important role it plays in absorbing, mobilizing and guiding other cities into the WCN. Therefore, a global city is exercising 'power to' secure the networks with others, or 'networked power', rather than 'power over' others, nor 'power as a structural capacity' (Parsons 1957). And such 'networked power' is expressed in commercial activities that are highly concentrated in global cities, such as forging connections, brokering ties and stabilizing relationships. In other words, a global city cannot show its power by simply 'possessing' corporate HQs or holding accumulated expertise 'in reserve'; instead, it mobilizes its power and influence through the networks (to seek out connections, aiming to enhance networked resources). Certainly, different cultural and regulatory codes which have shaped business behaviour in the two cities still remain in evidence, but they have been partially transformed through the fact of connection, more so through negotiation and inducement than diktat or strict authority (Morgan and Quack 2005).

The 'networked power' of a global city bridges what was previously separate and unconnected elements, and brings them into a collaborative networked space. Thus, it becomes a facilitative notion of power, whereby it is simply a means to an end, a general facility that is mobilized to hold the networks together. Therefore, the power itself is not conceived as a resource, but as something generated by the application of resources and skills over tracts of space and time. Since a global city is a rather fluid medium which can expand or contract in line with the resources available, its 'power to' do things is sustained through networked interaction; it is what enables the orchestration and coordination of action to take place along the length and breadth of the networks, and is used to fuse and modify patterns of interaction at a distance (Mann 1993). Therefore, in this kind of networked arrangement, global cities' functions cannot be defined by the practice of domination any more. The 'power to' secure networked relationships across tracts of space and time enable some global cities to occupy a dominant position in their networked interaction without actually dominating other cities. That is to say, global cities with such a power can dominate the WCN without necessarily dominating and controlling another city's expense.

The power to broker the networks, to reach across and between them, if it is to be at all effective, is just as likely to entail collaboration as much as competition, negotiation rather than constraint. In contrast to more strident forms of instrumental power, these quieter registers 'work' through varied powers of reach made possible by topological shifts in the networked architecture of globalization. Power topologies, as such, are part of the glue that both makes and binds cities in complex forms of networked interaction. As Allen (2003) has pointed out, here power works through quieter registers such as competition and negotiation, as well as collaboration, than its brash counterparts of command and constraint. Collaboration in such instances does not imply an absence of power, but rather a negotiable set of interactions in which management and professional authority is of a diffused nature across the global city networks, where outcomes are negotiated and mediated, and power itself exhibits a certain spatial ambiguity as to its whereabouts (Jones 2008).

In city networks, with the mix of economic, cultural and political resources giving shape to different organizational forms, power even as an exercise in facilitation can be about a soft constraint. City networks hold together because they hold out the prospect of positive gains that are too great for those involved not to want. The promise of network gains is held out for all involved. Inducement and incitement are arguably what drive these networked interactions between city actors. Therefore, the power of global cities can only be exercised on the premise of guaranteeing network gains. This means that mutuality, in the form of a close-knit network of transnational interdependencies, provided the framework for a plus-sum economic game to take place (Beck 2005). For example, London's global business outlook enables firms in Frankfurt to access global markets and the latter's European business provides an entry point for London's banks and professional services. London's importance as a global capital market, its concentration of financial skills and expertise, was found to add to Frankfurt's service role in the German and European markets, and the increased strength of Frankfurt was seen to benefit London through the enhanced business opportunities an expanding Europe brought. This reveals the growing interdependence of the two financial regions (Beaverstock et al. 2001). Of course, in such networked interactions, a 'plus-sum' outcome is predicated upon on the effectiveness of the 'work' put into holding the networked arrangements together, that is, to achieve greater complementarity and avoid substitutability as much as possible. The outcome may operate in a 'positive-sum' manner, but the global city management and performance benefits stem from their role in holding the loose arrangement together as a network. Of course, such 'positive-sum' gains do not automatically amount to equal-sum gains. Some subjects may receive more skewed gains than others, but on the whole it benefits all parties.

It is worth pointing out that the facilitative power of global cities can be made to 'work' for cities in a collaborative rather than a competitive manner within the WCN. 'Outside' the network framework, for some cities that are free or detached from the key network, this 'power to' promote city interactions can fold over into 'power over' them (Allen 2010), becoming a zero-sum game (Thompson 2003). However, seen from a different angle, the coeval nature of city networks suggests that power can be made to 'work' for cities by putting together connections that take them along quite different paths to that set out by varying trajectories. Therefore, what looks like a zero-sum game from a particular node in a hierarchical city network may look quite different from a position at the crossover of different kinds of networks and associations, each of variable reach and intensity. As extensive and intensive networks change, as weak ties come to the fore holding out the potential for new patterns of association, so these cities' trajectories may not so much lag behind as take a different direction. In short, this networked world of distributed authority will lead to more reciprocity, and outcomes are held out to be positive rather than zero-sum.

7.2.4. The Global Urban Development Focusing on Mid-Level Cities in the Urban Network

The purification of hierarchical WCNs means a shift from a pyramid-shaped structure to an olive-shaped structure, which is a new feature of the global urban evolution. On the one hand, there will not be a great increase in the number of global cities at the top level in the hierarchy, especially of the multifunctional metropolis, which will remain relatively concentrated and be only subject to some internal adjustments if new members join in. The newly emerged multifunction metropoles are expected to be cities mainly from emerging economies rather than developed countries. From the perspectives of strategic position, centrality, recursive centrality and power status, these top-level global cities may have relatively declined influence, but it certainly does not mean that they have weakening roles in the urban network. The development of ICT makes virtualization and real-time worldwide transactions on an almost 24-hour basis possible. However, the paradox is that the roles played by the top-level global cities are becoming more significant. It is because the new technology has promoted blizzard-like flows of global information, complex financial innovations and needs for specialized knowledge which requires the input of much-sought-after top-level skills that are often concentrated and transferred in top-level global cities. As a result, the centres of the world economic system are maintained and strengthened through global service production (Pain 2007). On the other hand, the number of global cities at the mid-level in the hierarchy of global urban network will increase dramatically. Under the influence of the 'nearshore' adjustment of global commodity chains of MNCs and their enhanced functions of regional HQs, global cities members at the mid-level will go through big changes, and there is a high possibility for second-tier cities in developed countries and cities in emerging economies to rise to the mid-level.

During this changing process, the most important thing is that mid-level cities will take a higher position as nodes in the global urban network in terms of its strategic position, centrality, recursive centrality and power status, narrowing the gap with the top-level global cities to weaken their functions as nodes. For example, from 2006 to 2012, the decrease of New York's CCI had a strong impact on the CCI of the USA, but cities such as San Jose, Washington and San Francisco witnessed the largest increase in their CCI. In 2006, the CCI of New York was surpassed by the cumulative CCIs of the six cities of Dallas, Washington, San Francisco, Chicago, Charlotte and San Jose. In 2012, it was surpassed by the cumulative CCIs of merely four cities, that is, San Jose, Washington, San Francisco and Dallas. In spite of this change, New York was still undoubtedly the major command and control centre of the USA in 2012, and its position is not challenged by any other city, but its gap with other cities is narrowing. In 2006, the CCI of New York was 4.3 times as much as that of Dallas, which ranked second, whereas in 2012, the CCI of New York was only 3.4 times as much as that of San Jose, which ranked second in that year (Csomós 2013).

The remarkable increase of mid-level global cities is mostly manifested in the rapid increase of regionally multifunction cities or specialized global cities. This is highly correlated with regional development around the world and the international division of labour, the two reasons behind the purification of hierarchical WCNs. A number of global cities, that is, regionally multifunction cities and specialized global cities, have risen or upgraded to the mid-level of network under the background of regional development and international division of labour, respectively.

In addition, the world city hierarchy has become flatter and, in a similar vein, the distribution of global city nodes in the network becomes less concentrated, scattering around the globe in clusters. Particularly in the Southern Hemisphere and the East, a large number of global cities connected by the network will emerge.

The Evolution of Space

8

The evolution of global cities, with its inherent characteristic of space expansion and unique spatial structure, is an important foundation for the global cities networks to exercise their functions. The expansion process of global cities is a part of the study on the dynamics of contemporary global cities and is, thus, an important element of its dynamic evolution.

8.1. SPACE EXPANSION

Based on the space of places and space of flows, and with a strong and inherent characteristic of space expansion in its evolution, global cities keep bringing peripheral regions into the flows of geography, and become functional urban regions in the context of globalization. This is closely connected with economic globalization that goes beyond a territorial and scalar reading of the position and function of urban economies and has become the crystallization of globalization processes on the geographic landscape. As such, the evolution of global cities is a certain process of space expansion.

8.1.1. Definition

Spatial expansion in the evolution of global cities is completely different from the traditional concept of spatial expansion that always occurs along with urban growth. As such, we must first make clear the definition of the spatial expansion of global cities.

The traditional concept of urban sprawl is the expansion of city boundaries or the enlargement of regional physical scale based on space of places, largely driven by the accumulation and concentration of capital. The level of accumulation and concentration of capital is closely connected with the dominant forms of production in history. As such, we can distinguish three different historical phases, each with its characteristic dominant form of production, its related set of agglomeration economies and its dominant urban form (Kloosterman and Lambregts 2007). These three phases are, respectively, the pre-industrial era, the industrial era and the post-industrial era. In the pre-industrial era (roughly 1500–1750), most urban economies were mainly based on the transformation of agricultural commodities (Phelps and Ozawa 2003), which, therefore, became the main source of capital accumulation. As returns to scale were mainly internal to firms, the level of accumulation of capital was still relatively low, while the level of concentration of capital within its urban system was considerable, resulting in comparatively small agglomerations or cities. Primate city became the dominant urban form. In the second phase, that of industrial capitalism (roughly 1750–1975), as the mechanization of production lifted economic growth to a higher level and a deepening division of labour (inter- and intra-firm, intra-sectoral) and capital intensification were sources of economic growth, the level of accumulation of capital rose remarkably. Increasing internal and external returns to scale contributed to a growing average firm size as well as to a growing average city size, notably the expansion of city boundaries or the enlargement of regional physical scale. The post-industrial era (1975 onwards) has seen service economy playing a leading role in urban development, with business services serving as a key sector. The handling of highly complex forms of knowledge and information is increasingly central to business services but also to many other contemporary economic activities. A local labour force's 'knowledge-handling skills' can, accordingly, be seen as an increasingly important but scarce resource for post-industrial economies. Under this circumstance, firms and suppliers can benefit from spatial clustering as this reduces search costs on both sides. Proximity enables and enhances accessibility to these various but strategic resources and so constitutes a strong incentive to co-location.

The high level of centralization of industries and businesses has led to the expansion of city boundaries to some extent.

Unlike before, during the process of globalization, the business services sector has gradually begun to play a vital role in global coordination and provide support for the global economy, and is closely intertwined with the expanding and strengthening economy in the rest of the world. While progress in transportation and communication technologies have not eliminated the needs for important business proximity, they enable companies to sell their products and gain inputs at low cost in increasingly distant markets. Meanwhile, such an increasing number of business activities and highly concentrated cities are embedded in multiple global network exchanges. The interactions between the dynamic local networks based on mutually beneficial economic relations and the global network with inter-regional competition and exchanges strictly conform to the law of increasing returns and, thus, open up new potential for consumption and production and create more possibilities for advanced urban economy. More importantly, they have given birth to increasingly dense urban nodes. During this process, as 'key spatial nodes', some city regions have become 'motors' of the global economy (Scott, Agnew et al. 2001). Unlike before, the spatial expansion of global cities generally refers to as functionally interdependent sets of cities, that is, a set of interdependent nodes and the spatial interactions among them, for example, commuting, investment, shopping trips and inter-firm trade (Berry 1964). In essence, it is not about physical urban expansion, but a regional expansion of urban networks based on location and the space of flows urban networks, which is a special phenomenon beyond the city per se.

In Castells' (1989) view, general spatial forms are associated with leading social organizations in the society, that is, a new organization brings about new spatial forms or even an entirely 'new spatial logic'. In this regard, new organizations play a vital role in global cities as a new spatial logic. Knowledge-intensive business services (KIBS) play a leading role in service economy, and their strategies wield great influence over the spatial expansion of global cities. These strategies can also be seen as resulting from a series of tensions, one of which is a 'locational tension' (Hoyler and Pain 2001). The city centre has better access to customers, human resources, infrastructure (transportation), related professional services and office buildings at good locations as a form of investment and, thus, has more opportunities for (idle) office space to rent, proximity to amenities and boasts better urban environment (including social opportunities). Its appeal to KIBS has formed 'clusters', making it a battleground for them and bringing about 'location tension'. Despite this, the city centre also has disadvantages, including traffic congestions, high costs for employees' accommodation and board, and inadequate parking spaces for employees and customers, all of which will lead to decentralization. Therefore, KIBS take location as a key factor of cost management in dealing with competition pressure. Thanks to new information technologies, large office-based information-intensive corporations are dramatically transforming their organizational and spatial structure, resulting in a complex, hierarchical, diversified organizational structure characterized by a variable geometry depending upon time, place and realm of activity.

In terms of spatial structure, these corporations have undergone a twofold process of simultaneous centralization and decentralization. Centralization means metropolitanization of service activities or reinforcement of decision-making in corporate cores of major central business districts (CBD). Decentralization means a spread of service activities or the relocation of some more routine, back office operations to suburbs or further afield which covers different spatial levels. As Cochrane and Pain ([2000] 2004) pointed out, in the context of new service economy in the era of globalization, flows of people, information, goods and finance have stretched and intensified between cities, and across national borders and continents, also transforming city regions.

Despite some common features, a huge diversity was found among KIBS firms. Besides, there are big differences both between and within KIBS sectors. Thus, the process of office centralization or decentralization is differentiated according to the different types of office functions and their place in the hierarchy of the corporation. One way or another, some KIBS firms may have a bigger potential to fuel decentralization, while other firms display a tendency to centralization owing to the inertia effect of labour markets' spatial rigidity. The bottom line is that there is no universal organizational–spatial logic of large-scale organizations. This complex process where neither centralization nor decentralization is dominant transforms metropolitan areas into multifunctional, multinuclear spatial structures, resulting in a complex territorial development process. But more importantly, all various office functions within a corporation (from head office to back offices) regardless of their actual location have to be interrelated and interconnected by the means of communication flows via ICT infrastructure. There is one shared logic among all KIBS—a business logic of profit-making (Sokol 2004), which is critical for the economic fortunes of firms, organizations, people and places. This actually reveals the inherent functional connections of spatial expansion beyond the city boundaries. Indeed, the examination of geographies of economies may be more fruitfully approached through the inclusion of the prism of value networks (Smith et al. 2002). It follows that cities are increasingly engaged in worldwide systems of economic exchange and financial flows, and this intense global–local interaction gives rise to new functional relations that cross-established urban administrative perimeters, making 'the category ("the City") theoretically and practically obsolete', which can be identified as a global city region phenomenon (Scott 1988).

From this perspective, the research into the spatial expansion of global cities has gone beyond some relevant factors including average density and city size, changing the dynamics of spatial expansion based on capital accumulation and concentration, and drawing focal attention to the driving forces of economic globalization. Economic globalization has given global cities a key role in articulating flows in advanced, knowledge-intensive business and professional services, turning them into places for production and trade in global production networks. This role has also been given to these expanded city regions. As articulated by Hall (2001), these spatial units incorporate suburbs and nearby cities surrounding the CBDs of global cities. The activity in these locations could include some of the broader array of global economic forces, constituting the spatial nodes of global economy. Therefore, the spatial expansion in the evolution of global cities is a spatial process in which new functional relationships expand. Since it is not restricted by physical boundaries, it becomes sustainable and has a greater possibility of spatial expansion with retentive and even enhanced economic vitality.

The two key features of global city relations—rescaling and complexity—play a vital role in the spatial expansion of global cities. We know that the global economic relations of contemporary cities are increasingly constructed by connectivity and flows associated with forms of network organization. Cities that are more complex and more strongly integrated in global-scale service networks are conferring complexity on proximate towns and cities which have complementary roles and functions (Pain and Hall 2006). Producer service networks are flexible structures. They comprise dynamic flows of people and knowledge, and they use cities strategically to engage with competitive markets at different scales. Therefore, relations conferred on cities by service networks are multi-scalar and fluid; they are determined by markets and organizational operations which are cross-border and dynamic. Thus, the spatial expansion of global cities can be measured by different intersecting scales of network organization or, in other words, by different geographical scales. Moreover, these geographical scales are hard to define. In practice, the degree of the spatial expansion of global cities varies. The spatial expansion of some global cities is interlinked with proximate towns and cities by global-scale service networks but the other global cities are conferring less global service network integration on a civil or regional scale. However, in all cases, the spatial expansions of global cities are not defined by natural boundaries, and intercity relations do not coincide with existing regional administrative and political unit boundaries.

8.1.2. Analytical Paradigm

As mentioned earlier, globalization and knowledge-intensive service enterprises' strategies are the endogenous drivers of the spatial expansion of global cities. Then what are the dynamics of the spatial expansion of global cities? There are different answers to this question according to different analytical paradigms.

A rather mature analytical paradigm has been developed to analyse the traditional way of the spatial expansion of global cities from the perspective of space of places called agglomeration externalities, also known as 'spatially constrained external economies of scope'. It explains the spatial expansion of the city and its boundaries through the dynamic balance of the benefits and costs of its agglomeration economies. According to the traditional agglomeration theory, the city's agglomeration externality is confined to its boundary. This contrasts sharply with the fact that a city's functions cover greater spatial scales and extend beyond its boundary through the expansion of spaces. Hence, the traditional theory cannot be used to explain the mechanism of the spatial expansion of global cities.

However, global cities are not defined or measured by their size. At the extreme, some megalopolises are not defined as global cities. But undeniably, relative size is a fundamental measure of global cities and their functions. The theories on the space of places and space of flows, used to explain the spatial expansion of global cities, is still inevitably related to the size of the cities. The external network connections of global cities and their functions are closely related to their agglomeration externalities, which are based on the critical scale of the cities. From this perspective, a global city must reach a minimum size. Of course, the minimum size is only a theoretical assumption rather than an exact figure. The size of a global city depends on its type and functions as a node. More importantly, it is obvious that being home to large number of global functional institutions (enterprises), global cities themselves have urban agglomeration externalities, which are one of the basic requirements for their operation. Indeed, this kind of urban agglomeration externalities are not a distinctive characteristic of global cities—they are also found in other large cities. Therefore, it is necessary to start with the analytical paradigm of agglomeration externalities.

Generally, the larger a city, the more such externalities are present (Melo, Graham and Noland 2009). Larger cities profit from larger input markets, larger labour pools, the presence of better infrastructure, public facilities and more specialized business services, all facilitating better matches between supply and demand. Also, the presence of a large internal market offers a larger degree of stability and lower transport costs (Siegel, Johnson and Alwang 1995). Large cities are also more likely to be home to universities, R&D facilities and other knowledge-generating institutions (Isard 1956) and facilitate the transmission of information and provide a good environment for consumption as well (Glaeser, Kolko and Saiz 2001). In addition, the often diverse industry mix in large cities stimulates the generation, replication, modification and recombination of ideas and applications across different industries by providing better opportunities through face-to-face contact and protects a city from a volatile demand (Frenken, Van Oort and Verburg 2007). Thus, larger, denser and more diverse cities allow for cost reductions, output enhancements and utility gains for both firms and households. According to Duranton and Puga (2004), there are three main underlying channels through which firms and households can benefit from co-locating in cities which can be seen as external economies: sharing, matching and learning. While it remains uncertain whether small cities offer firms and households potential cost savings, an abundance of literature stresses that firms and households are sensitive to agglomeration benefits offered through large cities (Erickcek and McKinney 2006). Therefore, agglomeration benefits are important for being the underlying driving force of much of the contemporary urban dynamics and the theoretical models of the NEG tend to predict the development of larger cities (e.g., Fujita et al. 1999). But there are also prices to pay for agglomeration. A city may catch 'big city diseases' with the large-scale expansion of its physical border. Traffic congestion, fierce competitions in the city centre, crime and exposure to environmental pollution increase in a larger city size and are harder to tackle. It appears that smaller cities have a greater endogenous capacity to keep these social, economic environmental cost under control (Capello and Camagni 2000). In the dynamic process of city evolution, agglomeration diseconomies accumulate and a city may go into a stage when the costs of agglomeration surpasses its benefits, a tipping point at which city expansion became unsustainable and the signal that a city is about to enter a period of (terminal) decline and disintegration. Mumford (1938) called a city at this stage 'megalopolis' (a city of exaggerated size) and said it was 'the last vestige of urban development'. Though Gottmann (1961) did not agree with Mumford's suggestions that unsustainable equalled irreversible fatality, he noted that 'megalopolis stands indeed at the threshold of a new way of life, and upon [the] solution of its problems will rest civilization's ability to survive'.

Some researchers have found that agglomeration externalities seemed well capable of explaining developments in the urban system, but it failed to explain current population and growth dynamics (Glaeser and Kohlhase 2004), particularly for mature, developed urban systems (Partridge et al. 2009). Dijkstra, Garcilazo and McCann (2013) suggest that, at least since the beginning of the new millennium, large city urbanization effects have not been the primary economic drivers within the EU15 in the same way they have been elsewhere in the world. It is also proved that agglomeration externalities are not the answers for either why global cities develop or how they sprawl. But the city size of agglomeration externalities helps explain an apparent (positive) disconnection between size and function of cities. Some cities may 'borrow size' from other cities in the network and, thus, have more metropolitan functions than would be expected given their size. Contrarily, some cities face agglomeration shadows cast by others. This shows that metropolitan functions may not be confined by the boundaries of cities through borrowing size.

The concept of 'borrowed size' was proposed by Alonso (1973) to explore a disconnection between size and function of smaller urban areas that form part of a polycentric metropolitan entity. Smaller urban areas 'borrow' some of the agglomeration benefits of their larger neighbours while avoiding the agglomeration costs. The concept of borrowed size is a manifestation of the complementarity between the advantages (low rental cost and reduced traffic congestion) firms draw from their locality with those they draw from other nearby settlements through their business transactions and interactions. Their people can use the shopping and entertainment facilities of other cities to complement their own, their businessmen can share such facilities as warehousing and business services and their labour markets enjoy a wider and more flexible range of demand and supply (Phelps, Fallon and Williams 2001). Small cities in multi-centric metropolitan areas perform more favourably than isolated small cities largely due to the former's superior balance of agglomeration benefits and costs. Yet it also should be noted that balance of agglomeration benefits and costs varies in different areas (Camagni, Capello and Caragliu 2013). This corresponds to types of externalities that can be borrowed according to Polèse and Shearmur (2006). Therefore, small cities in multi-centric metropolitan areas are more attractive compared with isolated small cities because of spillover effect from metropolitan cities. This effect makes high-order services and scale-sensitive institutions and infrastructure transfer to small cities (Henderson 1997). But there are two problems to be fixed or improved.

First, the concept of 'borrowed size' is not a one-way process, that is, small cities borrowing from larger cities to expand their own size. In fact, metropolitan areas also borrow from adjacent small cities to obtain diverse inputs, including APS and command and control functions (Puga 2010). In addition, borrowed size (in functional terms) is not reserved to small cities, but instead occurs more often in larger cities, especially among those that form part of a polycentric metropolitan entity. They demonstrate a higher tendency to borrow size compared with smaller cities. In this sense, the concept of 'borrowed size' need not be limited to small cities. Not only small cities capitalize on agglomeration economies of larger nearby cities, but that the opposite frequently occurs as well. Rather smaller cities help large cities maintain more metropolitan functions than they could originally support independently. Broadly speaking, different agglomeration can also be borrowed or shared within networks at similar spatial scales.

Second, contrary to Alonso's original conceptualization, the size borrowing phenomenon does not just happen between neighbouring cities or, in other words, is not just dependent on proximity and/or accessibility to neighbouring areas. According to Polèse and Shearmur (2006), differences between small cities and surrounding non-urban areas within larger metropolitan areas are growing less distinct. In this sense, borrowing can happen at a larger spatial scale. More importantly, size borrowing is likely to be fostered by proximity and accessibility, but not necessarily. The existence of neighbouring cities does not automatically set size borrowing in motion. In fact, it is interaction between cities that stimulate borrowing. Borrowing is rarely the product of proximity and accessibility, other than true intercity interaction. In other words, geographical proximity and/or accessibility is a necessary condition for size borrowing to happen, whilst interaction among cities is a sufficient one. Borrowing size or significance no longer relies on physical proximity between the cities, but on embeddedness in overarching networks between and within polycentric city regions, via corporate relations, market pervasion and, last but not least, information and communication networks (Hesse 2014).

When borrowed size is incorporated into the networks, another important analytical paradigm 'urban network externalities' (Boix and Trullen 2007) has been coined. It captures such network outcomes and their significance in local connectivity and also emphasizes the role that interaction in city networks may have on the performance of places that are linked by these networks. The logic that underlies the paradigm is that the spatial organization in which cities operate is essential to understanding their efficiency, growth, factor productivity and sometimes their specialization (Capello and Camagni 2000). Along these lines, the spatial expansion of global cities can be interpreted based on network connectivity. However, it should be noted that network connectivity would not replace local size in terms of some urban functions. Networks cannot substitute for proximity for all types of metropolitan functions, and that in particular larger cities are especially capable of capitalizing on network connectivity (Meijers and Burger 2015). Therefore, it may not be sufficient to reveal the mechanism of the spatial expansion of global cities by the general proposition that network economies may substitute for agglomeration economies (Johansson and Quigley 2004).

So the three analytical paradigms, namely agglomeration externalities, borrowed size and network externalities, are interrelated but still different. The mechanism through which global cities expand their spatial scales cannot be sufficiently explained by any of them alone. Therefore, we should not rely solely on any of them or use one at the exclusion of others to understand such a mechanism. Instead, useful elements of these concepts should be extracted, adjusted and integrated to produce a new analytical paradigm. In other words, we combined agglomeration externalities of cities with the borrowed size effect that goes beyond city boundaries to form a 'functionally networked interaction externalities' theory. This new theory is defined as urban functions or performance that can be 'shared' or 'borrowed' through functional interactions in a city network of multiple spatial scales. It means that external economies are not confined to a single urban core or boundary, but instead appear to borrow size through functional agglomeration, generating agglomeration effects of sharing, matching and learning through interactions in networks across multiple scales.

8.1.3. Mechanism

In this section, the mechanism of the spatial expansion of global cities is examined through the lens of 'functionally networked interaction externalities'.

First, the spatial expansion of global cities should not be interpreted as being reserved to a certain zone surrounding a city, but rather as a network phenomenon. Only in this way can network-based interaction be both a measure of, and the mechanism enabling, borrowed size (Phelps et al. 2001), and can global cities and many other types of cities borrow size from each other, 'share' agglomeration externalities in city networks and expand their spatial scales. In the spatial expansion of global cities, interactions take place from metropolitan to global scales. However, different agglomeration externalities can be borrowed on various scales.

Second, unlike most studies that focus on general connectivity of city networks, we focus more on the role of functional integration, that is, its positive effect on borrowed size. General network connectivity has both positive and negative effects on borrowed size, the latter of which is called 'agglomeration shadow' (Krugman 1993), a concept that implies that growth will be limited by competition effects. When two or more cities form part of the same functional urban area, the strongest degree of functional integration between two cities occurs. In this case, cities that are strongly integrated with other cities perform better than those that are only moderately or weakly integrated. On the contrary, while agglomeration shadows continue to dominate, the shadow cast over the others is more pronounced in the absence of strong ties. In other words, a higher degree of functional integration between neighbouring cities may override negative effects of competition, diminishing agglomeration shadows. Therefore, space expansion, as a way of extending urban functions across different spatial scales, is focused on greater functional integration or interaction by means of network interaction. Only in this way can the positive process of agglomeration shadow dominance by scale be a reality. Otherwise, it is probable that the agglomeration externalities cannot be better borrowed or shared within networks at different spatial scales, which impairs the driving forces behind such processes.

Also, the borrowed size of a city can be due to its positioning within a network of cities. Borrowed size becomes evident in a (positive) disconnection between the size and a particular characteristic of a city that can be attributed to the city's positioning within a network of cities (Alonso 1973). Through networks from other cities, the relatively inadequate size or agglomeration of a city can be compensated, and will be integrated into the city network. However, a further distinction should be made about what kind of city network we are talking about, and whether it's a local, national or global network. Cities integrated into different networks will have different borrowed size. Burger et al. (2015) found that the biggest cities in an area are in a better position to borrow size than other cities through local and (global) national network, as they have stronger agglomeration economy and serve as the centre for all the activities of connected cities in the world. That is to say, the connection between global and national network contributes to a city's functions. Being well embedded in national and international networks allows to borrow size in the sense that cities that are very well connected have more metropolitan functions, though the authors also show that networks cannot substitute for proximity for all types of metropolitan functions, and that in particular larger cities are especially capable of capitalizing on network connectivity. Compared with the global and national network, stronger regional network embeddedness generally produces competition effects for certain metropolitan functions, resulting in agglomeration shadow dominance rather than borrowed size on the regional scale. Indeed, greater connectedness and access to large city benefits may also expose firms and households to fiercer competition (Meijers et al. 2012).

Of course, cities in the network system can be embedded at the same time into local, national and global networks. But in terms of the spatial expansion of global cities, the first step is integration into the global network, and then different space locations are covered with different functions. This is one significant feature with which a city can distinguish itself from others. That is to say, global cities and beyond that are well embedded into the global and national network will be allowed to borrow size and gain more city functions. Of course, it is allowed to borrow size by means of the local network which plays its role under the leadership and dominance of the global network. In this sense, spatial development of global cities will be possible if they are embedded into different networks to borrow size, which will help gain more functions of global cities. As a matter of fact, the reality is more complicated. Many cities are embedded into different networks and at the same time are located in different areas of spatial scales, both within global cities and in the areas of global cities and megacities. Therefore, in the spatial expansion of global cities, many cities are related on multiple scales with functional agglomeration happening at different levels. In this process, it is totally possible that functional agglomeration varies in strength at different levels. This, thus, constitutes different space structures during the spatial expansion of global cities.

8.2. EVOLUTIONARY TREND OF SPATIAL EXPANSION PROCESSES

The spatial expansion of global cities manifests itself as the expansion of urban functions at different levels or, to more specifically, global cities, global city clusters and MCR. It is worth noting that such spatial expansion can occur simultaneously at all three levels, though the three urban spaces are products of a sequential evolution. The evolutionary trend of global urban expansion is a direct result of spatial allocation driven by globalization, and marks a significant change in urban spaces.

8.2.1. The Evolution of Global Cities

The evolution of global cities mainly refers to the spatial expansion process in which a functional central urban area expands to surrounding suburban areas, and then form a network of cities. The process somewhat mirrors the four successive phrases under the urban development model proposed by van der Berg et al. (1982), but with a major difference, that is, the evolution of global cities is a process in which city networks come into being.

Similar to the evolution of other things, the path dependency of global cities starts from a traditional urban space comprising an urban centre (district) and its surrounding suburbs. Historically, global cities originated from a central city, and then spread over the neighbourhoods. The decentralization of production activities worldwide requires coordination, a whole set of professional support activities (producer services), as well as a higher quality of life. These special and strategically significant requirements have fostered a surge of agglomeration economies particularly beneficial to the development of large cities. These cities, based on HQs of transnational companies and APS, on (international) accessibility (both physical and virtual), and on perceived quality of life, constitute the higher echelons of a global network of cities. In this scenario, globalization has led to a surge in capital accumulation and concentration that translates into a shift towards a megalopolis: a very large urban complex with multiple centres of economic gravity including one spatially concentrated economic base focused on high-end international services. This urban spatial structure with a single core (or a single centre) is nearly the same as that in the first phase (urbanization) as proposed by van der Berg et al. (1982) in their urban development model, when central cities play a leading role.

However, the requirements for functions of global cities to be connected in a network are fundamentally contrary to the single-core spatial pattern, given that the development of central cities under this pattern is highly subject to shifts in demand and supply of inputs (labour and capital) on global markets. This kind of expansion has led to limited decentralization, such as the so-called 'suburbanization' of commercial activities and the decentralization of corporate organizations, that is, the relocation of HQs from large cities to suburban areas (Florida and Jonas 1991) and regional decentralization of 'edge cities' (Hall and Pain 2006), etc. As early as the 1980s, one important area of investigation focused on the 'flight' or the 'exodus' of corporate complexes (HQs and APS) from traditional CBDs to the peripheries of city regions. This process, which was once seen as adding to urban sprawl, was depicted as a third wave of deconcentration, following the residential and industrial deconcentration of the fordist city region. This process of urban expansion is much like the second phrase (suburbanization) and the third phrase (counter-urbanization) under the urban development model proposed by van der Berg et al. (1982). In the second phase, suburbanization, the centre of gravity of both population and land-intensive uses, moves to suburban locations. The central city, however, still performs as the region's employment core. In the third phase, desurbanization, the metropolis tends to split into many urban centres, some located on the rim of the urban fringe (Johnson 1974).

But in the two phases which van der Berg et al. (1982) portrayed, the metropolis loses its compact nodal structure, and the central city tends to decline both in population and employment. At the fourth phase, re-urbanization is viewed as a remedy for the split structure of the metropolis. Since the late 1980s, many European governments have initiated a rigorous re-urbanization strategy aimed at the revival of their old established metropolitan cores as high-density function-intensive 'compact cities' (Shachar 1997).

Obviously, this is completely different from the global urbanization process whose decentralization is an integral part of adapting to a changing economy and does not mean disappearance of the central city. Although the decentralization model is diverse, as it is largely related to its historical traditions, geographical conditions and development status, etc., the common result is a major change in the suburban network in the metropolitan areas—the suburbs begin to play an active role in the economy (Garreau 1991). New suburban towns with self-circulating functions begin to emerge. Thus, a multi-centre model emerges in global cities, which constitutes a large commute–work area.

In other words, it was itself regarded as a system, and a network city based on a multi-centre, multi-core spatial structure. Among justifications for the urban network strategy, two seem to have a common ground, namely 'society is developing in the direction of network-based rather than area-based relations' and 'global competition favored larger urban areas rather than smaller ones'.

In the evolution of global cities, its spatial expansion is achieved through interactions between polarization and diffusion (Myrdal 1957b) and the mechanism of 'borrowing size'. The concept of economic rent is the best explanation for the balance between polarization and diffusion, that is, the need to pay local 'factors of production' for a given urban function/activity, allowing it to operate in the local economy. The most cited factors of production were land, labour and capital, signifying the key resources employed to produce goods and services (Lipsey and Harbury 1992). As factors of production in central areas of global cities reach the saturation point, backwash (polarization) effects are replaced by a spread (trickle-down) trend, with the city's economic rent and the increasingly strengthened spreading. The mainstay of this manuscript then is the assumption that spread effects are the product of a continuous dwindling of production factors, the most important of which, in order of decreasing elasticity, are land, labour and capital. When shortage of a given factor of production occurs, urban functions that are unable to pay their increased economic rent tend to trickle down. This will lead to two effects: for one thing, it creates new openings for higher threshold activities, mainly of the quinary and quaternary sectors, usually followed by enhanced supply of local psychological rewards, a result of a continuous upgrading course of the first city's economy, culture and society. The outcome of the upgrading process is the enduring dominant position of the first city in the context of the evolving national network of cities. For another, it creates a large periphery and develops it as a new city, expanding the economy and other functions of the downtown areas to some well-selected new suburban towns designated as growth centres (Small and Witherick 1986). This development should be aimed at target growth centres, most of which will evolve into regional first cities and service hubs for their immediate hinterlands. The evolution of regional first cities into national sub-anchors of a national global network demands high commitment and the investment of every effort in order to allow them to absorb the spread opportunities and functions from the nation's first city. These efforts include the development of facilities to accommodate high-tech and APS, and diverse local 'psychological rewards', a prerequisite for the attraction of today's high status labour. The process will be effective only if and when an extensive infrastructure, primarily of transport and communication networks, develops in the periphery.

Therefore, saturation and spread are allied with swift upgrading of the national first city's economic base and its psychological rewards. Instead of weakening the dominant position of first cities (many of which hold a world city status), it would further advance the first city's functional primacy through drawing away urban functions that are unable to pay their increased economic rent, and meanwhile retain its expanding dominant position in the economy, culture and society. The secondary cores formed as a result of spread effects reduce the national periphery to a few smaller inter-metropolitan peripheries. The secondary urban cores, which perform as growth centres/growth poles, seem best to resemble the aspired-for urban network concept.

In this urban network, the former dominant urban cores that appear to possess all the functions totally changed, producing a strong connection between size and function, providing possibilities for borrowed size processes to occur between different centres, that is, a more polycentric structure can strike a better balance between agglomeration of benefits and agglomeration of costs and, thus, have direct and positive effects on global city performance. Only in this way can the concept of 'borrowed size' be employed to explain economic developments in edge cities, or suburban places (Phelps et al. 2001). Partridge et al. (2009) found that population growth in a small city is positively associated with its proximity to the centre of a higher tier city. Although small cities are faced with competition effects, they tend to grow faster because they have access to agglomeration benefits of larger neighbouring cities.

8.2.2. The Process of Global City Regions

The spatial extension trend of global cities do not stop because of the emergence of new cores at city peripheries, but rather break up urban boundaries and enter a process dominated by global city regions, in which global cities are highly connected and integrated with neighbouring cities, turning the region into a spatial node of globalized economy. The driving forces behind the process of global city regions are basically the same as behind the formation process of global cities, or economic globalization. The only subtle difference between them lies in the reliance on the second opportunity opened up by the process of globalization as depicted by Storper (1997) in his *Regional World*. To survive the onslaught of low-wage competitors, firms in this part of the world have to compete on something different than just price. Their products have to be endowed with special qualities either in technological or in conceptual terms on a continuous basis to keep ahead of competitors. Therefore, they need to continuously innovate and prosper in certain circumstances, and carry out corporate vertical separation by deploying different corporate functions in different locations of physical separation. This will result in specialization of regional functions, where some regions are specialized in production, while others in delivery, and still others in HQ activities. In fact, cities might form new industrial clusters around these specialized functions (Duranton and Puga 2005). Continuous innovation thrives in specific milieus where firms, educational and other institutions are not only spatially concentrated but also embedded in dense webs of traded and untraded interdependencies (Boschma 2005), regional worlds of innovative production—'new industrial districts'—have their own agglomeration logic (based on more narrow 'localization economies' that mainly pertain to one specific industry), which results in decentralized polycentricity. However, the decentralized polycentricity breaks through urban boundaries or space of metropolis and steps up the ladder of spatial scales, with the relevant scale becoming that of the region. In this case, the global city is giving rise to a functionally polycentric MCR process on the basis of its exceptionally strong global multi-sector service network connectivity. In fact, the expansion and diffusion of 'industrial urbanism' on a global scale which is led by the formation of global production networks with local anchoring points in urban regions all over the world is a most distinctive feature of the current phase of globalization (Soja 2000).

Global city regions have a variable and functional definition concerning its geometrical structure and geographical characteristics, which is described as a series of anything between 10 and 50 cities and towns physically separate but functionally networked, clustered around one or more larger central cities and drawing enormous economic strength from a new functional division of labour (Hall and Pain 2006) or 'integrated sets of cities and their surrounding suburban hinterlands' (Florida, Gulden and Mellander 2008). So far, global city regions are a process that can be observed in both developed and developing countries (Phelps and Ozawa 2003). Scott, Soja and Agnew (2001) listed 30 global city regions in the world for the first time. There are marked differences between these global city regions, ranging from familiar metropolitan agglomerations dominated by a strongly developed core such as the London region or Mexico City, to more polycentric geographic units as in the case of Randstad. Global city regions are recognized as key spatial organizations for human development in the context of the C21st information-/innovation-driven economy and intensified globalization. Scott, Soja et al. (2001) have argued that the new urban form emerging under conditions of contemporary globalization are global city regions rather than global cities that are regarded as the growth nodes of world economy.

This new phenomenon, which comes with the rise and expansion of global cities into city regions, is a form of new regionalism to a certain extent. Many people have recognized that regions are the pivotal socio-spatial formation since the end of the 1970s (Ohmae 1995) and that regions represent the only scale. In an increasingly mobile world characterized by all kinds of flows and networks, this avowedly territorial and scalar logic is today challenged by those advocating a more radically 'relational' approach to the study of cities and regions. Attaching particular significance to transnational relations, connections and flows, research on the geographies of networks has resulted in an approach where space and regions are conceptualized as open, fluid and unbound (Amin 2004). Space is no longer seen as a nested hierarchy moving from 'global' to 'local'. Emerging socio-spatial formations are not necessarily territorial-scalar but constituted through the flow of spatiality, juxtaposition, porosity and connectivity, and supported in policy terms by the emergence of an expanding plethora of 'unusual regions'—so-called because they do not conform to any recorded territorial units (Deas and Lord 2006). These regions are spaces for the movement and circulation of goods, technologies, knowledge, people, finance and information, which reveals a complex and unbounded lattice of articulations (Allen, Massey and Cochrane 1998). Therefore, we might now be living in a 'regional world' where regions are the fundamental building blocks of a globally interconnected modern world (Storper 1997). In such 'regional world', capital accumulation and governance is 'about exercising nodal power and aligning networks in one's own interest, rather than about exercising territorial power for there is no definable territory to rule over' (Amin 2004). This absurd scale-dependent notion is replaced by the notion that what counts is connectivity (Thrift 2004), implying that regions must be conceptualized as 'central rather than merely derivative of nonspatial processes' (Agnew 2000). It follows that the global city region process is a product of global economic integration and the consequent formation of megacities, and this, thus, expands the 'pointed' global city logic that is defined by external linkages. In other words, global cities are networked externally on a global scale, as key staging posts for the operation of MNCs, and internally on a regional scale, as city expansion sees the functional economies of large cities extend beyond their traditional administrative boundaries to capture physically separate but functionally networked urban settlements in the surrounding hinterland.

Global city regions are the important new 'regional social formations', with external and internal functional linkages being the determining attribute (Hall 2001) and, therefore, they are functionally dominant, that is, just because two urban systems are located proximate to each other does not mean they can be aggregated up to form a single, larger, more coherent and more competitive urban economic unit. To take one example, Liverpool and Manchester are UK cities located less than 50 km apart. As single urban systems, they do not have the critical mass to register as a global city region. Therefore, network connectivity is a defining sign of the global city region. It is correlated with distance, and similar with the nodes of APS industry in the globalization process. The global city region is not just the spatial representation of an interconnected network of corporations, institutions and people, but more of a specific multi-core structure that complicates the network and is defined by less localization, permanent macro-geographical distribution and globalization.

As we know, urban areas are traditionally defined as monocentric, containing a principal centre and several surrounding subordinate centres of different hierarchical orders that are part of the principal centre's market area (Haggett 1965). Such an urban system is characterized by a hierarchy of centres that is rank-ordered on the basis of the size of their market areas and their complexity in terms of the number of functions provided (Davies 1967). From a network point of view, such a monocentric urban system is best represented by a star-shaped pattern of interactions, where the flows of goods, services and commuters between centres of different hierarchical orders are one-sided and centralized (Haggett and Chorley 1967), whereas the nodality of a centre can be expressed by its size and the range of functions it offers (Lukermann 1966), the centrality of a centre is typically defined as the part of its importance that can be ascribed to the provision of goods, services and jobs in excess of those demanded by the centre's own inhabitants (Marshall 1989). Apparently, in traditional city regions, centres at the top of the urban hierarchy in an urban system are disproportionally connected to this 'outside world' because of better accessibility and the higher order functions they provide, while other centres fulfil a more regional or local function (Lambregts 2009). On the contrary, the global city region based on networks seems to be more characterized by a polycentric spatial organization than by a hierarchy at all functional levels. The hierarchical central place model, with its emphasis on monocentricity, has increasing difficulty explaining this spatial reality (Coffey et al. 1998). One of the reasons is its inability to deal with the more polycentric spatial organization of metropolitan areas that appears to be inherent to the post-industrial era and that is fuelled by globalization (Kloosterman and Musterd 2001). Therefore, a strong fusion theory has come up in identifying 'polycentricity' and 'multi-core' as the defining characteristics of global city regions in the 21st century, that global city regions are the result of coordination and interactions among multiple centres, cities and clustering economies in the same places.

The formation of global city regions can be viewed as a tangible, local spatial convergence process, with more general technological, economic and regulatory changes being the product of market forces, unnamed matrices and complex interdependencies. Indeed, city regions are no longer seen as static places defined by a set of resources. They are described as dynamic arrangements facilitating innovation or, in other words, as incubators or commutator processing flows of ideas, people, capital and goods. A city region can be a node, full of lateral flows of tangible, intangible and virtual types from all directions though, and does not follow an organized pattern. Therefore, global city regions have more interaction with their 'hinterworld' than with their 'hinterland' (Taylor 2001b). The twofold dimensionality of global city regions gives themselves a substantial advantage in the global flow-based and knowledge-driven economy: these regions are not only focal points for knowledge creation, learning and innovation—capitalism's new post-Fordist economic form (Morgan 1997) but also important sites for fostering new post-national identities, increasing social cohesion and encouraging new forms of social and political mobilization (Keating 1998). Thus, these global city regions are becoming the core components (elements) of the more complex and extensive global social, economic and information exchange networks, and the key to generation, transmission and reception of cross-border flows of capital, goods and services, information and people.

In global city regions, external economies are not confined to a single urban core, but instead appear to be shared among a group of functionally linked settlements (Phelps and Ozawa 2003). Such 'regionalization' of urbanization externalities has been conceptualized and described as 'urban network externalities' (Capello 2000), 'spatial externality fields' (Phelps et al. 2001) or 'regional externalities' (Parr 2002). These concepts build on the concept of 'borrowed size', coined by Alonso (1973), who used it to explain why smaller cities that are part of a mega-politan urban complex had much higher incomes than self-standing cities of similar size. This is because agglomeration costs are more confined to city boundaries than agglomeration benefits (Parr 2002) and, thus, cities within a polycentric global city region enjoy favourable location conditions for 'borrowing size' to a greater extent, while the positive and negative agglomeration externalities are balanced (Meijers and Burger 2010). Besides, global city regions 'are based predominantly on some combination of pecuniary and technological externalities open to service industries across a group of settlements, rather than the technological externalities available at the localized scale of discrete towns or cities' (Phelps and Ozawa 2003), which will strengthen their interactions with neighbouring cities, and may also influence the presence of agglomeration externalities.

The city region is not defined by natural boundaries, because it is essentially the artefact of the cities at their nuclei; the boundaries move outward—or halt—only as city economic energy dictates (Jacobs 1984), hence the obvious duality of the governance of global city regions, that is, territory/function governance. Western countries adopted the metropolitan model in the 20th century, thinking this way of space governance was at least possible in form, and they even arranged metropolitan areas in highly connected rings to enable the metropolis to implement space governance. However, this metropolitan governance was destroyed in a global city region, which became the fundamental difference between a city region and a metropolis. To overcome the debilitating binary division between territorial and relational geography, one needs to recognize that political space is bounded and porous (Morgan 2007). Jones and Jessop (2010) further the 'approach that can grasp the inherently polymorphic, multidimensional character of socio-spatial relations' that matters more in analysing these socio-spatial territories, places, scales and networks connected across space–time, and in analysing increasing configurations and possible combinations of these socio-spatial dimensions and their coherence in spatio-temporal fixes. Some scholars point out that in the quest to present the new regionalism as a new institutionalist paradigm for development, it is guilty of bundling together the different dimensions of socio-spatial relations (i.e., work on territorial restructuring, new regional geography, state rescaling and the network society; Painter 2008). But at the same time, it provides a useful empirical test bed for considering the degree to which various dimensions of socio-spatial relations can be deemed complementary alternatives.

8.2.3. The Process of Megacity Region

On the basis of global city region, the expansion of global cities into larger city regions is being superseded by trans-metropolitan landscapes comprising networked urban centres and their surrounding area, resulting in the formation of MCR. As Hall and Pain (2006) have defined, an MCR is the wider functional urban region surrounding major global cities through APS networks.

The major driving force behind the evolution from global city regions to MCRs is also global connectivity, and its mechanism is again based on locations and practices of APS firms and their professionals. It connects places into a flowing geography, leading to the interconnected development of urban system functions covering a wider regional range. We know that as globalization progresses, market competition intensifies at every scale, while the horizontal urban network linkages are seemingly thickened and expanded. Corporations increasingly need to operate across cities to stay competitive, which contributes to intercity synergies. This might suggest a development model shifting from low-value, offshore and general activities to high-skilled and high-profit functions, which is different from the traditional market development model based on low-cost labour. It reflects that, in a wider regional space, there is a specific geographical logic of APS industries 'for which dispersal and centralization are "two sides of one ball"'. The knowledge-intensive production and trade activities qualify APS as a central 'anchor' in global city connectivity (Hall and Pain 2006) and, thus, the global connectivity expanded through functional polycentric APS networks plays a vital role in the economic dynamics and, especially, the expansion of MCRs. However, this is ably supported by a geopolitical logic that the scale and pace of urbanization in these locations is now so pervasive that new supra-local scales of urbanization are being created, which to function effectively requires economic systems and political systems to be geographically aligned. From this point of view, how the type of MCR varies depends on whether you take rapid urbanization (form) or global economic integration (function) as your starting point for framing globalized urbanization (Harrison and Hoyler 2014).

The formation of mega-regions is significant in the evolution of global cities for two reasons: first, it implies that there is an unbreakable logic linking mega-regions (as space) and mega-regionality (as process) with the most advanced elements of the 21st-century globalization; second, it reveals the search for a post-national spatial/scalar fix for globalized capital accumulation and organizing (inter) national space economies. As new urban configurations, mega-regions are fast 'becoming the new engines of global and regional economies' (UN-Habitat 2010: 1). The 2003–2006 EU 'Polynet' study supported by European Regional Development Fund conducted rigorous research on the regional growth phenomenon associated with highly globally networked cities active in financial and business services in Northwest Europe. The findings shed light on the complex webs of city interlinkages specifically generated by APS networks in extensive functional areas, termed global 'MCR', around nine major European global cities. And the 'MCR' concept was discussed by providing empirical evidence from the Paris and London case studies (Halbert and Pain 2009). At the current stage of global urban expansion, mega-regions are playing an increasingly dominant role. Florida (2008: 38) asserts that 'bigger and more competitive economic units—mega-regions—have superseded cities as the real engines of the global economy'.

> The world's 40 largest mega-regions...cover only a tiny fraction of the habitable surface of the earth and are home to less than 18% of the world's population; yet, they are responsible for 66% of global economic activity and about 85% of technological and scientific innovation. (Florida et al. 2008: 474)

The Regional Plan Association (RPA; 2016) considers making their own statement on what they saw as the current and near-future 'mega-regional' geography of the USA. America 2050 is that vision. It identifies 11 emerging mega-regions as prototypes for balanced and sustainable growth across the USA during the first half of the 21st century.

It is particularly worth noting that the 'mega-region' concept totally differs from the term 'megacity' that is proposed by Perlman and O'Meara (2007) to describe the largest contiguous urban areas or metropolitan areas in the world. Marked by local functional connectivity and flows such as daily commuting to work and shopping trips, megacities have their local social and economic priorities. They are focal points of social reproduction disconnected from vibrant economic globalization, irrespective of their overall degree of global economic integration, and economic vibrancy associated with global city expansion. By contrast, global MCRs are not simply a new scale of a long-standing process of urbanization, but are becoming increasingly globally constituted and integrated, and this spatial logic of territorial space is increasingly dominated by spaces of flows (Castells 1989). This is a 'reconstitution of the concept of region' that is linked into 'global circuits' (Sassen 2002b). The more globally connected these regions become, the more regionally connected they will be. Although convenient transportation and Internet networks give us the feeling of a 'shrinking' world, the 'real geographical distance' still matters and, of course, the neighbouring regions are of greater importance. Therefore, rescaling of localized network connections, the development of external urban relations, and the ways in which these relations define and construct city regions, are key determinants of the degree to which global cities are really expanding, functionally. For example, the 'mega-region' identified by the RPA on the north-east coast of the USA will differ in its scale of external economic relations from that of the 'megalopolis' identified by Jean Gottmann in roughly the same location 50 years ago (Gottmann 1961).

The MCR process is morphologically integrated, and it can also promote economic growth in geographically independent and remote cities. What's more, it is a phenomenon of 'functional polycentricity', emphasizing the functional connectivity and, precisely, the global functional connectivity, which is formed by the APS network through the expansion of big city region process. The MCR, if only morphologically integrated but with surprisingly weak functional connectivity between cities and regions, is not the MCR in the true sense of the word, which means that cities with only transportation connections (railway and air transportation), similar economic bases and similar economic cycles do not necessarily develop into an MCR. On the contrary, as long as the functional connectivity between cities develops, even if their economic bases and development trajectories are completely different, the cities may form an MCR.

The phenomenon of MCR is composed of three different yet mutually interfering and interlinked types of interaction between the city and the world. We have attributed purely network/exchange quality to the first and called it a network level. It is well described by the global network of flows of business connectivity and concentration of processes between non-territorial nodes. The interactions that constitute connectivity or flows of processes between agents (companies) in the nodes (cities) take place very fast and in many different directions. We have also attributed purely central place/agglomeration quality to the latter and called it a regional level. It is well described by the concentric areas of resources gravity to the central point inside and are processed. Eventually, the third level, representing an interaction of a city within itself, is called municipal or internal level. It is well described by the level and intensity of an interaction of city within itself. This is where basically quality of both public space and living emerges and manifests. It is worth noting that the municipal level has relatively strong ties not to the regional but to the network level. The core basic mechanism of multiplied value creation by global MCRs is reflected in: optimization of three crucial resources (capital, human and ideas) are absorbed through the regional level and from the network, and processed in central cities; then a small amount of the processed resources are released back into the region; most of the resources focus within global cities building up a critical mass needed for a new solution (products, services, professionals). The new solution is then sent into the metronetwork. At the same time, other new solutions are received from the network. Global cities accumulate the global ideas and creativities—both own and those acquired from the metronetwork to create new solutions. And finally they are exchanged for value through the network level which induces growth of accumulated value on the municipal level.

In the global MCR, intercity relations were found to extend far beyond the metropolitan boundary and statutory boundaries. While sub-regional business markets influence office network location outside global cities, because APS networks supply services to each other at different geographical scales, their functional relations do not relate to territorially fixed government administrative areas at any level, emphasizing that boundaries must be regarded as 'porous' as argued within new regionalism literature (Harrison 2011), and the importance of acknowledging spatial relations that criss-cross the space of places (Storper 1997). The porosity of boundaries makes effective democratic and institutional policy engagement with the development issues presented by global MCR emergence highly challenging. Yet because the development of a whole range of global MCR infrastructures, resources and services, including transportation and housing, require coordinated, long-term planning and investment, policy networking across administrative boundaries is essential (Pain 2006). However, the existing governance system in the global MCR lacks institutional structures beyond global urban boundaries to ensure strategic planning policy cooperation at appropriate functional scales, which clearly poses major dilemmas for representative sub-national governance for strategic planning and development in the megacity and for MCR as a whole (Macleod and Jones 2007). The conflicting interests and tensions between constituent democratically elected local authorities comprising the functional space of the global MCR will not disappear with its regional structures.

A Case Study of 'Shanghai 2050' Global City Vision (Part I)

In this and the next chapters, we will apply the principles of the evolution of global cities and to the case of Shanghai for analysis on the future evolution of global cities. Specifically, we will analyse the main variables and their interrelationships to interpret the dynamic process of evolution, synthetically deduce (estimate) the evolutionary possibilities and visions of Shanghai towards a global city and sketch out the core functions of Shanghai being a global city, with a view to test the predictive power of this evolutionary theory.

We need to put the 'Shanghai 2050' case study under the goal-oriented framework of global cities to examine it as a general evolution case of global cities in a macro-dynamic context of the coming 30 years. We will look into the variables that will influence and determine the evolution of Shanghai towards a global city, including, among others, globalization and informationization, long-term economic cycles and changes in the world economic structure at the macro level, the national economic strength and national economic arrangements at the meso level and the urban genetics, development level and infrastructures at the micro level.

9.1. STRATEGIC DRIVE: PROSPECTS OF GLOBALIZATION

Global cities are the outcomes of globalization, and the globalization process dominates the evolution of global cities as a core variable among all impact factors around the world. In the upcoming 30 years, the basic developments of globalization and the new changes or features in its process will directly drive the evolution of global cities. Therefore, prospects of globalization make the primary analysis in the case study of 'Shanghai 2050' global city evolution.

9.1.1. The Fate of Globalization

As contemporary globalization has facilitated the flows of commodities, services and all kinds of factors across the globe, through which resources are allocated on a larger scale, it greatly changes the world and people's lives. Therefore, globalization has become a worldwide issue of great concern. When it comes to the significance and influence of globalization, opposing viewpoints always clash, even at the time when globalization was growing rather rapidly. On the one hand, changing local–global relations have been interpreted negatively by Cochrane and Pain ([2000] 2004) as representing the increasing power and dominance of major economic and political interests and the spatially and socially uneven consequences of globalization. In a word, globalization can lead to polarization. On the other hand, a more positive interpretation has seen the expansion of global communications and stretching socio-spatial processes as presenting opportunities for increasing economic development worldwide, ultimately improving general living conditions. Alongside these opposing interpretations, so-called 'traditionalists' have taken issue with the notion that globalization is actually a new phenomenon, seeing contemporary change simply as a continuation of previous global power relations. In that case, globalization can neither cause polarization nor improve general living conditions. But an emergent 'transformationalist' perspective is identified which recognizes global change as a development from pre-existing spatial relations but also sees the implications of advances in informational and communications technologies and high-speed travel as requiring in-depth study and serious policy attention. Emergent understandings instead conceptualize contemporary global interactions *as a complex relational and spatial process,* in which power is less directly associated with specific cities and nations but is increasingly *diffused through networks.* When the financial crisis burst in 2008, the debate over globalization reached a fever pitch and, once again, the fate of globalization is seriously discussed: re-globalization or de-globalization? The choice that affects how global cities will develop in the future undoubtedly plays a decisive role in their evolution. Similarly, it determines whether emerging cities like Shanghai can rise or not. That's why we are required to have a basic judgement about the fate of globalization.

An increasingly prevalent argument which blames globalization for the happening of the financial crisis follows such a logic that the global dispersion of production has led to the current geographic dispersion of HQs and their subsidiaries, and the further expansion of global commodity chains. In pursuit of cost reduction and profit maximization, these firms utilize their commodity chains in order to organize value added production stages, coordinate various levels of distribution, employ a governance structure which controls the allocation of resources and facilitate an institutional framework that coordinates between national and international policies (Gereffi 1994). Nonetheless, although corporate networks are evidently increasing in reach, it is equally apparent that investments are only becoming more concentrated within and between particular nations (Driffield and Love 2005). In this sense, it appears that global corporate networks are only integrating particular nations of the world, resulting in a higher relative polarization between countries. Additionally, since such corporate activities that utilize global commodity chains are often unstable and even in disorder, they are unable to lay a solid foundation for the growth of national economy. Consequently, this process leads to increasing uncertainty concerning the future of nations within the globalizing economy (Kentor 2005). As such, instead of continuing to promote globalization, an internationalized development based on other countries' experience in driving national economic growth should be pursued. During the pursuit, some major economies made big moves to adjust strategies and policies, which resulted in the re-emergence of trade protectionism. Noticeably, some developed countries that used to play a dominant role in the process of globalization have now showed signs of setting inward-looking policies and quitting their dominant role in stages. Accordingly, 'de-globalization' or 'anti-globalization' is becoming increasingly influential and considered as the right strategy to adopt.

It is undeniable that the Global Financial Crisis in 2008 has had a strong impact on the world economy, leading to the stagnation of globalization. To some extent, this is an instinctive safe haven response and a temporary callback to the global economic 'balance of terror' affected in the past. The current sharp fall in the growth of world trade and the rise of trade protectionism are more of a phenomenon in the process of world economic re-balancing than of 'de-globalization'. Moreover, the current slowdown in the growth rate of world trade is also related to some cyclical factors. According to the *World Economic Outlook* issued by the International Monetary Fund (IMF) in October 2016, three quarters of the decline in real trade growth between 2012 and 2016 could be attributed to the weak global economic growth as compared with that between 2003 and 2007, especially in investments. In addition, the slowdown in trade growth may also reflect that the extraordinary momentum that promoted trade growth in the past has reached natural maturation. Therefore, even if the income elasticity of trade (the ratio of trade growth rate to GDP growth rate) is less than 1, we cannot owe it to the mechanism of 'de-globalization'. It is more related to the downturn and the tough recovery of macroeconomy instead. At the same time, we also recognize that globalization will inevitably cause profound income redistribution effects, which will bring unequal interests to each country and different classes of it and perhaps conflicts of interests. However, through the transnational flows of production factors, globalization brings together the potential production factors of different countries to achieve practical efficiency and increase the world's total production. In this process, countries participating in the international division of labour share unequal interests. Globalization accelerates the transnational transfer of technology and will promote the continuous adjustment of the economic structure of each country. The institutional arrangements for global economic governance brought about by globalization have far-reaching influence on the current and future evolution of economic systems. The economic prospects of all countries are closely related to the process of globalization and, thus, every country need and must observe and think about their economic operations, especially future development trends, from the perspective of globalization. For developing countries, their economic development must be based on the openness to the outside world, because self-enclosure can only lead to poverty and backwardness. For developed countries, their development issues need to be addressed in the process of globalization.

On the basis of earlier analysis, we can come to the conclusion that the current stagnation or obstruction of globalization is only a temporary phenomenon. Although globalization has brought some negative effects, the dominant are positive effects and no evidence shows any tendency of de-globalization. In the next 30 years, globalization will continue to progress, and this trend will not change easily. No country can get rid of the influence of globalization whether it wants or not, and the only way out is to find its own position in this process. With long-term upside momentum and the corresponding structural adjustment, globalization will continue to deepen in the future.

9.1.2. Long-Wave Fluctuations

The progression of globalization, taking place at a specific time and space, is subject to the influence of synchronic and diachronic global changes, including long-term economic cycles, scientific and technological revolutions and urbanization, thus presenting a fluctuating, non-linear feature in its speed, direction and degree. These fluctuations in the course of globalization, to a large extent, correlate to global economic trends. It is hypothesized that globalization gains speed when the world economic growth accelerates and slows down as world economic growth decelerates. Therefore, if we want to predict the trends of globalization in the next three decades, we need to analyse world economic trends, especially long-term economic cycles and technological revolutions that may have significant impacts on the world economy.

Such prediction should be based on Kondratieff's long wave theory, which proposes long-term economic cycles as a result of technological innovation. Since 1991, the world has stepped into the Fifth Wave, with its core technology being information technology and the Internet (Table 9.1). Then, as the 2008 Global Financial Crisis broke out, the world economy entered a recession, and has since been stuck in a volatile quagmire characterized by stagnation, a widening gap between

Table 9.1 *Groundbreaking Innovations Marking the Long Waves*

	Wave Length	Innovations
First Wave	1782–1845	Textile machine Steam engine
Second Wave	1845–1897	Steel Railway
Third Wave	1897–1948	Electro-technology Chemical industry
Fourth Wave	1948–1991	Automobile Computer
Fifth Wave	1991–2035	Information technology and the Internet
Sixth Wave	2035	—

Source: Compiled by author and his research team.
Note: The data and analysis are derived from the research project China Economic Growth Prediction in the Next 30 Years funded by Shanghai Development Strategy Research Institute and lead by Dr Daming Zhu.

different economies, and mounting uncertainties and risks. It is projected that in the near future, the world economy will experience a depression protracting until around 2025, then embrace a recovery, and finally witness the end of the Fifth Wave around 2035 (Table 9.2).

Table 9.2 *Analyses and Predictions on World Economic Growth Based on the Long-Wave Theory*

	Prosperity	Recession	Depression	Recovery
First Wave	1782–1802	1815–1825	1825–1838	1838–1845
Second Wave	1845–1866	1866–1873	1873–1883	1883–1897
Third Wave	1897–1917	1917–1929	1929–1937	1937–1948
Fourth Wave	1948–1966	1966–1973	1973–1982	1982–1991
Fifth Wave	1991–2008	2008–2016	2016–2025	2025–2035
Sixth Wave	2035–2055	—	—	—

Source: Compiled by author and his research team.
Note: The data and analysis are derived from the research project China Economic Growth Prediction in the Next 30 Years funded by Shanghai Development Strategy Research Institute and lead by Dr Daming Zhu.

However, the technologies that triggered the Fifth Wave differ from the former ones. During the long waves in industrial times, major groundbreaking technologies, as a core independent variable of the economy, directly stem from and find their applications in the manufacturing sector. That explains why such technologies release their power of promoting economic booms in a pattern of sudden surges and plunges. Consequently, when the technologies mostly exhausted their power, economic crisis came with heavy downward economic pressure and turbulent fluctuations, which persisted until a new batch of groundbreaking technologies emerged to take their place. In contrast, modern information technology is widely applicable and intensely employed across the economic sectors and is highly compatible with other technologies. Moreover, the more it is integrated with other technologies, the more applicable it becomes. In this sense, its power of driving economic growth is released at a gradual pace. Therefore, according to our observations, information technology and the Internet have not yet fully unleashed their potential for inspiring industrial revolutions and will continue to have a significant impact on the global economy. Evidently, the power to be further released from these technologies will serve as a countering force to the downward economic pressure, possibly abating it and easing economic fluctuations, thus producing a less steep downward track. In addition, the information technology has laid the groundwork for breakthroughs in other technologies, especially enabling major innovative technologies for the next cycle to come into being. No matter from which sector the new round of world technological revolution arises, be it bioscience, new material or new energy, modern information technology will accelerate its arrival. Nonetheless, the aforementioned factors can only change the sharp downward curve of the fifth long wave. They cannot overturn the internal patterns of the long wave, particularly the wavelength and the basic rhythm.

When the sixth long cycle will start depends, to a large extent, on the new round of global technological and industrial revolution. Despite various predictions, it is still unclear what the new technology marking the sixth wave will become. This uncertainty is a result of the increasing unpredictability of technologies which develop in a way that is hard to imagine. Nevertheless, a general consensus is that the world is now on the eve of a new scientific and technological revolution, towards which some marked changes have taken place. First, signs of revolutionary breakthroughs appear in some significant scientific issues and key technologies, such as brain science, quantum computing and material genome, which have a bright prospect for application. Second, scientific and technological innovations keep occurring in diverse fields, but none of them has a dominant position or a leading explicit technology road map. Third, IT, biotechnology, clean energy, new materials and intelligent manufacturing and other technological fields have been integrating with one another, making breakthroughs together and rapidly translating into productivity, which, in turn, make technologies and industries more 'intelligent, ubiquitous, interconnected, green, and sound'. Fourth, as the elements of innovation are flowing and allocated on a global scale, a world innovation network featuring multiple nodes and levels has taken shape. In the light of this, major developed countries began to launch innovation strategies, hoping to either become the centre or consolidate their central position in the innovation network, a measure that can advance the accumulation of innovation elements such as talent, intellectual properties and innovative brands.

Although it is not easy to forecast which innovative technology or leading industry will carry the sixth cycle, history does tell us that every scientific and technological revolution is triggered by strong demands from economy, society or people's livelihood, as well as technology breakthroughs. A foreseeable trend is that in the next three decades, the rapid development of high technologies will occur in groups, composed of IT, biotechnology, new materials technology, new energy technology, new manufacturing technology, marine technology and space technology. From a vertical perspective, the shared theoretical basis of these technology groups is the quantum theory, yet at different microscopic levels. From a horizontal perspective, they are all within the research scope of complexity science, with their elements, structures, functions, information and environments interconnected and mutually restraining. It can be sure that the new round of global technological and industrial revolution will have a huge impact on the world economy, no matter in which area or areas it takes place.

In a word, this new revolution will not only be a powerful engine for the world economic growth but also dramatically change the structures of economic and industrial systems and labour markets, leading the global economy into the sixth long cycle. An optimistic forecast is that the world economy will enter the prosperity period in the sixth long cycle around 2035 and then last till 2050, while a vaguer prediction states that this economic boom will start before 2050. But one thing is for sure: when such boom starts, the pace of globalization will also increase. By then, more attention will be paid to the management of globalization, with attempts to find a governance mechanism and effective measures to address its adverse impacts.

9.1.3. The Future of Globalization

Over the next 30 years, globalization, as an ongoing process, will expand its scope, experience new changes and present new characteristics and forms that are different from the past. In this section, we will forecast its future process from three dimensions.

1. Globalization will deepen with its scope expanding and interdependence between countries strengthening.

   Although many countries and regions have been involved in globalization, TNCs, as basic units to conduct and integrate global production, can only carry out transnational activities in limited geographical areas and, thus, the transnational corporate networks will continue to be asymmetric (Carroll 2007). The uneven geographical distribution of capital reveals the territorial rights of transnational HQs, because the existence of capital requires safe and relatively fixed social and physical infrastructures (Harvey 1982). There are signs that corporate internationalization remains restricted to the 'happy few' (Mayer and Ottaviano 2007), and that corporate network connections are polarized into the core regions of North America, Europe and Asia-Pacific, since these regions claim for 98 per cent outward FDI and 82 per cent foreign investment. These signs not only indicate disproportionate distribution of power globally but also show how the world depends on these core regions. Global connections will present a clear North–South divide.

However, TNCs have made new strategic adjustments, indicating future directions for development. They shifted their deployment of global production chains from 'offshore' to 'nearshore', shortening global supply chains; meanwhile, they also facilitated greater specialization of industries based on modularization and integration, thus further extending the 'length' of GVCs. In addition, they adopted a common strategy of 'reverse innovation', paying more attention to the rise of emerging economies and accordingly adjusting their deployment of GVCs by gradually relocating more innovation activities to emerging economies and then selling innovative products to the global market including developed economies. This has accelerated the transfer of related and supporting industries and will eventually lead to the integrated transfer of R&D, manufacturing and marketing. Such transfer of industrial chains has changed the competition between individual enterprises to that between global production systems or chains, which not only indicates the formation of a new global layout of TNCs but will also change the forms and characteristics of global industrial transfer and integrated production. More specifically, there will be three notable trends.

First, TNCs from developed economies and emerging ones will coexist and interact with each other, which will change the traditional pattern of one-way industrial transfer (from developed countries to developing countries) to a global pattern of interactive two-way industrial transfer, resulting in a larger scale of global trade, capital flow, immigration and information exchange, an increasingly interconnected world and a complex network that covers the entire world. The complexity and speed of interconnection will take globalization to a new level and bring unexpected opportunities but impose great risks as well.

Second, the asymmetric TNC network will be improved to some extent to adjust the division of labour among different countries, which will increase nodes of GVCs and intensify the connection of production network around the world.

Third, the global production network will become more intensive so that there will be more major network nodes, instead of a few centres, focusing on global investment and trade.

Therefore, globalization will deepen in the next 30 years. The scope of globalization will be extended with more countries involved in the process. But more importantly, the interdependence between countries will become stronger, mainly reflected by the participation of more emerging economies and developing countries which will move from the edge of globalization to its periphery, then to the sub-core and finally even to the core.

2. The fields of globalization will not only expand with the emergence of new fields but also become increasingly 'dematerialized'.

In the next 30 years, apart from global flows of goods (in traditional manufacturing industry) and capital flows (in the financial sector), economic globalization will increasingly demonstrate a tendency of 'dematerialization', especially in two aspects. One is the soaring cross-border data flow. According to the reports by the MGI, global flow of data has more than doubled between 2013 and 2015, reaching 290 megabytes per second, then increased another one-third by the end of 2016, which means that the amount of cross-border data sent by enterprises and individuals worldwide is 20 times higher than that in 2008. Thus, the economic value of this new type of globalization is rather evident. In 2014, the cross-border flows of capital, goods, services and data have created an added value of $7.8 trillion to the global economy, in which data flows alone account for $2.8 trillion, slightly higher than global commodity trade ($2.7 trillion). Digital economy arrives hand in hand with the shortening of global supply chains; and global data flow surges as the growth of trade in commodity and capital slows down. This shows that digital economy of the 21st century has begun to disintegrate the old economic order, meaning that globalization has dramatically changed and is moving towards a higher level of digitalization.

The other is the rapid growth of emerging service trade. The continuous upgrade in and greater specialization of globalized industries facilitated the separation of services that were originally part of the production process for more professional operation and cooperation. The application of new technologies and the further advancement and intelligent development of information technology have also created many new service models and patterns. As developed countries seek to establish a new real economy grounded in technological innovation, producer services associated with these emerging technology industries, such as R&D subcontracting, marketing, consulting, technical support and after-sales services, patents and expertise trade is growing at a fast pace. Meanwhile, the development of modern information technology has greatly reduced time and space, and also enhanced the 'tradability of services'. Public consumption in all countries has truly entered an era of internationalization, and the consumption pattern of the middle class, in particular, will shift from thrifty-focused to one that can drive growth (Laermans 1993), as the pursuit of a new lifestyle triggers the expansion of demands for global services. Therefore, global service trade will have greater development potential, especially the burgeoning trade in services such as education and training, healthcare, cultural creation, media and cultural relics.

As the areas of economic globalization continue to broaden, another new change will take place—globalization of labour. Normally, compared to other resources, labour is relatively fixed due to the restriction of borders and is, thus, less globalized. However, in the next 30 years, the globalization of labour will be greatly enhanced due to an array of new factors:

- The high-speed, reliable Internet bolsters the global information environment, enabling people to see more, share more, create more and become organized faster. This will give rise to a low-cost and high-quality global labour force that can meet the needs of economic growth in this century and also push the integration of workers from developing countries into the global labour pool. Meanwhile, AI-powered machine translation is expected to break language barriers, thus promoting cross-border labour flow.
- Education levels have increased in many parts of the world, boosting labour turnover and allowing more people to immigrate.
- These changes will be accentuated by the demographic trend towards the larger share of elderly people. It is estimated that, by 2050, the amount of older population will have surpassed that of the youth for the first time to reach 2 billion (21% of the total), 30 per cent of which will come from developed

countries. In some sense, this can also facilitate cross-border and cross-ocean immigration, as economic considerations facing serious challenges brought by population ageing will counter public opposition to immigration.
- The competition for human resources is becoming a key factor in all countries' efforts to achieve their strategic goals. Such increasingly fierce competition can also speed up global labour flow. In this context, today's emigration is less related to predicaments, as was in the 1960s and 1970s, than to globalization (Massey 2003).

Recently, globalization has also showed growing influence over scientific research, environment and some social and political areas. For example, the rapid development of modern ICT is breaking the connection between the flow of human capital and labour service (such as service outsourcing), and this trend will only become amplified in the future. Of course, no evidence can prove that such disconnection will interfere the flow of skilled labour force, but it can promote the flow of technology. This shows that technological globalization will further develop in future and reach a new level.

Besides, as international and intercity cooperation in scientific research expands, global network links keep increasing and the globalization of academic research is emerging. The analysis in Oner et al. (2010) shows that from 1991 to 2009, the international collaboration in urban studies and planning saw a fourfold increase, while the intercity collaboration a twofold increase. And 'the number of ties within the network of international and intercity co-publications has marked considerable growth as well'—'the number of linkages increased from 12 links in the first half of the 1990s to the current number of 100'. Moreover, similar changes also occur in other subjects of globally joint research, including biotechnology, nanotechnology, ICT (Matthiessen, Schwarz and Find 2006), information system (Cunningham and Dillon 1997), physics, biomedical research, computer science (Newman 2001 2001b), psychology (Cronin, Shaw and Barre 2003), medicine and math (Glänzel and Schubert 2004).

What's more, with the development of knowledge economy, a growing number of countries shift their economic structure towards a knowledge-intensive one, which calls for advanced education (Romer 1990). This boosts the demand for alternative education services, thus encouraging trade in education and training services and education globalization. The examples include the increase in international exchange programmes, integration of globalization-related materials into courses and the introduction of foreign education franchises (Ali and Doan 2006). Therefore, education services trade in future is expected to be more diversified; and its spatial distribution will become more extensive and intensive globally and feature two-way and circular flow.

From the perspective of global civil society, globalization will also move forward with the articulation of cultural sensibilities, notably 'the ecological concern with global resources and environments and the postmodern condition of pluralistic, multicultural, non-hierarchical, and de-centered world society' (Bauman 1998). Although it is commonly agreed that global civil society is a 'fuzzy concept' (An-Na'im 2002; Anheier, Glasius and Kaldor 2001: 11; Chandhoke 2002) with its 'organizational infrastructure' still in a 'state of flux' (Anheier and Themudo 2002: 191), nevertheless the description in Keane (2001: 23) points out the essence of the subject: 'Global civil society is a vast, interconnected, and multilayered social space that comprises many hundreds of self-directing or non-governmental institutions and ways of life'. Through its 'cross-border networks', global civil society is constituted of 'chains of interactions linking the local, regional and planetary orders' (Keane 2001: 24). And leading NGO operatives are equally part of the 'transnational class' (Townsend Porter and Mawdsley 2002: 830) and the NGOs are creating such a global civil society via countless interconnected networks.

Sassen (2002b) has also turned her eyes from the global services market to global civil society, believing that the 'strategic cross-border geography that by-passes national states' is part of 'the infrastructure of global civil society' (Sassen 2002a: 217). This is because cities provide a 'thick enabling environment' through which transnational and sub-national activities can be brought together: 'The density of political and civic cultures in large cities localizes global civil society in people's lives. We can think of these as multiple localizations of civil society that are global in

that they are part of global circuits and trans-boundary networks' (Sassen 2002a: 218). 'Thus, although the non-economic circuits of flows are through different networks, NGOs and MNCs are both integral to the same overall global space of flows that defines contemporary globalization' (Taylor [2003] 2004).
3. The structure of globalization will be complex and diversified, especially with the appearance of new regionalization.

   In theory, there are two trends in the global economy: the first is integration in the forms of free trade zones, customs unions, common markets, economic alliances, political alliances, political unifications, etc. Nations between which economic integration can happen often have similar social conventions, diplomatic policies and economic development level. The second is the so-called 'regionalization'—a tendency of increased cooperation within one region. Although without any formal treaties or agreements, deepened cooperation between nations within a region in trade, investment and other economic areas also produce the same economic benefits as from economic integration. In the process of globalization, the trends of integration and regionalization coexist, so do the multilateral and bilateral cooperation.

   Over the past 30 years, the world trade has largely followed the multilateral trading system dominated by developed country members, such as the World Trade Organization (WTO), the IMF and the World Bank, which are known as *troika* of the world economy. However, after the 2008 financial crisis, although the WTO remained a major player in world trade governance, it is stuck in a mire, hardly be able to push world trade forward. Meanwhile, the wave of regionalization has sprung up, with strengthened efforts in establishing regional economic and trade alliances. Such trends may reshape the post-Western world trading patterns, which might rebalance the economic order between developed countries and emerging markets and determine whether the future multilateral relations will continue be characterized by 'open global arrangements' or 'competitive groups'. The gradual integration of nations within our globalizing world is strongly characterized by the economic networks formed by MNC HQs and their subsidiaries located across the globe (Brakman and Garretsen 2008), which is also the embryonic form of the future world economic pattern—the new regionalization appeared in the process of globalization.

Most of our previous studies define regionalization as a scale in traditional economic geography (Grabher 2006), by dividing the world into regions and being all-inclusive. Although such regionalization transcends territories as it avoids using nation states as modules in its composition, it remains in essence a delineation of the world based on super-localism by defining boundaries. It equates regionalization with classification and tends to produce regional patterns that are neatly demarcated as a simple, mosaic geography, thus inheriting a strong feature of traditional international division of labour and international trade. As the globalization advances, 'most studies fail to conceptualize regional development in an era of globalization' (Dicken and Malmberg 2001). Different from the traditional regionalization, the foregoing bilateral, regional and inter-regional investment and trade agreements imply the new regionalization as they are ostensibly negotiated by countries while, in fact, based on the key institutions relied on globalization, especially advanced producer firms and their global network 'in which activities are mediated across different geographical and organizational scales' (Coe et al. 2004), thus forming a new regional pattern. Rather than the persistent focus on regions as locally embedded entities or orderly organized and meaningful world spaces, they should be seen as 'new islands of an archipelago economy' (Hein 2000) 'in which a process of transnational network embedding exists, creating interpersonal relationships of trust at different, interrelated geographical scales' (Henderson et al. 2002).

Thus, such new regionalization in the context of globalization displays some key features.

> It is the non-territorialist world regionalization based upon connections rather than divisions. We replace neat territorialism with untidy connections. Regional labels are provided by home-regions, but the subsequent regional content always includes an outreaching global pattern of important cities. In addition, there is much overlap, not at the 'edges' as in territorial thinking, but right at the center across the home-regions themselves. Our regionalization still leaves much of the world and its people 'off the map' as Jennifer Robinson (2002) tells it; this is in keeping with our regionalization not being all-inclusion

as in traditional world regional geographies. Thus we can interpret our regionalization as a basic structure of the contemporary world economy, which can provide a framework for global conflict with a more complex geography of multiple global integrations. (Taylor, Derudder et al. 2013)

Of course, the regionalization does not mean the end or complete replacement of the multilateral trading system which will sustain in the next 30 years. In fact, WTO remains advancing, though its further advancement in the future will be a problem. If the situation remains unimproved, then the WTO might be marginalized. In addition, the Group of Twenty (G20), a broadly representative forum for economic governance which should play a more important role in global trade and investment, mainly discusses issues of trade and investment at the macro level without the necessary binding force over its members. Likewise, the Asia-Pacific Economic Cooperation (APEC), a forum for economic governance in the Asia-Pacific region which consists of 21 members and has a broad representation, should take more efforts in promoting the establishment of the Free Trade Area of the Asia-Pacific (FTAAP), but hasn't made any substantial progress. In future, whether the G20 and APEC can assume more responsibility for global trade governance depends on whether they can make breakthroughs. Therefore, in the next 30 years, we expect to see an increasingly complex and diversified structure of globalization and related institutional arrangements—a pattern of 'the multilateral system WTO plus various regional and bilateral investment and trade agreements'. In the process, long-term new 'rules of the game' of globalization may take shape, especially by evolving towards high-standard trade and investment agreements. Probably, the new rules will serve as strategic tools to reshape international trade, investment and the world economy.

9.1.4. Globalization Drives the Evolution of Global Cities

In the next 30 years, the process of globalization will definitely create wider and more intensive connections among cities within the world system, thus enhancing its functional and spatial structure. In this context, the WCN will undergo significant changes, which will consequently influence the evolution of global cities. Therefore, globalization will not only change the way how existing global cities grow but will also determine whether those emerging global cities can successfully evolve into new global cities and how to make that happen.

9.1.4.1. Increasing the Number of Global Cities

In the next 30 years, as globalization deepens and the economic sector grows, global firms will build new offices in more and more cities, especially those in developing countries, thus contributing to the expansion of the WCN. As Cerny (1991) points out that shifts in competitive advantage in the global marketplace have increased the global reach of economic activity, driven by competitive market mechanisms, technological change and space–time compression. In this process, developing countries, especially those emerging economies, will show faster economic growth, and give full play to their latecomer and comparative advantages through opening up. As a result, they will be more quickly integrated into the process of economic globalization, with a large number of cities joining in the WCN. Developing countries will also witness complex geographical distribution of intercity services (as intercity complementarity has already existed between Brazil and other South American countries), which will undoubtedly promote the expansion of the increasingly integrated WCN.

However, the expansion of the WCN does not necessarily mean the increase in the number of global cities, as the WCN is not only composed of global cities but also of a larger number of globalizing cities as basic nodes. Thus, the expansion may also result from an increase of globalizing cities. But we can make a hypothesis that the expansion of the network may lead to an increase in the number of global cities. The hypothesis is based on the premise that globalizing cities, driven by the improved network connectivity, can evolve into new global cities without replacing the old ones. The premise is true for now, considering the fact that some global cities, whose connectivity remains at the same level or is even slightly improved, slipped down the rankings relative to others. Obviously, this is not because they are replaced by new global cities, but because the overall connectivity of the WCN strengthened with more and more cities joining the network. From this perspective, with the expansion of the WCN, the number of global cities will increase, representing a major trend in their evolution.

9.1.4.2. Enhancing the Function of Global Cities as Nodes

In the next 30 years, due to the geographical imbalance of globalization, expansion of WCN and rise of new cities as nodes that connect business activities around the world will mainly be seen in developed countries, but it may occur in developing countries as well.

In the next 30 years, the WCN will be expanded in a way that still represents the geographical imbalance in the reach of globalization with more cities (both in developed and developing countries) rising as new nodes that connect business activities around the world.

The WCN expansion is characterized by the increase in overall connectivity, which is made possible by both the entrance of more cities into the network (i.e., additional network connectivity) and improved connectivity of current members of the network. Although the current WCN, especially the top part of its hierarchical structure, is already dominated by cities of developed countries, this does not mean that these cities won't expand further. On the contrary, since the beginning of the 21st century, the connectivity of these cities in the WCN has also been on the rise. The most typical example of such developed countries is the United Kingdom. London ranked the first in the measurement of GNCs in 2000, but it was the only UK city ranked in the top 100 (Beaverstock et al. 2001). However, the measurement in 2004 showed that some of the UK cities had undergone rapid growth in connectivity, the most impressive ones being Edinburgh, Bristol, Cardiff and Leeds (Taylor and Aranya 2006). The measurement in 2008 revealed that 17 UK cities 'have proportionate connectivities above 0.05—these measures show how well the different cities are integrated into the world city network (Taylor 2011b).... Among these cities, Manchester, Edinburgh and Birmingham each have at least one-fifth of the highest connectivity'. This means that 'UK cities right across the country have been integrated into the world city network to varying degrees', significantly improving the country's hierarchical structure of cities, which used to be dominated by London, despite the fact that the UK has yet to ensure balanced development of all cities economically. Similarly, cities of other developed countries in Europe are also experiencing further growth in network connectivity, and an urban area consisting of numerous cities is emerging in the inland of Europe.

This change did not lead to the decline in the position of the old global cities such as London as nodes, but instead has improved it. On the one hand, for global cities that are main nodes, as the density of the city network surrounding them increase, their connections will become more extensive (which means increased length of connectivity) and more frequent (which means increased density of connectivity), so that they will function better as nodes. On the other hand, when more and more cities emerge as nodes of the network around a global city, this urban area will expand into a global city region or MCR with this global city as the core, which will play a more important role in the network. Therefore, the progressing of globalization will further enhance the function of global cities as nodes and enable these cities to contribute even more in global resource allocation.

9.1.4.3. Growing Diversity amongst Global Cities

With the scope of globalization widening, globalization structures tend to be more complicated and diverse, accordingly with the nodes becoming diversified, more complicated and extending themselves within WCN. In the process, different types of city networks are going to take shape. Meanwhile, a great number of new global cities with the exception of economic function will come forth, including global cities dominated by culture, technology, media, education and global governance with new advantages in the future. Some original global cities will take new functions to be more comprehensive, and New York and London as the paradigmatic global cities obviously fall into this category. These two cities used to mainly take economic function but now become comprehensive global cities added with technological innovation and cultural functions. In addition, emerging global cities may have chances to directly transform into comprehensive global cities. Still, cities within different types of networks are, respectively, distributed and not connected closely enough, only leading to more major nodes growing in different networks. Viewed from the general evolution trend, specialized global cities will be mostly on rise rather than comprehensive cities. Therefore, further development of globalization will bring about more new global cites, especially those characterized with distinctive functions. The evolutionary path can signal a future direction of global cities development, which is the important way to boost more diverse global cities.

9.2. STRATEGIC OPPORTUNITIES: RESHAPING OF WORLD PATTERN

It is a ubiquitous phenomenon that the development of the world is imbalanced. This is a known factor amid the uncertainty of the future and will be profoundly reflected in the reshaping of world pattern. Great changes have taken place in the world pattern, which indicates that globalization flow may change its route and the world centre of gravity is shifting, structurally affecting and even determining the evolution of global cities. In other words, the reshaping will manifest future regional distribution and structural characteristics of the evolution of global cities and, thus, pass on the key message of the rise and decline of global cities in different countries or regions. In the process of great adjustment in world economy, former world pattern dominated by 'Northern Hemisphere' and driven by developed countries in Europe and America in a unipolar situation will be replaced by a new tendency of multi-polarity of growth with the global economy's centre of gravity shifting east. Admittedly, these new tendencies still face instability and uncertainties. To this end, we need to provide insights into whether these tendencies of new changes will remain in 30 years and how the world economic pattern will be changed.

9.2.1. Adjustment in Global Economic Landscape

9.2.1.1. Multi-Polarization of World Economic Growth

At the start of each long-term economic cycle, the world witnesses significant new changes, one of which is the collective rise of emerging economies with an increasingly vital role in the world economy, and the world economy is heading towards a multi-polarity of growth.

Emerging economies have made tremendous progress in the past 20 years and have rose as influential regional powerhouses. The share of emerging economies in global GDP rose from about 35 per cent in 1993 to about 50 per cent in 2013, contributing almost as much to global GDP growth as the developed countries of the Group of Seven (G7). Their holdings of foreign exchange reserves have increased from nearly one-half of developed countries in 2000 to about twice in 2015. In 2014, 10 of the 20 countries with the largest FDI in the world were emerging market countries. And FDI in emerging economies has also grown rapidly, with Brazil, China, India and Russia claiming $850 billion offshore investment capital. In addition, with emerging market countries accounting for the majority, the G20 have took over the management of the global financial system from the hands of the industrialized countries of G7. These emerging economies also play an important role in other global issues such as climate change, migration, human rights and intellectual property rights. In the context of the long downward wave of the world economy, the performance of emerging economies is not as 'eye catching' as in the past. Especially in recent years, emerging economies have experienced serious economic setbacks, including the slowdown of China's economic growth and even negative economic growth in Russia, Brazil and South Africa. Raising doubts about emerging economies has led to some assertions that the most dynamic growth periods in emerging market countries are coming to an end. The fate of emerging economies is a matter of interpretation related to the adjustment of world economic growth pattern, whether it will return to the traditional unipolar growth pattern or the ongoing multi-polar growth pattern. Therefore, this requires a basic study.

We believe it is a normal phenomenon that the economic growth remains sluggish and uneven in emerging economies in the context of the Global Financial Crisis and the feeble recovery of the world economy. Sharing the fate with many developed countries, emerging economies are unlikely to disengage from the increasingly turbulent global economy. In today's globalized world, a country's economy is highly integrated with others, which means emerging economies will inevitably be affected by the external impact of the Global Financial Crisis. Moreover, emerging economies themselves constitute an entire industrial chain in the very crisis and bothered by excess capacity too. From this point of view, emerging economies have to hedge against external shocks, including global demand reduction, trade protection, quantitative easing and other major impacts, and need to digest internal overcapacity, solve supply-side structural problems, but emerging economies are more fragile in terms of resistibility compared to developed countries. Under this circumstance, the function of emerging economies as global 'economic engine' is bound to be greatly weakened, with their economic growth rates even be zero or negative that clearly contrasts with the past. However, this is a 'temporary problem' and cannot be used as a basis to mark the end of the era of emerging economies. Although the current growth of emerging economies is not as conspicuous as it used to be, overall, the rising trend of emerging economies in the global economic landscape has not been fundamentally reversed. As is estimated by the IMF, the average annual growth rate of GDP in new economies, whose share of the global economy will increase to 55.1 per cent, will reach about 5.9 per cent during 2013 and 2018, much higher than the growth rate (2.3%) in developed economies. More importantly, new economies are resilient, many of which not only survived two major financial crises (the Asian Financial Crisis in 1998 and the Global Financial Crisis in 2008) but also grew stronger afterwards as they learned from the crises and adjusted their policies accordingly, taking positive measures such as turning to a flexible exchange rate system resistant to the effect of speculation or adapting prudent debt management policies to reduce bankruptcies. From a profounder perspective, the formation and rise of new economies are not the result of 'random factors' but based on some deeper rules of history. The first one is the pendulum theory that development centre is moving southwards and eastwards; the second is a new round of the Kondratiev cycle. New economies, which have undergone deeper structural adjustments during the crisis, will resume great energy and power as the world economy greets a long-term upturn.

Therefore, the time for new economies is still at its early stage with great development potential rather than approaching towards the end. McKinsey predicts that by 2025 the number of consumers in the world will increase by 1.8 billion to 4.2 billion with a total consumption capacity of 64 trillion dollars, nearly half of which will be contributed by new economies (Figure 9.1). By then, new economies will become important producers and consumers for global goods, services, capitals, human resources and data. Currently, there are about 8,000 large corporations around the world whose annual revenue is over 1 billion dollars; by 2025, according to McKinsey, the number will increase by 7,000, with the total revenue doubled to 130 trillion dollars. One of the greatest changes is that 70 per cent of these new corporations are going to be located in new economies. That is to say, about 4,800 large corporations are expected to be introduced into new economies, which will bring along more decision-making, capital and innovation (Figure 9.1). By then, the number of large corporations in new economies will probably be tripled or more, rising from the current 2,000 to about 7,000 by 2025. Large corporations in new economies will take

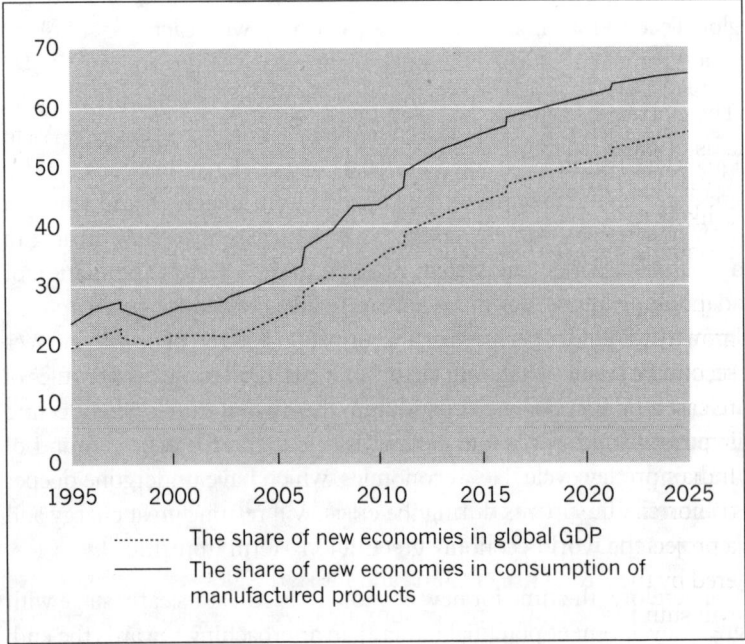

Figure 9.1 *The Share of New Economies in Global GDP and Consumption*

Source: McKinsey Global Institute.

up 46 per cent of the total large corporations in the world in 2025, compared with 27 per cent in 2010; meanwhile, their proportion in the global revenue will increase from 24 per cent to 46 per cent. This means the number of the HQs of MNCs controlled by new economies will quickly approach that of developed Western countries, among which the number of those controlled by China will very likely exceed Japan and Europe, only next to America.

In the next 30 years, while America will still remain an important pole in the world economy, it will no longer play a dominant role in the world economy, and a pattern in which America must work with great powers like China on major issues of the world will, hence, take shape. The EU could still be a pole in the world economy if it still unites as a whole at that time, but its influence will not increase greatly. New economies represented by China and India, as a whole, will increasingly improve their influence on the world affairs and economy.

9.2.1.2. Shift of the World's Economic Centre of Gravity

The global economic order has been going through big changes as the axis of global economic and geopolitical powers is shifting from the West to the East and from the Global North to the Global South and is likely to keep drifting. Asia is expected to witness the world's fastest economic growth, with East Asia contributing the most.

Looking forward, China and Japan are projected to lead global growth in 2050 and, respectively, become the world's largest and second largest economy. According to a report titled 'World in 2050' released in 2015 by the consulting firm PwC, China's projected GDP in purchasing power parity (PPP) terms will amount to US$61 trillion. India's projected GDP will rise to US$17 trillion in 2030 from US$7 trillion in 2014, and overtake America (US$41 trillion) in 2050 with a projected GDP of US$42 trillion. It is obviously observed that, powered by the strong rise of China and India, the global economic power will shift to Asia. More projections about Asia's economic growth are made: Indonesia could become the fourth largest economy in 2050 with a projected GDP of US$12 trillion, up from the ninth in 2014; Pakistan could move from the 25th to the 15th with a projected GDP

Table 9.3 Projections for Asia Economic Growth and Its Share of the World's GDP in 2050

	2010	2020	2030	2040	2050
Global output (market exchange rates, USD trillions)	62	90	132	195	292
Asian share of global output (%)	27.4	33.5	38.9	44.5	50.6
Global growth (%)	–	4.0	3.9	3.8	3.6
Asia growth (%)	–	5.8	5.2	4.8	4.4
Asian share of global growth (%)		55.7	59.3	62.8	66.0
Global GDP per capita (PPP)	10,700	14,300	19,400	26,600	36,600
Asian GDP per capita (PPP)	6,600	10,600	16,500	25,400	38,600

Source: Asian Development Bank (2011).

of US$4 trillion in 2050; the Philippines could move from the 28th to the 20th with US$3.5 trillion; Thailand to the 21st; Bangladesh from the 31st to the 23rd and Malaysia from the 27th to the 24th. However, some countries may witness falls: Japan could fall from the 4th to the 7th; South Korea from the 13th to the 17th and Australia from the 19th to the 28th. As projected in 'Asia 2050: Realizing the Asian Century', a report issued by Asian Development Bank in 2011, Asia will account for 36 per cent of the global GDP, more than 50 per cent of the global output and 50 per cent of the global trade and investment in 2030. By 2050, the Asian GDP per capita will have reached US$38,600, overtaking the global GDP per capita of US$36,600 (Table 9.3).

It should be noted that these are mere projections for linear trend and can only make sense on condition that low- or middle-income countries can keep benefiting from the export-oriented development mode, which worked well in the past mostly thanks to (a) a larger number of consumers in developed countries and (b) its own cost advantages as well as spillover effects generated by the investment from developed economies. However, the fact is that the first condition has been reversed. A decade ago, the total population of Japan, South

Korea and the Taiwan region of China was only about 150 million, while the developed economies had a total population of around 400 million. But now, the developed economies have only 1 billion or so consumers, while the population of developing countries in East Asia totals about 2 billion. As for the second condition, it remains true for today but may well face changes. For example, the technological development, including the invention of industrial robots and 3D printing, is expected to change the way of products manufacturing and value creation and alter the basic cost structure of production, which will reform the way to gain added value and profits. As a result, MNCs in developed countries may adjust the layout of their production network by, for example, bringing back jobs in manufacturing, which will be a huge threat to the cost advantages owned by developing countries in East Asia. Hence, the linear inference, based on previous data about the global and regional economic growth, will not be quite accurate when it comes to predicting the future geopolitical power of Asia. In addition, Asia itself had many drawbacks or risks that may hinder its development: failure of economic reforms in some countries, falling into the middle-income trap, population aging, reduced economic vitality or even stagnant economic growth, political upheavals, institutional difficulties in handing common problems faced by different countries and possibility of starting wars.

But we don't believe it to be 'the end of the Asian century' as framed by Auslin (2017). Excluding those unpredictable factors like war, several prominent but foreseeable elements will also bring us to the conclusion that the world's economic centre of gravity is moving eastwards to Asia: (a) the population of Asia may increase by 3 billion in 2050, making it home to the largest fraction of global residents; (b) Asia is projected to witness remarkable development in urbanization and may report an estimated 65 per cent of urban dwellers in 2050; (c) the middle class is expected to grow most rapidly in Asia. According to the OECD, the size of global middle class (defined as households with daily expenditures between US$10 and US$100 per person in 2005 PPP terms) is predicted to increase from 1.8 billion in 2009 to 4.9 billion in 2030. By then, Asia will represent two-thirds of the global middle-class population, compared to 28 per cent in 2009;

(d) Asia is expected to be the biggest consumer market across the world. Not only will it accommodate two-thirds of the global middle class but also more than 60 per cent of the 1.7 billion wealthiest residents in the world by 2030. Capitalizing on these opportunities, Asia can be thoroughly transformed into a motor of consumption from a global manufacturing centre that it was previously known for, and a retail market worth US$7 trillion; (e) Asia will develop into a region with the most global capital deposit. In the upcoming several decades, Asia could contribute to nearly 45 per cent of the net increase in global capital deposit, and meanwhile significantly stimulate the absolute increase in its own capital deposit, accounting for approximately three quarters of the global share before 2050. Moreover, Asia has the most comprehensively distributed and organically connected network of global supply chain, which features a high level of economic coordination among its members. The interdependence of these Asian economies is primarily reinforced through the global trading system instead of the bilateral or regional trade arrangements.

It is worth pointing out that, in spite of past practices, the economic centre of gravity may not be closely associated with the distribution of economic benefits any more in the future. In other words, the eastward movement of the world's economic centre of gravity, under certain circumstances in a given time, may not be accompanied with the transfer of scientific and technological R&D capabilities or economic dominance. We believe that today's developed countries will remain to be in a dominant position in terms of technology and economy in the next 30 years, yet leading to an inconsistence between the shift of economic centre of gravity and the transfer of the two capabilities. The economic growth rate of these developed countries and regions may not be very high, but with their advanced technologies and economic dominance, they could receive extra economic benefits generated by the core regions of economic development. Such a pattern, where economic growth centre does not bring economic dominance, may constitute an important factor in world economic structure reshaping in the future. In this sense, the global economy of the next 30 years could not be summarized as 'Asianized'. Certainly, this pattern is not stable and will inevitably transition into a more stable one where economic growth, scientific and technological innovation, and economic system and rulemaking share the same core and, thus, feature a consistent pattern of benefits distribution.

9.2.2. Changes of World Cities Pattern

The 21st century is referred to as an urban century, because the large-scale urbanization not only has brought profound changes in production mode and living styles to a large part of the world's population, what's more, it also brought connections of larger scales among world cities, which indicates a significant change of world city relations. Therefore, the fact that there is an internal relation among the development trend of world cities, the WCN and the evolution of global cities is an important background for studying the evolution of global cities in the future.

9.2.2.1. World Urbanization

By 2008, more than half the world's population, or about 3.3 billion people, were living in towns and cities, which symbolizes a significant transformation of the world development in the 21st century. As humanity's 'greatest invention' (Glaeser 2011), cities enable people to become smart by learning from other smart people (Glaeser 2010), they unleash human potentials with results that can be best described as extraordinary (Taylor 2013). This is a consequence of unparalleled communication densities within and between cities, or again quoting Glaeser (2011), cities speed innovation by connecting their smart inhabitants to each other. Therefore, urbanization is of great significance in human history.

In the following 30 years, the world will urbanize more rapidly, and more people will choose to move from rural areas to urban areas. UNFPA (2007) predicts that by 2030, towns and cities will be home to almost 5 billion people, over two-thirds of the world's population. By 2050, the urban population is due almost to double (UNDP 2009), and to make up around 70 per cent of the total world population, shaping the world into a world of cities, among which the urbanization rate of most areas in Northern Hemisphere would reach 84 per cent at least, Africa 62 per cent and Asia 65 per cent. By 2015, although developed countries still lead the rate of urbanization, most of this urban growth, including but not limited to that driven by population growth, will be concentrated in developing countries in the following 30 years, especially in Asia and Africa. To be specific, Africa is expected to increase by 40–60 per cent, China and Nigeria combined are expected to account for 37 per cent of this global increase by 2050. India will add 404 million urban citizens, China 292 million and Nigeria 212 million.

Another feature of the urbanization around the world is that megacities, metropolitan areas with a total population of 10 million or more people, spring up like mushrooms, whose number has increased from 10 in 1990 to 28 currently, with 16 in Asia. Urbanization, a kind of special restructuring, is the final chapter in developed countries while an ongoing process in developing countries. The Asia-Pacific region, especially China, has long time witnessed income gaps between urban and rural dwellers, namely the so-called urban–rural gap. As working in urban areas can significantly improve one's living, it marks the best way of getting out of poverty; thus, moving from rural areas to cities, especially megacities, becomes a main solution to shake off poverty. It is for this reason that domestic migration is still one of the important features of developing countries like China.

9.2.2.2. Urban Space Restructuring

Global urbanization is usually considered as a mere phenomenon of rising urban population. However, the world has been trending towards globalization and informatization since the late 20th century, which restructured the urban space for human beings to live in, giving global urbanization a new connotation.

First of all, cities are becoming increasingly important as social and economic entities interacting with each other globally. Although there are speculations about the 'death of distance' (Cairncross 1997), technological development continues to make cities more significant as a location for economic activities. As Kay (2001) said, we are told again and again that geography is no longer important, but it will exert a great impact on the purpose and function of cities, which are dominant by the ever-growing population as the centre of modern economy. Besides, serving as the strategic location for the development of advanced service economy, cities provide the space for the decentralization of population generated by technology. 'In a globalized world where capital and the growing population move freely, only social capital is still bound within a specific location'.

Second, cities across the world are undergoing globalization in their development. In the process, more cities are becoming 'well connected' in global economy and upgrading their 'WCN' connectivity, because without connectivity to the WCN, even megacities are unsustainable socially, politically and environmentally (Segbers 2007), thus becoming the location of the world's poorest expanding population. Currently, commercial organizations in the urban network has created specialized knowledge-intensive jobs, facilitating the connection and flows of business among different cities. It has been a key issue concerning city development and of pivotal importance for both developed and developing countries to support the national economy in a more extensive location. Therefore, as more cities begin to upgrade their global service connectivity, some major cities in the world are undergoing the restructuring of their urban space, indicating a new performance of city development.

In the next three decades, as the world economic pattern changes profoundly due to the shift of the world economic centre, subsets of the WCN may vary in two major characteristics. On the one hand, connection areas in the urban network will further to concentrate in the Asia-Pacific region, which will weaken the function of the core region in Western Europe. In the case of the leading economies of the Asia-Pacific region, the major command and control functions are concentrated in the Beijing–Shanghai–Hong Kong triad in China (Lin 2004), the Tokyo–Osaka–Nagoya triad in Japan (Hill and Fujita 1995) and the Mumbai–New Delhi–Kolkata triad in India (Panagariya 2008). By contrast, the European Union is bipolar due to the dominant position of the London–Paris city pair (Halbert and Pain 2009). On the other hand, more scattered nodes will be integrated into small groups of global cities. Besides, more city nodes will spring up during the rapid development of the emerging economies, such as 'CIVETS' and 'Next-11'. Their integrations with the original scattered nodes will expand the connection areas of the city network, thus diversifying the geographical distribution of subsets of the WCN.

9.2.3. World System Reconstruction

Wallerstein (2004) describes the modern world system as a space economy based upon a core–periphery division of labour that is reflected in the distribution of power in the interstate system. As globalization process and new technologies develop and national economic strength adjusts, the world system dominated by developed economies is tending to be oscillated and disintegrated, leading to a new world system reconstruction process.

9.2.3.1. New World Order

In the existing world system, the international order defined in 1945 was based on a hierarchy determined by the prevailing powers after the Second World War and a code of conduct established by nations at the top of the hierarchy. This world order is currently subject to the major impacts from all sides. First, increasing new roles in the globalization process are emerging, and gradually getting involved in the impact. Second, the scale and speed of the redistribution of economic strength among major powers may be unprecedented in history, especially after the 2008 financial crisis. Moreover, new technologies not only empower small organizations and individuals but also multiply the power of non-state actors, so as to further weaken the country's monopoly on violence. The formation of a multi-polar world has the potential to break the old world order. There is growing evidence that emerging countries will become important players and developers of international rules.

It is certain that the differentiation and restructuring of developing countries have also developed significantly, making them less capable of accumulating power as a whole. In many worldwide dialogues and interests, the interests cannot always be brought together, and presented at the same position, which weakens the influence of developing countries to a certain extent and makes their position in the world economic structure not substantially improved as expected. Even the BRICS countries are currently uncertain and unclear that unite countries and promote close proximity to each other thanks to the huge differences in their economic development levels and directions, and the lack of common political and economic factors. However, once the BRICS countries become the main core of the world today, the international order will undergo a fundamental change and move in a positive direction. This is because the BRICS countries are not five separate countries; on the contrary, they are emerging powers with unique cultural backgrounds, representing the five major civilizations. Unlike the rise of the USA and Germany in the 19th century, today's emerging powers have civilizations that are completely new to the West, among which some countries have thousands of years of cultural continuity. This cultural factor will lead to 'unknown unknowns', because between the West and the East, the North and the South, different nations have a preference for different realities. In a sense, the impact of today's power transfer is much more complicated than the transfer of power that had shattered geopolitical patterns 100 years ago.

It is foreseeable that in the next few decades, global power and presence will continue to dilute, so that there will be less concentration of power, but greater cooperation and dialogue on a global scale will become even more necessary. This will lead to more equal exchanges, closer political, economic and cultural relations and more free dissemination of ideas between the West and the East, the North and the South, along with partnerships rather than hegemonism. We predict that the next 30 years will be an era in which the world's various power relations are greatly adjusted, and major checks and balances are created to create a new pattern and order. An upcoming new world order will tend to strengthen partnerships, increase economic exchanges, avoid wars in major powers and provide a political foundation for human freedom.

9.2.3.2. The Revolution of the Global Governance System

The current global governance system is a modern spatial organization between countries at local levels on the premise of spatial consistency within national boundaries. That is to say, modern governance is to integrate politics, economy, culture and society into 'national state' with a view to create national economy, culture and society that are managed by national government. The national state with spatial consistency provides a thorough solution to the problems faced by governance: the differentiated process is packaged into certain manageable units. These basic governance units are eager to control the flows at their borders, while the states negotiate the cross-border flows in international relations. Therefore, such global governance is essentially to adapt the flows to region.

In the next 30 years, the increased role of cities and the active participation of many NGOs will be important factors in the revolution of the global governance system. With the development of globalization, the sense of belonging in sovereign countries will gradually weaken. On the one hand, globalization has further promoted the individual empowerment, the governing bodies have become more diversified and the world has moved towards polycentric governance. The development and popularization of technology have greatly increased the ability of individuals, groups and organizations, which has attacked the monopoly of the country. On the other hand, globalization has also exacerbated some small problems, leading to the so-called 'gap of rule', namely the distance between the target of the governing body and its mobility poses the question of whether the ability of the state to rule is reliable. In fact, the MNC can be seen as the first continuous 'offense' against the national state since it appeared 100 years ago, allowing the world to enter an era where the most powerful law is supply and demand rather than sovereignty. The establishment of the UN in 1945 marked the beginning of an era in which national sovereignty get weakened by global organizations, because the UN and 'international law' could persuade a particular country to act in accordance with rules set by other countries. So far, a large number of NGOs have joined this trend. Of course, this phenomenon will never reduce the importance of the country. Because national sovereignty is unshakable currently, other bodies cannot have the resources and integration capability that the state has. Moreover, the big problems across national borders need each country to solve, respectively. But in such process, more NGOs will participate in the global governance to improve global standards and rules such as the cooperation between governments and NGOs in the fields of accounting, auditing and insurance. With the deepening of interactions between countries, we will see more and more cooperation between governments and NGOs to improve global standards in a wide range of fields such as environment, safety and health.

In addition, with the rise of networked society, the global governance system will be network oriented, and this new way for promoting the transition of global governance, known as the networked global governance, is a system for the space of flows based on spatial inconsistency, featuring multilevels, multi-organizations and multi-sectors. For example, the networks for diplomacy, the UN and the NGOs are political networks at international, supranational and transnational levels, respectively. Although these networks all have contributed to the establishment of modern politics, they are greatly different. The supranational and transnational networks can not only improve the existing political system but also destroy it. Apart from that, these networks operate through cities in different continents, which means those that used to operate only through capital cities of countries are being replaced by networks operating through diversified cities, as they can overlap the sub-nets in global networks. In stark contrast to the competitive (realism-based) international relations, the current networked global governance is characterized by cooperative (interrelation-based) intercity relations, which, totally different from those relying on the modern regional spatial organizations that operate through systems at the national level, is what can substantially promote the global governance in the future. It is worth studying the issue on how to build the global governance network and establish a supportive intercity relation through connectivity based on the space of flows across cities in the 21st century.

Another trend for the development of global governance system is to focus more on the governance in particular regions, which might lead to various regional governance models. Although global governance mechanisms based on multilateral consultations still exist and will continue to play an important role, with the development of worldwide regionalization, regional governance will become increasingly significant and prominent. The European Union, a typical example of regional governance, has established its own governance model, which might not be suitable to be applied to regions elsewhere as they have different paths for future development, but each region will certainly find a model that suits itself. This is especially true in Asia, which is likely to create a new model of world governance. With the rise of emerging economies such as China and India, there is no doubt that the international order in the Asia-Pacific region, which was based on the free trade system and dominated by the USA, will finally change. This will make it possible for bilateral relations to develop in multiple ways so that each party can exert its competence to the fullest without damaging the interest of the other. Striking a balance between cooperation and competition will be the new quest in the long run. Though hard to maintain, a balanced relation might be the lasting solution for global governance because this is a model that encourages close proximity without integration and cooperation without alignment, and it may be the model of governance for Asia in the 21st century.

9.3. THE RISE OF CHINA AS STRATEGIC SUPPORT

Although the influence of global cities has gone beyond the boundaries in the globalized world, they belong to their own nation states under restrictions as a result of the system development and spatial evolution of the countries where they are located, following the rules of public institutions within the national territory. Therefore, the form of a global city depends greatly on what role the country plays in globalization and its geopolitical and geo-economic power.

9.3.1. China's Role in Global Economy

As a new power with great economic strength, China has become the world's second largest economy with profound global influence and has shifted its role from a participant to a leader in globalization, offering a platform and strategic support for Shanghai to rise and evolve into a global city.

China is the world's second largest economy, but its per capita income remains below the global average. Whether China can overcome the middle-income trap, continue to show supernormal growth potential or achieve sustainable growth and join the ranks of high-income countries as the world's largest economy in next three decades is the key success factor that determines if it can realize the 'Chinese Dream'. According to the theory of economic convergence, theoretically China's low GDP per capita indicates supernormal growth potential in economic growth. But certainly, some related variables are likely to change in the next 30 years, among which the higher costs, changes in demand and environmental protection are rather common with less impact on the economic growth, while the changes in capital deposit, population and labour force (such as the population size and the trend of aging) and total factor productivity (TFP) are the engines powering China's economy. My research team has projected the potential of China's economy growth in the next 30 years by analysing the data of the dominant variables mentioned earlier. A similar research was conducted by Shanghai Development and Strategy Research Center with Dr Daming Zhu as the lead author.

We use models of Grey system theory to project how China's capital deposit will change in the next 30 years (Figure 9.2). To ensure reliability of data, two different methods were adopted: (a) the differences

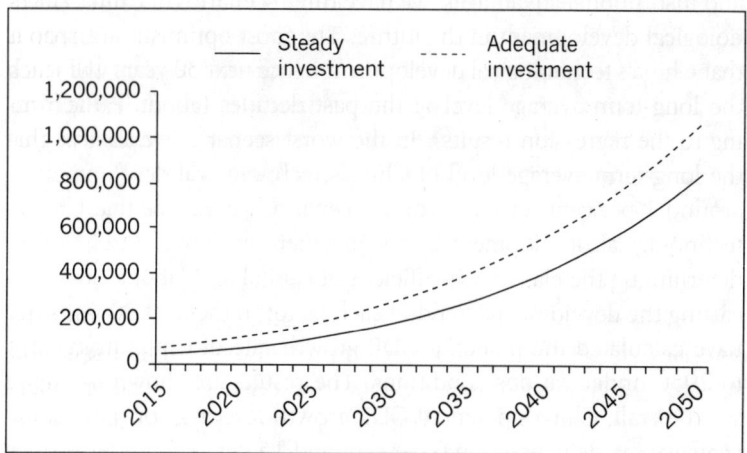

Figure 9.2 *Projection of China's Capital Deposit in the Next 30 Years (in Billions of RMB)*

Source: Compiled by author and his research team.
Note: The data and analysis are derived from the research project China Economic Growth Prediction in the Next 30 Years funded by Shanghai Development Strategy Research Institute and lead by Dr Daming Zhu.

of annual capital deposit from 1993 to 1998 are used as initial values and the result shows a steady investment; (b) the differences of annual capital deposit from 2008 to 2013 are used as initial values and the result shows a sufficient investment.

Inspired by Men Kepei (2004), we use the same method based on Grey system theory to project the population of China by 2050 and the result indicates that China (excluding Hong Kong, Macau and Taiwan) will witness a steady population growth in the next few decades. Despite the slowdown in population growth, the population policies will be optimized and China's population is expected to reach 1.4 billion by 2020 and 1.45 billion by 2030 and steadily increase to 1.6 billion by 2050 (Table 9.4).

The projection shows that though China's total population is likely to grow at a steady pace over the next 30 years, the employment-to-population ratio is likely to decline, and may even fall below 50 per cent by 2050 (Figure 9.3), close to the employment-to-population ratio in 2014 or so. Considering China's late developing advantages and institutional advantages, we have three scenarios of China's technological development in the future. The most optimistic scenario is that China's technological development in the next 30 years will reach the long-term average level of the past decades (about 3% according to the regression results). In the worst scenario, we assume that the long-term average level of China's technological development is around 1 per cent. In the medium scenario, we assume that China's technological development falls somewhere in between (2%). After determining the elasticity coefficient of capital and labour, and forecasting the development trend of each factor in the next 30 years, we have calculated the potential GDP growth rate of China from 2015 to 2050 under various conditions. The results are shown in Figure 9.4. Overall, China's potential GDP growth forecasts for the next 30 years vary widely, between 6 per cent and 15 per cent, under various assumptions (Figure 9.4). Assuming that the annual growth of TFP remains stable, the potential growth range of GDP is between 6.18 per cent and 9.04 per cent. But, in general, with weakening institutional advantages in China and uncertainty about technological development, the annual growth rate of TFP will decline, similar to what happened in the USA in the 1980s. The annual growth rate of TFP is likely to

Table 9.4 China's Total Population Forecast for the Next 30 Years (Unit: 10,000)

Year	Prediction 1	Prediction 2	Prediction 3	Year	Prediction 1	Prediction 2	Prediction 3
2003	129,207			2027	136,711	145,888	147,818
2004	129,909			2028	136,792	146,611	148,834
2005	130,557			2029	136,865	147,336	149,877
2006	131,154			2030	136,931	148,065	150,947
2007	131,704			2031	136,990	148,797	152,045
2008	132,212			2032	137,043	149,532	153,171
2009	132,679			2033	137,090	150,270	154,326
2010	133,108			2034	137,133	151,012	155,511
2011	133,502			2035	137,171	151,756	156,726
2012	133,865			2036	137,206	152,504	157,973
2013	134,197			2037	137,236	153,254	159,250
2014	134,502			2038	137,263	154,008	160,560
2015	134,780	137,443	137,499	2039	137,287	154,765	161,903
2016	135,035	138,135	138,237	2040	137,309	155,525	163,280
2017	135,268	138,827	138,996	2041	137,328	156,289	164,691
2018	135,481	139,521	139,779	2042	137,345	157,055	166,138

(Continued)

(Continued)

Year	Prediction 1	Prediction 2	Prediction 3	Year	Prediction 1	Prediction 2	Prediction 3
2019	135,675	140,211	140,578	2043	137,360	157,825	167,620
2020	135,852	140,915	141,402	2044	137,373	158,598	169,139
2021	136,013	141,615	142,248	2045	137,385	159,375	170,695
2022	136,160	142,319	143,117	2046	137,395	160,154	172,290
2023	136,293	143,027	144,008	2047	137,404	160,937	173,923
2024	136,413	143,738	144,924	2048	137,412	161,723	175,597
2025	136,523	144,451	145,863	2049	137,418	162,512	177,310
2026	136,622	145,168	146,828	2050	137,424	163,305	179,066

Source: Compiled by author and his research team.

Note: The data and analysis are derived from the research project China Economic Growth Prediction in the Next 30 Years funded by Shanghai Development Strategy Research Institute and lead by Dr Daming Zhu.

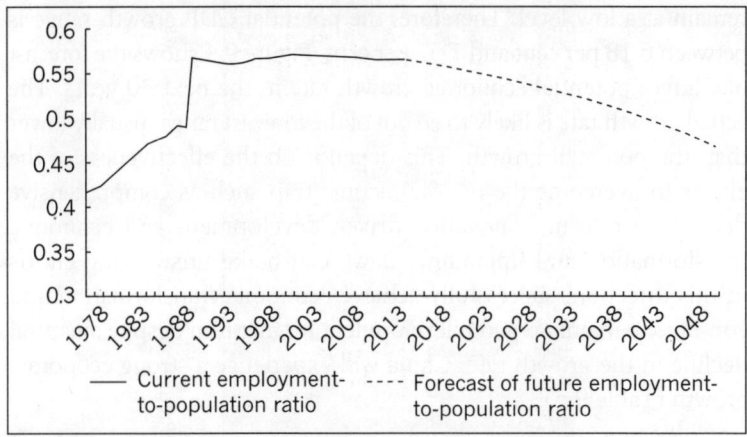

Figure 9.3 *China's Employed Population Forecast for the Next 30 Years*

Source: Compiled by author and his research team.
Note: The data and analysis are derived from the research project China Economic Growth Prediction in the Next 30 Years funded by Shanghai Development Strategy Research Institute and lead by Dr Daming Zhu.

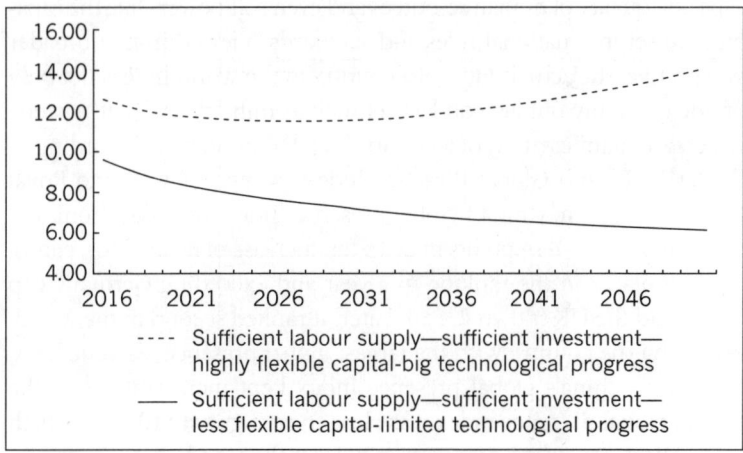

Figure 9.4 *Forecast of China's Potential Economic Growth Rate in the Next 30 Years (Unit: 10,000)*

Source: Compiled by author and his research team.
Note: The data and analysis are derived from the research project China Economic Growth Prediction in the Next 30 Years funded by Shanghai Development Strategy Research Institute and lead by Dr Daming Zhu.

remain at a low level. Therefore, the potential GDP growth range is between 6.18 per cent and 7.57 per cent. Figure 9.4 shows the forecast of China's potential economic growth rate in the next 30 years. The actual growth rate is likely to go out of the forecast range, usually lower than the potential growth. This depends on the effectiveness of the efforts to overcome the middle-income trap such as comprehensive deepening reform, innovation-driven development and economic transformation and upgrading. If we can make unswerving efforts in this direction, successfully achieve economic transformation and continue to maintain good development momentum despite a natural decline in the growth rate, China will experience a strong economic growth (Table 9.5).

China will become the world's biggest economy in the next 30 years, which will bring a significant impact to the world. However, being the largest economy does not necessarily mean being the strongest. The economic strength of a country is not only based on the size of economy but also depends on strengths in technologies and finance, competitiveness of industries and enterprises, global resource allocation capacity, quality of human resources and even soft powers like the capability to set international rules and standards. Viewed from a broader perspective, the actual status of a country in the world hinges not only on the economy but also on factors such as military and soft powers, which are manifestation of a country's global influence. According to the '2016 Elcano Global Presence Index', a report by Elcano Royal Institute of Spain, China's global presence index increased from 387 points in 2014 to 414 points in 2015 (an increase of nearly 7%), climbing two places in the ranking in a year and exceeding Germany (up 2.5%) and the UK (down 2.4%). Later, it ranked second in the world, becoming the country with the largest global presence after the USA. Moreover, China's global presence index kept increasing when the overall global presence index was close to zero growth (0.4%), which fully reflects its strong momentum against the trend.

In terms of global influence, there is still a big gap between China and the USA (the global presence index exceeded 1,098 points). It is even more so when taking a closer look at the composition of their global influence, since China is heavily biased towards economic factors. As China's economic growth shifted its mode, its growth rate will

Table 9.5 Forecast of China's Economic Growth Rate (%)

Year	Sufficient Labour Supply—Sufficient Investment—Highly Flexible Capital			Sufficient Labour Supply—Sufficient Investment—Less Flexible Capital			Insufficient Labour Supply—Sufficient Investment—Highly Flexible Capital			Insufficient Labour Supply—Sufficient Investment—Less Flexible Capital		
	TFP (1%)	TFP (2%)	TFP (3%)	TFP (1%)	TFP (2%)	TFP (3%)	TFP (1%)	TFP (2%)	TFP (3%)	TFP (1%)	TFP (2%)	TFP (3%)
2016	10.29	11.40	12.52	9.50	10.60	11.71	9.13	10.22	11.33	8.41	9.50	10.60
2017	10.00	11.14	12.31	9.23	10.36	11.53	9.07	10.19	11.36	8.35	9.47	10.63
2018	9.72	10.89	12.12	8.98	10.14	11.36	9.00	10.16	11.38	8.29	9.44	10.66
2019	9.45	10.66	11.94	8.74	9.93	11.21	8.93	10.13	11.41	8.22	9.41	10.68
2020	9.24	10.48	11.82	8.54	9.77	11.11	8.86	10.09	11.44	8.16	9.38	10.71
2021	9.04	10.31	11.72	8.36	9.62	11.02	8.79	10.06	11.46	8.09	9.35	10.75
2022	8.85	10.15	11.63	8.19	9.48	10.95	8.72	10.02	11.50	8.03	9.32	10.78
2023	8.68	10.02	11.56	8.03	9.37	10.90	8.65	9.99	11.53	7.96	9.29	10.82
2024	8.53	9.90	11.52	7.90	9.26	10.87	8.58	9.95	11.57	7.89	9.26	10.86
2025	8.38	9.80	11.48	7.76	9.17	10.85	8.51	9.92	11.61	7.83	9.23	10.91
2026	8.25	9.70	11.46	7.64	9.09	10.84	8.43	9.89	11.66	7.76	9.21	10.96
2027	8.13	9.62	11.46	7.53	9.02	10.85	8.36	9.86	11.71	7.69	9.18	11.01
2028	8.01	9.55	11.47	7.43	8.95	10.87	8.29	9.83	11.76	7.63	9.16	11.07

(Continued)

(Continued)

Year	Sufficient Labour Supply—Sufficient Investment—Highly Flexible Capital			Sufficient Labour Supply—Sufficient Investment—Less Flexible Capital			Insufficient Labour Supply—Sufficient Investment—Highly Flexible Capital			Insufficient Labour Supply—Sufficient Investment—Less Flexible Capital		
	TFP (1%)	TFP (2%)	TFP (3%)	TFP (1%)	TFP (2%)	TFP (3%)	TFP (1%)	TFP (2%)	TFP (3%)	TFP (1%)	TFP (2%)	TFP (3%)
2029	7.91	9.48	11.49	7.33	8.90	10.90	8.23	9.81	11.82	7.56	9.13	11.14
2030	7.81	9.42	11.52	7.24	8.85	10.94	8.16	9.78	11.88	7.50	9.11	11.21
2031	7.71	9.37	11.56	7.16	8.81	10.99	8.09	9.76	11.95	7.44	9.10	11.28
2032	7.62	9.33	11.62	7.08	8.78	11.05	8.02	9.74	12.03	7.38	9.08	11.36
2033	7.54	9.29	11.68	7.00	8.75	11.12	7.96	9.72	12.11	7.32	9.07	11.45
2034	7.46	9.26	11.75	6.93	8.72	11.20	7.90	9.70	12.20	7.26	9.06	11.54
2035	7.39	9.24	11.83	6.87	8.70	11.29	7.83	9.69	12.29	7.20	9.05	11.64
2036	7.32	9.21	11.92	6.80	8.69	11.38	7.77	9.68	12.39	7.15	9.04	11.74
2037	7.25	9.20	12.02	6.74	8.68	11.49	7.71	9.67	12.50	7.09	9.03	11.85
2038	7.19	9.19	12.13	6.69	8.67	11.60	7.65	9.66	12.61	7.04	9.03	11.97
2039	7.13	9.18	12.24	6.63	8.67	11.72	7.60	9.66	12.73	6.98	9.03	12.09
2040	7.07	9.18	12.37	6.58	8.68	11.85	7.54	9.66	12.86	6.93	9.03	12.22
2041	7.02	9.18	12.50	6.53	8.68	11.99	7.49	9.66	13.00	6.88	9.04	12.36

2042	6.96	9.18	12.64	6.48	8.69	12.14	7.43	9.66	13.14	6.83	9.05	12.51
2043	6.91	9.19	12.80	6.44	8.70	12.30	7.38	9.67	13.29	6.78	9.06	12.66
2044	6.87	9.20	12.96	6.40	8.72	12.46	7.33	9.67	13.45	6.74	9.07	12.82
2045	6.82	9.22	13.13	6.36	8.74	12.63	7.28	9.69	13.61	6.69	9.08	12.99
2046	6.78	9.23	13.31	6.32	8.76	12.82	7.23	9.70	13.79	6.65	9.10	13.17
2047	6.74	9.26	13.49	6.28	8.79	13.01	7.18	9.72	13.97	6.60	9.12	13.35
2048	6.70	9.28	13.69	6.25	8.82	13.21	7.42	10.02	14.46	6.82	9.41	13.82
2049	6.66	9.31	13.90	6.21	8.85	13.42	7.11	9.78	14.39	6.54	9.19	13.77
2050	6.62	9.34	14.12	6.18	8.89	13.64	7.57	10.32	15.13	6.96	9.68	14.47

Source: Compiled by author and his research team.

Note: The data and analysis are derived from the research project China Economic Growth Prediction in the Next 30 Years funded by Shanghai Development Strategy Research Institute and lead by Dr Daming Zhu.

slow down, and accordingly its supportive influence on China's global existence index will weaken, which means that China's global influence in the future will be more soft power oriented. At present, China's soft power is obviously a 'short slab' compared with its economic power. However, China still has great potential in tourism, sports, culture, education, science, technology, cooperation and development, which will lead to a strong momentum of development. For instance, according to the China's national development plan, it aims to establish a national innovation system with Chinese characteristics and become an innovation-driven country by 2020, and fundamentally change its mode of development and become one of the most innovative countries by 2030, and become a great power of science and technology innovation and a major hub of science and innovation platform by 2050. It is predictable that in the next 30 years, as China's soft power continues to rise, its global influence will be further expanded. Not only will it remain in the second place in the world but it would also narrow the gap with the USA.

In addition to the prospect of becoming the world's largest economy with enhanced global presence, China is expected to undertake and cement a leading role, gradually yet steadily, in the new stage of globalization in the next three decades, notably through its Belt and Road Initiative (BRI). With the potential to become the largest economic development project in the world, the BRI involves numerous extensive investment programmes for infrastructure construction and industry park development that will create enormous job opportunities and is, thus, likely to boost and revitalize business and trade in almost every sector in the countries and regions along the BRI routes. BRI will have a knock-on effect, giving new impetus to the global economy and offering new business and industry models, discoveries, ideas, inventions and cultures. Once completed, the BRI areas will become the world's largest economic corridor connecting Asia, Europe and Africa that covers a population of 4.4 billion and an economic output of US$21 trillion, accounting for 63 per cent and 29 per cent of the world's total, respectively. It may redefine the strategic and economic landscape across the Eurasia and Indian Ocean, which virtually means a revolutionary change in the global economic map. Meanwhile, with a network linking the major civilizations across the globe, the BRI may present new opportunities and possibilities for globalization. Leveraging this connectivity project straddling the Pacific and the Indian Ocean, China may go beyond its connections in the East Asia or around the Pacific, and network with the whole Eurasia to diversify its markets of export and foreign investment, secure imports of energy and food, and expand the scope where RMB is widely accepted as a trade and reserve currency, thus raising China's position in the global economy as compared to that of the USA. More importantly, China will be able to share with the rest of the world more solutions with Chinese wisdom and provide more public goods for the international community under the BRI cooperation framework, which indicates that China will transform from a participant of globalization to a leader in the new stage of the global trend, and serve as a normative power to shape a century of globalization together with the international community.

9.3.2. The To-Be-Expected Chinese Cycle in the Modern World System

Among all the core states, a hegemonic state is considered as a 'core within the core' in the modern world system, which typically emerges with a dominance cycle. Each hegemonic state, along with its dominance cycle, is created and indexed by concentrated explosive city growths through the most creative economic processes featuring 'high tech and high wage'. These economic processes deliver economic prosperity followed by cultural and political dominance, which is how a hegemon attains its admirable success that other countries try to emulate (Wallerstein 1984). In the next 30 years to come, a cycle catalyzed by concentrated explosive city growths in China will take shape in the modern world system, which will contribute to a conducive environment for Shanghai to become a global city.

Taylor et al. (2010) provided a geohistorical empirical description and analysis of the history of the Earth and the modern world system as a mega-process led by dynamic city economies, and provided a list of explosive city growths happened in the modern world system. Although currently the modern world system is still in an American cycle, major US cities have been seeing significantly smaller explosive growths since the second half of the 20th century, and their growth continues to slow down in the first decade of the 21st century. From a global perspective, China is likely to witness concentrated explosive city growths in the next three decades. In the second half of the 20th century, Beijing and Shanghai took the first and second place on the list of cities with explosive growths. This reflects a very typical hegemonic cycle. The previous hegemonic cycles are usually represented by the leading cities on the list of cities with explosive growths at the time, especially the top three, and meanwhile supported by a number of city 'groups' with exceptional growth. Aside from Beijing and Shanghai, no other Chinese cities have been included in the list till today. In addition, only Hong Kong, Shanghai and Beijing are considered as the cities with the best network connectivity in the world; while Guangzhou and Shenzhen fit into the global city network on a moderate level, and the remaining 14 Chinese cities are only weakly connected to the network (Table 9.6). Nevertheless, China has laid

Table 9.6 Changes of Population and City Area in Major Cities

	Population (in 10,000)*		Total Area (sq. km)		Built-Up Area (sq. km)	
Year	2002	2015	2002	2015	2002	2015
Tianjin	616	941	7,417	10,171	453	885
Guangzhou	583	854	3,718	7,434	553	1,237
Hangzhou	231	517	1,079	4,876	255	506
Nanjing	480	653	4,989	6,589	438	755
Chengdu	439	594	2,177	2,173	290	615
Chongqing	972	2,137	7,583	34,519	437	1,329
Shenzhen	232	1,137	355	1,997	168	900
Suzhou	168	341	1,730	2,827	129	458
Qingdao	241	372	1,349	3,231	133	566
Dalian	273	304	2,415	2,567	248	395
Xi'an	357	701	1,256	3,874	186	500
Xiamen	137	211	1,565	1,569	94	317

Source: Ministry of Housing and Urban-Rural Development, P. R. China (2002, 2015).

Note: *The data of 2002 include all of the urban population, while the data of 2015 only include the population of permanent residents and excludes the non-resident population.

a solid foundation and gained a great momentum. Cities such as Shenzhen, Guangzhou, Hangzhou and Nanjing are witnessing rapid development, while other new cities also make remarkable progress. In the following 30 years, clusters of explosive growths will take turn to happen in China, and a Chinese cycle will arrive, which will alter or replace the current hegemonic cycle in the modern world system. Since cycles are not simple sequences, they will overlap: one country's cities can be rising during the high hegemony of another country. Therefore, there might occur an overlap of the Chinese and American cycles if the latter continues to dominate in the first half of the 21st century or further into the future; if the American cycle terminates, the Chinese cycle will take over the dominant position in the modern world system.

9.3.3. A New Model of Regional Development

As the development of BRI and the Yangtze River Economic Belt is picking up speed, China will promote regional development beyond the existing four regions (the western, north-eastern, central and eastern regions) and a new model of H-shaped regional development will take shape.

On the basis of transformation and upgrading, China's eastern coastal area will further utilize its major infrastructure, such as high-speed rails and the coastal highways, ports and international hub airports, and form a highly opened-up and well-developed eastern economic development belt with a spillover effect on the adjacent areas. China's eastern coastal area has built a solid foundation for its development, and in the future efforts will be focused on facilitating integration through a comprehensive and organized exchange of productive factors, as well as building up connections through its node cities. This belt will not only give new vigour to the eastern coastal area, enabling it to take lead in China's economic growth, but will also effectively accelerate the development of China's inland regions. However, a bigger change is to happen in a similar economic development belt in the western area. Despite this area's poor existing conditions, such as scant and scarce growth poles, and poor flow and connections of productive factors, its location advantage will be changed fundamentally, thanks to China's BRI. The BRI opens two 'gates' for China's inland regions, respectively, represented by the Silk Road Economic Belt in the north and the 21st-century Maritime Silk Road in the south, as well as the new railway corridor that links China's northern and southern areas, stretching from Haikou, and passing through Nanning and Guiyang, all the way to Lanzhou and, thus, enables the inland regions to connect other parts of the country. In this case, it will be much easier for China's western area to give full play to its natural endowments and comparative advantages, and to facilitate its exchange of productive factors, while further opening up to be better integrated into the world economy. If the western area successfully seizes this opportunity to promote its regional transformation and economic growth, it is entirely possible to form a western economic development belt composed of node cities including Urumqi, Lanzhou, Xi'an, Chengdu, Chongqing, Guiyang, Kunming and Nanning. Certainly, it will take rather a long time to build this belt, and it also depends on the progress of BRI. This is especially so for cities along the new Silk Road such as Urumqi, Lanzhou, Xi'an and cities along the Maritime Silk Road such as Guiyang, Kunming and Nanning.

Yangtze River Economic Belt that runs throughout China's core hinterland is the 'horizontal' connection between the eastern and western economic development belts. This globally important inland economic belt covers an area of up to 2.05 million sq. km encompassing nine provinces and two cities in China, accounts for more than 40 per cent of the country's total population and GDP, and enjoys a growth rate higher than China's national average, making it a major driving force pivotally positioned in the country's overall strategy. Moreover, the Yangtze River Economic Belt is not merely an ordinary economic zone, but it is a new type of geographic area centred on giant developmental ecosystems. To better develop the regions along this belt, further efforts shall be primarily put in optimizing the Yangtze River Economic Belt through adjusting its existing industries, improving the quality of newly emerging industries and upgrading its modern industrial system. With scientific and technological innovation, as well as institutional innovation as parallel drivers of development, an all-round innovation-based system will be built in the regions along the belt, where science and technology, industry, education and finance are to be fully integrated to establish a comprehensive cooperative mechanism for exchanging and sharing productive factors and resources, where regional blockades and barriers caused by different interests can be broken down. By 2030, the Yangtze River Economic Belt will build up an innovation-driven industrial system and economic growth model, with world leading innovation capacity and significant achievements made through coordinated regional cooperation and balanced development. It will become an important engine that leads China's economic transformation and upgrading, and supports the coordinated development of the country. The rise of the belt gives full play of the advantages of China's golden waterway—Yangtze River in terms of promoting the flow of resources and making different regions more complementary to each other. Therefore, it can provide all-round support for other regions, promote the transformation of resources into productivity and facilitate the cooperation and concerted development among eastern, central and western regions, so as to drive China's next round of economic development.

In the H-shaped regional development pattern, there are also a number of strategic belts that connect north with south, and east with west, including the Pearl River–Xijiang River economic belt, Harbin–Changchun economic belt in the north-east, Longhai–Lanxin Railway economic belt, Baotou–Kunming economic belt and Huaihe River green economic belt, which will become important links to promote balanced regional development and great economic leap forward.

9.4. SHANGHAI'S ENDOGENOUS FOUNDATION FOR GLOBAL CITIES EVOLUTION

Although the aforementioned factors at the global and national levels (exogenous selection environment) are indispensable conditions and driving force for the evolution of global cities, according to the duality of the selection environment in the ontological assumption of 'living organism', Shanghai's own foundation for evolution constitutes the endogenous factors of the selection environment, including historical trajectory and city genes investigated from the historical perspective, and the actual development foundation and trend in reality. The key of evolution of an individual global city depends on how well the endogenous evolutionary foundation fits in or matches the exogenous selection environment, which, to some extent, decides the probability of evolution.

9.4.1. Genetic Information of Cities

During the evolution of global cities, although opportunity is the main driving force for the change of the set of possible states, a fundamental breakthrough inspired by an exogenous crisis is rarely seen, and path dependence always exists in the process. The so-called path dependence refers to the phenomenon that what has occasionally happened in the past still significantly affects our decision-making (Mahoney 2000). As a complex phenomenon of urban system with high sunk cost in physical and social aspects, the evolution of global cities exhibits strong tendency of path dependence. Therefore, it is necessary to carefully examine the historical trajectory of Shanghai's development.

As the halfway point of China's coastline, Shanghai lies at the estuary of the Yangtze River, faces Japan's Kyushu Island across the East China Sea and neighbours the Hangzhou Bay in the south and Jiangsu and Zhejiang provinces in the west. Enjoying an advantageous location, the city keeps playing an important role in Shanghai's development in different ways and at different periods of time. Since Shanghai became a port, it was renowned as a world-class commercial city and Asia's most well-developed and important financial centre known for its attraction for international capital, professionals and new ideas (Wei 1987). The process of globalization in Shanghai paused for a period from 1949 when China centralized resource inputs under the framework of planned economy, which had an impact on the city's international trade, shipping and finance. But then it was still China's economic centre, thanks to its industrial and commercial strengths. When China began to adopt the policies of reform and opening-up 40 years ago, Shanghai started its process of globalization again. Through structural adjustments and the development of Pudong New Area, Shanghai was revived and regenerated with enhanced comprehensive functions, and transformed from an industrial and commercial city to a multifunctional international economic centre of national strategic importance supported by finance, trade and shipping. Shanghai keeps driving the development of its neighbouring cities and strengthening cooperation and competition with them to facilitate the economic growth in Yangtze River region and to integrate its finance and trade with the world economy (Yusuf and Wu 2002). Shanghai is not always striding on the path towards globalization, and there were even serval serious deviations. However, its function and status as an economic centre have never been changed. It keeps playing a significant role in national and global economic and social development at different periods of time. This may be a core of Shanghai's urban development and has become one of the city's features. In addition, Shanghai has showed its strong gene of openness and globalization. The planned economy may restrict Shanghai's development for a while, but once the external environment was changed, the city would show its desire for openness and globalization, and its excellent capacities, thus attracting and assimilating cross-border institutions (enterprises) and their cultures. It is a great asset for a city to grow up by building global connections, and this is the case for Shanghai. We can say that openness and globalization is Shanghai's special traits throughout its history.

These two pieces of genetic information of Shanghai are embodied and reflected in its urban existence. It is known that urban existence is materialized in the form of urban morphologies and structures based on built environment and infrastructure. The durability of built environment and infrastructure, especially of existing housing and commercial properties, is one of the momentums for path dependency (Storper and Manville 2006). Moreover, urban systems connected by infrastructural links are robust. (Le Galès 2002). The unchanged function and lasting position of Shanghai as a central city and its level of openness and globalization have been deeply ingrained in its urban morphologies and structures. The buildings of various architectural styles in the Bund, old-style garden villas and *Shikumen*-style buildings, for example, are the architectural environment created throughout the history. They are the proof that Shanghai has long been a highly globalized city and a paradise for businessmen and adventurers. And the built environment and infrastructure along the Suzhou Creek and Huangpu River provide a glimpse of Shanghai in its old days, when a considerable amount of national, foreign and bureaucrat capital flew in. Urban morphologies, to put it more generally, are very tenacious. Once in place, they tend to be hard to change. Planning traditions, being institutions themselves, are also subject to path-dependent effects (Needham 2006). As the built environment itself constrains new spatial interventions in specific ways, they can be modified, streets can be broadened, new buildings can be erected, but the weight of history is always there. Cities and urban systems mostly adapt to changes by adding new layers to the existing outlay. Urban morphologies and structures of a city will be taken into consideration when individuals and firms choose locations for their business, which largely prevents Shanghai from derailing from its history trajectory. In this sense, such inertia contributes to the future development of the city.

Certainly, the immaterial form of urban existence is more about the broader sense of institutional frameworks. The unchanged function and lasting position of Shanghai as a central city and its level of openness and globalization are more deeply reflected in its pattern of behaviours, routinized mode of operation, ways of organization and how it is connected with other cities. For example, Shanghai is marked with the traits of inclusiveness, modesty, respect for rules and meticulous care for details, and they are all the result of the city's long-standing tradition of openness. Apparently, path-dependent trajectories are not limited to the built environment exclusively as institutional frameworks can also be characterized by high set-up costs, learning effects, mutually adaptive expectations and by coordination effects. These last three factors are particularly relevant when one looks at social structures. Such institutional frameworks, in this sense, is more path-dependent than the durability of built environments and infrastructures. As Taylor ([2003] 2004) points out, notwithstanding the fact that many urban systems are affected by roughly similar processes of economic restructuring and changes in the way forces of concentration and deconcentration interplay, their shapes and, to a certain extent, their destinies are still significantly affected by how they were shaped and how they were related to their national economies centuries ago. This even applies, we argue, to one of the most influential factors determining the status and dynamics of global city regions in our time. That is the way in which they are inserted in the global economy.

Overall, the unchanged function and lasting position of Shanghai as a central city and its level of openness and globalization are two important pieces of genetic information retained after a long time of historical selection, and have become assets that make Shanghai distinct from other cities. These are vital endogenous bases for Shanghai's future evolution into a global city, and may become the constraints and boundaries for its new characteristics.

9.4.2. Existing Strengths of Shanghai

The (re)emergence of Shanghai as a world city has been noted by many scholars as the city experiencing a process of urban development arguably unmatched in scale and speed in recent urban history, in terms of infrastructural projects, urban growth and redevelopment and industrial transformation (Cai and Sit 2003). More importantly, infrastructure plays a far-reaching role in the rise of global cities. For example, Shanghai has built a multifunctional and well-connected infrastructure system, which is indispensable in promoting global flows. The four terminals of Pudong Airport and Hongqiao Airport cover 1.2 million m^2, boast five cargo areas and six runways and the Pacific-Asia gateways and aviation hubs for international and domestic passenger and cargo transportation. In 2016, Shanghai's airline passengers exceeded 100 million, making the city the fifth member of the billion-level passenger aviation 'club' following London, New York, Atlanta and Tokyo. The annual cargo and mail throughput of Pudong Airport held third place for nine years. Thanks to the third phase expansion of Pudong Airport in 2019, the total annual passenger throughput of both airports is expected to exceed 120 million. The position of Shanghai as a global hub port city has been strengthened. In 2015, cargo throughput reached 717.3964 million tonnes, ranking first in the world. The international container throughput of Shanghai's ports was 36.537 million international standard containers, ranking the first in the world for the sixth consecutive year. Shanghai has made remarkable achievements in building railways that link the rest of the country, and a railway hub has been built that include Hongqiao Railway Station, Shanghai Railway Station, Shanghai South Railway Station and Shanghai East Railway Station. The intercity transportation infrastructure for the Yangtze River Delta region has been completed. Port and airport expressways that connect Shanghai and the rest of the country have been improved. The highway network has been upgraded to better connect Jiangsu Province and Zhejiang Province. A rail transit network (including urban and local lines) has been built in Shanghai. By building a world-leading information infrastructure and IPv6 transformation of key network facilities, Shanghai aims to become a smart city offering a wide coverage of integrated services and a next-generation Internet demonstration city. Moreover, submarine cables have been built and existing optical cables have been expanded to greatly enhance the city's export and interconnectivity with the world. Shanghai has been making progress in energy, water supply and drainage, disaster prevention, ecology and infrastructure, which have laid the foundation to attract big flows of people, logistics, information, capital and technology to the city, and made it a hub for global, intercontinental and domestic transportation and information.

A new industrial system that underpins the global city's network has taken shape in Shanghai. Its industrial structure has been transformed, in which the service economy plays the leading role, accounting for 70 per cent of the total economy, and advanced manufacturing accounting for about 25 per cent. A new model based on the industrial Internet has been built in order to boost high-end and smart manufacturing and make the city a world-class centre for innovation by emerging industries. The most remarkable feature of the city's new industrial system is integrated development, especially that of modern service industry and advanced manufacturing. Rapid growth in manufacturing has enabled Shanghai to attain a wealth of non-material expertise, and develop special types of financial, accounting and legal services and global logistics. This makes Shanghai different from global cities such as New York, London and Hong Kong, whose knowledge-oriented economies are not stemmed from their development of real economies.

In contrast, Shanghai is one of the hubs of industrial globalization, which is the one of the main reasons why it is chosen as the destination for many multinational manufacturing companies' HQs and high-end value chains, giving the city some unrivalled advantages. This will help the producer services industries to become more specialized and get closer to the higher end of the value chain, and make the consumer services industries become more specialized, sophisticated and achieve higher quality. Building on the advantages of the leading role of Yangtze River Delta industrial chain, Shanghai has seen the emergence of several industry clusters, built a more environment-friendly and resource-saving manufacturing industry, and enhanced international competitiveness and brand influence, making itself one of the international high-end smart manufacturing centres with high added value, high tech and high TFP. At the same time, the regional spillover effect and influence of the producer services industries have also been expanding. Shanghai's industrial development is becoming more sophisticated, smart, environment-friendly and service oriented. It is dominated by modern service industries, spearheaded by strategic emerging industries and supported by advanced manufacturing industries, which provides perfect industry connection and support to the aggregation of HQs for MNCs.

A network platform for flux economy has been established. A sound financial system including stock, bonds, futures, currency, foreign exchange, gold, insurance markets has taken shape, and the market scale has significantly increased. Shanghai's major financial markets such as stock, bond, futures and gold markets are rising fast on the global ranking, and the trading volume of several financial products ranked top in the world, thus wielding increasing influence over the world. Market platforms for international service trade, technology trade, entrepot trade and offshore trade have been built, making Shanghai a magnet for entrepreneurs, information and factors of production, a decision-maker of pricing and a hub of ports. Shanghai has established trading markets for non-ferrous metals, steel, chemicals, oil and natural gas, and will further expand its presence in the international market, diversify its functions, enhance the connection between spot market and futures market, build an all-weather trading system that provides a full set of services for all kinds of financial products, and further enhance the ability of price discovery, in order to improve the international influence of Shanghai Price and Shanghai Index. An international shipping cargo trading platform has grown to a large size. At the same time, a derivatives market platform is under construction which provides services for shipping insurance, ship aircraft financing leases and shipping freight exchange, so as to standardize the ship trading market, shipping brokerage, ship management and maritime arbitration. A comprehensive and professional exhibition platform with international influence has been built, which boasts 14 exhibition venues with a total area of 1 million m². The indoor exhibition area of the National Exhibition and Convention Center (Shanghai) is 400,000 m², and the outdoor exhibition area is 100,000 m², making Shanghai one of the cities with the largest venue and largest total area in the world. Shanghai's information, transactions, intermediaries and service platforms based on the market system will become more well developed, well supported and diversified, providing a powerful boost and catalyst for the flow and allocation of resources.

A large number of global functional institutions have settled in Shanghai. Since 2000, a rapidly increasing number of MNCs, foreign-invested companies and foreign-invested R&D centres have entered Shanghai (Figure 9.5). As of August 2015, there were 522 regional HQs of MNCs in Shanghai, making it the city with the largest number of regional HQs of MNCs. The regional HQs settled in Shanghai usually performed high-level management functions. Among them, 82 per cent performed investment decision-making functions, 61 per cent capital management functions, 54 per cent R&D functions and 35 per cent procurement and sales functions. Moreover, more than 95 per cent of them performed two or more functions. In the same year, there were 429 foreign-funded financial institutions in Shanghai, accounting for about 30 per cent of the total number of Shanghai's financial institutions. And there were 306 foreign-invested companies, in which 70 per cent of the projects and 90 per cent of the funds are invested in various provinces and cities across the country.

There are 390 foreign-funded R&D centres, accounting for about 25 per cent of those in the Chinese mainland, of which more than 30 are global and 15 are regional centres. Having gathered a large number

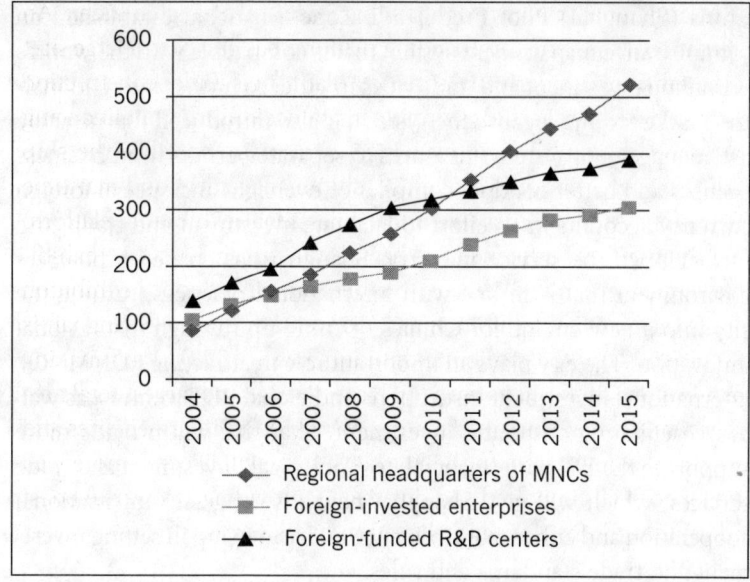

Figure 9.5 *Regional Headquarters of Multinationals in Shanghai 2004–2015*

Source: Compiled by author and his research team.
Note: The data and analysis are derived from the research project China Economic Growth Prediction in the Next 30 Years funded by Shanghai Development Strategy Research Institute and lead by Dr Daming Zhu.

of regional HQs of MNCs, global investment corporations and global R&D centres, Shanghai is characterized by its extensive connectivity, high capacity and high network power, which provides a solid foundation for the formation of the needed connectivity to turn Shanghai into a global city.

A business environment that is in line with high-standard international practices has been formed. In the process of building itself into an international economic, financial, trade and shipping centre, Shanghai proposed to adopt international practices in terms of market access, supervision, taxation and legal system, and took the lead in piloting the value added tax (VAT) reform, which replaced all business tax with VAT. While perfecting the institutional design of the

China (Shanghai) Pilot Free Trade Zone, Shanghai established an administrative management system that is compatible with the world's prevailing investment and trade rules in order to further internationalize, marketize and legalize the system. It also introduced the 'negative list' management system, measures to separate permits from business licenses and better conduct compliance oversight and special foreign currency accounts in an effort to facilitate investment and trade, and further open the service industry. Shanghai has created a business environment that is in line with international practices, turning the city into a new engine for China's opening up through institutional innovation. The city plays an important role in attracting FDI, MNCs, international investment institutions and global R&D centres, as well as in facilitating outbound investment. Shanghai will provide more support to the BRI with financial, technological, investment and trade services, which will give Shanghai new advantages in international cooperation and enhance its influence and leadership in setting investment and trade standards and rules.

A Case Study of 'Shanghai 2050' Global City Vision (Part II)

10.1. PROSPECTS OF SHANGHAI'S EVOLUTION TO A GLOBAL CITY

The evolution of a city is a dynamic process, and it remains uncertain whether Shanghai will successfully grow into a global city by 2050. It is impossible to accurately map the process through the use of any econometric model, nor can any subjective estimation be fully justifiable. But still we can apply the trend forecasting method to extrapolate some relatively certain factors and trends from the uncertain dynamic process, and to forecast the prospect of Shanghai's evolution into a global city by measuring the probability of certain scenarios.

10.1.1. Shanghai's Emergence as a Future Global City

In the dynamic, yet uncertain evolution of the city of Shanghai, all kinds of scenarios are likely to occur, each with a different probability of occurrence. In order to assess the probability, we will have to find some relatively certain factors from the uncertain dynamic process to identify most likely scenario.

Relatively, greater uncertainty exists in the global context because what will happen in the next 30 years is unpredictable. There might be geopolitics or geo-economic changes, or potential risks such as wars and disasters. But these extreme world-changing incidents aside, we can still identify some relatively certain and predictable trends. The recovery and prosperity of the world economy and the further deepening of globalization will serve as a powerful tailwind to Shanghai's continuous evolution. The great changes in the structure of the world economy and the redistribution of MNCs will bring a rare opportunity for the leapfrog development of Shanghai. The further expansion of globalization and the intensification of various forms of interactions and flows around the world will provide greater possibilities for Shanghai to evolve into a global city in innovative ways.

On national level, the macro environment in the next three decades is also favourable for Shanghai's evolution. According to the long-term road map charted by the Chinese leadership, China will encourage economic transformation and upgrading, deepen overall reform and resolve international frictions to avoid the middle-income trap. As China rises, it is expected to lead global development and globalization. This requires major cities and city clusters in China to compete in the international arena and develop into key nodes or agglomerations in the WCN, in line with China's goal of promoting economic development and international status. As one of China's first-tier cities, chances are high that Shanghai will evolve into an important global city. Shanghai's global city construction plan has been included in the national strategy, making the city a preferred recipient of national resources and a pilot city for new policies. The city cluster that is growing around Shanghai, which has the potential to become a world-class city cluster, will also propel Shanghai's evolution.

Despite present constraints and underlying challenges, Shanghai has great room to develop. Shanghai has not been in steady evolution and its status in the WCN has not been acknowledged as generally as New York and London. In the next decades, the city will also face challenges and risks of innovative transformation. However, as a hub for both the BRI and the Yangtze River Economic Belt, Shanghai will become a key port in global flows, whose route will affect the dynamic evolution of global cities. Metropolises located off the new route will decline, while those along it, such as Shanghai, will rise. This will give Shanghai a bigger chance to become a global city and improve its functions and status as a node in the WCN. The city's attributes and achievements will also make it attractive and influential in broader global interactions.

Given these reasons, the rise of Shanghai is in line with the trend of the evolution of global city, which means it has great possibilities to become a global city.

10.1.2. Prospect of Ecological Niche in the Evolution of Global City

From a broader perspective, Shanghai's evolution in the next three decades will not be an isolated event. World-class city clusters will rise and increase in China as Shanghai develops into a global city. The agglomeration of rising global cities will create a biotope for the evolution of global city and spatial distribution, thus providing a unique environment for Shanghai's evolution.

Historically, global cities have emerged in countries or regions leading globalization and the world economy, a phenomenon called 'the agglomeration of global cities'. In the next three decades, the centre of the world economic activity will continue to shift towards Asia. As the biggest economy in the region, China will become one of the drivers of the world economy and globalization, and see the rise of global city clusters. Currently, many Chinese cities are being incorporated into the global city network and, as a result, China's global city network connectivity has risen substantially. In 2008, 19 Chinese cities were on the GaWC connectivity list, accounting for 5.3 per cent of the world's total. China came second in terms of global city connectivity, followed by the USA (Table 10.1). China (including Taiwan, Hong Kong and Macau) had 18 cities on GaWC's 2012 Global Connectivity List. While in the next years no more Chinese cities joined the list, the ranking of the existing cities was upgraded. For example, Qingdao was upgraded from the Sufficiency subgroup in 2010 to High Sufficiency now, with an evidence that the general connectivity was improving. One of the impressive achievements is that three Chinese cities—Hong Kong, Shanghai and Beijing—are on the alpha category, ranking among top 10 in terms of global connectivity. No other countries have yet been as successful as China. China achieved this result not just because of its vast territory (the USA and Russia as two of the largest countries in the world each have only one city ranked above Alpha) but also because of the tremendous momentum of China's rise since reform and opening-up in the late 1970s and the connection of its cities to the global economy. In addition, it seems that a pyramid-shaped four-tier city system has formed in China's high connectivity network. The first tier includes three cities (Hong Kong, Shanghai and Beijing);

Table 10.1 *Top 10 Country's GaWC Connectivity in 2008*

Country	GaWC City Number	GaWC Connectivity (Country-Based)	GaWC Connectivity Global Share	Global GDP Share (%)
USA	61	1,135,819	15.8	25.5
China	19	382,285	5.3	8.6
UK	16	297,292	4.1	4.5
Germany	14	292,635	4.1	5.8
India	9	226,578	3.2	2.6
Canada	11	210,644	2.9	2.4
Australia	7	200,925	2.8	1.7
Italy	8	168,379	2.3	3.3
France	9	154,764	2.2	4.3
Japan	13	153,588	2.1	8.7
Total	167	3,222,909	44.9	67.2

Source: GaWC database (2008).

the second tier includes four cities (Taipei, Guangzhou, Shenzhen and Tianjin); the third tier includes five cities (Chengdu, Qingdao, Hangzhou, Nanjing and Chongqing); and the fourth tier includes six cities (Dalian, Kaohsiung, Xiamen, Wuhan, Xi'an and Macao).

As empirical studies have shown, there is a clear positive correlation between the total strength of a country's network connectivity and the number of global cities it has, with the only exception of Singapore, which is a city state. Generally speaking, a country with high global connectivity has several global cities. For example, New York ranks on top globally in terms of its own network connectivity. But on the other hand, it only accounts for 8.4 per cent of the total share of the US network connectivity, the rest of which is contributed by other US cities. Compared with the fragmented urban system in the USA, Frankfurt only represents 16.5 per cent of the total connectivity in Germany given the country's vertical structural urban system. Paris, France's capital with a vertical structural urban system, accounts for less than half (48.7%) of the country's total share of global connectivity. This suggests that countries with high network connectivity usually have several global cities. As the centre of the world's economic activity moves eastwards, Asia will become the core region of globalization. China, as a rising economy, will play an important role both in Asia's regional development and new round of globalization. In this sense, there will be more global cities that serve as decisive nodes in economic connectivity in the world. This demand will further lead to the rise of global city clusters in China.

As Shanghai evolves into a global city, other future global cities in China are also rising. How these rising global cities function in the process is worth exploring. Shanghai's functions in the future global city constellation will be dependent on its relationship with other major cities in China, especially in terms of divisions of labour and cooperation in the GNC.

First, it is found that different patterns of connectivity can be indicated by a city's hinterworld (Taylor 2001b). Two measures of hinterworld are used as follows: (a) the average of a city's hinterworld linkages to London and New York as representing the globalist orientation in a city's hinterworld; and (b) the average of a city's residual linkages to other inter-regional (e.g., Asia-Pacific) cities as representing the regionalist (local) orientation in a city's hinterworld. In reality, a city's hinterworld is measured by hybrid criteria, including both globalist- and regionalist-oriented connectivity, and the result depends on whether the city is more globalist or not in the pattern of its linkages. The orientation of a city's hinterworld is a major measure to classify the evolution of global cities.

According to empirical research on city connectivity in Asia-Pacific, cities such as Bangkok, Kuala Lumpur, Jakarta and Seoul are more regionalist, while Shanghai, Hong Kong, Tokyo, Singapore and Beijing are more globalist in terms of connectivity (Table 10.2). Compared with global cities in Europe and America, those in Asia-Pacific appear to concentrate in their home region and do not even feature in the global outreach. For example, Tokyo, a leading global city in the globalist group, is highly connected with those in Japan and other Asia-Pacific cities instead of those in the West. However, the importance of Chinese globalizing cities is increasing as the size of

Table 10.2 Hinterworld Properties of Asia-Pacific Cities

City	Globalist Orientation	Regionalist Orientation
Shanghai	1.167	−0.938
Hong Kong	1.110	−1.012
Tokyo	0.949	−1.006
Singapore	0.640	−0.912
Beijing	0.591	−0.715
Bangkok	−0.401	1.067
Kuala Lumpur	−0.704	0.315
Jakarta	−0.819	1.244
Seoul	−0.939	0.844
Taipei	−1.593	1.113

Source: Taylor (2006).

their global reach is more extensive. In particular, Shanghai ranks first in Asia in terms of its globalist connectivity which exceeds that of Tokyo and Singapore. China, an emerging developing country in Asia-Pacific, stands out for its unique strategy in the globalization of world economy and could also bring about a new type of intervention in the WCN. The globalizing cities in China are generating global reach beyond Asia-Pacific home region which is concentrated in New York and Miami of the USA (representing an alternative Latin American penetration since no cities from that region feature in this service geography), London in Western Europe, the five cities in Eastern Europe and others in Arabian Gulf region and Africa (e.g., Johannesburg). Taylor (2006) found by fuzzy set analysis that the Shanghai–Beijing group has three overlaps: to Western Europe cities through Sydney, to US cities through Los Angles and to Eastern European cities through Munich. In addition, through the Western European link, it has an indirect overlap with the cities just below London and New York through Frankfurt. This is a clear case of overlapping regions since Chinese cities are featured in Asia-Pacific home region while also constituting their own home region, which demonstrates a unique service geography in the WCN.

It brings out the distinctiveness of Beijing and Shanghai in the WCN. Clearly more connected than the other cities of their connectivity strata, they have a globality like the top-tier strata, which shows the centrality of Beijing and Shanghai to the early 21st-century global economy. The relationship among Shanghai, Hong Kong and Beijing, which constitutes a globalist group of connectivity, is very special. In terms of ecological constellation, they are closely connected and prosper through their interaction. Because city networks operate through mutuality, it follows that instead of the rise of Shanghai and Beijing implying a decline in Hong Kong, the latter can continue to prosper through repositioning itself within the WCN. Also, the increase of Shanghai and Beijing's connectivity is similar to a win–win game rather than a zero-sum competition, because under any circumstances these two cities both rank in the top 10 worldwide.

In the following three decades, Asia-Pacific will become the central region of globalization as the world's economic centre of gravity shifts eastwards. In this way, Chinese cities in the Asia-Pacific home region will enhance their global connectivity. In addition, a growing number of Chinese companies are pursuing the strategy of 'going global', investing in Western countries and increasing investment in countries covered by the BRI. As a result, China's global outreach will extend beyond home regions, mostly to Eastern Europe, the Arab Gulf and Africa, especially for globalist cities such as Shanghai, Hong Kong and Beijing. These overlapping regions where Chinese cities are featured in the Asia-Pacific home region, while also constituting their own home region, will greatly increase the importance of Chinese emerging global cities in the WCN, overshadowing other global cities in the Asia-Pacific.

Second, different kinds of connectivity models can be analysed through a city's connectivity functions, specifically comprehensive and professional functions. The cities connected through comprehensive functions are referred to as comprehensive global cities, while those through professional functions are known as professional functional global cities. However, in practice, the line between these two types of cities is blurred, even though professional functional global cities have multiple network connectivity. This classification just means that a city has powerful strengths in some aspects of network connectivity, and it has a markedly imbalanced connectivity structure. Besides, each type can be broken down to different sub-categories, depending on a city's position and function in the WCN and hierarchical tendencies to operate within the same network.

As mentioned earlier, Shanghai and Beijing are globalist cities, but their network connectivity has different functional focus—Shanghai's is economic, whilst Beijing's is political (Table 10.3). Also, this kind of difference, to a large extent, leads to their distinctive geographies of links and respective city-dyads. Detailed geographical outcomes of

Table 10.3 *A Comparison between Beijing and Shanghai's Connections*

Orientation	City	Link Difference
Cities more connected to Beijing	New York	52
	Tokyo	21
	Rome	17
	Los Angeles	10
	Sydney	6
	Singapore	5
	Seoul	5
	Mosco	5
	Hong Kong	4
Cities more connected to Shanghai	São Paulo	−5
	London	−10
	Mexico City	−13
	Vienna	−15
	Jakarta	−15
	Frankfurt	−16
	Chicago	−16
	Bangkok	−17
	Toronto	−21
	Milan	−21

Orientation	City	Link Difference
	Dublin	−21
	Buenos Aires	−21
	Paris	−22
	Lisbon	−26
	Zürich	−27
	Amsterdam	−27
	Warsaw	−28
	Kuala Lumpur	−29
	Mumbai	−31
	Taipei	−37
	Stockholm	−42
	Brussel	−43
	Madrid	−44

Source: Taylor, Derudder, Hoyler et al. (2014).

city repositioning empirically show the political role and commercial role of these two cities. To compare the WCN connectivity of Beijing and Shanghai, Taylor subtracted the sum of city-dyad connections of Shanghai from that of Beijing. A positive difference would indicate that Beijing has stronger connectivity than Shanghai and vice versa (Table 10.4). As the result turned out, Beijing has stronger political connections with other world cities, such as strong links with New York (UN HQs) and major neighbouring Pacific Rim cities (plus neighbouring Eurasian Moscow) (Table 10.5). Shanghai, however, has stronger economic links with other world cities than Beijing, especially closer connections with important commercial centres in both the USA and Europe, such as London, Paris, Frankfurt, Chicago, Toronto and Mumbai. The fact that Beijing is more linked to Italy's capital city Rome (also with UN offices) whilst Shanghai has stronger connections to Italy's 'economic capital' Milan is particularly noteworthy. With linkages to different cities in the world, Beijing and Shanghai complement each other in the WCN (Taylor et al. 2014).

Table 10.4 *Sectors Where Shanghai Has Stronger Connectivity than Beijing*

Rank	City	Financial Services (%)	Rank	City	Advertising (%)
1	London	100	1	New York	100
2	New York	96	2	London	75
3	Hong Kong	93	3	Paris	75
4	Tokyo	82	4	Hong Kong	73
5	Singapore	82	5	Tokyo	71
6	Paris	79	6	Singapore	70
7	Shanghai	77	7	Moscow	65
8	Sydney	77	8	Shanghai	64
9	Seoul	70	9	Warsaw	63
10	Madrid	70	10	Sydney	63
12	Beijing	69	18	Beijing	60

Source: Taylor (2012).

Other than the difference between Beijing and Shanghai in economic or political functions in the WCN, if seen from an economic perspective only, the two cities are integrated into the WCN through different patterns of sector workflows. Judging from the five component service sectors (financial services, legal services, advertising, accountancy and management accountancy) in the overall network connectivity, Shanghai ranks in the top 10 for financial services (7th) and advertising (8th). Beijing, although at 12th and 18th places, respectively, in terms of these two modern core commercial service sectors, remains in the top 10 for accountancy (8th), management accountancy (10th) and legal services (10th), compared to 14th, 23rd and 11th places that Shanghai occupies, respectively. It would seem that at this time, Beijing presents more of a global city than Shanghai in terms of accountancy and management accountancy, with a similar connectivity rating in respect of legal services to Shanghai. But overall, firms in different sectors tend to use Beijing and Shanghai in different ways, thus providing them with complementary roles in the WCN (Taylor 2012).

In the next 30 years to come, such classification of world city connectivity is expected to be more diversified and refined as more sectors

Table 10.5 Sectors Where Beijing Has Stronger Connectivity than Shanghai

Rank	City	AC (%)	Rank	City	MC	Rank	City	LS (%)
1	London	100	1	New York	100	1	London	100
2	New York	79	2	London	67	2	New York	89
3	Hong Kong	74	3	Paris	65	3	Paris	70
4	Sydney	69	4	Chicago	62	4	Frankfurt	59
5	Singapore	67	5	Hong Kong	61	5	Washington	58
6	Milan	67	6	Singapore	56	6	Brussels	54
7	Paris	66	7	Tokyo	56	7	Hong Kong	53
8	Beijing	64	8	Zürich	55	8	Moscow	50
9	Buenos Aires	63	9	Madrid	55	9	Tokyo	48
10	Kuala Lumpur	62	10	Beijing	53	10	Beijing	45
14	Shanghai	60	23	Shanghai	44	11	Shanghai	42

Source: Taylor (2012).
Note: AC is accountancy; MC is management consultancy; LS is legal services.

experience globalization. This indicates that in China, the rise of global city clusters will foster a diversified model of city connections, in which each individual global city will have a clearer function to perform in more complex intercity relationships. In general, most of China's future global cities will fulfil a professional function, and only a few of them will become comprehensive world cities. Thus, their relationships in global services are more complementary than competitive.

10.1.3. Potential Position of Cities in the World City Network

In the next 30 years, as China's global city clusters come to the fore, what position will they occupy in the WCN? Since they will partly follow the evolutionary pattern of global cities, we can make possible predictions despite the world economic dynamics and uncertainty.

It is known that globalization originated from the economic heartland of the world, and it does not have a one-way process in a homogenous world. For a long time, New York and London (or USAL for USA plus London), being the two most important overlaps in the centre of the world economy, have been the locus for generating two distinctive globalization strategies. As the global economic centre of gravity continues to shift to Asia in the next 30 years, there will be three important overlaps in the world economic centre against the three main core economic areas of the world: Asia, the Americas and Europe. According to the law of large numbers, top positions in the WCN are likely to be occupied by global cities in these three regions. In the Americas, once again New York dominates the command cities with the USA being a world power (its world position might be weakened). Back in the traditional centre of the world economy, Europe, it is uncertain which city will represent the region (in the context of EU integration), leaving the question open as to whether London, a traditional global city that was the undisputable European representative, would retain its top global city or representative position in the scenario of 'Brexit'. A report by the *Economist* forecasts that by 2050, Germany will be the only European country in the world's top 7 economies. Certainly it's possible that another EU global city (such as Frankfurt) will overtake London as the European representative although the supplanter will have to meet certain standards for economic infrastructure and facilities. Therefore, a possible scenario would be that Europe loses its share of top global cities in the WCN as London's world position weakens because of 'Brexit' and a new substitute is nowhere to find. On other side of the globe, as the centre of global economic activity shifts to Asia, more Asian cities, in particular Chinese cities, will enter the list of top 10 global cities (Table 10.6).

Table 10.6 *Top 20 City-Dyads That Include Chinese Cities*

China Rank	World Rank	City-Dyad	CDC*
1	2	Hong Kong and London	75.0
2	3	Hong Kong and New York	69.0
3	6	London and Shanghai	62.1
4	10	New York and Shanghai	58.7
5	14	Beijing and London	55.6
6	19	Beijing and New York	52.3
7	20	Hong Kong and Singapore	51.6
8	31	Hong Kong and Shanghai	47.5
9	32	Hong Kong and Paris	47.2
10	37	Hong Kong and Tokyo	44.9
11	39	Beijing and Hong Kong	43.9
12	44	Shanghai and Singapore	41.1
13	45	Paris and Shanghai	40.4
14	46	Dubai and Hong Kong	39.8
15	47	Chicago and Hong Kong	39.7
16	50	Hong Kong and Sydney	39.2
17	52	Beijing and Singapore	38.8
18	54	Shanghai and Tokyo	38.4
19	56	Beijing and Shanghai	38.0
20	57	Hong Kong and Milan	37.0

Source: Taylor, Derudder, Hoyler et al. (2014).
Note: *CDC is city-dyad connectivity and is shown as percentage of the most connected city-dyad (London–New York).

In terms of GNC, Hong Kong, Shanghai and Beijing now rank among the top 10, indicating their important roles in the WCN. City-dyad analyses, however, enhance the prominence of these Chinese cities compared with simple rankings by total GNC. Of the top 20 city-dyads, 7 across the world feature Chinese cities that occupy more than one-third of the places. Besides, Hong Kong, Shanghai and Beijing are all connected with London and New York. This suggests that they have developed more strategically important roles in the WCN than previously understood in terms of simple connectivity rankings.

Yet in some ways, this actually under-reports the role of the three cities in the WCN. Taylor, Derudder et al. (2014) measured the relative concentration of the two cities' potential working flows in this particular dyad. High values indicate many firms choosing to locate offices, often important offices, in both cities suggesting extra business being conducted through this city-dyad. Therefore, such city-dyads are relatively over-connected, and it indicates an enhanced 'strategic-ness'. The result indicates that the three Chinese cities feature in over half of the top 38 highest over-connected city-dyads, and the three all-China city-dyads are ranked from 4th to 6th places (Table 10.7). Hong Kong is most over-connected to Singapore, followed by Shanghai and Beijing. Shanghai is most over-connected to Hong Kong, followed by Beijing, but the latter city ranks Shanghai before Hong Kong in over-connectedness, followed by Hong Kong's over-connections with New York and London, Shanghai's over-connections with New York and London. In terms of the three Chinese cities, Hong Kong strongly continues in its position just below London and New York; Shanghai rises above Singapore to be 4th and Beijing rises second-most place to 7th above Paris. Thus, the key finding is that in terms of strategic potential working flows, the Chinese cities appear even more important than recent studies of global network analyses have indicated, and their flows strongly feature both intra-China and global connections, which is a remarkable show of concentrated potential working flows displaying all symptoms of being strategic places.

Considering that China is growing to be the world's largest economy, and that the modern world system is undergoing an overlap

Table 10.7 Top 20 City-Dyad Over-Connections That Include Chinese Cities

China Ranking	World Rank	City-Dyad	CDO*
1	3	Hong Kong and Singapore	97.4
2	4	Hong Kong and Shanghai	96.4
3	5	Beijing and Shanghai	96.4
4	6	Beijing and Hong Kong	95.7
5	7	Hong Kong and London	95.5
6	9	Hong Kong and New York	93.0
7	10	New York and Shanghai	92.1
8	12	London and Shanghai	91.9
9	14	Beijing and Singapore	91.6
10	16	Beijing and Frankfurt	90.2
11	17	Shanghai and Singapore	90.1
12	19	Hong Kong and Tokyo	89.6
13	21	Beijing and Tokyo	89.3
14	25	Shanghai and Tokyo	89.2
15	26	Frankfurt and Hong Kong	89.1
16	29	Beijing and London	88.5
17	33	Beijing and New York	88.2
18	35	Hong Kong and Paris	88.0
19	37	Paris and Shanghai	87.6
20	38	Frankfurt and Shanghai	87.1

Source: Taylor, Derudder, Hoyler et al. (2014).
Note: *CDO are measures of city-dyad over-connections presented as percentages of largest over-connection (Chicago–Los Angeles). Only cities in the top 20 of GNC are included.

period of American cycle and Chinese cycle, China's global cities are likely to represent Asia. China is very likely to be the only Asian country to have three global cities in the top 10 ranking by WCN connectivity that exert unique influence on the WCN. Moreover, the three cities will develop powerful strategic connectivity and support while playing their unique roles, forming a 'city-triad' where Shanghai is the fastest growing finance centre and Beijing the fastest growing political centre. Hong Kong has the role of being the fastest growing global platform. The initial globalizing impetus for network formation seems to have created a New York–London–Washington city-triad with each city having a distinctive role. New York is the leading financial centre and Washington is the leading political centre (including finance governance of the IMF and the World Bank), whilst London plays the role of a global platform. Taylor (2012) contended that the development of the WCN seemed to have involved creation of two city-triads, each related to key stages of network formation and reproduction with respect to leading states. Currently, the parallel between the two city-triad processes is remarkable, suggesting a necessary underlying structure that could only be recognized using relational thinking about win–win results. However, the former city-triad reflects an 'old' globalization structure, while the latter epitomizes the future of globalization.

10.2. SHANGHAI'S VISION OF BECOMING A GLOBAL CITY

The 'Shanghai 2050' vision represents the pinnacle of Shanghai's evolution towards the global city status. This vision should be seen as an achievable goal based on existing conditions, instead of wishful thinking. In order to make this vision look 'appropriate' or moderate, we will directly link Shanghai's roles to attributes of the WCN to forecast the city's prospects in global urban evolution, and propose the positioning that it should have, combining the application of global urban typology.

10.2.1. A Comprehensive Globalist City

Past experience shows that when a country becomes a global economic power and opens its own world dominant cycle in the modern world system, comprehensive globalist cities will emerge. The rise of London when the UK dominated the world economic and that of New York in the US-led cycle are good examples. Such globalist cities are few in number in the WCN, but occupy top positions, with the most extensive global reach, the most diversified network connections and strong presence in world city connections. In the next 30 years, China will rise to become the world's largest economy and start a China-dominated cycle, leading a new round of globalization. In such a case, it's natural or necessary that a global city will appear in China. Among domestic cities, Shanghai stands out because of its great potential for both global coverage and functional integration.

In terms of network connectivity coverage, Shanghai has a high degree of centrality, with the most obvious globalist orientation. More importantly, Shanghai is more connected to the core nodes of the WCN, especially to the top global cities in Europe and the Americas. This kind of network connection, which has both a high degree of eigenvector centrality, is one of the key features of a globalist city. From the perspective of network connectivity, the globalist orientation of Shanghai is higher than that of Hong Kong, and Hong Kong is more connected to cities in the Asia-Pacific region (Taylor 2006). Taylor, Derudder et al. (2014) compared Shanghai and Beijing's city-dyads, and the results suggest two main geographical differences. First, Beijing's city-dyads include all Pacific city links (including two Australian cities) except for Hong Kong, while Shanghai is more strongly linked to European and US cities (Table 10.8). Second, Beijing has a tendency to be linked more strongly to capital cities (such as Washington, Brussels, Madrid, Moscow, etc.), while Shanghai is more strongly linked to economical centres, suggesting that Shanghai is developing commercially as the more strategic place. Statistics show that European cities are generally more strongly linked to Shanghai—13 compared with 6 for Beijing, while amongst US cities, it is 6 to 4 in Shanghai's favour but the latter consists of the top 5 US cities in terms of GNC plus Miami (7th ranked in the USA), which is the main link to Latin America. It can also be seen that there are four Latin American cities in these data and they break 3 to 1 in favour of Shanghai, with Sao Paulo and Shanghai having particularly strong links. Therefore, it can be concluded that Shanghai has an obvious tendency of globalization in terms of GNC, and a globally wider coverage can be observed.

Table 10.8 Relative Strengths of Shanghai and Beijing in City-Dyads with Other Top 50 GNC Cities

Cities Tending Towards Shanghai	Difference*	Cities Tending Towards Beijing	Difference*
Munich	1.09	Washington	−0.86
Milan	1.04	Seoul	−0.73
Madrid	1.01	Dublin	−0.66
Sao Paulo	0.81	Kuala Lumpur	−0.52
Santiago	0.70	Johannesburg	−0.50
Mumbai	0.69	Frankfurt	−0.48
New York	0.61	Melbourne	−0.34
London	0.53	Moscow	−0.30
Lisbon	0.52	Dallas	−0.24
Stockholm	0.51	Atlanta	−0.23
Warsaw	0.51	Singapore	−0.23
Prague	0.46	Philadelphia	−0.22
Miami	0.46	Brussels	−0.20
Istanbul	0.37	Zürich	−0.19
Boston	0.32	Delhi	−0.16
Barcelona	0.30	Dubai	−0.16
Paris	0.24	Taipei	−0.13
Vienna	0.23	Bangkok	−0.12
Los Angeles	0.17	Mexico City	−0.10
Buenos Aires	0.15	Sydney	−0.09
Hong Kong	0.11	Jakarta	−0.08
San Francisco	0.09	Tokyo	−0.03
Toronto	0.07	Düsseldorf	−0.00
Amsterdam	0.01		
Chicago	0.00		

Source: Taylor, Derudder, Hoyler et al. (2014).
Note: *Difference is computed as (CDRShanghai-i − CDRBeijing-i). These values are very small and, therefore, they are multiplied by 10,000 for presentation). Top 20 GNC cities are emboldened.

In terms of the comprehensiveness in cities' general functions judged from the categorical scale of network connectivity, Hong Kong apparently favours economic links, Beijing being a political centre boasts stronger political connectivity, whereas Shanghai is in between. In terms of political connectedness, the difference between Shanghai and Beijing lies in the number of comprehensive transnational organizations (embassies and consulates) they have. Total 150 embassies are located in Beijing, which accounts for 50 per cent of the comprehensive transnational organizations, while Shanghai only has 63 consulates. But the difference between Beijing and Shanghai in terms of technical transnational organizations (international media, cultural organization and business organizations) is very limited, with 20 such organizations located in Beijing and 15 in Shanghai. In the current global governance system, unofficial diplomatic networks, including international organizations, NGOs and civil society diplomatic organizations are playing increasingly larger roles, aside from official diplomatic networks. Non-capital cities can also take important roles in global governance as long as they have a lot of entities operating within these unofficial diplomatic networks. Even though it is not a political capital, Shanghai can attract more transnational organizations of the unofficial diplomatic networks and grow towards a more comprehensive city such as New York. In other words, being a non-capital city does not hinder Shanghai from expanding its general functions. Finally, in terms of global science and culture connectivity, Beijing and Shanghai are on a par.

In effect, the connectivity to economic service is the most important, powerful and influential among all network connectivity types of global cities, followed by the connectivity to political capitals. Shanghai takes advantages in the comprehensiveness in its (economic) functions in a narrow sense, and notably the diversity in connectivity. As an international financial, trade, shipping, economic, science and technology centre, Shanghai boasts a complete financial market system, various trading and investment platforms, a great number of regional HQs of transnational companies, foreign investment firms, foreign-invested R&D centres and a wide array of specialized service firms. As is showed in Taylor's (2011) empirical research, Shanghai ranked 7th by its financial network connectivity, 11th for law, 8th by advertising,

14th by accountancy and 23rd by management consultancy. In fact, Shanghai's potential for comprehensive development based on a globalist orientation is not random or unstable but supported by a solid foundation and competitive advantages.

10.2.2. Strategic Cities with High Mobility

Functions of global cities lie in the GNC, which are mainly reflected by the levels of strategicness for cities' network positions and the levels of mobility for their networks. Different combinations of strategicness and mobility at various levels define different types of global cities. Among all combinations, strategic cities with high mobility are the global cities with highest levels of strategicness and mobility.

Based on the current developments and trends, Shanghai has been an outstanding strategic place in terms of its network position and mobility. Some empirical studies showed that Shanghai ranked 11th in GNC (Table 10.9). The number of strategic offices in Shanghai reached 23, only two fewer than that in New York and London, and above than in cities such as Paris, Hong Kong, Singapore and Tokyo. However, Shanghai has a relatively low connectivity per strategic firm office (261.70), much lower than that of New York (438.04), London (372.64) and Singapore (360.35). This is because Shanghai is more often the location of regional HQs (not the corporate HQs) for transnational companies, and the functional institutions with high strategicness such as law firms and management consultancy firms located in the city are relatively weak. Some empirical studies further regressed strategic network connectivity against GNC and recorded the residuals. These are standardized (0 mean and a standard deviation of 1) so that positive numbers indicate relative strategic over-connectedness, and negative numbers indicate relative strategic under-connectedness. In Table 10.10, cities are ranked by size of their residuals to show the importance of their strategic connectivity relative to overall connectivity. According to the findings, although Chinese cities are increasingly important in terms of GNC, this is not being reflected in strategicness—only Shanghai is recorded as strategically over-connected and above the average (ranked 19th).

A Case Study of 'Shanghai 2050' Global City Vision (Part II)

Table 10.9 Strategic Network Connectivity

Rank	City	Strategic Network Connectivity	Number of Offices	Connectivity per Office
1	New York	10,951	25	438.04
2	London	9,316	25	372.64
3	Chicago	7,629	24	317.88
4	Paris	7,023	22	319.23
5	Hong Kong	6,744	20	337.20
6	San Francisco	6,484	24	270.17
7	Los Angeles	6,325	23	275.00
8	Sydney	6,219	18	345.50
9	Singapore	6,126	17	360.35
10	Tokyo	6,110	22	277.73
11	Shanghai	6,019	23	261.70
12	Milan	5,731	19	301.63
13	Frankfurt	5,613	20	280.65
14	Beijing	5,581	22	253.68
15	Moscow	5,201	17	305.94

Source: Taylor, Derudder, Faulconbridge et al. (2014).

Table 10.10 Residuals from Regressing Strategic Network Connectivity against GNC

Rank	City	Residual
1	New York	2.53
2	San Francisco	2.36
3	Chicago	2.26
4	Palo Alto	1.51
5	Los Angeles	1.36
6	Bangkok	0.98
7	Auckland	0.93
8	Düsseldorf	0.92
9	Miami	0.79

(Continued)

(Continued)

Rank	City	Residual
10	Riyadh	0.78
11	Johannesburg	0.74
12	Frankfurt	0.74
13	Paris	0.63
14	Stockholm	0.48
15	Sydney	0.47
16	Dallas	0.26
17	Washington	0.24
18	Milan	0.11
19	*Shanghai*	0.01
20	Tokyo	0.00
21	Moscow	−0.01
22	Beijing	−0.02
23	Rome	−0.26
24	Munich	−0.27
25	Taipei	−0.29
26	London	−0.31
27	Hong Kong	−0.32
28	Melbourne	−0.40
29	Houston	−0.43
30	Singapore	−0.45

Source: Taylor, Derudder, Faulconbridge et al. (2014).

Although the aforementioned analysis of strategic network connectivity offers a different measure from that offered by the analysis of global city network connectivity, it merely shows a city's overall level of connectivity and tells us nothing about the specific intercity connections that constitute it: how many connections it is composed of (i.e., the number of other cities it shares firms with), which cities it is more strongly connected to and where it is relatively weakly connected. In order to solve these questions, the city-dyad connectivity (CDC) analysis has to be applied. Among the top 20 GNC cities ranked by top 40 dyad memberships, Shanghai is ranked the fourth with

8 dyad memberships, which is 2 fewer than that of New York who is ranked the 1st, 1 fewer than that of London, and the same as the number of Hong Kong. Moreover, Shanghai has more cities (11) in the top 20 and these are generally ranked higher including both London and New York (Table 10.11). This suggests that Shanghai tends to have a more concentrated pattern of intercity connections constituting its GNC, particularly featuring other major cities. Additionally, it

Table 10.11 Top 20 GNC Cities Ranked by Top 40 Dyad Memberships

City	Dyad Memberships*	Membership Rank**	GNC Rank
New York	10	1	2
London	9	2	1
Hong Kong	8	3	3
Shanghai	8	4	7
Singapore	8	5	5
Frankfurt	8	6	19
Beijing	7	7	12
Paris	7	8	4
Tokyo	6	9	6
Los Angeles	4	10	17
Chicago	3	11	8
Sydney	1	12	10
Madrid	1	13	15
Toronto	0 (59)	14	13
Mumbai	0 (67)	15	16
Milan	0 (100)	16	11
São Paulo	0 (109)	17	14
Moscow	0 (120)	18	18
Dubai	0 (132)	19	9
Mexico City	0 (174)	20	20

Source: Taylor, Derudder, Hoyler et al. (2014).
Notes: *For cities with zero membership in the top 40, their highest ranked dyad membership is given in brackets for ranking purpose.
**For cities with dyad membership that have equal totals, they are ranked by their lowest average of ranks from Table 10.9.

Table 10.12 Changes in City-Dyad Connectivity (2000–2010)

City-Dyads	Change of CDC (%)
Beijing–Shanghai	69.40
Hong Kong–Shanghai	39.58
Beijing–Hong Kong	20.54
London–Shanghai	37.91
London–Beijing	16.73
London–Hong Kong	–11.04
New York–Shanghai	38.84
New York–Beijing	20.22
New York–Hong Kong	–14.85
London–New York	–12.65

Source: Taylor, Derudder, Hoyler et al. (2014).

has a more strategic position within the WCN than the cities that are more generally integrated into the network. In terms of trends in the changing CDC, Shanghai has been on a growing trend. Table 10.12 shows that over the period 2000–2010, among all city-dyads, the London–New York CDC has declined by 12.65 per cent, while the Shanghai–Beijing CDC increased the most by 69.4 per cent. Second to the Beijing–Shanghai CDC, the New York–Shanghai CDC has grown by 38.84 per cent and the London–Shanghai CDC by 37.91 per cent. Whereas the Shanghai–Hong Kong CDC and the Beijing–Hong Kong CDC have gone up, the London–Hong Kong CDC and the New York–Hong Kong CDC have dropped by 11.04 per cent and 14.85 per cent, respectively. This clearly demonstrates that Shanghai has developed strategically a more important role in the WCN.

Given the categorization based on functions of connectivity, the Shanghai 2050 Plan aims to build Shanghai into a strategic global city with high mobility by providing various gateways for resource circulation and platforms for resource allocation and as a hub controlling and serving the large-scale circulation and allocation of global resources. To this end, Shanghai strives to lead the concentration and diffusion of factors such as capital, information, commercial services and high-level professionals in the process of global resource allocation, through housing the HQs of a great number of transnational and global firms with control and coordination functions, especially those that are domestically owned. In this way, Shanghai will become a major innovation incubator for innovative thoughts, creative activities and start-up models and play a pivotal role in global governance and international affair coordination.

10.2.3. Hub Cities Acting as a Gateway

Global cities are always part of the interconnected structure, with positions at multiple dimensions in the WCN, which indicates the different roles they play in the world system. Different combinations of the recursive centrality of hub global cities and the recursive power of gateway global cities shape different types of global cities based on the interconnected structure.

In terms of GNC, Shanghai displays characteristics of both a hub city and a gateway city, seen from its current developments and trends, though such characteristics are assessed in two different spatial scales. On a global scale, Shanghai shows more characteristics of hub cities, with its recursive centrality represented by strong capabilities of accumulation and dissemination, and consequently sizable flows of economic elements. Nevertheless, on this scale, Shanghai's role as a gateway (passage) to the rest of the world is relatively smaller because it has limited capability of guiding and controlling resources flows in foreign cities, unlike those typical gateway cities such as New York and London, only through which can flows of resources in other cities access the world market. This gap should be attributed to Shanghai's lack of management and control functions over the GVC and the 'out-degree'-based global linkage. On the domestic spatial scale, Shanghai is more of a gateway city than of a hub city. That is to say, it obtains more influence (power) by providing other cities in China with access to the global market. Shanghai has historically been a natural gateway city of great importance due to its unique geographic advantage of being in the estuary of the Yangtze River and facing the East China Sea. Since the implementation of the reform and opening-up policy, China has attracted sizable FDI and developed an export-oriented growth model. During the process, Shanghai has strengthened its role as a gateway connecting Chinese cities with the world market.

Thus, although Shanghai shows characteristics of both hub cities and gateway cities, it does not enjoy high centrality or high power in the interconnected structure because these two different sets of characteristics are represented by different spatial scales. But as long as the basis for these characteristics exists, Shanghai may possibly evolve towards high centrality and high power, or at least have more potential to do so. And during this evolution, three variables will play main parts: (a) China-based MNCs or global firms are expanding and implementing 'overseas investment' via Shanghai to developed countries such as the USA and European countries and developing countries in Africa and Latin America, especially those along the Belt and Road. To establish connectivity with the ill-connected cities in these countries is to build strategic connections. If new connections with well-connected cities are to enhance the possibility of resource concentration (centre), then the new connections with ill-connected cities are to strengthen the possibility of command and control (power). Thus, Shanghai will be able to enhance its high power in the interconnected structure and function as a global gateway city; (b) quite a number of Chinese cities will enter the rank of global cities, hence the change in the nature of their connections with Shanghai. Rather than the gateway facing domestic cities, Shanghai will increasingly become the gateway facing global cities; (c) as China continues on the road to RMB internalization and makes its currency a major international reserve currency, Shanghai will develop into an international financial centre befitting China's economy size and RMB's international position, and a global centre for RMB product-dominated innovation, trading, pricing and clearing. And Shanghai's emergence into an inevitable destination for the world banking and financial industries will highlight its significance as a global gateway city.

Therefore, based on the typology of interconnected structure, the Shanghai 2050 Plan is targeting at a gateway hub city. At that time, Shanghai, as a hub city with high centrality, will have a large number of direct connections as well as indirect connections from remote places, thereby effectively attracting and distributing resources worldwide. Meanwhile, as a gateway city of 'high power', Shanghai can extend the connection to cities with little connectivity, so that these cities can be included into the WCN through their only portal (channel) and, thus, it can further control and influence the element flows in certain parts of the network. It means that Shanghai, a city with high centrality and high power in the interconnected structure of WCN in the future and an important outpost of globalization, has the structural advantages of resource gathering/dissemination and resource flow control. It will provide not only greater opportunities for actors (such as MNCs, political leaders, cultural organizations and social movements) in cities to develop strategies and innovation initiatives but also a more effective path for actors in other cities to enter the global market.

10.2.4. Unification of Three Targets: An Excellent Global City

The three targets based on the characteristics of global city types as analysed and defined earlier are not completely unrelated but have certain intersection and internal unity. First, they are all based on GNC, which manifest the features of key network nodes. Second, they are all at the highest level of the evolution of their respective global urban types, which means that they are the most powerful in terms of the range, frequency, intensity and type of external connectivity in the network, with the highest network position and mobility in terms of connectivity functions, as well as the strongest centrality and power in the interconnected structure. Thus, they play the most important role in the interconnected structure. Third, given the conditions earlier, they all perform strategic functions in coordinating and allocating global resource flows, that is, the functions influencing and determining the scale of global resource flows, the main flow direction, the emphasis in allocation and the means of allocation. Finally, in line with the strategic functions of the global resource allocation and flow coordination, they must be able to provide integrated services globally. Obviously, from the perspective of unity, a city that can reach the highest level of all three types of global cities at the same time must be an excellent global city with great global influence and strong capabilities of coordination and control, such as New York and London.

Therefore, considering the high degree of unity of the three targets based on the characteristics of global city types, we can set 'an excellent global city' as the overarching goal of the Shanghai 2050 Plan. The core of an excellent global city is its strategic functions of global resource allocation and flow coordination, which are generally characterized by: (a) the strong creativity in global resource flows and allocations, which affects and dominates the flow direction and allocation methods. This is a concentrated manifestation of the inherent vitality and innovation of Shanghai being a global city in the flows and allocation of global resources; (b) the broad influence in global resource allocation, which affects and guides the flow volume and allocation scope of global resources. This is a concentrated manifestation of Shanghai being a global city with external network connectivity in the flows and allocation of global resources; (c) the appeal in global resource allocation, which affects and guides the flow rate and allocation efficiency of global resources. This is a concentrated manifestation of Shanghai being a global city with inherent advantage in the flows and allocation of global resources. These basic characteristics are interrelated and mutually supportive, and each of them indispensable. To conclude, Shanghai will be a creative, influential and glamorous global city in the future.

The Shanghai 2050 goal of leaping to an excellent global city will, of course, encounter some interferences and risks. But as long as China keeps pursuing national rejuvenation, Shanghai would not be deterred from achieving this overarching goal. Although there is a significant gap between Shanghai and existing global cities such as New York and London, which cannot be closed in a short time, Shanghai's potential to evolve into an excellent city will be fully unleashed with various favourable conditions and the support of national strategies. It's totally possible that Shanghai would stand as an excellent global city full of creativity, impact and charm, and equipped with the strategic functions in global resource allocation and flows that are commensurate with China's economy size and international status by 2050. At that time, Shanghai, New York and London (presuming that it will still serve as the representative of European cities) will become a trio of global cities at the highest level (New York–London–Shanghai).

10.3. CORE FUNCTIONS OF SHANGHAI AS A GLOBAL CITY

Although all global cities contribute to resource flows across the globe, they don't carry out the same series of activities or show the same significance when performing functions with international influence. On the contrary, decided by their positions in the WCN, each global city has its own core functions. This also applies to Shanghai. In accordance with the vision of a comprehensive globally oriented excellent global city, the Shanghai 2050 Plan seeks to bestow upon Shanghai strategic core functions featuring high integration of economy (finances), technology and culture. The fundamental effects of these core functions may not change, but their meanings could be expanded and adjusted with time.

10.3.1. Function of Global Value Chain Governance

As economic globalization goes further, especially as transnational firms grow rapidly and evolve into global companies, the global allocation of resources becomes increasingly important and stimulates the integration of investment, trade, finance and industrial activities, which is increasingly reflected in the networked operation of GVCs. Therefore, when Shanghai plays the role of strategic global resource allocation, it will be mainly reflected in its core function of robust GVC governance.

According to the definition of GVC, global production should be understood as the transnational trading of a series of goods produced at different production stages among different enterprises and institutions (Gereffi and Korzeniewicz 1994). Unlike the earlier vertically integrated structure derived from economic globalization, it is characterized by a distributed resource network, which has its grounds in the NIDL and acts as an advanced form of global production and resource allocation. GVC has two basic traits: (a) its connectivity is distributed across a range of locations and achieved through the necessary transnational flows between their respective spatial node activities; (b) being a type of highly diversified industrial activities, it enables the sharing at stages of investment, financing, production, technology and trade, which varies with specific commodity chains. Besides, it is also a fluid industry that relies on different infrastructure and transportation modes. That's why GVC is marked by the 'dual crossing of the borders' in resource flow and allocation—crossing the borders of enterprises and organizations, and of national territories.

The current trend of economic globalization shows that global production is increasingly growing towards GVCs, which will result in a new system of international division of labour dominated by GVCs. Specifically, it is manifested in the following three aspects. First, the investment-driven trade and the intra-firm and intra-industry trade promoted by investment will constitute the largest share of trade under GVCs. Second, as GVCs are shifting from 'offshoring' to 'near-shoring' strategies, the tendencies of international dispersion and regional agglomeration will be seen. Third, GVCs are becoming more networked. Compared with the previous simple 'value chains', the networked GVCs will produce more 'chemical reactions' that contribute to technical integration, product integration, market integration and industrial integration. Meanwhile, networked GVCs are expected to bring more 'spillover effects' by strengthening the connections of knowledge, technology and capability among value chains.

As the world economic centre of gravity moves eastwards and the production networks in the Asia-Pacific region continue to evolve, GVCs will prevail in the Asia-Pacific and other regions. China being a regional economic power with fully integrated sub-systems will surely play a crucial role in the Asia-Pacific production networks. With enhanced economic performance and innovation capability, China is seeing an increasing number of domestic multinational companies going global, which will facilitate the emergence of more GVCs dominated by Chinese companies. In this process, aiming to develop into an 'excellent global city', Shanghai will certainly become a place where the relevant nodes or linkages of GVCs tend to converge, equipped with the function of GVC governance.

The well functioning of GVCs is realized through governance. 'A chain without governance would just be a string of market relations' (Humphrey and Schmitz 2001). In other words, the governance of GVCs refers to the management and control of a string of market relations. The issue here is who should manage and control these chains. Although there are numerous participants in GVCs, they differ from each other in terms of their capacity to 'appropriate rents and the barriers to entry of the different nodes', which 'have a dynamic character, and may be eroded by potential competition' (Kaplinsky and Morris 2001). Only key actors in the chains are the lead firms involved in the governance structure of GVCs. While the lead firms in different value chains may compete against each other, those in the same value chain are not competitors since they all lead and promote the growth of the chain they are in and, thus, exert management and control functions. The behaviour of the lead firms may involve direct coordination of activities on a global scale, the identification and appropriation of dynamic rents, the assignment of specific roles to chain agents, as well as indirect rule setting for the chain. These key actors in the governance of GVCs fall into two categories: MNC HQs or regional HQs, and global APS firms.

By establishing networks of procurement, production and marketing on a global scale, MNCs have built various GVCs and propelled the rapid growth of R&D, manufacturing and sales along the value chains, thereby establishing themselves as a backbone force in the development and deployment of GVCs. The HQs of MNCs, which govern GVCs and the vital parts within, play the significant role as network coordinators in the allocation of production factors and key resources. With the growing trend of 'nearshoring', the regional HQs of MNCs also play an increasingly significant role in the management and governance of GVCs, and are expected to become another backbone force in the development and deployment of GVCs. However, the role of global producer service firms in GVCs has yet to be deeply analysed (Brown et al. 2010). Although global producer service firms do not directly create GVCs, they have the professional competitive advantage to serve the GVCs through their internal networks distributed around the world, resources shared by their long-term foreign partners and their own well-trained professionals. This is critical for companies seeking to 'go global', and connect and manage the decentralized production and consumption sites. In fact, producer service firms provide services for the entire GVC, from market research, provision of legal information, such as corporate laws, criminal laws and tax and tariff laws, and of risk assessments, and management of debts and receivables worldwide to human resources management, advertising services and more. Moreover, when providing services, producer service firms exert pressure on the clients' decision-making process by, for example, requiring and supervising corporate compliance operations, and establishing rules and procedures on corporate governance and corporate decision-making. By providing services in relation to business target positioning and location selection, tax issues, labour legislation, risk management and entry barriers, they actually help clients to manage and control GVCs. The pre-structured participation of producer service firms in decision-making is a kind of embedded governance. Through the temporary cooperation team, this kind of 'embedded governance' can also incorporate strategic concerns into specific services in the form of indirect decision-making, or producer service firm can participate in the decision-making process directly as a consultant or independent director to the client. In a word, governance is defined by the role global producer service firms play in managing and adjusting their clients' GVCs as 'authority and power relationships that determine how financial, material and human resources are allocated and flow within a chain' (Gereffi 1994: 97). Therefore, Shanghai's core function of GVC governance lies above all in the clustering of such organizations as leaders and promoters of GVCs, and it is then manifested by their direct or cross-governance of GVCs.

To approach the issue from another angle, global cities' function of GVC governance is also the specialized allocation function of elements along the value chain, which is mostly reflected in the large-scale and high-frequency flows of resources, such as capital, commodities, information, services and talents through the node cities around the world that causes multi-polarized distribution of locations for different activities in the value chain. Regardless of whether the different types of value chains are constructed and specified by the leading companies in the upstream or in the downstream, the core types of production factors always control other types of factors and play the dominant role in the governance structure. Following this logic, Shanghai's function of GVC governance should focus on certain activities that are based on core production factors. Global cities' function of governing or driving GVCs is performed by merely gathering senior management and international affairs management, strengthening knowledge work and conducting some vertical market management activities, which is reflected in, specifically, coordinating cross-border economic relationships, integrating value chains, guiding the distribution of interest, integrating knowledge flows, leading the innovation of technology and business models and so on. The links of a single GVC tend to separate vertically, while different GVCs are interconnected and cross-coordinated and even horizontally reorganized together to create value more efficiently and gain more network rents. The value chain governance function of global cities is, therefore, also reflected in the powerful network radiation, which makes it possible for complementary optimization among GVCs, improvement in productivity and rationalized allocation of resources.

Obviously, in order to better perform this function, Shanghai needs a broad and multi-layered operational platform for high-end activities along the GVC. The more powerful and convenient these platforms are, the more high-end activities they can attract, and the more efficiently they can promote complementarities among different value chains. At the same time, in order to strengthen knowledge sharing in the value chain, Shanghai needs to take measures to promote the flow of knowledge on both global and local scales and turn the functional geographical distribution of APS into the knowledge flow space and the 'nerve centres' of knowledge flow in the GVC. In addition, given the need of a substantial input of energy, resources and capital to achieve global coverage of the value chain, Shanghai, as it seeks to integrate more small-sized enterprises into the wider global network, needs to provide a favourable environment and a complete market system encouraging domestic and cross-border corporate merges, acquisitions and joint ventures and facilitating the establishment of new operational companies, strategic alliances and partnerships which are connected by various contracts. Besides, Shanghai needs to have in place stronger connections in the world network, super resource pools and extensive mobility, so as to meet the requirements for: the variable operations and cross-regional purchasing and logistics within the GVC, the techniques and skills of international labours necessitated by the increasingly complicated 'mixed' operational models, the miscellaneous dynamic service, procurement and logistical arrangements caused by specific projects and the difficult clarification and definition of the changing relations between entities. Last but not least, Shanghai needs to develop sets of clear and coherent institutions and policies accustomed to common international practices, especially by improving the regulatory standards for labour flexibility, taxation, migration, education, political stability, cultural and space planning. All this is of paramount importance to the flows of elements, knowledge and value in the GVC.

10.3.2. Function of Global Wealth Management (GWM)

Though the preceding section on the function of GVC governance has dealt with the activities of finance, trade and investment, as well as shipping and logistics as a whole, it mainly addresses financial activities directly related to the industrial value chain, which partially covers the topic. As the core of economic activities, finance has its own mode of operation which is unique and undergoing constant change and refinement. Existing studies concerned have also taken financial activities as one of the key functions of global cities. Therefore, in this section, finance is set apart as one of the core functions of the future global city Shanghai, with its focus on GWM according to the vision of future international financial centre. Judging from the present developments and trends, the form and function of international financial centres will go through further changes, placing ever-increasing stress on the wealth management function. In the coming three decades, Shanghai, on its way of upgrading and development towards an international financial centre as well as the global RMB centre, will enhance its function of GWM after it becomes a hub for capital markets.

Economic development offers more opportunities for individuals to build wealth. As a result, the global personal wealth accumulates fast, which creates a strong demand for wealth management. Goldman Sachs has predicted that by 2050, the average GDP per capita of all countries of the world will reach US$30,000, and that the global total of assets under management (AUM) including funds managed by the insurance industry, mutual fund assets and charitable funds will be close to the world's GDP, which shows a significant positive correlation between the average GDP per capita and the asset management. If the US Dollar is assumed to remain stable and the global wealth is projected to increase at an average annual growth rate of 4 per cent, the global wealth will amount to US$1,200 trillion in 2050. By 2030, the size of middle-income group across the globe with yearly income levels from US$6,000 to US$30,000 will rise to 2 billion. According to the estimates by the European Union Institute for Security Studies, the size of the middle class all over the world will increase to 4.9 billion. Apparently, all this shows that there will be a huge increase in the demand of private wealth management. As estimated by the Citibank, the wealth management industry revenue now accounts for 20 per cent of the total revenue in the global financial service sector while the global total of AUM is about US$87 trillion (The City UK 2013), equal to the world's GDP in one year. Over the past 20 years, London, New York, Singapore and Hong Kong have become the most important international financial centres offering onshore private assets management services. And now, Shanghai, located in the Asia-Pacific region, is confronted by compelling historic opportunities to establish its GWM capabilities, as the global investments and wealth shift eastwards and the number of China's high-net-worth individuals (HNWIs) grows drastically. According to statistics of the Boston Consulting Group (BCG), the Asia-Pacific region (excluding Japan) has undergone the highest relative growth rate of wealth, from US$11.1

trillion in 2005 to US$21.7 trillion in 2010, increasing by 95.5 per cent (Table 10.13). In the next 30 years, the global wealth will further shift to Asia. By 2050, the population of the middle class in Asia will occupy 60 per cent of that of the world's middle class (Table 10.14). If the wealth grows at an average annual rate of 8 per cent, by 2050, Asia's total wealth will reach to US$1,800 trillion and 40 per cent of

Table 10.13 Assets under Management (2005–2010)

	AUM by Region (in Trillion USD)					
	2005	2006	2007	2008	2009	2010
North America	31.3	35.1	37.5	31.2	34.6	38.2
Europe	31.3	33.6	34.8	33.1	35.4	37.1
Asia-Pacific (excluding Japan)	11.1	12.8	15.5	14.9	18.5	21.7
Japan	16.7	17.3	17.3	16.6	16.8	16.8
Middle East and Africa	3.2	3.6	3.9	3.6	4.1	4.5
Latin America	2.3	2.5	2.8	2.9	3.2	3.5
Total	95.8	104.9	111.8	102.3	112.8	121.8

Source: Boston Consulting Group (2011).

Table 10.14 Size of the Middle Class (2009–2050; Millions of People and Global Share)

	2009		2020		2050	
North America	338	18%	333	10%	322	7%
Europe	664	36%	703	22%	680	14%
Central and South America	181	10%	251	8%	313	6%
Asia-Pacific	525	28%	1,740	54%	3,228	66%
Sub-Saharan Africa	32	2%	57	2%	107	2%
Middle East and North Africa	105	6%	165	5%	234	5%
World	1,845	100%	3,249	100%	4,884	100%

Source: Kharas (2010).

the world's wealth management services will be performed in Asia. In addition, the personal wealth in China also accumulates very rapidly. Credit Suisse's Global Wealth Report 2014 shows that the wealth of mainland China grows at 8.1 per cent while the number of households with millions of dollars in assets ranks third in the world only after the USA and Japan, and that China's assets per capita have increased from US$5,670 in 2000 to about US$21,300 in 2014, with the median value of US$7,033.

As a new function of the city derived from its position as an international financial centre, GWM involves the management, allocation and control of assets on a global scale, which influences the direction and distribution of global capital flows. Its key indicator is not the amount of assets in transaction, but that of AUM—disposable and controllable assets, especially the size and structure of offshore assets (including the structure of asset sources and investment). GWM includes services such as investment management and asset allocation for various institutions and individuals across the globe, with the primary aim to preserve and increase their wealth, which requires appropriate global strategic decisions. Its major principles are long-term planning, sound management, reasonable debt structure and effective risk aversion.

Though different from the asset, currency and derivative trading in the traditional capital market, currency market and derivatives market, respectively, GWM still builds on sound financial systems, mature capital markets and sophisticated financial instruments, and must be conducted through various platforms. Also, despite a few new institutions that were set up to deal with GWM specifically, the majority of this business is handled by existing financial institutions which have undergone business transformation or expansion—changes leading to the specialization of the services of these institutions as professional institutional investors. They have their own target clients and business scope and use different combination of financial instruments. But, at the same time, their businesses also have some similarities and overlap to some degree. This allows them to coordinate and cooperate with each other and, thus, in some sense operate as a whole.

Besides, GWM also needs a large number of supportive service agencies. For example, accounting firms predominantly give clients in the HNWI to ultra-HNWI market advice on personal taxation (including filing returns), financial planning, setting up and managing trusts (for inheritance) and the management of estates (private property portfolios). And the third-party financial institutions, as independent intermediaries, focus on offering personalized financial services to HNWI. Therefore, the principal condition for GWM is the cluster of a large group of financial and related professional institutions that manage global wealth with different financial instruments through different financial platforms. These institutions have not only engrained a tradition of credibility, trust and safety in the deposit of wealth, such as London's world-class reputation in traditional private banking which has not only laid the foundation for the new private wealth sector (Cassis and Cottrell 2009) but also created a milieu of expertise, knowledge and financial instruments which spill over into similar financial sectors. Based on this, London has developed as an important location for GWM and a residential magnet for the global HNW and UHNW population.

At present, wealth management is still at its infancy in China, which is mostly product oriented, while, in fact, it is better achieved through personalized financial planning. Moreover, the necessary infrastructure for its smooth operation has yet to be put in place, for example, an electronic wealth management and trading platform that is cross-border, account connected and asset allocation oriented. However, with the further reform and improvement of China's financial system, Shanghai's functions as an international financial centre will be upgraded and a unique model will be established for better performance in GWM—a model featuring highly professional services, better use of IT, diversified services and products, and efficient management platforms offering offshore and international management, so as to enable IT-driven and customized wealth management services.

10.3.3. A Global Technology Innovation Hub

In the next three decades, a global innovation network (GIN) will take shape and become a new network system connecting the whole world in addition to existing global production networks. As Shanghai evolves into a comprehensive global city, it will have a new function as a global technology innovation hub that can take the lead in global innovation and resource allocation.

Building Shanghai into a global science and technology innovation centre is undoubtedly important to its shift towards innovation-driven development and represents an inevitable road to an excellent global city. But this strategy is more about supporting China's rejuvenation. In the next 30 years, as the world will witness a new round of technological and industrial revolution, the global innovation landscape will undergo profound changes: many countries including the USA, Europe and China are likely to become centres for the new round of technology innovation. Although China still lags far behind developed countries in terms of technological innovation ability and output, it maintains strong momentum which has attracted worldwide attention. In addition, although the globalization process currently led by Chinese enterprises still mainly focuses on manufacturing, it will ultimately be driven by a global innovation system to be established based on Chinese traditional culture and current market conditions. Therefore, Shanghai's reinforcement of its function as a global technology innovation hub is a drive to support China in leading the new round of scientific and technological revolution and facilitate Chinese enterprises to make innovations of global significance.

To fulfil this new function means that Shanghai, as a global city, needs to give full play to its function of global resource allocation, thus enabling flows of diverse resources and services based on its network connections. Moreover, 'global science and technology innovation centre' should not be simply regarded as a global knowledge centre, or a centre for creation and application of achievements in science and technology in the narrow sense. Rather it calls for integration of innovation, creativity and entrepreneurship, and interaction between technological innovation and service innovation, which will not only boost technological innovation in existing industrial sectors but also give rise to new industries, new supply chains and new business models that are cross-boundary or where boundaries blur.

Meanwhile, to be a key node of the global technological innovation network, Shanghai should also adopt a new model that facilitates participation of multiple players, cross-boundary flow and allocation of innovation resources, international cooperation in innovation projects and rapid dissemination and integration of new technologies. Such a model is more open and flexible than the traditional one which emphasizes independence and self-reliance throughout the whole process of R&D, production and application of scientific and technological achievements. It can enable dynamic and cross-disciplinary innovation with global vision that features modularization and parallel processing.

In addition, in terms of spatial organization, innovation resources should be pooled in line with value chains to form widely distributed small clusters (like 'silicon lanes' or 'silicon zones') that are intertwined with or embedded within other functional areas, so as to promote the integration of university campuses, science and technology parks, public communities and urban blocks.

Based on the aforementioned considerations, as a global science and technology innovation centre, Shanghai will be able to chart the map for global innovation activities by serving as a hub for the allocation of global innovation resources and developing platforms for competition and cooperation, and to support a large number of Chinese enterprises in making innovations of global influence. Specifically, the city will have strong capabilities of attracting, allocating and integrating innovation resources, spreading technological innovations and translating them into productivity. It will focus on cutting-edge innovations with wide influence and a significant application potential and create platforms for their display with a view to promote innovation and shape its future landscape. As a major node of the GIN, the city will effectively perform organizational and control functions in the innovation network to establish extensive connections, hold innovation activities frequently and promote intensive innovation exchange and cooperation. Finally, it will use and integrate global innovation resources to strengthen the innovation capacity of Chinese enterprise, thus turning itself into an innovation powerhouse.

To achieve these goals, Shanghai itself should invest more on innovation to produce richer and higher level outcomes and, more importantly, it should equip itself with the ability to allocate global innovation resources and lead in related rulemaking processes. First, it should ensure that its basic research institutes reach the world-class level, especially in frontier areas such as material structure, evolution of the universe, origin of life and the essence of consciousness. Currently, major breakthroughs are being or expected to be made in these areas, which will greatly spur innovation and take it to a higher level—a prerequisite for a technological innovation centre with global influence. Second, the city should indicate the future trends in technological innovation by showcasing the world's most cutting-edge innovations, facilitate the flow and allocation of resources worldwide and act as a coordinator in the GIN. Third, it should have a strong capability of applying innovations, especially those motivated by people's increasing demand for new lifestyles. To this end, innovation incubators are needed: not only platforms for facilitating widely applicable technologies but also multidisciplinary, application-oriented integrated service providers that can offer efficient and customized resource allocation solutions for innovative activities. Finally, the city must be able to organize and control innovation resources efficiently based on diversified and extensive connections in the GIN. As a key node of the network, it should provide a favourable institutional environment, a mature market system and effective trading platforms that can boost the flow of innovation resources and outcomes. In addition, it should seek to establish technological innovation alliances or partnerships involving different industries, enterprises (or innovation teams) and geographical locations for the application of certain advanced technologies, which will catapult it to positions such as key player in the formulation of innovation competition rules and significant initiator of new competition platforms.

Shanghai's new function of effective integration and utilization of global innovation resources will have to rely on the GIN featuring multiple players, knowledge sharing and collaboration, as well as various kinds of new innovation alliances that have three functions, that is, network-based new market think tanks, new motivators of technological development and creators of innovative knowledge network. Generally speaking, especially in the context of globalization, 'growth in international collaborations may be due more to the dynamics created by the self-interests of individual scientists rather than to other structural, institutional or policy-related factors' (Wagner and Leydesdorff 2005). Therefore, seeking opportunities of foreign cooperation is mainly a result of the participators' own choices with their own efforts. The complex dynamics of network resulting from those choices shows spontaneous self-organization, which becomes the structure of many of today's knowledge systems (Wagner and Leydesdorff 2006).

The GIN first comes into being as new nodes form links between them, and then more links appear between these existing nodes as participants of the collaboration increase. When major structural transformations occur in the network, the occasional, spontaneous cooperation in the initial network evolves into a structured relationship between more partners who seek to maintain stable and coherent clusters. Meanwhile, the large number of new participants illustrates trends of seeking variety and exploring new sources of knowledge and ideas. The online globalization research community is a case in point. As a communication platform for scholars from all over the world to share ideas and present diversified perspectives on issues of common interest, it will be more influential as the number of its members grows.

In addition, to create a solid knowledge base for the city to serve as a GIN-based global technology innovation hub, clusters such as those comprised of universities, research institutions, enterprises and entrepreneurs need to interact with each other rapidly and efficiently, which calls for a series of platforms that can facilitate the flow and distribution of innovation resources, for example, platforms encouraging and enhancing global knowledge exchange, international R&D cooperation, R&D public services, generic technology services, industrialization acceleration, intellectual property exchange, technology-powered financial service promotion and R&D personnel mobility, respectively.

Finally, a favourable environment needs to be created for innovative activities, which means that the government should introduce systematic incentives aiming to spur innovation without interfering market coordination (or, in other words, undermining the dynamic balance between market and administrative coordination). However, when being put into practice, some policies in the name of innovation motivation actually produce negative impact on the innovation environment.

10.3.4. Converging and Leading Global Cultural Development

In modern society where cities are major spaces for cultural transmission, global cities play a more important role in converging and leading global cultural transmission, which has become an indispensable function of the top-level global cities in particular. Global cities of excellence are not only where global resources are strategically allocated but also vibrant, buzzing, fun places where international cultural and artistic services are provided and consumed in profusion. In addition to having a number of thriving local creative quarters, these global cities also host many large-scale international art festivals, radiating influences as art hubs beyond their national borders. They are viewed as providing quality, inspiring urban environment that are conducive to creation and innovation, enriching the lives of local residents and attracting talent from other countries to settle and work (Evans 2009). They are 'liveable, investible, and visitable' cities that find themselves popular among residents, workers, enterprises and tourists (Kotler, Haider and Rein 1993). Therefore, many major global cities have put cultural development on their agenda, seeking to enhance the cities' roles as global cultural and art centres. For example, to build itself into 'an exemplary, sustainable world city', London has developed a cultural strategy as one of its eight major strategies for the development of the Greater London, aiming at turning itself into a global innovation and cultural centre. Similarly, Tokyo has made 'developing into a cultural city with riveting charms' one of its priorities in its development vision for the 21st century published in the National Capital Region Development.

For Shanghai, strengthening this function in its evolution towards a global city is both natural and inevitable.

First, a primary driving force behind this aim stems from global urbanization. Human communication is a process of cultural transmission and convergence. In the age of globalization, this happens more frequently as a huge number of activities involving information transmission and cultural exchange occur between people from different cultural backgrounds. Globalization lies at the heart of modern culture; and cultural practices lie at the heart of globalization. The primary agent of the reciprocal relationship between culture and globalization is global urbanization, a product of the transnational practices carried out by the TCC who are indispensable to globalization. Representing something of entanglement, intermixing and commonness born of transcultural environments (Welsch 1999), such transnational practices of the TCC start to give rise to new cultural institutions and processes, and are transmitted and reflected across the world via other daily practices and spatial organizations in the 'fast' world, the relationship between transnational practices transcending a mere correlating and sharing and extending beyond the culture ideology of consumerism. The rise of these new cultural institutions and processes entail both the universalization of particularism (i.e., breaking the traditional boundaries of time and space, continuing the spread of the postmodernity of relativism and redefining uniqueness, variety and particularity) and the particularization of universalism (i.e., the particularization of transnational practices centring around some particular localities, classes, genders and groups; Robertson 1992). Therefore, global urbanization adjusted by and reborn from global cities is complex, dynamic and multifarious. The new cultural institutions and processes that it generates via global cities contain not only cultural homogenization, synchronization and convergence but also cultural diversity, differentiation and diffusion. In this sense, we should not define these new cultural institutions and processes as global cultural integration, but as global cultural convergence.

On the other hand, modern information technologies and the Internet have not only greatly enriched the content and increased the quantity of information but also brought about revolutionary changes in the ways that people acquire and spread information and cultural products, which, in turn, led to fundamental changes in ways of thinking and activity patterns. Such revolutionary changes in cultural terms have four characteristics:

- The instant and rapid dissemination of global information have furthered global cultural exchange and the rapid rise of popular culture.
- The sharing of information resources via the Internet has boosted the popularity and sharing of cultural products worldwide.
- With the help of modern information technologies and the Internet, the cultural and creative industries had been advanced and the global cultural market expanded.
- The global cultural network has strengthened international cultural exchange and cooperation, and promoted global allocation of cultural resources.

In this context, as the traditional bonds between families, neighbours, regions and countries have been dramatically changed by high-tech and high-speed networks and facilities, different groups of people have begun to contact and communicate with each other and even be mutually integrated. Owing to the influence of mass media, the instant and rapid information dissemination allowed more people to examine their lives by observing others' lives through the Internet. As a result, yearning for another life has become a feature of global urbanization. However, the expectations will be captured by the antinomies between social spaces in the fast-paced world, resulting in further blurring of spatial and temporal boundaries.

The driving force from the two aspects mentioned earlier are both intrinsic to the dual spaces (physical space and flow space) of global cities. The lifestyles pursued by the TCC have broadened the cultural horizons of global cities. Meanwhile, through the rapid coverage and dissemination of the new media, they have been further accepted as a fashion by consumers of the mass market, especially those who have more choices, flexibility, interactions, goals and imaginations in the fast-paced world, thus becoming a popular culture and a new lifestyle. Therefore, global cities generally have a large number of high-quality cultural facilities, art groups and creative industries which are impossible to be found in ordinary cities. In addition, they also boast big cultural markets, extensive and frequent cultural activities, and a variety of audiences. These all enable the continuous convergence and integration of cultural elements from all over the world.

Given the circumstances, Shanghai will play an important role in the eastward shift of the world cultural centre and the formation of the oriental cultural centre which will be mainly influenced by Chinese culture, thus becoming one of the major hubs for integrating and leading global culture. History tells us that the rise of a powerful country is often accompanied by the popularity of its culture in the global arena. Over its 5,000 years of history, China has developed unique ideas, values and customs, including the concepts of 'the unity of man and nature', 'all under heaven are of one family' and 'the doctrine of the golden mean', which represent the Chinese people's unremitting pursuit of peace, amity and harmony. These values are the driving force behind China's development and growth, and are also its outstanding advantages and soft power. Such inclusiveness and openness have enabled the Chinese culture to constantly develop and prosper in its communication and exchange with other cultures.

In today's world, with the deepening of economic globalization and political multi-polarization, the exchange, integration and collision between different ideas and cultures will be more active. As such, a country or city needs to bolster broader, more intensive and more inclusive cultural integration, so as to take the lead in the great cultural change, rapidly improve its cultural soft power and have a bigger say.

The hosting city of numerous transnational activities, Shanghai has gained much experience in the process of global urbanization and built up its image as a growing global city. In addition, its *Haipai* (literally 'Shanghai style') culture fits well with the function of converging and leading global culture, as it integrates both Chinese and Western cultural elements, representing a subtle blend of exquisite Jiangnan-style elegance on the one hand and the modernity and stylishness of a global metropolis on the other. Based on its *Haipai* culture, Shanghai champions inclusiveness, openness, diversity, innovation and pursuit of excellence. Shanghai provides precious opportunities for Chinese traditional culture to interact, exchange and blend with cultures from around the world—a role that will become more important as the city keeps evolving with the times.

This function of Shanghai as an excellent global city reflects its pursuit of cultural prosperity, which is also the ultimate goal of development, and represents one of the common features of global cities, namely that all global cities have their own distinctive culture. More specifically, this function involves four aspects: cultural convergence, integration, creativity and influence.

Cultural convergence refers to the ability of a city to bring together different cultures around the world. To acquire this ability, a global city should be open and inclusive, meaning that it should be able to accommodate various organizations from across the globe, facilitate extensive and intensive flow of people, welcome immigrants of different ethnic groups and allow their cultures to blossom. However, the key factor of cultural convergence is the attractiveness of the city's own culture, which is made up of: (a) rich and profound cultural heritage which arouses the eagerness of people from other parts of the world to know more about it; (b) distinctive cultural elements that make the city a place of mystery and enchantment to these people due to cultural differences and (c) advanced, cutting-edge and fashionable cultural elements that stimulate imitation.

Cultural integration is the ability to encourage exchange, and mutual influence, inspiration and understanding among different cultures. The progress of human civilizations is largely a result of interactions, including even debates, among them. To a certain extent, the greater the differences between cultures, the greater the possibility of their mutual influence, enlightenment and advancement. To promote cultural integration is to actively advocate mutual understanding in a multicultural context. In other words, it requires people to respect, understand and interpret other cultures despite the fact that it differs from their own, and to expand one's horizon through cross-cultural understanding, in order to gain an open-mindedness and learn a variety of problem-solving approaches. Moreover, interaction and integration will allow different cultures to merge into a global culture.

Therefore, cultural integration needs a climate of respect for cultural diversity, a large number of cultural facilities and cultural exchange platforms and ubiquitous public cultural spaces.

Cultural creativity refers to the creative transformation and innovative development of culture. It involves retaining the essence and wisdom of traditional culture accumulated over generations and adapting them to contemporary values, so that they can be carried on and well expressed in their modern contexts. The adaptation is a process of getting inspiration from foreign cultures and integrating their advanced elements into local traditional culture, so as to create an emerging culture and various creative cultural products that are qualified as icons of the era. Therefore, cultural creativity requires the city to be endowed with a rich culture that has great potential for further development, to have a high concentration of cultural industries and a large culture-related talent pool and to provide strong impetus to cultural innovation, creation and entrepreneurship through high-level platforms.

Cultural influence is the ability of a city to export its culture to other parts of the world and have a significant impact on other sectors thanks to its great cultural vitality and vibrancy. Cities of such capability are often cultural powerhouses who play a predominant role in the global cultural market. With rich and unique culture, they usually possess premium cultural brands that can lead the global trend and 'communicate' with all mankind. With extensive network connections, they are powerful in disseminating culture and promoting cultural products across the world. Equipped with effective methods and solutions, they can organize all-round cultural exchange activities frequently in a mature cultural market and to sophisticated audiences. On the other hand, such cultural influence may also arise from flows of high-end consumer products and services, such as fashion, design and decoration, and catering, which reflect the taste and characteristics of consumer culture spread by the TCC.

In particular, unlike that of traditional cultural metropolis, the global cities' function of converging and leading cultural development is fulfilled by the transmission through the global cultural network which is spatially based on intercity connection. Such transmission is made possible by the cross-border activities and operations of transnational cultural institutions and companies. In this sense, it is these organizations that built the global cultural network. Krätke (2003) points out that the globally operating media firms are at least as influential as the global providers of corporate services, because they create a cultural market space of global dimensions, providing economic and cultural networks that extend throughout the global urban system. Therefore, Shanghai should not only attract large multinational media firms and subsidiaries but also be home to many small media organizations and relative service companies, so as to create a unique media service cluster and connect with other cities through the cultural network. Similarly, to exert its cultural influence, Shanghai also needs to gather a large number of cultural leaders, as well as creative and media talent who can conduct multicultural exchange and transnational business activities. What's more, Shanghai should foster a group of outstanding figures of global influence in a wide range of fields, such as music, film, literature, politics, economy, science, sports and environmental protection. Their words, behaviours, manners, dressings, etc., will constantly convey cultural messages to foreigners who know them, thus exerting a subtle influence on or even set an example for their way of life.

In addition, Shanghai should establish an array of multifunctional platforms, especially for organizing cultural events of global influence. Also, it should focus on building trading channels for cultural products and services, such as copyright transactions, antiques and art auctions, cultural brokering and crowdfunding. Large-scale cultural infrastructure and landmarks are also needed as they can be popular destinations for locals and people outside the city, thus serving as windows into the city's cultural charm and becoming the city's symbols. Therefore, Shanghai should build a number of cultural infrastructure with specific functions and launch grand cultural programmes such as the Disneyland Resort to turn itself into a cultural metropolis and enhance its international influence. Meanwhile, Shanghai should design and build cultural landmarks featuring distinctive Shanghai style, and make it a popular tourist attraction for visitors both at home and abroad.

Finally, as a leader in global cultural integration, Shanghai should not only develop its own distinctive culture but also turn itself into a major world cultural hub. To this end, Shanghai needs to redefine and reshape 'Haipai culture', creating its own cultural symbols and vigorously promoting its image in international communication. It should enhance its exchange with other cultures in the world by exploring new ways of interaction and building more exchange platforms, so as to improve its ability to conduct cross-cultural communication. In addition, it should better display its cultural style and creativity as a global city and make new inventions in blending Chinese and foreign cultural elements.

BIBLIOGRAPHY

Abu-Lughod, J. 1991. *Changing Cities, Urban Sociology*. New York, NY: Harper Collins Publishers.
Ackers, L. 2005a. 'Moving People and Knowledge: Scientific Mobility in the European Union'. *International Migration* 43 (5): 99–131.
———. 2005b. 'Scientific Migration within the EU: Introduction to the Special Issue'. *Innovation* 18 (3): 275–276.
Acuto, M. 2011. 'Finding the Global City: An Analytical Journey through the "Invisible College"'. *Urban Studies* 48 (14): 2953–2973.
Agnew, J. 2000. 'From the Political Economy of Regions to Regional Political Economy'. *Progress in Human Geography* 16: 99–121.
Aharoni, Y., and L. Nachum. 2000. *Globalisation of Services: Some Implications for Theory and Practice*. London: Routledge.
Albrechts, L. 2001. 'How to Proceed from Image and Discourse to Action: As Applied to the Flemish Diamond'. *Urban Studies* 38: 733–745.
Alchian, A. A. 1950. 'Uncertainty, Evolution and Economics Theory'. *Journal of Political Economics* 58: 211–221.
Alderson, A. S., and J. Beckfield. 2004. 'Power and Position in the World City System'. *American Journal of Sociology* 109: 811–851.
———. 2007. 'Globalization and the World City System: Preliminary Results from a Longitudinal Dataset'. In *Cities in Globalization: Practices, Polices and Theories*, edited by P. J. Taylor, B. Derudder, P. Saey, and F. Witlox, 21–36. London: Routledge.
Alderson, A., J. Beckfield, and J. Sprague-Jones. 2010. 'Intercity Relations and Globalization: The Evolution of the Global Urban Hierarchy, 1981–2007'. *Urban Studies* 47: 1899–1923.
Ali, A. K., and P. L. Doan. 2006. 'A Survey of Undergraduate Course Syllabi and a Hybrid Course on Global Urban Topics'. *Journal of Planning Education and Research* 26 (2): 222–236.

Allen, J. 1997. 'Economies of Power and Space'. In *Geographies of Economies*, edited by R. Lee and J. Wills, 59–70. New York, NY: Arnold.

Allen, J. 1999. 'Cities of Power and Influence: Settled Formations'. In *Unsettling Cities*, edited by J. Allen, D. Massey, and M. Pryke, 181–218. New York, NY: Routledge.

———. 2002. 'Living on Thin Abstractions: More Power/Economic Knowledge'. *Environment and Planning A* 34: 451–466.

———. 2003. *Lost Geographies of Power*. Oxford: Blackwell Publishing.

———. 2008. 'Powerful Geographies: Spatial Shifts in the Architecture of Globalization'. In *The Handbook of Power*, edited by S. Clegg and M. Haugaard. Los Angeles, CA, and London: SAGE Publications.

———. 2010. 'Powerful City Networks: More than Connections, Less than Domination and Control'. *Urban Studies* 47 (13): 2895–2911.

Allen, J., and A. Cochrane. 2007. 'Beyond the Territorial Fix: Regional Assemblages, Politics and Power'. *Regional Studies* 41: 1161–1175.

Allen, J., D. Massey, and A. Cochrane. 1998. *Rethinking the Region*. London: Routledge.

Allmendinger, P., and G. Haughton. 2007. 'The Fluid Scales and Scope of UK Spatial Planning' *Environment and Planning A* 39 (6): 1478–1496.

Alonso, W. 1973. 'Urban Zero Population Growth'. *Daedalus* 102: 191–206.

Altbach, P. G. 2005. 'Globalization and the University: Myths and Realities in an Unequal World'. In *The NEA 2005 Almanac of Higher Education*, 63–74. Washington, DC: National Education Association.

Alvesson, M. 2001. 'Knowledge Work: Ambiguity, Image and Identity'. *Human Relations* 54 (7): 863–886.

American National Intelligence Council. 2013. *The Global Trends for 2030—The Transforming World*. Washington, DC: Current Affairs Press.

Amin, A. 2002. 'Spatialities of Globalisation'. *Environment and Planning A* 34: 385–399.

———. 2004. 'Regions Unbound: Towards a New Politics of Place'. *Geografiska Annaler* 86B: 33–44.

Amin, A., D. Massey, and N. Thrift. 2003. *Decentering the Nation: A Radical Approach to Regional Inequality*. London: Catalyst.

Amin, A., and N. Thrift. 1992. 'Neo-Marshallian Nodes in Global Networks'. *International Journal of Urban and Regional Research* 16: 571–587.

———. 2002. *Cities: Reimagining the Urban*. Cambridge: Polity.

Andersen, J. E., and E. Van Wincoop. 2004. 'Trade Costs'. *Journal of Economic Literature* 17: 691–751.

Anderson, B. 1983. *Imagined Communities*. London: Verso.

Andersson, A. E. 2005. 'Globalisation in Stages'. In *Economics of Globalisation*, edited by P. Gangopadhyay and M. Chatterji. Aldershot: Ashgate.

Andersson, A. E., and D. E. Andersson, eds. 2000. *Gateways to the Global Economy*. Cheltenham: Edward Elgar.

Andrade, G., M. Mitchell, and E. Stafford. 2001. 'New Evidence and Perspective on Mergers'. *Journal of Economic Perspectives* 15: 103–120.

Angew, J. 1994. 'The Territorial Trap: The Geographical Assumptions of International Relations Theory'. *Review of International Political Economy* 1 (1): 53–80.

Anheier, H., M. Glasius, and M. Kaldor, eds. 2001. 'Introducing Global Civil Society'. In *Global Civil Society*, edited by H. Anheier, M. Glasius, and M. Kaldor. Oxford: Oxford University Press.

Anheier, H., and N. Themudo. 2002. 'Organisational Forms of Global Civil Society: Implications of Going Global'. *Global Civil Society* 2 (1): 42–47.

An-Na'im, A. A., ed. 2002. *Cultural Transformation and Human Rights in Africa*. Vol. 2. London: Zed Books.

Appadurai, A. 1996. *Modernity at Large: Cultural Dimensions of Globalization*. Minneapolis, MN: University of Minnesota Press.

Arrighi, G. 1994. *The Long Twentieth Century: Money, Power, and the Origins of Our Times*. London: Verso.

———. 2007. *Adam Smith in Beijing: Lineages of the Twenty-First Century*. London: Verso.

Arthur, W. B. 1994. *Increasing Returns and Path Dependence in the Economy*. Ann Arbor, MI: University of Michigan Press.

Asian Development Bank. 2011, May. 'Asia 2050: Realizing the Asian Century'. Mandaluyong: Asian Development Bank.

Auslin, M. R. 2017. *The End of the Asian Century: War, Stagnation, and the Risks to the World's Most Dynamic Region*. New Haven, CT: Yale University Press.

Badiou, A. 2003. *Infinite Thought*. London: Continuum.

———. 2006. *Theoretical Writings*. London: Continuum.

Bagchi-Sen, S., and J. Sen. 1997. 'The Current State of Knowledge in International Business in Producer Services'. *Environment and Planning A* 29: 1153–1174.

Bailey, N., and I. Turok. 2001. 'Central Scotland as a Polycentric Urban Region: Useful Planning Concept or Chimera?' *Urban Studies* 38: 697–715.

Bair, J. 2003. 'From Commodity Chains to Value Chains and Back Again?' Paper presented at 'Rethinking Marxism', University of Massachusetts at Amherst. Available at http://www.csiss.org/events/meetings/time-mapping/files/bair_paper.pdf (accessed on 13 January 2020).

Bakis, H. 1993. 'Economic and Social Geography—Toward the Integration of Communications Networks Studies'. In *Corporate Networks, International Telecommunications and Interdependence*, edited by H. Bakis, R. Abler, and R. Roche, 1–15. London: Belhaven Press.

Bakis, H., R. Abler, and R. Roche, eds. 1993. *Corporate Networks, International Telecommunications and Interdependence*. London: Belhaven Press.

Baldwin, R. E., and R. Forslid. 2000. 'The Core-Periphery Model and Endogenous Growth: Stabilizing and Destabilizing Integration'. *Economics* 67: 307–324.

Barba, N. G., and A. J. Venables. 2004. *Multinational Firms in the World Economy*. Princeton, NJ: Princeton University Press.

Barham, J. 1990. 'A Poincaréan Approach to Evolutionary Epistemology'. *Journal of Social and Biological Structure* 13 (3): 193–258.

Barley, S. R., J. Freeman, and R. C. Hybels. 1992. 'Strategic Alliances in Commercial Biotechnology'. In *Networks and Organizations*, edited by N. Nohria and R. G. Eccles, 311–347. Boston, MA: Harvard Business School Press.

Barnett, R., and A. Phipps. 2005. 'Academic Travel: Modes and Directions'. *The Review of Education, Pedagogy, and Cultural Studies* 27 (1): 3–16.

Bartlett, C. A., and S. Ghoshal. 1989. *Managing across Borders: The Transnational Solution*. London: Century Business.

———. 2002. *Managing Across Borders: The Transnational Solution*, 2nd ed. Boston, MA: Harvard Business School Press.

Bassens, D., B. Derudder, and F. Witlox. 2011. 'Setting Shari'a Standards: On the Role, Power and Spatialities of Interlocking Shari'a Boards in Islamic Financial Services'. *Geoforum* 42: 94–103.

Bathelt, H., A. Malmberg, and P. Maskell. 2004. 'Clusters and Knowledge: Local Buzz, Global Pipelines and the Process of Knowledge Creation'. *Progress in Human Geography* 28: 31–56.

Batten, D., J. Casti, and B. Johnsson, eds. 1987. *Economic Evolution and Structural Adjustment*. Berlin: Springer.

Batten, D. F., and R. Thord. 1995. 'Europe's Hierarchical Network Economy'. In *Networks in Action: Communication, Economics, and Human Knowledge*, edited by David Batten, J. Casti, and R. Thord, 251–266. New York, NY: Springer-Verlag.

Batten, D. F. 1995. 'Network Cities: Creative Urban Agglomerations for the 21st Century'. *Urban Studies* 32: 313–327.

Batty, M. 1997. 'Virtual Geography'. *Futures* 29: 337–352.

Baum, S. 1997. 'Sydney, Australia: A Global City? Testing the Social Polarisation Thesis'. *Urban Studies* 34 (11): 1881–1901.

Bauman, Z. 1998. *Globalization: The Human Consequences*. New York, NY: Columbia University Press.

———. 2000. *Community: Seeking Security in an Insecure World*. Cambridge: Polity.

Beauregard, R. A., and A. Haila. 2000. 'The Unavoidable Continuities of the City'. In *Globalizing Cities: A New Spatial Order?* Edited by P. Marcuse and R. Kempen, 22–36. Oxford: Blackwell.

Beaverstock, J. V. 1996. 'Subcontracting the Accountant! Professional Labour Markets, Migration, and Organizational Networks in the Global Accountancy Industry'. *Environment and Planning A* 28: 303–326.

———. 2004. 'Managing across Borders: Knowledge Management and Expatriation in Professional Legal Service Firms'. *Journal of Economic Geography* 4: 1–25.

———. 2007. 'World City Networks "From Below": International Mobility and Inter-City Relations in the Global Investment Banking Industry'. In *Cities in Globalization: Practices, Policies and Theories*, edited by P. J. Taylor, B. Derudder, P. Saey, and F. Witlox, 52–71. London: Taylor & Francis.

———. 2010. 'Immigration and the UK Labour Market in Financial Services: A Commentary'. In *Who Needs Migrant Labour? Shortages, Immigration and Public Policy*, edited by M. Ruhs and B. Andersen, 290–294. Oxford: OUP.

Beaverstock, J. V. 2011. 'German Cities in the World City Network: Some Observations'. *Raumforschung und Raumordnung* 69: 213–217.

Beaverstock, J. V., M. Hoyler, K. Pain, and P. J. Taylor. 2001. *Comparing London and Frankfurt as World Cities: A Relational Study of Contemporary Urban Change*. London: Anglo-German Foundation.

Beaverstock, J. V., P. J. Hubbard, and J. R. Short. 2004. 'Getting Away with It? Exposing the Geographies of the Super-Rich'. *Geoforum* 35: 401–407.

Beaverstock, J. V., M. A. Doel, P. J. Hubbard, and P. J. Taylor. 2002. 'Attending to the World: Competition, Cooperation and Connectivity in the World City Network'. *Global Networks* 2 (2): 111–132.

Beaverstock, J. V., R. G. Smith, P. J. Taylor, D. R. F. Walker, and H. Lorimer. 2000. 'Globalization and World Cities: Some Measurement Methodologies'. *Applied Geography* 20 (1): 43–63.

Beck, U. 2005. *Power in the Global Age*. Cambridge: Polity.

Beckfield, J., and A. S. Alderson. 2006. 'Whither the Parallel Paths? The Future of Scholarship on the World City System'. *American Journal of Sociology* 112 (3): 895–904.

Begg, I. 1999. 'Cities and Competitiveness'. *Urban Studies* 36 (5–6): 795–809.

Bel, G., and X. Fageda. 2008. 'Getting There Fast: Globalization, Intercontinental Flights and Location of Headquarters'. *Journal of Economic Geography* 8: 471–495.

Bender, T., and I. Farias, eds. 2009. *Urban Assemblages: How Actor-Network Theory Changes Urban Studies*. London: Routledge.

Benmergui, L. 2009. 'The Alliance for Progress and Housing Policy in Rio de Janeiro and Buenos Aires in the 1960s'. *Urban History* 36 (2): 303–326.

Berry, B. J. L. 1964. 'Cities as Systems within Systems of Cities'. *Papers of the Regional Science Association* 13: 146–163.

Berry, B. J. L., and F. E. Horton. 1970. *Geographic Perspectives on Urban Systems*. Englewood Cliffs, NJ: Prentice-Hall.

Bertaud, A. 2004. 'The Spatial Organization of Cities: Deliberate Outcome or Unforeseen Consequence?' (IURD Working Paper Series WP–2004–01, Institute of Urban and Regional Development, CA).

Bhagwati, J. N., ed. 1972. *Economics and World Order*. New York, NY: Macmillan.

Bianconi, M., J. A. Yoshino, and M. O. M. de Sousa. 2013. 'BRIC and the U.S. Financial Crisis: An Empirical Investigation of Stock and Bond Markets'. *Emerging Markets Review* 14: 76–109.

Biehl, D. 1991. 'The Role of Infrastructure in Regional Development'. In *Infrastructure and Regional Development*, edited by R. W. Vickerman. London: Pion Limited.

Bird, J. H. 1973. 'Central Places, Cities and Seaports'. *Geography* 58 (259): 105–118.

Boix, R., and J. Trullen. 2007. 'Knowledge, Networks of Cities and Growth in Regional Urban Systems'. *Regional Science* 86: 551–574.

Boland, K. E. 1981. *Evolutionary Economics*. Beverly Hills, CA: SAGE Publications.

Bordo, M., M. Taylor, and J. Williamson. 2005. *Globalization in Historical Perspective*. Chicago, IL: The University of Chicago Press.

Boschken, H. L. 2008. 'A Multiple-Perspectives Construct of the American Global City'. *Urban Studies* 45: 3–28.

Boschma, R. A. 2005. 'Proximity and Innovation: A Critical Assessment'. *Regional Studies* 39: 61–74.

Boston Consulting Group. 2011. *Global Asset Management 2011*. Boston, MA: Boston Consulting Group.

Bosworth, A. 1996. 'The World-City System by the Year 2000'. *Journal of Developing Societies* 12 (1): 52–67.

Bourdeau-Lepage, L. 2007. 'Advanced Services and City Globalization on the Eastern Fringe of Europe'. *Belgeo* 1: 133–146.

Bourdieu, P. 1989. 'Social Space and Symbolic Power'. *Sociological Theory* 7: 14–25.

Bowen, J. 2002. 'Network Change, Deregulation, and Access in the Global Airline Industry'. *Economic Geography* 78 (4): 425–439.

Brakman, S., and H. Garretsen. 2008. 'Foreign Direct Investment and the Multinational Enterprise: An Introduction'. In *Foreign Direct Investment and the Multinational Enterprise*, edited by S. Brakman and H. Garretsen, 1–10. Cambridge, MA: MIT Press.

Brakman, S., and C. Van Marrewijk. 2008. 'It's a Big World after All: On the Impact of Location and Distance'. *Cambridge Journal of Regions, Economy and Society* 1.

Brand, S. 2010. *Whole Earth Discipline*. London: Atlantic Books.

Braunerhjelm, P. 2004. 'Heading for Headquarters? Why and How the Location of Headquarters Matter among EU Countries'. In *European Union and the Race for Foreign Direct Investment in Europe*, edited by L. Oxelheim and P. N. Ghauri, 123–148. Amsterdam: Emerald.

Brenner, N. 2002. 'Decoding the Newest "Metropolitan Regionalism" in the USA: A Critical Overview'. *Cities* 19 (1): 3–21.

———. 2004. *New State Spaces: Urban Governance and the Rescaling of Statehood*. Oxford: Oxford University Press.

———. 2009a. 'A Thousand Leaves: Notes on the Geographies of Uneven Spatial Development'. In *Leviathan Undone? Towards a Political Economy of Scale*, edited by R. Keil and R. Mahon, 27–49. Vancouver: UBC Press.

———. 2009b. 'Open Questions on State Rescaling'. *Cambridge Journal of Regions, Economy and Society* 2: 123–139.

Brenner, N., and R. Keil, eds. 2006. *The Global Cities Reader*. London: Routledge.

Brown, E., B. Derudder, C. Parnreiter, W. Pelupessy, P. J. Taylor, and F. Witloxe. 2010. 'World City Networks and Global Commodity Chains: Towards a World-System's Integration'. *Global Networks* 10 (1): 12–34.

Brueckner, J. K. 2003. 'Airline Traffic and Economic Development'. *Urban Studies* 40 (8): 1455–1469.

Brunn, S. 2003. 'A Note on the Hyperlinks of Major Eurasian Cities'. *Eurasian Geography and Economics* 44 (4): 321–324.

Buck, N., I. Gordon, A. Harding, and I. Turok. 2005. *Changing Cities: Rethinking Urban Competitiveness, Cohesion and Governance*. London: Palgrave.

Bunge, M. 1977. *Treatise on Basic Philosophy: Ontology I: The Furniture of the World*. Vol. 3. Dordrecht: Springer.

Burger, M., and E. Meijers. 2012. 'Form Follows Function? Linking Functional and Morphological Polycentricity'. *Urban Studies* 49: 1127–1149.

Burger, M. J., B. De Goei, L. Vanderlaan, and F. M. J. Huisman. 2011. 'Heterogeneous Development of Metropolitan Spatial Structure: Evidence from Commuting Patterns in English and Welsh City-Regions'. *Cities* 28: 160–170.

Burger, M. J., E. J. Meijers, M. M. Hoogerbrugge, and J. Masip Tresserra. 2015. 'Borrowed Size, Agglomeration Shadows and Cultural Amenities in North-West Europe'. *European Planning Studies* 23 (6): 1090–1109.

Burghardt, A. F. 1971. 'A Hypothesis about Gateway Cities'. *Annals of the Association of American Geographers* 61 (2): 269–285.

Burt, R. S. 1976. 'Positions in Networks'. *Social Forces* 55: 93–122.

———. 1992. *Structural Holes: The Social Structure of Competition*. Boston, MA: Harvard University Press.

Cai, J., and V. F. S. Sit. 2003. 'Measuring World City Formation—The Case of Shanghai'. *The Annals of Regional Science* 37: 435–446.

Cairncross, F. 1997. *The Death of Distance: How the Communications Revolution Will Change Our Lives*. New York, NY: McGraw-Hill.

Callan, H. 2000. 'Internationalisation in Europe'. In *The Globalisation of Higher Education*, edited by P. Scott, 44–57. Buckingham: Society for Research into Higher Education and Open University Press.

Callon, M., and J. Law. 2004. 'Guest Editorial'. *Environment and Planning D* 22: 3–11.

Camagni, R. 1993. 'From City Hierarchy to City Network: Reflections about an Emerging Paradigm'. In *Structural and Change in the Space Economy*, edited by T. R. Lakshmanan and P. Nijkamp, 66–87. Berlin: Springer-Verlag.

Camagni, R., R. Capello, and A. Caragliu. 2013. 'One or Infinite Optimal City Sizes? In Search of an Equilibrium Size for Cities'. *Annals of Regional Science* 51 (2): 309–341.

———. 2015. 'The Rise of Second-Rank Cities: What Role for Agglomeration Economies?' *European Planning Studies* 23 (6): 1069–1089.

Cantwell, J. 1995. 'The Globalization of Technology: What Remains of the Product Cycle Model?' *Cambridge Journal of Economics* 19.

Capello, R. 2000. 'The City Network Paradigm: Measuring Urban Network Externalities'. *Urban Studies* 37 (11): 1925–1945.

Capello, R., and R. Camagni. 2000. 'Beyond Optimal City Size: An Evaluation of Alternative Urban Growth Patterns'. *Urban Studies* 37 (9): 1479–1496.

Carroll, W. K. 2007. 'Global Cities in the Global Corporate Network'. *Environment and Planning A* 39: 2297–2323.

———. 2009. 'Transnationalists and National Networkers in the Global Corporate Elite'. *Global Networks* 9: 289–314.

Cartier, C. 1999. 'Cosmopolitics and the Maritime World City'. *The Geographical Review* 89 (2): 278–289.

Cassis, Y., and P. L. Cottrell, eds. 2009. *The World of Private Banking*. Farnham: Ashgate.

Castells, M. 1989. *The Informational City, Information Technology, Economic Restructuring, and the Urban-Regional Process*. Oxford: Blackwell.

———. 1996. *The Rise of the Network Society*. Oxford: Blackwell.

———. (1996) 2001. *The Information Age: Economy, Society and Culture*. Vol. I: The Rise of the Network Society. Oxford: Blackwell.

———. 2000. 'Materials for an Exploratory Theory of the Network Society'. *British Journal of Sociology* 51 (1): 1–24.

———. 2007. 'Why the Megacities Focus? Megacities in the New World Disorder'. In *The State of the World: Our Urban Future*, edited by J. Perlman and S. O'Meara, 1–16. Available at http://www.megacitiesproject.org/ (accessed on 14 January 2020).

———. 2009. *Communication Power*. Oxford: Oxford University Press.

Castells, M., and P. Hall. 1994. *Technopoles of the World*. London; New York, NY: Routledge.

Cerny, P. G. 1991. 'The Limits of Deregulation: Transnational Interpenetrations and Policy Change'. *European Journal of Political Research* 19: 173–196.

Chalaby, J. K. 2005. 'From Internationalization to Transnationalization'. *Global Media and Communication* 1: 28–33.

Champion, T. 1995. 'Internal Migration, Counterurbanisation and Changing Population Distribution'. In *Europe's Population: Towards the Next Century*, edited by R. Hall and P. White. London: UCL Press.

Champion, T., and T. Fisher. 2004. 'Migration, Residential Preferences and the Changing Environment of Cities'. In *City Matters: Competitiveness, Cohesion and Urban Governance*, edited by M. Boddy and M. Parkinson. Bristol: Policy Press.

Chandhoke, N. 2002. 'The Limits of Global Civil Society'. In *Global Civil Society*, edited by M. Glasius, M. Kaldor, and H. Anheier. Oxford: Oxford University Press.

Chen, Xiangming. 2005. *As Borders Bend: Transnational Spaces on the Pacific Rim*. Lanham, MD: Rowman & Littlefield Publishers.

Cheshire, P. 1995. 'A New Phase of Urban Development in Western Europe? The Evidence for the 1980s'. *Urban Studies* 32 (7): 1045–1063.

———. 2006. 'Resurgent Cities, Urban Myths and Policy Hubris: What We Need to Know'. *Urban Studies* 43 (8): 1231–1246.

Cheshire, P., and D. Hay. 1989. *Urban Problems in Western Europe*. London: Unwin Hyman.

Choi, J. H., G. A. Barnett, and B. Chon. 2006. 'Comparing World City Networks: A Network Analysis of Internet Backbone and Air Transport Intercity Linkages'. *Global Networks* 6: 81–99.

Christaller, W. 1933. *Central Places in Southern Germany*. Englewood Cliffs, NJ: Prentice-Hall.

Christopherson, S., and J. Clark. 2007. 'Power in Firm Networks: What It Means for Regional Innovation Systems'. *Regional Studies* 41: 1223–1236.

Ciccone, A. 2002. 'Agglomeration Effects in Europe'. *European Economic Review* 46: 213–227.

Clancy, M. 1998. 'Commodity Chains, Services and Development: Theory and Preliminary Evidence from the Tourism Industry'. *Review of International Political Economy* 5: 122–148.

Clark, G. 2005. 'Money Flows Like Mercury: The Geography of Global Finance'. *Geografiska Annaler* 87B (2): 99–112.

Claval, P. 1981. *La Logique des Villes: Essai d'Urbanologie*. Paris: Litec.

Cochrane, A., and K. Pain. (2000) 2004. 'A Globalising Society?' In *A Globalising World?* Edited by D. Held, 5–45. London: Routledge.

Coe, N. M., P. Dicken, M. Hess, and H. W. C. Yeung. 2010. 'Making Connections: Global Production Networks and World City Networks'. *Global Networks* 10: 138–149.

Coe, N. M., M. Hess, H. W. C. Yeung, P. Dicken, and J. Henderson. 2004. 'Globalizing' Regional Development: A Global Production Networks Perspective'. *Transactions of the Institute of British Geographers* 29: 468–484.

Coe, N. M., J. Johns, and K. Ward. 2007. 'Mapping the Globalization of the Temporary Staffing Industry'. *Professional Geographer* 59: 503–520.

Coffey, W. J., L. S. Bourne, J. E. Randall, W. K. D. Davies, and R. White. 1998. 'Urban Systems Research: Past, Present and Future, a Panel Discussion'. *Canadian Journal of Regional Science* 21: 327–364.

Cohen, R. B. 1981. 'The New International Division of Labor, Multinational Corporations and Urban Hierarchy'. In *Urbanization and Urban Planning in Capitalist Society*, edited by D. Michael and A. J. Scott, 287–315. New York, NY: Taylor & Francis.

Cook, G. A. S., N. R. Pandit, J. V. Beaverstock, P. J. Taylor, and K. Pain. 2007. 'The Role of Location in Knowledge Creation and Diffusion: Evidence of Centripetal and Centrifugal Forces in the City of London Financial Services Agglomeration'. *Environment and Planning A* 39: 1325–1345.

Cook, K. S., R. M. Emerson, M. R. Gillmore, and T. Tamagishi. 1983. 'The Distribution of Power in Exchange Networks: Theory and Experimental Results'. *American Journal of Sociology* 89: 275–305.

Cooke, P., C. Delaurentis, F. Tödtling, and M. Trippl. 2007. *Regional Knowledge Economies*. Cheltenham: Edward Elgar.

Cooley, A. 2005. *Logics of Hierarchy*. Ithaca, NY: Cornell University Press.

Cowan, R. 1991. 'Tortoises and Hares: Choice among Technologies of Unknown Merit'. *Economic Journal* 101: 801–814.

Crague, G. 2004. 'Commutation. Essai sur l'économie de l'agglomération'. *Géographie, Economie, Société* 6: 9–21.

Crang, M. 2003. 'Telling Materials'. In *Using Social Theory: Thinking through Research*, edited by M. Pryke, G. Rose, and S. Whatmore, 137–144. London: SAGE Publications.

Cronin, B., D. Shaw, and K. L. Barre. 2003. 'A Cast of Thousands: Co-Authorship and Sub-Authorship: Co-Authorship Sub-Authorship Collaborations in the Twentieth Century as Manifested in the Scholarly Literature of Psychology and Philosophy'. *Journal of the American Society for Information Science and Technology* 54: 855–871.

Cronin, M. 2003. *Translation and Globalization*. London: Routledge.

Csomós, G. 2013. 'The Command and Control Centers of the United States (2006/2012): An Analysis of Industry Sectors Influencing the Position of Cities'. *Geoforum* 50: 241–251.

Cunningham, S. L., and S. Dillon. 1997. 'Authorship Patterns in Information Systems Research'. *Scientometrics* 39 (1): 19–27.

Currid, E. 2006. 'New York as a Global Creative Hub: A Competitive Analysis of Four Theories on World Cities'. *Economic Development Quarterly* 20 (4): 330–350.

———. 2007. *The Warhol Economy: How Fashion, Art and Music Drive New York City*. Princeton, NJ: Princeton University Press.

Currie, M., and I. Kubin. 2003. *Chaos in the Core-Periphery Model*. Vienna: University of Economics and Business Administration.

Daniels, P. W., and J. R. Bryson. 2002. 'Manufacturing Services and Servicing Manufacturing: Changing Forms of Production in Advanced Capitalist Economies'. *Urban Studies* 39 (5–6): 977–991.

David, P. A. 1993. 'Path-Dependence and Predictability in Dynamical Systems with Local Network Externalities: A Paradigm for Historical Economics'. In *Technology and the Wealth of Nations*, edited by D. G. Foray and C. Freeman, 208–231. London: Pinter.

Davies, W. K. D. 1967. 'Centrality and the Central Place Hierarchy'. *Urban Studies* 4: 61–79.

Daviron, B., and S. Ponte. 2005. *The Coffee Paradox, Global Markets, Commodity Trade and the Elusive Promise of Development*. London; New York, NY: Zed Books.

Davis, K. 1959. *The World's Metropolitan Areas*. Berkeley, CA: University of California Press.

De Certeau, M. 1986. *Heterologies: Discourse on the Other*. Manchester: Manchester University Press.

De Filippis, J. 2001. 'The Myth of Social Capital in Community Development'. *Housing Policy Debate* 12: 781–806.

de Vries, I. 2006. 'Propagating the Ideal: The Mobile Communication Paradox'. In *Information Communication Technology and Emerging Business Strategies*, edited by S. Van Der Graaf and Y. Washida, 1–19. Hershey, PA: Ideas Group.

Dear, M., and A. Scott, eds. 1981. *Urbanisation and Urban Planning in Capitalist Society*. London: Methuen.

Deas, I., and A. Lord. 2006. 'From a New Regionalism to an Unusual Regionalism? The Emergence of Non-Standard Regional Spaces and Lessons for the Territorial Reorganisation of the State'. *Urban Studies* 43: 1847–1877.

Debbage, K., and D. Delk. 2001. 'The Geography of Air Passenger Volume and Local Employment Patterns by U.S. Metropolitan Core Area: 1973–1996'. *Journal of Air Transport Management* 7: 159–167.

Deinema, M. N. 2012. 'The Culture Business Caught in Place: Spatial Trajectories of Dutch Cultural Industries, 1899–2005' (PhD thesis, Faculty of Social and Behavioral Science, University of Amsterdam, Amsterdam).

Deleuze, G., and F. Guattari. 1988. *A Thousand Plateaus: Capitalism and Schizophrenia*. London: Athlone.

Denstadli, J. M. 2004. 'The Impact of Videoconferences on Business Travel: The Norwegian Experience'. *Journal of Air Transport Management* 10 (6): 371–376.

Derudder, B. 2006. 'On Conceptual Confusion in Empirical Analyses of a Transnational Urban Network'. *Urban Studies* 43 (11): 2027–2046.

———. 2008. 'Mapping Global Urban Networks: A Decade of Empirical World Cities Research'. *Geography Compass* 2: 559–574.

Derudder, B., and P. J. Taylor. 2005. 'The Cliquishness of World Cities'. *Global Networks* 5 (1): 71–91.

Derudder, B., M. Hoyler, and P. J. Taylor. 2011. 'Goodbye Reykjavik: International Banking Centres and the Global Financial Crisis'. *Area* 43 (2): 173–182.

Derudder, B., M. Hoyler, P. J. Taylor, and F. Witlox, eds. 2012. *International Handbook of Globalization and World Cities*. Cheltenham: Edward Elgar Publishing.

Derudder, B., P. J. Taylor, P. Ni, A. De Vos, M. Hoyler, H. Hanssens, D. Bassens, J. Huang, F. Witlox, W. Shen, and X. Yang. 2010. 'Pathways of Change: Shifting Connectivities in the World City Network 2000–2008'. *Urban Studies* 47 (9): 1861–1877.

Derudder, B., P. J. Taylor, F. Witlox, and G. Catalano. 2003. 'Hierarchical Tendencies and Regional Patterns in the World City Network, a Global Urban Analysis of 234 Cities'. *Regional Studies* 37 (9): 875–886.

Derudder, B., and F. Witlox, eds. 2010. *Commodity Chains and World Cities*. New York, NY: John Wiley & Sons.

Devriendtl, L., A. Boulton, S. Brunn, B. Derudder, and F. Witlox. 2011. 'Searching for Cyberspace: The Position of Major Cities in the Information Age'. *Journal of Urban Technology* 18 (1): 73–92.

Devriendt, L., B. Derudder, and F. Witlox. 2008. 'Cyberplace and Cyberspace: Two Approaches to Analyzing Digital Intercity Linkages'. *Journal of Urban Technology* 15 (2): 5–32.

Dicken, P. 1998. *Global Shift: Transforming the World Economy*. London: Paul Chapman.

———. 2003a. *Global Shift, Reshaping the Global Economic Map in the 21st Century*, 4th ed. London: SAGE Publications.

———. 2003b. '"Placing" Firms: Grounding the Debate on the "Global" Corporation'. In *Remaking the Global Economy: Economic-Geographical Perspectives*, edited by J. Peck and H. W. C. Yeung, 27–44. London: SAGE Publications.

Dicken, P., and A. Malmberg. 2001. 'Firms in Territories: A Relational Perspective'. *Economic Geography* 77: 345–363.

Dicken, P., P. F. Kelly, K. Olds, and H. W. C. Yeung. 2001. 'Chains and Networks, Territories and Scales, Towards a Relational Framework for Analysing the Global Economy'. *Global Networks* 1: 99–123.

Dieleman, F., and C. Hamnett. 1994. 'Globalisation, Regulation and the Urban System'. *Urban Studies* 31: 357–364.

Dijkstra, L., E. Garcilazo, and P. McCann. 2013. 'The Economic Performance of European Cities and City Regions: Myths and Realities'. *European Planning Studies* 21 (3): 334–354.

DiMaggio, P. J., and W. W. Powell. 1983. 'The Iron Cage Revisited: Institutional Isomorphism and Collective Rationality in Organizational Fields'. *American Sociological Review* 48: 147–160.

DiMuccio, R. B. A., and J. N. Rosenau. 1992. 'Turbulence and Sovereignty in World Politics'. In *Globalization and Territorial Identities*, edited by Z. Mlinar, 60–76. Aldershot: Avebury.

Dixit, A. K., and J. E. Stiglitz. 1977. 'Monopolistic Competition and Optimum Product Diversity'. *American Economic Review* 67 (3): 297–308.

Dobkins, L. H., and Y. M. Ioannides. 2001. 'Spatial Interactions among U.S. Cities: 1900–1990'. *Regional Science and Urban Economics* 31: 701–731.

Dodge, M., and N. Shiode. 2000. 'Where on Earth is the Internet? An Empirical Investigation of the Geography of the Internet Real Estates'. In *Cities in the Telecommunications Age: The Fracturing of Geographies*, edited by J. Wheeler, Y. Aoyama, and B. Warf, 42–53. London: Routledge.

Doel, M. A. 2001. 'Qualified Quantitative Geography'. *Environment and Planning D: Society and Space* 19 (5): 555–572.

Doppel, Kurt. 2004. *Evolutionary Economics*. Beijing: Higher Education Press.

Dosi, G. 1997. 'Opportunities, Incentives and the Collective Pattern of Technological Change'. *Economic Journal* 14: 33–65.

Doucet, P. 2010. '1950–2050: Sunset and Sunrise over the Eurasian Continent'. In *China and Europe: The Implications of the Rise of China for European Space*, edited by K. R. Kunzmann, W. A. Schmid, and M. Koll-Schretzenmayr, 256–270. London; New York, NY: Routledge.

Douglass, M. 1998. 'World City Formation on the Asia Pacific Rim: Poverty, "Everyday" Forms of Civil Society and Environmental'. In *Cities for Citizens*, edited by M. Douglass and J. Friedmann, 107–138. Chichester: John Wiley & Sons.

Drennan, M. P. 1992. 'Gateway Cities: The Metropolitan Sources of US Producers Service Exports'. *Urban Studies* 29 (2): 217–235.

Driffield, N., and J. H. Love. 2005. 'Intra-Industry Foreign Direct Investment, Uneven Development and Globalization: The Legacy of Stephen Hymer'. *Political Economy* 24: 1.

Ducruet, C. 2004. *Les Villes-ports: Laboratoires de la mondialisation*. Le Havre: Université du Havre.

Dunning, J. H. 1993. *Multinational Enterprises in the Global Economy*. Wokingham: Addison-Wesley.

Dunning, J. H., and S. M. Lundan. 2008. *Multinational Enterprises and the Global Economy*. Cheltenham: Edward Elgar.
Dunning, J. H., and G. Norman. 1983. 'The Theory of the Multinational Enterprise: An Application to Multinational Office Location'. *Environment and Planning A* 15: 675–692.
———. 2005. 'From Sectoral to Functional Urban Specialisation'. *Journal of Urban Economics* 157 (2).
Elliott, D. 2000. 'Internationalizing British Higher Education: Policy Perspectives'. In *The Globalisation of Higher Education*, edited by P. Scott, 32–43. Buckingham: Society for Research into Higher Education and Open University Press.
Englund, P., A. Gunnelin, P. Hendershott, and B. Soderberg. 2008. 'Adjustment in Commercial Property Space Markets: Taking Long-Term Leases and Transaction Costs Seriously'. *Real Estate Economics* 36: 81–109.
Erickcek, G. A., and H. McKinney. 2006. 'Small Cities Blues: Looking for Growth Factors in Small and Medium-Sized Cities'. *Economic Development Quarterly* 20 (3): 232–258.
Esping-Andersen, G. 1990. *The Three Worlds of Welfare Capitalism*. Cambridge: Polity Press.
European Commission. 2006. *Cities and the Lisbon Agenda: Assessing the Performance of Cities*. Brussels: Directorate-General for Regional and Urban Policy.
Evans, G. 2009. 'Creative Cities, Creative Spaces and Urban Policy'. *Urban Studies* 46 (5–6): 1003–1040.
Fainstein, S. 2001. 'Inequality in Global City-Regions'. In *Global City-Regions, Trends, Theory, Policy*, edited by A. A. Scott, 285–298. Oxford: Oxford University Press.
Faulconbridge, J. R. 2007. 'Relational Networks of Knowledge Production in Transnational Law Firms'. *Geoforum* 38 (5): 925–940.
———. 2008. 'Managing the Transnational Law Firm: A Relational Analysis of Professional Systems, Embedded Actors and Time-Space Sensitive Governance'. *Economic Geography* 84; 185–210.
Faulconbridge, J. R., J. V. Beaverstock, C. Nativel, and P. J. Taylor. 2011. *The Globalization of Advertising: Agencies, Cities and Spaces of Creativity*. London: Routledge.
Faulconbridge, J. R., S. J. E. Hall, and J. V. Beaverstock. 2008. 'New Insights into the Internationalization of Producer Services: Organizational Strategies and Spatial Economies for Global Headhunting Firms'. *Environment and Planning A* 40: 210–234.
Featherstone, D., R. Phillips, and J. Waters. 2007. 'Introduction: Spatialities of Transnational Networks'. *Global Networks* 7 (4): 383–391.
Flora, P. 2000. *Stein Rokkan: Staat, Nation und Demokratie in Europa*. Frankfurt am Main: Suhrkamp.
Florida, R. (2002) 2004. *The Rise of the Creative Class: And How It's Transforming Work, Leisure, Community and Everyday Life*. New York, NY: Basic Books.
———. 2005. 'The World Is Spiky'. *Atlantic Monthly* 296 (3): 48–51.

Florida, R. 2008. *Who's Your City? How the Creative Economy Is Making Where to Live the Most Important Decision of Your Life*. New York, NY: Basic Books.

Florida, R., and A. Jonas. 1991. 'U.S. Urban Policy: The Postwar State and Capitalist Regulation'. *Antipode* 23 (4): 349–384.

Florida, R., T. Gulden, and C. Mellander. 2008. 'The Rise of the Mega-Region'. *Cambridge Journal of Regions, Economy and Society* 1 (3): 459–476.

Folker, F., J. Heinrichs, and O. Kreye. 1977. 'The Tendency Towards a New International Division of labor: The Utilization of a World-Wide Labor Force for Manufacturing Oriented to the World Market'. *Review (Fernand Braudel Center)* 1 (1): 73–88.

Folkman, P., J. Froud, S. Johal, and K. Williams. 2007. 'Working for Themselves? Capital Market Intermediaries and Present Day Capitalism'. *Business History* 49: 552–572.

Foss, N. J. 1994. 'Realism and Evolutionary Economics'. *Journal of Social and Biological Systems* 17: 21–40.

Fouré, J., A. Bénassy-Quéré, and L. Fontagné. 2012. 'The Great Shift: Macroeconomic Projections for the World Economy at the 2050 Horizon' (CEPII working paper 2012–03, February, Paris).

Frank, A. G. 1969. *Latin America: Underdevelopment or Revolution: Essays on the Development of Underdevelopment and the Immediate Enemy*. New York, NY: Monthly Review Press.

———. 1998. *Reorient: Global Economy in the Asian Age*. Berkeley, CA: University of California Press.

Freeman, L. C. (1978) 1979. 'Centrality in Social Networks: Conceptual Clarification'. *Social Networks* 1: 215–239.

Frenken, K., F. G. Van Oort, and T. Verburg. 2007. 'Related Variety, Unrelated Variety and Regional Economic Growth'. *Regional Studies* 41: 685–697.

Friedman, T. L. 2005. *The World Is Flat: A Brief History of the Twenty-First Century*. New York, NY: Farrar, Straus, and Giroux.

Friedmann, J. 1986. 'The World City Hypothesis'. *Development and Change* 17: 69–83.

———. 1995. 'Where We Stand: A Decade of World City Research'. In *World Cities in a World System*, edited by P. Knox and P. J. Taylor, 21–47. Cambridge: Cambridge University Press.

Friedmann, J., and G. Wolff. 1982. 'World City Formation: An Agenda for Research and Action'. *International Journal of Urban and Regional Research* 6: 309–344.

Fröbel, F., J. Heinrichs, and O. Kreye. 1977. *Die neue internationale Arbeitsteilung: Strukturelle Arbeitslosigkeit in den Industrieländern und die Industrialisierung der Entwicklungsländer*. Reinbek: Rowohlt.

Fujita, M., and J. F. Thisse. 2002. *Economics of Agglomeration: Cities, Industrial Location and Regional Growth*. Cambridge: Cambridge University Press.

Fujita, M., P. Krugman, and A. J. Venables. 1999. *The Spatial Economy: Cities, Regions, and International Trade*. Cambridge: The MIT Press.

Fujita, M., J. F. Thisse, and Y. Zenou. 1997. 'On the Endogenous Formation of Secondary Employment Centres in a City'. *Journal of Urban Economics* 41: 337–357.

Fulford, T., D. Lee, and P. J. Kitson. 2004. *Literature, Science and Exploration in the Romantic Era*. Cambridge: Cambridge University Press.

Garreau, J. 1991. *Edge City*. New York, NY: Doubleday.

GaWC database, 2008. Available at https://www.lboro.ac.uk/gawc/data.html (accessed on 8 April, 2020).

Geddes, P. 1915. *Cities in Evolution*. London: Williams and Norgate.

Gereffi, G. 1994. 'The Organization of Buyer-Driven Global Commodity Chains: How U.S. Retailers Shape Overseas Production Networks'. In *Commodity Chains and Global Capitalism*, edited by G. Gereffi and M. Korzeniewicz, 95–122. Westport: Praeger.

———. 1999. 'International Trade and Industrial Upgrading in the Apparel Commodity Chain'. *Journal of International Economics* 48 (1): 37–70.

Gereffi, G., and R. Kaplinsky, eds. 2001. 'The Value of Value Chains: Spreading the Gains from Globalization'. *IDS Bulletin* 32 (3).

Gereffi, G., and M. Korzeniewicz, eds. 1994. *Commodity Chains and Global Capitalism*. Westport, CT: Praeger.

Gereffi, G., M. Korzeniewicz, and R. P. Korzeniewicz. 1994. 'Introduction: Global Commodity Chains'. In *Commodity Chains and Global Capitalism*, edited by G. Gereffi and M. Korzeniewicz, 1–14. Westport, CT: Praeger.

Gershon, R. A. 1997. 'The Transnational Media Corporation: Global Messages and Free Market Competition'. Mahwah, NJ: Lawrence Erlbaum Associates.

Gertler, M. S. 1992. 'Flexibility Revisited: Districts, Nation-States and the Forces of Production'. *Transactions of the Institute of British Geographers* 17.

Ghoshal, S., and C. A. Bartlett. 1990. 'The Multinational Corporation as an Interorganizational Network'. *The Academy of Management Review* 15: 603–625.

Gibbons, M. 2000. 'A Commonwealth Perspective on the Globalisation of Higher Education'. In *The Globalisation of Higher Education*, edited by P. Scott, 70–87. Buckingham: Society for Research into Higher Education and Open University Press.

Girardet, H. 2008. *Cities/People/Planet: Urban Development and Climate Change*, 2nd ed. Chichester: John Wiley.

Glaeser, E. 2010. 'Why Cities Matter'. *The New Republic January* 19: 1–5.

———. 2011. *Triumph of the City: How Our Greatest Invention Makes Us Richer, Smarter, Greener, Healthier and Happier*. London: Macmillan/New York: Penguin Press.

Glaeser, E., J. Kolko, and A. Saiz. 2001. 'Consumer City'. *Journal of Economic Geography* 1: 27–50.

Glaeser, E. L., and J. Kohlhase. 2004. 'Cities, Regions and the Decline of Transport Costs'. *Regional Science* 83: 197–228.

Glänzel, W., and A. Schubert. 2004. 'Analyzing Scientific Co-Authorships through Co-Authorship'. In *Handbook of Quantitative Science and Technology Research*, edited by H. F. Moed, W. Glänzel, and U. Schmoch, 257–276. Dordrecht: Kluwer Academic Publishers.

Goddard, J., and I. Smith. 1978. 'Changes in Corporate Control in the British Urban System, 1972–1977'. *Environment and Planning A* 10: 1073–1084.

Godfrey, B. J., and Y. Zhou. 1999. 'Ranking World Cities: Multinational Corporations and the Global Urban Hierarchy'. *Urban Geography* 20 (3): 268–281.

Goerzen, A., C. G. Asmussen, and B. B. Nielsen. 2013. 'Global Cities and Multinational Enterprise Location Strategy'. *Journal of International Business Studies* 44: 427–450.

Goldfeld, K. S., ed. 2007. *The Economic Geography of Mega-Regions*, 59–83. Princeton, NJ: The Policy Research Institute for the Region.

Gordon, I., and I. Turok. 2005. 'How Urban Labour Markets Matter'. In *Changing Cities: Rethinking Urban Competitiveness, Cohesion and Governance*, edited by N. Buck, I. Gordon, A. Hardin, and I. Turok, London: Palgrave.

Gottmann, J. 1961. *Megalopolis: The Urbanized Northeastern Seaboard of the United States*. New York, NY: Twentieth Century Fund.

Grabher, G. 2001. 'Ecologies of Creativity: The Village, the Group, and the Heterarchic Organisation of the British Advertising Industry'. *Environment and Planning A* 33: 351–374.

———. 2006. 'Trading Routes, Bypasses, and Risky Intersections: Mapping the Travels "Networks" between Economic Sociology and Economic Geography'. *Progress in Human Geography* 30: 163–189.

Grabher, G., and W. W. Powell. 2004. 'Exploring the Webs of Economic Life'. In *Networks*, edited by G. Grabher and W. W. Powell, 1–36. Cheltenham: Edward Elgar.

Granovetter, M. 1973. 'The Strength of Weak Ties'. *American Journal of Sociology* 78: 1360–1380.

Green, N. 2007. 'Functional Polycentricity: A Formal Definition in Terms of Social Network Analysis'. *Urban Studies* 44: 2077–2103.

Gritsai, O. 1997. 'Business Services and the Restructuring of Urban Space in Moscow'. *GeoJournal* 42 (4): 365–376.

Growe, A., and H. H. Blotevogel. 2011. 'Knowledge Hubs in the German Urban System: Identifying Hubs by Combining Network and Territorial Perspectives'. *Raumforschung und Raumordnung* 69 (3): 175–185.

Guillaume, M. 1999. *L'Empire des Réseaux*. Paris: Descartes & Cie.

Guimera, R., S. Mossa, A. Turtschi, and L. A. N. Amaral. 2005. 'The Worldwide Air Transportation Network: Anomalous Centrality, Community Structure, and Cities' Global Roles'. *Proceedings of the National Academy of Sciences* 102: 7794–7799.

Guisinger, S. 1985. *Investment Incentives and Performance Requirements*. Santa Barbara, CA: Praeger.

Gulati, R., and M. Garguilo. 1999. 'Where Do Interorganizational Networks Come from?' *American Journal of Sociology* 104: 1439–1493.

Hack, G. 2000. 'Infrastructure and Regional Form'. In *Global City Regions, Their Emerging Forms*, edited by R. Simmonds and G. Hack, 183–192. London: Spon Press.

Haggett, P. 1965. *Locational Analysis in Human Geography*. London: Edward Arnold.

Haggett, P., and R. J. Chorley. 1967. *Network Analysis in Geography*. London: Edward Arnold.

Halbert, L., and K. Pain. 2009. *PAR-LON—Doing Business in Knowledge-Based Services in Paris and London: A Tale of One City?* Available at http://www.lboro.ac.uk/gawc/rb/rb307.html (accessed on 14 January 2020).

Hall, P. 1998. *Cities in Civilisation: Culture, Innovation, and Urban Order*. London: Weidenfeld & Nicolson.

———. 2001. 'Global City Regions in the Twenty-First Century'. In *Global City-Regions: Trends, Theory, Policy*, edited by A. J. Scott, 59–77. Oxford: Oxford University Press.

Hall, P., and D. Hay. 1980. *Growth Centres in the European Urban System*. London: Heinemann Educational.

Hall, P., and K. Pain, eds. 2006. *The Polycentric Metropolis: Learning from Mega-City Regions in Europe*. London: Earthscan.

Hall, P. A., and D. Soskice, eds. 2001. *Varieties of Capitalism, the Institutional Foundations of Comparative Advantage*. Oxford: Oxford University Press.

Hall, P. G. 1966. *The World Cities*. London: Weidenfeld & Nicolson.

Hall, T., and P. Hubbard, eds. 1998. *The Entrepreneurial City: Geographies of Politics, Regimes and Representations*. London: Wiley.

Hamnett, C. 1996. 'Why Sassen Is Wrong: A Response to Burgers'. *Urban Studies* 33 (1): 107–110.

———. 2003. *Unequal City: London in the Global Arena*. London: Routledge.

Hang Seng Bank. 1999. 'Hong Kong: The Road to Becoming a World City'. *Hang Seng Bank Economic Monthly* (November/December). Hong Kong: Hang Seng Bank.

Hannemann, R., and M. Riddle. 2005. *Introduction to Social Network Methods*. Riverside, CA: University of California.

Hanssens, H., B. Derudder, P. J. Taylor, M. Hoyler, P. Ni, J. Huang, X. Yang, and F. Witlox. 2011. 'The Changing Geography of Globalized Service Provision, 2000–2008'. *The Service Industries Journal* 31 (14): 2293–2307.

Harrington, J. W., and P. W. Daniels, eds. 2006. *Knowledge-Based Services, Internationalization and Regional Development*. Farnham: Ashgate.

Harris, C. 1954. 'The Market as a Factor in the Localization of Industry in the United States'. *Annals of the Association of American Geographers* 64: 315–348.

Harrison, J. 2010. 'Networks of Connectivity, Territorial Fragmentation, Uneven Development: The New Politics of City-Regionalism'. *Political Geography* 29: 17–27.

———. 2011. 'Configuring the New "Regional World": On Being Caught between Territory and Networks'. *GaWC Research Bulletin* 370. Available at http://www.lboro.ac.uk/gawc/rb/rb370.html (accessed on 14 January 2020).

Harrison, J., and M. Hoyler. 2014. 'Governing the New Metropolis'. *Urban Studies*. doi:10.1177/0042098013500699

Harvey, D. 1982. *The Limits to Capital*. Oxford: Blackwell.

———. 1989. 'From Managerialism to Entrepreneurialism: The Transformation in Urban Governance in Late-Capitalism'. *Geografiska Annaler* 71 (B): 3–17.

———. 1996. *Justice, Nature and the Geography of Difference*. Oxford: Blackwell.

———. 2006. *Spaces of Global Capitalism: A Theory of Uneven Geographical Development*. Brooklyn, NY: Verso.

Hausner, V., ed. 1986. *Critical Issues in Urban Economic Development*. Vol. 1. Oxford: Oxford University Press.

Hazell, R. 2000. *An Unstable Union: Devolution and the English Question*. State of the Union Lecture. London: Constitution Unit.

Healey, P. 2006. 'Relational Complexity and the Imaginative Power of Strategic Spatial Planning'. *European Planning Studies* 14: 525–546.

———. 2007. *Urban Complexity and Spatial Strategies: Towards a Relational Planning for Our Times*. London: Routledge.

———. 2010. *Making Better Places, the Planning Project in the Twenty-First Century*. New York, NY: Palgrave Macmillan.

Hedlund, G. 1986. 'The Hypermodern MNC—A Heterarchy'. *Human Resource Management* 25: 9–35.

———. 1994. 'A Model of Knowledge Management and the N-Form Corporation'. *Strategic Management Journal* 15: 73–90.

Heenan, D. A. 1977. 'Global Cities of Tomorrow'. *Harvard Business Review* 55: 79–92.

Held, D., A. McGrew, D. Goldblatt, and J. Perraton. 1999. *Global Transformations: Politics, Economics, and Culture*. Palo Alto, CA: Stanford University Press.

Henderson, J., P. Dicken, M. Hess, N. Coe, and H. W. C. Yeung. 2002. 'Global Production Networks and the Analysis of Economic Development'. *Review of International Political Economy* 9 (3): 436–464.

Henderson, J. V. 1974. 'The Sizes and Types of Cities'. *American Economic Review* 64: 640–656.

Henderson, V. 1997. 'Medium Size Cities'. *Regional Science and Urban Economics* 27 (6): 583–612.

Hennemann, S., and B. Derudder. 2013. 'An Alternative Approach to the Calculation and Analysis of Connectivity in the World City Network'. *GaWC Research Bulletin* 401. Available at http://www.lboro.ac.uk/gawc/rb/rb401.html (accessed on 14 January 2020).

Hepworth, M. 1989. *Geography of the Information Economy*. London: Belhaven Press.

Herman, E. S., and R. W. McChesney. 1997. *The Global Media: The New Missionaries of Global Capitalism*. London: Cassell.

Herrmann-Pillath, C. 1993. 'New Knowledge as Creation: Notes When Reading Nietzsche on Evolution, Power, and Knowledge'. *Journal of Social and Evolutionary Systems* 16 (1): 25–44.

Hesse, M. 2014. 'On Borrowed Size, Flawed Urbanisation and Emerging Enclave Spaces: The Exceptional Urbanism of Luxembourg, Luxembourg'. *European Urban and Regional Studies*. doi:10.1177/0969776414528723

Hill, R. C., and K. Fujita. 1995. 'Osaka's Tokyo Problem'. *International Journal of Urban and Regional Research* 19 (2): 181–193.

Hill, R. C., and J. W. Kim. 2000. 'Global Cities and Developmental States: New York, Tokyo and Seoul'. *Urban Studies* 37 (12): 2167–2195.

Hillis, K. 1998. 'On the Margins: The Invisibility of Communications in Geography'. *Progress in Human Geography* 22 (4): 543–566.

Hirshman, A. O. 1958. *The Strategy of Economic Development*. New Haven, CT: Yale University Press.

Hirst, P., and G. Thompson. 1996. *Globalization in Question: The International Economy and the Possibilities of Governance*. Cambridge: Polity Press.

Hodgson, G. M. 1995. 'The Evolution of Evolutionary Economics'. *Scottish Journal of Political Economy* 42: 469–488.

———. 2002. 'Darwinism in Economics: From Analogy to Ontology'. *Journal of Evolutionary Economics* 6: 589–781.

Hohenberg, P., and L. H. Lees. 1995. *The Making of Urban Europe 1000–1994*. Cambridge: Harvard University Press.

Hopkins, T. K., and I. Wallerstein. 1977. 'Patterns of Development of the Modern World System: Research Proposal'. *Review* 1: 111–145.

———. 1986. 'Commodity Chains in the World—Economy Prior to 1800'. *Review* 10 (1): 157–170.

Horan, B. 1995. 'The Statistical Character of Evolutionary Theory'. *Philosophy of Science* 61: 76–95.

Howard, E. 1902. *Garden Cities of Tomorrow*. London: Faber and Faber.

Hoyler, M., and K. Pain. 2001. 'London and Frankfurt as World Cities: Changing Local-Global Relations'. *GaWC Research Bulletin* 62.

Hoyler, M., R. C. Kloosterman, and M. Sokol. 2008. 'Polycentric Puzzles: Emerging Mega-City Regions Seen through the Lens of Advanced Producer Services'. *Regional Studies* 42: 1055–1064.

Hoylerm, M., and A. Watson. 2013. 'Global Media Cities in Transnational Media Networks'. *Tijdschrift voor Economische en Sociale Geografie* 104 (1): 90–108.

Hubbard, P., and T. Hall. 1998. 'The Entrepreneurial City and the "New Urban Politics"'. In *The Entrepreneurial City: Geographies of Politics, Regime and Representation*, edited by T. Hall and P. Hubbard, 1–23. Chichester: John Wiley.

Hudson, R. 2007. 'Regions and Regional Uneven Development Forever? Some Reflective Comments upon Theory and Practice'. *Regional Studies* 41: 1149–1160.

Hughes, A., and S. Reimer, eds. 2004. *Geographies of Commodity Chains*. London: Routledge.

Humphrey, J., and H. Schmitz. 2001. 'Governance in Global Value Chains'. *IDS Bulletin* 32 (3).

Hymer, S. 1972. 'The Multinational Corporation and the Law of Uneven Development'. In *Economics and World Order*, edited by J. N. Bhagwati. New York, NY: Macmillan.

Iredale, R., and R. Appleyard. 2001. 'International Migration of the Highly Skilled: An Introduction'. *International Migration* 39 (5): 3–6.

Irvin, G. 2008. *Super Rich, the Rise of Inequality in Britain and the United States*. London: Polity.

Irwin, M. D., and J. D. Kasarda. 1991. 'Air Passenger Linkages and Employment Growth in U.S. Metropolitan Areas'. *American Sociological Review* 56 (4): 524–537.

Isard, W. 1956. *Location and Space Economy*. Cambridge, MA: MIT Press.

Iyer, P. 2000. *The Global Soul: Jet Lag, Shopping Malls, and the Search for Home*. New York, NY: Knopf.

Jacobs, J. 1969. *The Economy of Cities*. New York, NY: Random House.

———. 1984. *Cities and the Wealth of Nations: Principles of Economic Life*. New York, NY: Random House.

———. 1993. *The Death and Life of Great American Cities*. New York, NY: Vintage Books.

———. 2000. *The Nature of Economies*. New York, NY: Vintage.

Jefferson, M. 1939. 'The Law of the Primate City'. *Geographical Review* 29: 226–232.

Jessop, B. 1997. 'The Entrepreneurial City: Re-Imagining Localities, Redesigning Economic Governance'. In *Realizing Cities: New Spatial Divisions and Social Transformations*, edited by N. Jewson and S. MacGregor, 28–41. London: Routledge.

Jessop, B., N. Brenner, and M. Jones. 2008. 'Theorizing Sociospatial Relations'. *Environment and Planning D* 26: 389–401.

Jiang, Y., and J. Shen. 2010. 'Measuring the Urban Competitiveness of Chinese Cities in 2000'. *Cities* 27 (5): 307–314.

Johansson, B., and J. M. Quigley. 2004. 'Agglomeration and Networks in Spatial Economies'. *Papers in Regional Science* 83: 165–176.

Johnson, J. H. 1974. 'Geographical Processes at the Edge of the City'. In *Suburban Growth*, edited by J. H. Johanson, 1–16. London: Wiley.

Jonas, A., and S. Pincetl. 2006. 'Rescaling Regions in the State: The New Regionalism in California'. *Political Geography* 25: 482–505.

Jones, A. 2002. 'The Global City: Misconceived: The Myth of Global Management in Transnational Service Firms'. *Geoforum* 33: 335–350.

———. 2005. 'Truly Global Corporations? Theorising Organizational' Globalization in Advanced Business Services'. *Journal of Economic Geography* 5: 177–200.

———. 2007. 'More Than Managing across Borders? The Complex Role of Face-to-Face Interaction in Globalizing Law Firms'. *Journal of Economic Geography* 7: 223–246.

———. 2008. 'The Rise of Global Work'. *Transactions of the Institute of British Geographers* NS 33: 12–26.

Jones, M., and B. Jessop. 2010. 'Thinking State/Space Incompossibly'. *Antipode* 42: 1119–1149.

Jöns, H. 2008. 'Academic Travel from Cambridge University and the Formation of Centres of Knowledge, 1885–1954'. *Journal of Historical Geography* 34 (2): 338–362.

Kaiser, A., and N. Ehlert. 2006. 'How and Why Do Political Institutions Matter? Federalism, Decentralisation and Macro-Economic Performance in OECD Countries' (Max Planck Summer Conference on Economic Sociology and Political Economy, Lake Como, Italy) 34.

Kaplinsky, R., and M. Morris. 2001. *A Handbook for Value Chain Research*. Available at http://www.ids.ac.uk/ids/global/pdfs/VchNov01.pdf (accessed on 14 January 2020).

Kay, J. 2001. 'Geography is Still Important'. *The Financial Times* (10 January).

Keane, J. 2001. 'Global Civil Society? Introducing Global Civil Society'. In *Global Civil Society*, edited by H. Anheier, M. Glasius, and M. Kaldor. Oxford: Oxford University Press.

Keating, M. 1998. *The New Regionalism in Western Europe: Territorial Restructuring and Political Change*. Cheltenham: Edward Elgar.

Keeling, D. J. 1995. 'Transport and the World City Paradigm'. In *World Cities in a World-System*, edited by P. L. Knox and P. J. Taylor, 115–131. Cambridge: Cambridge University Press.

Kellerman, A. 2002. *The Internet on Earth, a Geography of Information*. West Sussex: John Wiley & Sons Ltd.

Kenny, N. 2009. 'From Body and Home to Nation and World: The Varying Scales of Transnational Urbanism in Montreal and Brussels at the Turn of the Twentieth Century'. *Urban History* 36 (2): 223–242.

Kentor, J. 2005. 'The Growth of Transnational Corporate Networks 1962–1998'. *Journal of World Systems Research* 11.

Keohane, R. O., and J. S. Nye. 2000. 'Introduction'. In *Governance in a Globalizing World*, edited by J. S. Nye and J. D. Donahue, 1–45. Washington, DC: The Brooking Institution.

Kharas, Homi. 2010. *The Emerging Middle Class in Developing Countries*. Paris: OECD Development Centre.

Kindelberger, C. 1974. 'The Formation of Financial Centers: A Study of Comparative Economic History'. *Princeton Studies in International Finance* 36.

King, A. D. 1990. *Global Cities: Post-Imperialism and the Internationalisation of London*. London: Routledge.

King, R. 2002. 'Towards a New Map of European Migration'. *International Journal of Population Geography* 8 (2): 89–106.

Kloosterman, R. C., and B. Lambregts. 2007. 'Between Accumulation and Concentration of Capital: Toward a Framework for Comparing Long-Term Trajectories of Urban Systems'. *Urban Geography* 28 (1): 54–73.

Kloosterman, R. C., and S. Musterd. 2001. 'The Polycentric Urban Region: Towards a Research Agenda'. *Urban Studies* 38 (4): 623–633.

Knight, J. 1997. 'Internationalisation of Higher Education: A Conceptual Framework'. In *Internationalisation of Higher Education in Asia Pacific Countries*, edited by J. Knight and H. de Wit, 11–22. Amsterdam: European Association for International Education.

Knight, R. V., and G. Gappert, eds. 1989. *Cities in a Global Society*. Newbury Park, CA: SAGE Publications.

Knorr-Cetina, K. 1999. *Epistemic Cultures*. Cambridge, MA; London: Harvard University Press.

Knox, P. 1994. *Urbanization: An Introduction to Urban Geography*. Englewood Cliffs, NJ: Prentice Hall.

Knox, P., and P. Kathy. 2010. 'International Homogeneity in Architecture and Urban Development?' *Informationen zur Raumentwicklung* (IzR) 34 (2): 417–428.

Knox, P. L. 1996. 'Globalization and Urban Change'. *Urban Geography* 17: 115–117.

———. 2002. 'World Cities and the Organization of Global Space'. In *Geographies of Global Change*, 2nd ed., edited by R. J. Johnston, P. J. Taylor, and M. J. Watts, 328–338. Oxford: Blackwell.

Knox, P. L., and P. J. Taylor, eds. 1995. *World Cities in a World System*. Cambridge: Cambridge University Press.

Koestler, A. 1978. *Janus: A Summing Up*. New York, NY: Random House.

Kotler, P., D. Haider, and I. Rein. 1993. *Marketing Places: Attracting Investment, Industry, and Tourism to Cities, States, and Nations*. New York, NY: The Free Press.

Krätke, S. 1999. 'Berlin's Regional Economy in the 1990s: Structural Adjustment or Open Ended Structural Break'. *European Urban and Regional Studies* 6 (4): 323–338.

———. 2003. 'Global Media Cities in a Worldwide Urban Network'. *European Planning Studies* 11: 605–628.

———. 2011. 'How Manufacturing Industries Connect Cities across the World: Extending Research on "Multiple Globalizations"'. *GaWC Research Bulletin* 391. Available at http://www.lboro.ac.uk/gawc/rb/rb391.html (accessed on 14 January 2020).

Krätke, S., K. Wildner, and S. Lanz, eds. (2010) 2012. *Transnationalism and Urbanism*, 91–111. London: Routledge.

Krätke, S., and P. J. Taylor. 2004. 'A World Geography of Global Media Cities'. *European Planning Studies* 12: 459–477.

Krugman, P. 1991. 'Increasing Returns and Economic Geography'. *Journal of Political Economy* 99: 483–499.

———. 1993. 'On the Number and Location of Cities'. *European Economic Review* 37 (2): 293–298.

———. 2005. 'Second Winds for Industrial Regions?' In *New Wealth for Old Nations: Scotland's Economic Prospects*, edited by D. Coyle, W. Alexander, and B. Ashcroft, 35–47. Princeton, NJ: Princeton University Press.

Küblböck, K. 1999. 'Globalisierung und Peripherie'. In *Umstrukturierung in Lateinamerika, Afrika und Asien*, edited by Chr Parnreiter, A. Novy, and K. Fischer, 159–282. Frankfurt am Main: Brandes & Apsel.

Laermans, R. 1993. 'Learning to Consume: Early Departmental Stores and the Shaping of Modern Consumer Culture (1860–1914)'. *Theory, Culture & Society* 10: 79–102.

Lai, K. 2012. 'Differentiated Markets: Shanghai, Beijing and Hong Kong in China's Financial Centre Network'. *Urban Studies* 49 (6): 1275–1296.

Lambregts, B. 2009. *The Polycentric Metropolis Unpacked: Concepts, Trends, and Policy in the Randstad Holland*. Amsterdam: Amsterdam Institute for Metropolitan and International Development Studies.

Larsen, J., K. W. Axhausen, and J. Urry. 2006. 'Geographies of Social Networks: Meetings, Travel and Communications'. *Mobilities* 12: 261–283.

Lashinsky, A. 2002. 'Silicon Valley: The Lawyers Who Got Screwed Too'. *Fortune* 145: 133–140.

Latham, A., and D. McCormack. 2004. 'Moving Cities: Rethinking the Materialities of Urban Geographies'. *Progress in Human Geography* 28: 701–724.

Latour, B. 1987. *Science in Action: How to Follow Scientists and Engineers through Society*. Cambridge, MA: Harvard University Press.

———. 1993. *We have Never Been Modern*. London: Harvester Wheatsheaf.

———. 2005. *Reassembling the Social, an Introduction to Actor-Network Theory*. Oxford: Oxford University Press.

Latour, B., and E. Hermant. 1998. *Paris, Ville Invisible*. Paris: La Découverte.

Law, J. 2000. 'Transitivities'. *Environment and Planning D: Society and Space* 18: 133–148.

———. 2004. *After Method: Mess in Social Science Research*. London: Routledge.

Le Galès, P. 2002. *European Cities; Social Conflicts and Governance*. Oxford: Oxford University Press.

Lee, B., and P. Gordon. 2007. 'Urban Spatial Structure and Economic Growth in US Metropolitan Areas'. Paper presented at the 46th annual meeting of the Western Regional Science Association, Newport Beach, CA.

Lee, E. K. S., S. X. Zhao, and Y. Xie. 2012. 'Command and Control Cities in Global Space-Economy before and after 2008 Geo-Economic Transition'. *Chinese Geographical Science* 22 (3): 334–342.

Lefevre, H. 1991. *The Production of Space*. Oxford: Blackwell.

Leslie, D., and S. Reimer. 1999. 'Spatializing Commodity Chains'. *Progress in Human Geography* 23 (3): 401–420.

Letho, J. 2000. 'Different Cities in Different Welfare States'. In *Cities in Contemporary Europe*, edited by A. Bragnasco and P. Le Gales, 112–130. Cambridge: Cambridge University Press.

Levinson, P. 1988. 'Mind at Large: Knowing in the Technological Age'. *Research in Philosophy and Technology* Supplement 2.

Leydesdorff, L., and P. Zhou. 2005. 'Are the Contributions of China and Korea Upsetting the World System of Science?' *Scientometrics* 63 (3): 617–630.

Li, Gonghao. 2004. *The Rise of Shanghai: From a Fishing Village to a Cosmopolis*. Shanghai: Shanghai University Press.

Li, Xiangyang. 2011. 'The Prospect of a Shift in the Global Economic Centre of Gravity to the East'. *International Economic Review* 5 (5).

Limtanakool, N., T. Schwanen, and M. Dijst. 2007. 'Ranking Functional Urban Regions: A Comparison of Interaction and Node Attribute Data'. *Cities* 24: 26–42.

Lin, G. S. C. 2004. 'The Chinese Globalizing Cities: National Centres of Globalization and Urban Transformation'. *Progress in Planning* 61 (3): 143–157.

———. 2005. 'Service Industries and Transformation of City-Regions in Globalizing China: New Testing Ground for Theoretical Reconstruction'. In *Service Industries and Asia Pacific Cities: New Development Trajectories*, edited by P. W. Daniels, K. C. Ho, and T. A. Hutton, 283–300. New York, NY: Routledge.

Lind, H. 1993. 'A Note on Fundamental Theory and Idealizations in Economics and Physics'. *The British Journal for the Philosophy of Science* 44: 493–503.

Lipsey, R. G., and C. D. Harbury. 1992. *First Principles of Economics*, 2nd ed. London: Weidenfeld and Nicolson.

Liu, X., and D. Derudder. 2012. 'Two-Mode Networks and the Interlocking World City Network Model: A Reply to Neal'. *Geographical Analysis* 44: 171–173.

Liu, X., and P. J. Taylor. 2011. 'A Robustness Assessment of GaWC Global Network Connectivity Ranking'. *Urban Geography* 32 (8): 1227–1237.

Liu, X., J. Bollen, M. L. Nelson, and H. V. de Sompel. 2005. 'Co-Authorship Networks in the Digital Library Research Community'. *Information Processing and Management* 41: 1462–1480.

Lizieri, C. 2009. *Towers of Capital: Office Markets and International Financial Services*. Oxford: Wiley-Blackwell.

———. 2012. 'Global Cities, Office Markets and Capital Flows'. In *International Handbook of Globalization and World Cities*, edited by B. Derudder, M. Hoyler, P. J. Taylor, and F. Witlox, 162–176. Cheltenham; Northampton, MA: Edward Elgar.

Lizieri, C., and N. Kutsch. 2006. *Who Owns the City 2006: Office Ownership in the City of London Reading*. University of Reading Business School and Development Securities plc, 27 + iii.

Lizieri, C., A. Baum, and P. Scott. 2000. 'Ownership, Occupation and Risk: A View of the City of London Office Market'. *Urban Studies* 37 (7): 1109–1129.

Lo, F. C., and Y. M. Yeung, eds. 1996. *Emerging World Cities in Pacific Asia*. Tokyo: UNU Press.

———. 1998. *Globalization and the World Large Cities*. Tokyo: United Nations University Press.

Loasby, B. J. 1991. *Equilibrium and Evolution*. Manchester: Manchester University Press.

Lowendahl, B. 2005. *Strategic Management of Professional Service Firms*, 3rd ed. Copenhagen: Copenhagen Business School.

Lucas, R. E. B. 2003. *Migration and Lagging Regions*. Boston, MA: Boston University.

Lukermann, F. 1966. 'Empirical Expressions of Nodality and Hierarchy in a Circulation Manifold'. *East Lakes Geographer* 2: 17–44.

Lüthi, S., A. Thierstein, and V. Goebel. 2010. 'Intra-Firm and Extra-Firm Linkages in the Knowledge Economy: The Case of the Emerging Mega-City Region of Munich'. *Global Networks* 10: 114–137.

Lyons, D., and S. Salmon. 1995. World Cities, Multinational Corporations, and Urban Hierarchy: The Case of the United States. In *World Cities in a World-System*, edited by P. L. Knox and P. J. Taylor, 98–114. Cambridge: Cambridge University Press.

Ma, X., and M. Timberlake. 2012. 'World City Typologies and National City System Deterritorialisation: USA, China and Japan'. *Urban Studies* 50 (2): 255–275.

Machlup, F. 1962. 'The Supply of Inventors and Inventions'. In *The Rate and Direction of Inventive Activity*, edited by R. Nelson. Boston, MA: NBER.

Macleod, G., and M. Jones. 2001. 'Renewing the Geography of Regions'. *Environment and Planning D* 19: 669–695.

———. 2007. 'Territorial, Scalar, Networked, Connected: In What Sense a "Regional World"?' *Regional Studies* 41: 1177–1191.

Mahoney, J. 2000. 'Path Dependence in Historical Sociology'. *Theory and Society* 29: 507–548.

Mahutga, M. C., X. Ma, D. Smith, and M. Timberlake. 2010. 'Economic Globalization and the Structure of the World-City System: The Case of Airline Passenger Data'. *Urban Studies* 7 (9): 925–1947.

Malecki, E. 2002. 'The Economic Geography of the Internet's Infrastructure, Malecki'. *Economic Geography* 78: 399–424.

Malecki, E. J., and S. P. Gorman. 2001. 'Maybe the Death of Distance, But Not the End of Geography: The Internet as a Network'. In *Worlds of E-Commerce: Economic, Geographical and Social Dimensions*, edited by T. R. Leinbach and S. D. Brunn. West Sussex: Wiley.

Mann, M. 1986. *The Sources of Social Power*. Vol. I: A History of Power from the Beginning to AD 1760. Cambridge: Cambridge University Press.

———. 1993. *The Sources of Social Power*. Vol. II: The Rise of Classes and Nation States, 1760–1914. Cambridge: Cambridge University Press.

Marcuse, P., and R. van Kempen, eds. 2000. *Globalizing Cities: A New Spatial Order?* Oxford: Blackwell.

Marshall, J. U. 1989. *The Structure of Urban Systems*. Toronto: University of Toronto Press.

Maskell, P. 2001. 'The Firm in Economic Geography'. *Economic Geography* 77: 329–344.

Massey, D. 1993. 'Power-Geometry and a Progressive Sense of Place'. In *Mapping the Futures*, edited by J. Bird, B. Curtis, T. Putnam, G. Robertson, and L. Tickner, 59–69. London: Routledge.

———. 1994. *Space, Place and Gender*. Cambridge: John Wiley & Sons.

Massey, D. 1999. 'What Is a City?' In *Understanding Cities: City Worlds*, edited by D. Massey, J. Allen, and S. Pile. London: Routledge.

———. 2007. *World City*. Cambridge: Polity Press.

Massey, D. S. 2003. 'Patterns and Processes of International Migration in the 21st Century'. Paper presented at the Conference on African Migration in Comparative, Johannesburg.

Matthiessen, C. W., A. W. Schwarz, and S. Find. 2002. 'The Top-Level Global Research System, 1997–99: Centres, Networks and Nodality, an Analysis Based on Bibliometric Indicators'. *Urban Studies* 39 (5–6): 903–927.

———. 2006. 'World Cities of Knowledge: Research Strength, Networks and Nodality'. *Journal of Knowledge Management* 10 (5): 14–25.

Maude, D. 2006. *Global Private Banking and Wealth Management*. Chichester: Wiley.

May, R. M. 1997. 'The Scientific Wealth of Nations'. *Science* 275: 793–796.

Mayer, T., and G. Ottaviano. 2007. 'The Happy Few: New Facts on the Internationalisation of European Firms' (Bruegel-CEPR EFIM 2007 Report, Bruegel Blueprint Series, University of Bologna).

McCann, P. 2008. 'Globalization and Economic Geography: The World Is Curved, Not Flat'. *Cambridge Journal of Regions, Economy and Society* 1: 351–370.

McCann, P., and R. Mudambi. 2004. 'The Location Behavior of the Multinational Enterprise: Some Analytical Issues'. *Growth and Change* 25: 491–524.

McKenzie, R. D. 1933. *The Metropolitan Community*. New York, NY: McGraw-Hill.

McKinsey Global Institute. 2009. *Preparing for China's Urban Billion—Summary of Findings*. New York, NY: McKinsey & Company.

———. 2014. *Global Flows in a Digital Age: How Trade, Finance, People, and Data Connect the World Economy*. New York, NY: McKinsey & Company.

———. 2016. *Digital Globalization: The New Era of Global Flows*. New York, NY: McKinsey & Company.

McNeill, D. 2008. *The Global Architect: Firms, Fame and Urban Form*. London: Routledge.

McPherson, M., L. Smith-Lovin, and J. M. Cook. 2001. 'Birds of a Feather: Homophily in Social Networks'. *Annual Review of Sociology* 27: 415–444.

Meijers, E. J. 2005. 'Polycentric Urban Regions and the Quest for Synergy: Is a Network of Cities More Than the Sum of the Parts?' *Urban Studies* 42: 765–781.

———. 2008. 'Summing Small Cities Does Not Make a Large City: Polycentric Urban Regions and the Provision of Cultural, Leisure and Sports Amenities'. *Urban Studies* 45 (11): 2323–2342.

Meijers, E. J., and M. J. Burger. 2010. 'Spatial Structure and Productivity in U.S. Metropolitan Areas'. *Environment and Planning A* 42 (6): 1383–1402.

———. 2015. 'Stretching the Concept of "Borrowed Size"'. *Urban Studies*. doi:10.1177/0042098015597642.

Meijers, E. J., J. Hoekstra, M. Leijten, E. Louw, and M. Spaans. 2012. 'Connecting the Periphery: Distributive Effects of New Infrastructure'. *Journal of Transport Geography* 22: 187–198.

Melo, P., D. Graham, and R. Noland. 2009. 'A Meta-Analysis of Estimates of Urban Agglomeration Economies'. *Regional Science and Urban Economics* 39: 332–342.

Men, K., and W. Zeng. 2004. 'A Study on the Prediction of the Population of China over the Next 50 Years'. [In Chinese.] *Journal of Quantitative and Technical Economics* 21 (3): 12–17.

Metcalfe, J. S. 1998. *Evolutionary Economics and Creative Destruction*. London: Routledge.

Meyer, D. R. 1986. 'The World System of Cities: Relations between International Financial Metropolises and South American Cities'. *Social Forces* 64: 553–581.

Michelson, R., and J. Wheeler. 1994. 'The Flow of Information in a Global Economy: The Role of the American Urban System in 1990'. *Annals of Association of American Geographers* 84: 87–107.

Ministry of Housing and Urban-Rural Development, P. R. China. 2002. *China Urban Construction Statistical Yearbook 2002*. Beijing: China Planning Press.

———. 2015. *China Urban Construction Statistical Yearbook 2015*. Beijing: China Planning Press.

Mitlin, D., and D. Satterthwaite. 1996. 'What Is to be Sustained, What Developed? Sustainability and Sustainable Cities'. In *Sustainability, The Environment, and Urbanization*, edited by C. Pugh, 135–177. London: Earthscan Publications.

Mollenkopff, J. H. 1983. *The Contested City*. Princeton, NJ: Princeton University Press.

Mollenkopff, J. H., and M. Castells, eds. 1992. *Dual City: Restructuring New York*. New York, NY: Russell Sage.

Mommaas, H. 2004. 'Cultural Clusters and the Post-Industrial City: Towards the Remapping of Urban Cultural Policy'. *Urban Studies* 41 (3): 507–532.

Morgan, G. 2001. 'Transnational Communities and Business Systems'. *Global Networks* 1 (2): 113–130.

Morgan, G., and S. Quack. 2005. 'Institutional Legacies and Firm Dynamics: The Growth and Internationalization of UK and German Law Firms'. *Organization Studies* 26 (12): 1175–1785.

Morgan, K. 1997. 'The Learning Region: Institutions, Innovation and Regional Renewal'. *Regional Studies* 31: 491–503.

———. 2007. 'The Polycentric State: New Spaces of Empowerment and Engagement?' *Regional Studies* 41: 1237–1251.

Morley, D., and K. Robins. 1995. *Spaces of Identity: Global Media, Electronic Landscapes and Cultural Boundaries*. London: Routledge.

Morshidi, S. 2000. 'Globalising Kuala Lumpur and the Strategic Role of the Producer Services Sector'. *Urban Studies* 37 (12): 2217–2240.

Moss, M. L. 1987. 'Telecommunications, World Cities and Urban Policy'. *Urban Studies* 24 (6): 534–546.

Moss, M. L., and A. M. Townsend. 2000. 'The Internet Backbone and the American Metropolis'. *Information Society* 16: 35–47.

Moulaert, F., and F. Djellal. 1995. 'Information Technology Consultancy Firms: Economies of Agglomeration from a Wide-Area Perspective'. *Urban Studies* 32: 105–122.

Moulaert, F., A. Rodriguez, and E. Swyngedouw. 2003. *The Globalized City: Economic Restructuring and Social Polarization in European Cities*. Oxford: Oxford University Press.

Mumford, L. 1938. *The Culture of Cities*. Boston, MA: Harcourt.

Myrdal, G. 1957a. *Economic Theory and Underdeveloped Regions*. London: Duckworth.

———. 1957b. *Rich Lands and Poor: The Road to World Prosperity*. New York, NY: Harper.

Nachum, L. 2000. 'Economic Geography and the Location of TNCs: Financial and Professional Service FDI to the US'. *Journal of International Business Studies* 31 (3): 367–385.

Neal, Z. 2008. 'The Duality of World Cities and Firms: Comparing Networks, Hierarchies, and Inequalities in the Global Economy'. *Global Networks* 8: 94–115.

Neal, Z. P. 2010. 'Refining the Air Traffic Approach: An Analysis of the U.S. City Network'. *Urban Studies* 47 (10): 2195–2215.

———. 2011. 'Differentiating Centrality and Power in the World City Network'. *Urban Studies* 48 (13): 2733–2748.

———. 2012. 'Structural Determinism in the Interlocking World City Network'. *Geographical Analysis* 44 (2): 162–170.

Needham, B. 2006. *Planning, Law and Economics, an Investigation of the Rules We Make for Using Land*. London; New York, NY: Routledge.

Nelson, R., ed. 1962. *The Rate and Direction of Inventive Activity*. Boston, MA: NBER.

———. 1988. *National Innovation Systems*. Oxford: Oxford University Press.

Nelson, R., and B. N. Sampat. 1999. 'Making Sense of Institutions as a Factor Shaping Economic Progress' (Mimeo, Columbia University, New York, NY).

Nelson, R. R. and S. G. Winter. 1982. *An Evolutionary Theory of Economic Change*. Cambridge: Belknap Press.

Newman, M. E. J. 2001a. 'Scientific Collaboration Networks: I, Network Construction and Fundamental Results'. *Physical Review* E (64): 016131.

———. 2001b. 'Scientific Collaboration Networks: II, Shortest Paths, Weighted Networks, and Centrality'. *Physical Review* E (64): 016132.

Newman, P., and A. Thornley. 2005. *Planning World Cities: Globalization and Urban Politics*. London: Palgrave.

Ng, M. K., and P. Hills. 2003. 'World Cities or Great Cities? A Comparative Study of Five Asian Metropolis'. *Cities* 20: 151–165.

Niedzielski, M., and E. J. Malecki. 2012. 'Making Tracks: Rail Networks in World Cities'. *Annals of the Association of American Geographers* 102 (6): 1409–1431.

North, R. D. 2005. *Rich Is Beautiful, a Very Personal Defence of Mass Affluent*. London: Social Affairs Unit.

O'Connor, K., and P. Daniels. 2001. 'The Geography of International Trade in Services: Australia and the APEC Region'. *Environment and Planning A* 33: 281–296.

O'Connor, K., and K. Fuellhart. 2012. 'Cities and Air Services: The Influence of the Airline Industry'. *Journal of Transport Geography* 22: 46–52.

Ohlin, B., P. O. Hesselborn, and P. M. Wijkman. 1977. *The International Allocation of Economic Activity*. London: Macmillan.

Ohmae, K. 1990. *The Borderless World: Power and Strategy in the Interlinked Economy*. London: HarperCollins.

Ohmae, K. 1995. *The End of the Nation-State: The Rise of Regional Economies*. London: HarperCollins.

O'Kelly, M. E. and T. H. Grubesic. 2002. 'Backbone Topology, Access, and the Commercial Internet, 1997–2000'. *Environment and Planning B—Planning & Design* 29: 533–552.

Olalquiaga, C. 1992. *Megalopolis, Contemporary Cultural Sensibilities*. Minneapolis, MN: University of Minnesota Press.

Olds, K. 1995. 'Globalization and the Projection of New Urban Spaces: Pacific Rim Mega—Projects in the Late 20th Century'. *Environment and Planning A* 27: 1713–1743.

———. 1997. 'Globalizing Shanghai: The "Global Intelligence Corps" and the Building of Pudong'. *Cities* 14: 109–123.

Olds, K., and H. W. C. Yeung. 2004. 'Pathways to Global City Formation: A View from the Developmental City-State of Singapore'. *Review of International Political Economy* 11: 489–521.

Oncu, A., and P. Weyland. 1997. *Space, Culture, and Power, New Identities in Globalizing Cities*. Atlantic Heights, NJ: Zed Books.

Oner, A. C., D. Mitsova, D. Prosperi, and J. Vos. 2010. 'Knowledge Globalization in Urban Studies and Planning: A Network Analysis of International Co-Authorships'. *Journal of Knowledge Globalization* 3 (1): 2–30.

Owen, D. 2009. *The Green Metropolis*. New York, NY: Riverhead Books.

Paasi, A. 1986. 'The Institutionalization of Regions: A Theoretical Framework for Understanding the Emergence of Regions and the Constitution of Regional Identity'. *Fennia* 164: 105–146.

———. 2010. 'Regions are Social Constructs, But Who or What "Constructs" Them?' *Agency in Question, Environment and Planning A* 42: 2296–2301.

Pain, K. 2005. 'POLYNET Action 2.1: Qualitative Analysis of Service Business Connections: Summary Report'. London: Institute of Community Studies/The Young Foundation.

———. 2006. 'Policy Challenges of Functional Polycentricity in a Global Mega-City Region: South East England'. *Built Environment* 32 (2): 194–205.

———. 2007. 'City of London Global Village: Understanding the Square Mile in a Post-Industrial World Economy'. *GaWC Research Bulletin* 218.

———. 2008a. 'Gateways and Corridors in Globalization: Changing European Global City Roles and Functions'. *GaWC Research Bulletin* 287.

———. 2008b. 'Spaces of Practice in Advanced Business Services: Rethinking London–Frankfurt Relations'. *Environment and Planning D: Society and Space* 26 (2): 264–279.

Pain, K. 2008c. 'Urban Regions and Economic Development'. In *Connecting Cities: City-Regions*, edited by C. Johnson, R. Hu, and S. Abedin. Sydney: Metropolis Congress.

———. 2008d. 'Examining Core-Periphery Relationships in a Global Mega-City Region—The Case of London and South East England'. *Regional Studies* 42: 1161–1172.

Pain, K. 2008e. *Looking for the 'Core' in Knowledge Globalization: The Need for a New Research Agenda*. Available at http://www.lboro.ac.uk/gawc/rb/rb286.html (accessed on 14 January 2020).

Pain, K., and P. Hall. 2006a. 'Firms and Places: Inside the Mega-City Regions'. In *The Polycentric Metropolis: Learning from Mega-City Regions in Europe*, edited by P. Hall and K. Pain, 91–103. London: Earthscan.

———. 2008. 'Informational Quantity versus Informational Quality: The Perils of Navigating the Space of Flows'. *Regional Studies* 42, ISSN: 1360-0591 (electronic).

Pahl, R. 1986. 'On Hall's Social City'. *The Planner* (10 March).

Painter, J. 2008. 'Cartographic Anxiety and the Search for Regionality'. *Environment and Planning A* 40: 342–361.

Panagariya, A. 2008. *India: The Emerging Giant*. Oxford: Oxford University Press.

Parmar, I. 2002. 'American Foundations and the Development of International Knowledge Networks'. *Global Networks* 2 (1): 13–30.

Parnreiter, C. 2002. 'Mexico: The Making of a Global City'. In *Global Networks, Linked Cities*, edited by S. Sassen, 215–238. London; New York, NY: Taylor & Francis.

———. 2003. 'Global City Formation in Latin America: Socioeconomic and Spatial Transformations in Mexico City and Santiago de Chile'. Paper presented at the 99th Annual Meeting of the Association of American Geographers, New Orleans, 4–8 March 2003. *GaWC Research Bulletin* 103. Available at http://www.lboro.ac.uk/gawc/rb/rb103.html (accessed on 14 January 2020).

———. 2010. 'Global Cities in Global Commodity Chains: Exploring the Role of Mexico City in the Geography of Global Economic Governance'. *Global Networks* 10 (1): 35–53.

———. 2014. 'Network or Hierarchical Relations? A Plea for Redirecting Attention to the Control Functions of Global Cities'. *Tijdschrift voor Economische en Sociale Geografie* 105 (4): 398–411.

Parr, J. B. 2002. 'Agglomeration Economies: Ambiguities and Confusions'. *Environment and Planning A* 34 (4): 717–731.

———. 2004. 'The Polycentric Urban Region: A Closer Inspection'. *Regional Studies* 38: 231–240.

Parsons, T. 1957. 'The Distribution of Power in American Society'. *World Politics* 10: 123–143.

———. 1963. 'On the Concept of Political Power'. *Proceedings of the American Philosophical Society* 107: 232–262.

Partridge, M. D., D. S. Rickman, K. Ali, and M. R. Olfert. 2009. 'Do New Economic Geography Agglomeration Shadows Underlie Current Population Dynamics across the Urban Hierarchy?' *Regional Science* 88: 445–466.

Pelupessy, W. 2001. 'Industrialization in Global Commodity Chains Emanating from Latin America'. *UNISA Latin American Report* 17 (2): 4–14.

Pereira, R. A. O., and B. Derudder. 2010. 'Determinants of Dynamics in the World City Network, 2000–2004'. *Urban Studies* 47 (9): 1949–1967.

Perlman, J., and S. O'Meara. 2007. *The State of the World: Our Urban Future*. Megacities Project, 1–16.

Perlman, J., and M. O'Sheehan. 2007. *The State of the World 2007: Our Urban Future*. Megacities Project.

Perulli, P. 2012. *The Ontology of Global City-Region: A Critique of Statehood*. Available at http://www.lboro.ac.uk/gawc/rb/rb415.html (accessed on 14 January 2020).

Petrella, R. 1991. 'World City-States of the Future'. *New Perspectives Quarterly* 8: 59–64.

Pfeffer, J. 1982. *Organizations and Organization Theory*. Marshfield, MA: Pitman.

Phelps, N., and T. Ozawa. 2003. 'Contrasts in Agglomeration: Proto-Industrial, Industrial and Post-Industrial Forms Compared'. *Progress in Human Geography* 27: 583–604.

Phelps, N. A. 1998. 'On the Edge of Something Big: Edge-City Economic Development in Croydon, South London'. *Town Planning Review* 69 (4): 441–465.

Phelps, N. A., R. J. Fallon, and C. L. Williams. 2001. 'Small Firms, Borrowed Size and the Urban–Rural Shift'. *Regional Studies* 35 (7): 613–624.

Pierson, P. 2000. 'Increasing Returns, Path Dependency, and the Study of Politics'. *American Political Science Review* 94: 251–267.

Polèse, M., and R. Shearmur. 2006. 'Growth and Location of Economic Activity: The Spatial Dynamics of Industries in Canada 1971–2001'. *Growth and Change* 37 (3): 362–395.

Popper, K. 1985. *A World of Propensities*. Bristol: Thoemmes.

Porter, M. E. 1990. *The Competitive Advantage of Nations*. New York, NY: Free Press.

Powell, W. 1990. 'Neither Market nor Hierarchy: Network Forms of Organization'. *Research in Organizational Behavior* 12: 295–336.

Pratt, A. C. 2012. 'The Cultural Economy and the Global City'. In *International Handbook of Globalization and World Cities*, edited by B. Derudder, M. Hoyler, P. J. Taylor, and F. Witlox, 265–274. Cheltenham: Edward Elgar.

Pred, A. 1977. *City-Systems in Advanced Economies*. London: Hutchinson.

———. 1980. *Urban Growth and City Systems in the United States, 1840–1860*. London: Hutchinson.

———. 1984. 'Place as Historically Contingent Process: Structuration and the Time-Geography of Becoming Places'. *Annals of the Association of American Geographers* 74: 279–297.

Presas, L. M. S. 2005. *Transnational Buildings in Local Environments*. Aldershot: Ashgate.

Pryke, M. 1994. 'Looking Back on the Space of a Boom: (Re) Developing Spatial Matrices in the City of London'. *Environment and Planning A* 26: 235–264.

Puga, D. 2010. 'The Magnitude and Causes of Agglomeration Economies'. *Journal of Regional Science* 50: 203–219

Rabach, E., and E. M. Kim. 1994. 'Where Is the Chain in Commodity Chains? The Service Sector Nexus'. In *Commodity Chains and Global Capitalism*, edited by G. Gereffi and M. Korzeniewicz, 123–143. Westport, CT: ABC-CLIO.

Ratha, D., and W. Shaw. 2007. 'South-South Migration and Remittances' (Working Paper No. 102, World Bank, Washington, DC).

Reed, H. C. 1981. *The Pre-Eminence of International Financial Centers*. New York, NY: Praeger.

Regional Plan Association. 2016. *America 2050*. Available at http://www.america2050.org/images/2050_Map_Megaregions_Influence_150.png (accessed on 15 January 2020).

Reich, R. B. 1991. *The Work of Nations, Preparing Ourselves for 21st-Century Capitalism*. New York, NY: Vintage Books.

Reiffenstein, T. 2009. 'Specialization, Centralization, and the Distribution of Patent Intermediaries in the USA and Japan'. *Regional Studies* 43: 571–588.

Richardson, R., and A. Gillespie. 2000. 'The Economic Development of Peripheral Rural Areas in the Information Age'. In *Information Tectonics*, edited by M. I. Wilson and K. E. Corey. Hoboken, NJ: Wiley.

Rimmer, P. J. 1986. 'Japan's World Cities: Tokyo, Osaka, Nagoya or Tokaido Megalopolis?' *Development and Change* 17 (1): 121–157.

Robertson, R. 1992. *Globalization: Social Theory and Global Culture*. London: SAGE Publications.

Robinson, J. 2002. 'Global and World Cities: A View from Off the Map'. *International Journal of Urban and Regional Research* 26 (3): 531–534.

———. 2006. *Ordinary Cities: Between Modernity and Development*. London: Routledge.

Rodrigue, J. P., C. Comtois, and B. Slack. 2006. *The Geography of Transport Systems*. London; New York, NY: Routledge.

Romer, P. 1990. 'Endogenous Technology Change'. *Journal of Political Economy* 98: 71–102.

Rosenberg, N. 1982. *Inside the Black Box: Technology and Economics*. Cambridge: Cambridge University Press.

Rosenthal, S. S., and W. C. Strange. 2004. 'Evidence on the Nature and Sources of Agglomeration Economies'. In *Handbook of Regional Science and Urban Economics*. Vol. 4: Cities and Geography, edited by J. V. Henderson and J. F. Thisse, 2119–2171. Amsterdam: Elsevier.

Ross, B. H., and M. A. Levine. 2012. *Urban Politics: Cities and Suburbs in a Global Age*. New York, NY: M. E. Sharpe.

Ross, C. O. 1987. 'Organizational Dimensions of Metropolitan Dominance: Prominence in the Network of Corporate Control, 1955–1975'. *American Sociological Review* 52: 258–267.

Rossi, E. C., and P. J. Taylor. 2005. 'Banking Networks across Brazilian Cities: Interlocking Cities within and beyond Brazil'. *Cities* 22 (5): 381–393.

———. 2007. 'Gateway Cities: Círculos Bancarios, Concentración y Dispersión en el Ambiente Urbano Brasileño'. *Eure* 33 (100): 115–133.

Rossi, E. C., J. V. Beaverstock, and P. J. Taylor. 2007. 'Transaction Links through Cities: "Decision Cities" and "Service Cities" in Outsourcing by Leading Brazilian Firms'. *Geoforum* 38 (4): 628–642.

Rozenblat, C., and G. Melancon. 2009. 'A Small World Perspective on Urban Systems'. In *Handbook of Theoretical and Quantitative Geography*, edited by F. Bavaud and C. Mager, 431–457. Lausanne: UNIL.

Rozenblat, C., and D. Pumain. 2007. 'Firm Linkages, Innovation and the Evolution of Urban Systems'. In *Cities in Globalization: Practices, Policies, Theories*, edited by P. Taylor, B. Derudder, P. Saey, and F. Witlox, 130–156. London: Routledge.

Russett, B. M. 1967. *International Regions and the International System*. Chicago, IL: Rand McNally.

Rutherford, J., A. Gillespie, and R. Richardson. 2004. 'The Territoriality of Pan-European Telecommunications Backbone Networks'. *Journal of Urban Technology* 11 (3): 1–34.

Saey, P. 1996. 'Het Wereldstedennetwerk: De Nieuwe Hanze?' *Vlaams Marxistisch Tijdschrift* 30 (1): 120–123.

Salt, J., and H. Clout, eds. 1976. *Migration in Post-War Europe: Geographical Essays*. London: Oxford University Press.

Sassen, S. 1988. *The Mobility of Labor and Capital, a Study in International Investment and Capital Flow*. Cambridge: Cambridge University Press.

———. 1991. *The Global City: New York, London, Tokyo*. Princeton, NJ: Princeton University Press.

———. 1997. *Losing Control? Sovereignty in an Age of Globalization*. Chichester: Wiley.

———. 1999. 'Global Financial Centres'. *Foreign Affairs* 78 (1): 75–87.

———. 2001. *The Global City: New York, London, Tokyo*, 2nd ed. Princeton, NJ: Princeton University Press.

———. 2002a. 'Global Cities and Diasporic Networks: Microsites in Global Civil Society'. In *Global Civil Society*, edited by M. Glasius, M. Kaldor, and H. Anheier, H. Oxford: Oxford University Press.

———. 2002b. 'Locating Cities on Global Circuits'. *Environment and Urbanization* 14 (1): 13–30.

———. 2002c. 'Introduction, Locating Cities on Global Circuits'. In *Global Networks, Linked Cities*, edited by S. Sassen, 1–36. London: Routledge.

———, ed. 2002d. *Global Networks, Linked Cities*. London: Routledge.

Sassen, S. 2006a. *Cities in a World Economy*, 3rd ed. Thousand Oaks, CA: Pine Forge Press.

———. 2006b. 'Foreword'. In *Relocating Global Cities: From the Center to the Margins*, edited by M. M. Amen, K. Archer, and M. M. Bosman, ix–xiii. Lanham, MD: Rowman & Littlefield.

———. 2010. 'Global Inter-City Networks and Commodity Chains: Any Intersections?' *Global Networks* 10 (1): 150–163.

Sassoon, D. 2006. *The Culture of the Europeans: From 1800 to the Present*. London: Harper Press.

Savage, M., and K. Williams, eds. 2008. *Remembering Elites. Sociological Review Monograph*. Oxford: Blackwell's.

Saxenian, A. L. 2005. 'From Brain Drain to Brain Circulation: Transnational Communities and Regional Upgrading in India and China'. *Studies in Comparative International Development* 40 (2): 35–61.

Schafran, A. 2014. 'Rethinking Megaregions: Subregional Politics in a Fragmented Metropolis'. *Regional Studies* 48 (4): 587–602.

Schmitt, P., and L. Smas. 2012. 'Nordic "Intercity Connectivities" in a Multi-Scalar Perspective' (Nordregio Working Paper No. 7, Stockholm). Available at http://www.nordregio.se (accessed on 15 January 2020).

Schmitz, H. 2000. 'Global Competition and Local Cooperation: Success and Failure in the Sinos Valley, Brazil'. *World Development* 27: 1627–1650.

Scott, A. J. 1988. *Metropolis: From the Division of Labor to Urban Form*. Berkeley/Los Angeles, CA: University of California Press.

———. 2000. *The Cultural Economy of Cities: Essays on the Geography of Image-Producing Industries*. London: SAGE Publications.

———, eds. 2001a. *Global City-Regions: Trends, Theory, Policy*, 11–30. Oxford: Oxford University Press.

———. 2001b. 'Globalization and the Rise of City-Regions'. *European Planning Studies* 9 (7): 813–826.

Scott, A., E. Soja, and J. Agnew. 2001. 'Global City-Regions'. In *Global City-Regions: Trends, Theory, Policy*, edited by A. J. Scott. Oxford: Oxford University Press.

Scott, A. J., J. Agnew, E. Soja, and M. Storper. 2001. 'Global City-Regions'. In *Global City-Regions: Trends, Theory, Policy*, edited by A. Scott, 11–30. Oxford: Oxford University Press.

Scott, J. 1997. *Corporate Business and Capitalist Classes*. New York, NY: Oxford University Press.

Segbers, K., eds. 2007. The Making of Global City Regions Johannesburg, Mumbai/Bombay, São Paulo, and Shanghai. Baltimore, MD: John Hopkins University Press.

Shachar, A. 1997. 'A Metropolitan Approach in Planning the Urbanized Area of Tel Aviv'. In *Tel Aviv-Yafo, Social Processes and Public Policy*, edited by D. Nachmias and G. Nahum, 305–319. Tel Aviv: Ramot Press, Tel Aviv University.

Shanghai SWS Research Institute. 2009. 'The Globe Needs the Economic Growth by the Fifth Industrial Revolution'. *Shanghai Securities News* (5 Feb).

Shapiro, J. 2005. 'Smart Cities: Quality of Life, Productivity and the Growth Effects of Human Capital' (National Bureau of Economic Research Working Paper No. 11615, Cambridge, MA).

Sheller, M., and J. Urry. 2006. 'The New Mobilities Paradigm'. *Environment and Planning A* 38 (2): 207–226.

Sheppard, E. 2002. 'The Spaces and Times of Globalization: Place, Scale, Networks and Positionality'. *Economic Geography* 78: 307–330.

Shin, K. H., and M. Timberlake. 2000. 'World Cities in Asia: Cliques, Centrality and Connectedness'. *Urban Studies* 37: 2257–2285.

Short, J. R. 2004. 'Black Holes and Loose Connections in a Global Urban Network'. *The Professional Geographer* 56 (2): 295–302.

———. 2006. *Urban Theory: A Critical Assessment*. New York, NY: Palgrave.

Short, J. R., C. Breitbach, S. Buckman, and J. Essex. 2000. 'From World Cities to Gateway Cities Extending the Boundaries of Globalisation Theory'. *City* 4 (3): 317–340.

Short, J., Y. Kim, M. Kuss, and H. Wells. 1996. 'The Dirty Little Secret of World City Research'. *International Journal of Regional and Urban Research* 20: 697–717.

Schumpeter, Joseph. 1990. *The Theories of Economic Development*. Beijing: Commercial Press.

Shy, O. 2001. *The Economics of Network Industries*. Cambridge: Cambridge University Press.

Siegel, P., T. Johnson, and J. Alwang. 1995. 'Regional Economic Diversity and Diversification'. *Growth and Change* 26: 261–284.

Simmie, J., and W. F. Lever. 2002. 'Introduction: The Knowledge-Based City'. *Urban Studies* 39 (5–6): 885–857.

Simmonds, R., and G. Hack, eds. 2000. *Global City Regions: Their Emerging Forms*. London: Spon Press.

Sklair, L. 1991. *Sociology of the Global System*. Baltimore, MD: Johns Hopkins University Press.

———. 2001. *The Transnational Capitalist Class*. Oxford: Blackwell.

———. 2005. 'The Transnational Capitalist Class and Contemporary Architecture in Globalizing Cities'. *International Journal of Urban and Regional Research* 29 (3): 485–500.

Small, J., and M. Witherick. 1986. *A Modern Dictionary of Geography*. Baltimore, MD: Edward Arnold.

Smith, A., A. Rainnie, M. Dunford, J. Hardy, R. Hudson, and D. Sadler. 2002. 'Networks of Value, Commodities and Regions: Reworking Divisions of Labour in Macro-Regional Economies'. *Progress in Human Geography* 26 (1): 41–63.

Smith, D. A., and M. Timberlake. 1995a. 'World Cities: A Political Economy/Global Network Approach'. *Research in Urban Sociology* 3: 181–207.

Smith, D. A., and M. Timberlake. 1995b. 'Conceptualising and Mapping the Structure of the World System's City System'. *Urban Studies* 32: 287–302.

———. 2001. 'World City Networks and Hierarchies, 1977–1997: An Empirical Analysis of Global Air Travel Links'. *American Behavioral Scientist* 44 (10): 1656–1678.

Smith, M. P. 2001. *Transnational Urbanism, Locating Globalization*. Malden, MA: Blackwell Publishers.

———. 2005. 'Transnational Urbanism Revisited'. *Journal of Ethnic and Migration Studies* 31 (2): 235–244.

Smith, R. 2003. 'World City Actor-Networks'. *Human Geography* 27: 25–44.

———. 2008. 'Urban Studies without "Scale": Localizing the Global through Singapore'. In *Urban Assemblages: How Actor-Network Theory Changes Urban Studies*, edited by T. Bender and I. Farias. London: Routledge.

Smith, R. G. 2012. 'NY-LON'. In *International Handbook of Globalization and World Cities*, edited by B. Derudder, M. Hoyler, P. J. Taylor, and F. Witlox, 421–428. Cheltenham: Edward Elgar.

———. 2014. 'Beyond the Global City Concept and the Myth of "Command and Control"'. *International Journal of Urban and Regional Research* 38 (1): 98–115.

Smith, R. G., and M. A. Doel. 2010. 'Questioning the Theoretical Basis of Current Global-City Research: Structures, Networks, and Actor-Networks'. *International Journal of Urban and Regional Research* 34 (4).

Soja, E. 1996. *Thirdspace: Journeys to Los Angeles and Other Real and Imagined Space*. Oxford: Blackwell.

Soja, E. W. 2000. *Postmetropolis, Critical Studies of Cities and Regions*. Oxford: Blackwell.

Sokol, M. 2004. 'The "Knowledge Economy": A Critical View'. In *Regional Economies as Knowledge Laboratories*, edited by P. Cooke and A. Piccaluga, 216–231. Cheltenham: Edward Elgar.

Storper, M. 1995. 'The Resurgence of Regional Economies Ten Years Later: The Region as a Nexus of Untraded Interdependencies'. *European Urban and Regional Studies* 2: 191–222.

———. 1997. *The Regional World: Territorial Development in a Global Economy*. New York, NY: Guilford Press.

Storper, M., and M. Manville. 2006. 'Behaviour, Preferences and Cities: Urban Theory and Urban Resurgence'. *Urban Studies* 43 (8): 1247–1274.

Storper, M., and A. J. Venables. 2004. 'Buzz: Face-to-Face Contact and the Urban Economy'. *Journal of Economic Geography* 4 (4): 351–370.

Strassoldo, R. 1992. 'Globalism and Localism: Theoretical Reflections and Some Evidence'. In *Globalization and Territorial Identities*, edited by Z. Mlinar, 35–39. Aldershot: Avebury.

Su, N., and D. Xue. 2012. *The Spatial Distribution of Transnational Organizations in the Cities of Mainland China*. Available at http://www.lboro.ac.uk/gawc/rb/rb399.html (accessed on 15 January 2020).

Sudjic, D. 1992. *The 100 Mile City.* San Diego, CA: Harcourt Brace.

Taaffe, E. J. 1962. 'The Urban Hierarchy: An Air Passenger Definition'. *Economic Geography* 38: 1–14.

Taylor, J. B. 2007. 'Housing and Monetary Policy.' Working Paper 13682, National Bureau of Economic Research, Cambridge.

Taylor, M., and B. Asheim. 2001. 'The Concept of the Firm in Economic Geography'. *Economic Geography* 77: 315–328.

Taylor, P. J. 1995. 'World Cities and Territorial States: The Rise and Fall of Their Mutuality'. In *World Cities in a World-System*, edited by P. L. Knox and P. J. Taylor, 48–62. Cambridge: Cambridge University Press.

———. 1997. 'Hierarchical Tendencies amongst World Cities: A Global Research Proposal'. *Cities* 14: 323–332.

———. 1999. *Modernities: A Geohistorical Interpretation.* Cambridge: Polity Press.

———. 2000a. '"Izations" of the World: Americanization, Modernization and Globalization'. In *Demystifying Globalization*, edited by C. Hay and D. Marsh, 49–70. London: Macmillan.

———. 2000b. 'World Cities and Territorial States under Conditions of Contemporary Globalization'. *Political Geography* 19: 5–32.

———. 2001a. 'Specification of the World City Network'. *Geographical Analysis* 33: 181–194.

———. 2001b. 'Urban Hinterworlds: Geographies of Corporate Service Provision under Conditions of Contemporary Globalization'. *Geography* 86: 51–60.

———. (2003) 2004. *World City Network, a Global Urban Analysis.* New York, NY; London: Routledge.

———. 2005a. 'Leading World Cities: Empirical Evaluations of Urban Nodes in Multiple Networks'. *Urban Studies* 42: 1593–1608.

———. 2005b. 'New Political Geographies: Global Civil Society and Global Governance through World City Networks'. *Political Geography* 24 (6): 703–730.

———. 2005c. 'The New Geography of Global Civil Society: NGOs in the World City Network' *Globalizations* 1 (2): 265–277.

———. 2006. *Shanghai, Hong Kong, Taipei and Beijing within the World City Network: Positions, Trends and Prospects.* Available at http://www.lboro.ac.uk/gawc/rb/rb204.html (accessed on 15 January 2020).

———. 2010. 'Competition and Cooperation between Cities in Globalization'. In *International Handbook of Globalization and World Cities*, edited by B. Derudder, M. Hoyler, P. J. Taylor, and F. Witlox, 64–72. Cheltenham; Northampton, MA: Edward Elgar.

———. 2011a. 'Advanced Producer Service Centres in the World Economy'. In *Global Urban Analysis: A Survey of Cities in Globalization*, edited by P. J. Taylor, P. Ni, B. Derudder, M. Hoyler, J. Huang, and F. Witlox, 22–39. London: Earthscan.

Taylor, P. J. 2011b. 'UK Cities in Globalization'. In *Global Urban Analysis: A Survey of Cities in Globalization*, edited by P. J. Taylor, P. Ni, B. Derudder, M. Hoyler, J. Huan, and F. Witlox, 245–250. London: Earthscan.

———. 2012. The Challenge Facing World City Network Analysis. Available at http://www.lboro.ac.uk/gawc/rb/rb409.html (accessed on 15 January 2020).

———. 2013. *Extraordinary Cities: Millennia of Moral Syndromes, World-Systems and City/State Relations*. Cheltenham; Northampton, MA: Edward Elgar.

Taylor, P. J., and R. Aranya. 2006. 'Connectivity and City Revival'. *Town & Country Planning* 75: 309–314.

———. 2008. 'A Global "Urban Roller Coaster?" Connectivity Changes in the World City Network, 2000–2004'. *Regional Studies* 42 (1): 1–16.

Taylor, P. J., and G. Csomós. 2012. 'Cities as Control and Command Centres: Analysis and Interpretation'. *Cities* 29 (6): 408–411.

Taylor, P. J., M. Hoyler, K. Pain, and S. Vinciguerra. 2011. 'Extensive and Intensive Globalizations: Explicating the Low Connectivity Puzzle of US Cities Using City-Dyad Analysis'. *GaWC Research Bulletin* 369 (A).

Taylor, P., B. Derudder, and F. Witlox. 2007. 'Comparing Airline Passenger Destinations with Global Service Connectivities: A Worldwide Empirical Study of 214 Cities'. *Urban Geography* 28 (3): 232–248.

Taylor, P. J., and B. Derudder. 2004. 'Porous Europe: European Cities in Global Urban Arenas'. *Tijdschrift voor Economische en Sociale Geografie* 95 (5): 527–538.

Taylor, P. J., and K. Pain. 2007. 'Polycentric Mega-City Regions: Exploratory Research from Western Europe'. In *The Healdsburg Research Seminar on Megaregions*, edited by P. Todorovich. New York, NY: Lincoln Institute of Land Policy and Regional Plan Association.

Taylor, P. J., and D. R. F. Walker. 2004. 'Urban Hinterworlds Revisited'. *Geography* 89 (2): 145–151.

Taylor, P. J., G. Catalano, and D. R. F. Walker. 2002. 'Exploratory Analysis of the World City Network'. *Urban Studies* 39 (13): 2377–2394.

———. 2004. 'Multiple Globalisations: Regional, Hierarchical and Sectoral Articulations of Global Business Services through World Cities'. *Service Industries Journal* 24 (3): 63–81.

Taylor, P. J., B. Derudder, J. Faulconbridge, M. Hoyler, and P. Ni. 2014. 'Advanced Producer Service Firms as Strategic Networks, Global Cities as Strategic Places'. *Economic Geography* 90 (3): 267–291.

Taylor, P. J., B. Derudder, M. Hoyler, and P. Ni. 2012. 'Vital Positioning through the World City Network: Advanced Producer Service Firms as Strategic Networks, Global Cities as Strategic Places'. *GaWC Research Bulletin* 413. Available at http://www.lboro.ac.uk/gawc/rb/rb413.html (accessed on 15 January 2020).

———. 2013. 'New Regional Geographies of the World as Practised by Leading Advanced Producer Service Firms in 2010'. *Transactions of the Institute of British Geographers* 38 (3): 497–511.

Taylor, P. J., B. Derudder, M. Hoyler, P. Ni, and F. Witlox. 2014. 'City-Dyad Analyses of China's Integration into the World City Network'. *GaWC Research Bulletin* 407. Available at http://www.lboro.ac.uk/gawc/rb/rb407.html (accessed on 15 January 2020).

Taylor, P. J., B. Derudder, M. Hoyler, K. Pain, and F. Witlox. 2011. 'European Cities in Globalization'. In *Global Urban Analysis, A Survey of Cities in Globalization*, edited by P. J. Taylor, P. Ni, B. Derudder, M. Hoyler, J. Huang, and F. Witlox, 114–136. London; Washington, DC: Earthscan.

Taylor, P. J., B. Derudder, P. Saey, and F. Witlox, eds. 2006. *Cities in Globalization*. London: Routledge.

———, eds. 2007. *Cities in Globalization: Practices, Policies and Theories*. London: Routledge.

Taylor, P. J., D. M. Evans, M. Hoyler, B. Derudder, and K. Pain. 2009. 'The UK Space Economy as Practiced by Advanced Producer Service Firms: Identifying two Distinctive Polycentric Regional Processes in Contemporary Britain'. *International Journal of Urban and Regional Research* 33 (3): 700–718.

Taylor, P. J., A. Firth, M. Hoyler, and D. Smith. 2010. 'Explosive City Growth in the Modern World-System: An Initial Inventory Derived From Urban Demographic Changes'. *Urban Geography* 31 (7): 865–884.

Taylor, P. J., M. Hoyler, and R. Verbruggen. 2010. 'External Urban Relational Process: Introducing Central Flow Theory to Complement Central Place Theory'. *Urban Studies* 47 (13): 2803–2818.

Taylor, P. J., M. Hoyler, D. R. F. Walker, and M. J. Szegner. 2001. 'A New Mapping of the World for the New Millennium'. *The Geographical Journal* 167 (3): 213–222.

Taylor, P. J., P. Ni, B. Derudder, M. Hoyler, J. Huang, and F. Witlox, eds. 2011. *Global Urban Analysis: A Survey of Cities in Globalization*. London: Earthscan.

Taylor, P. J., P. Ni, B. Derudder, M. Hoyler, J. Huang, F. Lu, K. Pain, F. Witlox, X. Yang, D. Bassens, and W. Shen. 2008. 'Measuring the World City Network: New Developments and Results'. *GaWC Research Bulletin* 300. Available at http://www.lboro.ac.uk/gawc/publicat.html (accessed on 15 January 2020).

Terlouw, C. P. 1992. *The Regional Geography of the World-System: External Arena, Periphery, Semiperiphery, Core*. Utrecht: Faculteit Ruimtelijke Wetenschappen Universiteit Utrecht.

The City UK, 2013. Available at https://www.thecityuk.com/research/ (accessed on 8 April, 2020).

The Economist. 2004, 10 April. '(Still) Made in Japan' (Special Report: Manufacturing in Japan). *The Economist* 371 (8370): 577–593.

———. 2009. 'Spare a Dime? A Special Report on the Rich'. *The Economist* (4 April).

Thierstein, A., S. Luthi, C. Kruse, S. Gabi, and L. Glanzmann. 2008. 'Changing Value Chain of the Swiss Knowledge Economy: Spatial Impact of Intra-Firm and Inter-Firm Networks within the Emerging Mega-City Region of Northern Switzerland'. *Regional Studies* 42 (8): 1113–1131.

Thompson, G. F. 2003. *Between Hierarchies and Markets: The Logic and Limits of Network Forms of Organization*. Oxford: Oxford University Press.

Thrift, N. 1999. 'Cities and Economic Change: Global Governance?' In *Unsettling Cities*, edited by J. Allen, D. Massey, and M. Pryke. London: Routledge.

———. 2000. 'Afterwords'. *Environment and Planning D: Society and Space* 18: 213–256.

———. 2002. 'Performing Cultures in the New Economy'. In *Cultural Economy*, edited by P. du Gay and M. Pryke, 201–234. London: SAGE Publications.

———. 2004. 'Movement-Space: The Changing Domain of Thinking Resulting From the Development of New Kinds of Spatial Awareness'. *Economy and Society* 33 (4): 582–604.

———. 2008. *Non-Representational Theory: Space, Politics, Affect*. London: Routledge.

Throsby, C. D. 2010. *The Economics of Cultural Policy*. Cambridge: Cambridge University Press.

Tilly, C. 1992. *Coercion, Capital, and European States, AD 990–1992*. Cambridge, MA; Oxford: Blackwell.

Todeva, E. 2006. *Business Networks: Strategy and Structure*. New York, NY: Routledge.

Toly, N. J., S. Bouteligier, B. Gibson, and G. Smith. 2012. 'New Maps, New Questions: Global Cities beyond the Advanced Producer and Financial Services Sector'. *Globalizations* 9 (2): 289–306.

Torrance, M. I. 2008. 'Forging Glocal Governance? Urban Infrastructures as Networked Financial Products'. *International Journal of Urban and Regional Research* 32: 1–21.

Townsend, J. 1999. 'Are Non-Governmental Organizations Working in Development a Transnational Community?' *Journal of International Development* 11: 613–623.

Townsend, J., G. Porter, and E. Mawdsley. 2002. 'The Role of the Transnational Community of NGOs: Governance or Poverty Reduction?' *Journal of International Development* 14: 829–839.

Turok, I. 2009. 'The Distinctive City: Pitfalls in the Pursuit of Differential Advantage'. *Environment and Planning A* 41: 13–30.

Tushman, M., and P. Anderson. 1986. 'Technological Discontinuities and Organizational Environments'. *Administrative Sciences Quarterly* 31: 439–465.

Ullman, E., and C. D. Harris. 1945. 'The Nature of Cities'. *The ANNALS of the American Academy of Political and Social Sciences* 242: 7–17.

Umpleby, S. A. 2007. 'Academic Globalization: The Growth of International Collaboration in Education and Research'. Paper presented at the 11th World Multi-Conference on Systematics, Cybernetics, and Informatics, Orlando, FL, 8–12 July.

UNCTAD. 2001. *World Investment Report 2001, Promoting Linkages*. New York, NY; Geneva: UN.

UNDP. 2009. *Human Development Report 2009*. New York, NY: UNDP. Available at http://hdr.undp.org/en/reports/global/hdr2009/ (accessed on 15 January 2020).

UNFPA. 2007. *State of the World Population: Unleashing the Potential of Urban Growth*. New York, NY: United Nations Population Fund. Available at http://www.unfpa.org/swp/2007/ (accessed on 15 January 2020).

UN-Habitat. 2010. 'Urban Trends: Urban Corridors-Shape of Things to Come?' (UN-Habitat Press Release, Nairobi, 13 March).

Urry, J. 2000. *Sociology beyond Societies: Mobilities for the Twenty-First Century*. London: Routledge.

Uzzi, B. 1996. 'The Sources and Consequences of Embeddedness for the Economic Performance of Organizations: The Network Effect'. *American Sociological Review* 61: 674–698.

van den Berg, L., R. Drewett, L. H. Klassenn, A. Rossi, and C. H. T. Vijverberg. 1982. *Urban Europe: A Study of Growth and Decline*. Vol. 1. Oxford: Pergamon.

Van der Laan, L. 1998. 'Changing Urban Systems: An Empirical Analysis at Two Spatial Levels'. *Regional Studies* 32: 235–247.

Van Duijn. 1993. *Economic Long Wave and Innovation* [in Chinese]. Shanghai: Shanghai Translation Publishing House.

Van Oort, F. G., M. J. Burger, and O. Raspe. 2010. 'On the Economic Foundation of the Urban Network Paradigm, Spatial Integration, Functional Integration and Economic Complementarities within the Dutch Randstad'. *Urban Studies* 47: 725–748.

Vega-Redondo, F. 1996. *Evolution, Games and Economic Behavior*. Oxford: Oxford University Press.

Veneri, P., and D. Burgalassi. 2012. 'Questioning Polycentric Development and Its Effects, Issues of Definition and Measurement for the Italian NUTS–2 Regions'. *European Planning Studies* 20: 1017–1037.

Venturelli, S. 2004. *From the Information Economy to the Creative Economy*. New York, NY: Center for Arts and Culture.

Vertovec, S. 1999. 'Conceiving and Researching Transnationalism'. *Ethnic and Racial Studies* 22 (2): 447–462.

Wagner, C. S., and L. Leydesdorff. 2005. 'Network Structure, Self-Organization, and the Growth of International Collaboration in Science'. *Research Policy* 34: 1608–1618.

———. 2006. 'Measuring the Globalization of Knowledge Networks'. Presented at Blue Sky II Forum 2006: What Indicators for Science, Technology and Innovation Policies in the 21st Century? Ottawa, Ontario, Canada.

Wall, R. S. 2009. *Netscape: Cities and Global Corporate Networks*. Rotterdam: Haveka.

Wall, R. S., M. J. Burger, and G. A. van der Knaap. 2008. *National Competitiveness as a Determinant of the Geography of Global Corporate Networks*. Available at http://www.lboro.ac.uk/gawc/rb/rb285.html (accessed on 15 January 2020).

———. 2011. 'The Geography of Global Corporate Networks: The Poor, the Rich and the Happy Few'. *Environment and Planning A* 43 (4): 904–927.

Wall, R. S., and G. A. van der Knaap. 2011. 'Sectoral Differentiation and Network Structure within Contemporary Worldwide Corporate Networks'. *Economic Geography* 87: 267–308.

Wallerstein, I. 1974. *The Modern World-System*. New York, NY: Academic Press.

———. 1979. *The Capitalist World-Economy*. Cambridge: Cambridge University Press.

———. 1983. *Historical Capitalism*. London: Verso.

———. 1984. *Politics of the World-Economy*. Cambridge: Cambridge University Press.

———. 2004. *World-Systems Analysis: An Introduction*. Durham, NC: Duke University Press.

Wang, Chia-Huang. 2003. 'Taipei as a Global City: A Theoretical and Empirical Examination'. *Urban Studies* 40 (2): 309–334.

Warf, B. 1989. 'Telecommunications and the Globalization of Financial Services'. *Professional Geographer* 41 (3): 257–271.

Wasserstrom, J. N. 2009. *Global Shanghai, 1850–2010: A History in Fragments*. New York, NY: Routledge.

Watson, A., and M. Hoyler. 2010. 'Media Centres in the World Economy'. In *Global Urban Analysis: A Survey of Cities in Globalization*, edited by P. J. Taylor, P. Ni, B. Derudder, M. Hoyler, J. Huang, and F. Witlox, 40–47. London: Earthscan.

Wei, B. P. T. 1987. *Shanghai: Crucible of Modern China*. Hong Kong: Oxford University Press.

Weibull, J. W. 1995. *Evolutionary Game Theory*. Cambridge, MA: MIT Press.

Weise, P. 1996. 'Evolution and Self-Organization'. *Journal of Institutional Theoretical Economics* 152: 716–722.

Welsch, W. 1999. 'Transculturality: The Puzzling Form of Cultures Today'. In *Spaces of Culture*, edited by M. Featherstone and S. Lash, 194–213. London: SAGE Publications.

Wheeler, S. M., and T. Beatley, eds. 2004. *The Sustainable Urban Development Reader*. Abingdon; New York, NY: Routledge.

Willcocks, L., and M. Lacity. 1998. *Strategic Sourcing of Information Systems*. Chichester: Wiley.

Williams, J., and S. Brunn. 2004. 'Cybercities of Asia: Measuring Globalization using Hyperlinks (Asian Cities and Hyperlinks)'. *Asian Geographer* 23 (1–2): 121–147.

Wilson, A. 2008. 'Urban and Regional Dynamics–3: "DNA" and "Genes" as a Basis for Constructing a Typology of Areas' (CASA Working Paper No. 130, Centre for Advanced Spatial Analysis (UCL), London).

Winter, S. G. 1964. 'Economics Natural Selection, and the Theory of the Firm'. *Yale Economic Essays* 4: 225–272.

Wirth, L. 1938. 'Urbanism as a Way of Life'. *American Journal of Sociology* 44: 1–24.

Witt, U. 1985. 'Coordination of Individual Economic Activities as an Evolving Process of Self-Organization'. *Economie Appliquee* 37: 569–595.

———. 1987. 'How Transaction Rights Are Shaped to Channel Innovativeness'. *Journal of Institutional and Theoretical Economics* 143: 180–195.

———. 1993. 'Emergence and Dissemination of Innovations'. In *Nonlinear Dynamics and Evolutionary Economics*, edited by R. Day and P. Chen, 91–100. Oxford: Oxford University Press.

———. 2001. 'Evolutionary Economics: An Interpretative Survey'. In *Evolutionary Economics: Program and Scope*, edited by Kurt Dopfer. Boston, MA: Kluwer Academic Publishers.

Wójcik, D. 2011. 'Securitization and Its Footprint: The Rise of the US Securities Industry Centres 1998–2007'. *Journal of Economic Geography* 11: 925–947.

———. 2013. 'The Dark Side of NY-LON: Financial Centres and the Global Financial Crisis'. *Urban Studies*. doi:10.1177/0042098012474513

Wood, P. A. 2002. 'Knowledge-Intensive Services and Urban Innovativeness'. *Urban Studies* 39: 993–1002.

Woods, R. 1993. 'Classics in Human Geography Revisited: Commentary 1'. *Progress in Human Geography* 17 (2): 213–215.

Wu, J., and I. Radbone. 2005. 'Global Integration and the Intra-Urban Determinants of Foreign Direct Investment in Shanghai'. *Cities* 22 (4): 275–286.

Wu, N., and E. A. Silva. 2011. 'Urban DNA: Exploring the Biological Metaphor of Urban Evolution with DG-ABC Model'. Paper Sessions of the 14th AGILE International Conference on Geographic Information Science, Utrecht.

Yates, R. 1997. 'The City-State in Ancient China'. In *The Archaeology of City-States: Cross-Cultural Approach*, edited by D. Nicholas and T. Charlton. Washington, DC: Smithsonian Institution Press.

Yatsko, P. 2001. *New Shanghai: The Rocky Rebirth of China's Legendary City*. Fusionopolis Walk: John Wiley & Sons.

Yeaple, S. R. 2006. 'Offshoring, Foreign Direct Investment, and the Structure of U.S. Trade'. *Journal of the European Economic Association* 4: 602–611.

Yeung, H. W. C. 1998. 'Capital, State and Space: Contesting the Borderless World'. *Transactions of the Institute of British Geographers* 23: 291–309.

———. 2005. 'Organizational Space: A New Frontier in International Business Strategy?' *Critical Perspectives on International Business* 1: 219–240.

Yeung, Y. 1996. 'An Asian Perspective on the Global City'. *International Social Science Journal* 147: 25–31.

Yusuf, S., and W. Wu. 2002. 'Pathways to a World City: Shanghai Rising in an Era of Globalisation'. *Urban Studies* 39: 1213–1240.

Z/Yen Group. 2010. *Global Financial Centres Index* 7. London: Corporation of London.

Zelinsky, W. 1971. 'The Hypothesis of the Mobility Transition'. *Geographical Review* 61 (2): 219–249.

Zhang, Zhongli. 2008. *The Researches on Modern Shanghai (1840–1949)*. Shanghai: Shanghai Literature and Art Publishing House.

Zhao, S. X. B., L. Zhang, and D. T. Wang. 2004. 'Determining Factors of the Development of a National Financial Center: The Case of China'. *Geoforum* 35 (5): 577–592.

Zheng, Xiaoying, and Lixin Chen. 2006. 'The Characteristics of China's Aging Population and Its Policy Thinking'. *China's General Practice* 9 (23).

Zhou, Zhenhua. 2008. *The Rising Global Cities*. Shanghai: Shanghai People's Publishing House; Truth & Wisdom Press.

Zhou, Zhenhua et al. 2010. *Shanghai: Urban Transmutation and Prospect* (Trilogy). Shanghai: Shanghai People's Publishing House; Truth & Wisdom Press.

Zook, M., and S. Brunn. 2006. 'From Podes to Antipodes: Positionalities and Global Air Line Geographies'. *Annals of the Association of American Geographers* 96 (3): 471–490.

ABOUT THE AUTHOR

ZHOU Zhenhua is currently the Dean of Shanghai Institute for Global City, the People's Republic of China. He is an economist and was, until recently, the Director of the Development Research Center, Shanghai Municipal People's Government. He is also the President of Shanghai Economic Society. He graduated from Mudanjiang Teachers College in 1982 and Fujian Normal University in 1985, receiving a bachelor's degree in law and a master's degree in economics, respectively. During 1985–1987, he taught at the Department of Economics in Nanjing University. He completed his doctorate in Economics from Renmin University of China, in 1990.

ZHOU has taught and served as the Deputy Director at the Institute of Economic Research, Shanghai Academy of Social Sciences. For about three decades, he has been engaged in the study of urban development strategies and policies and has published several books and journal articles. The books he has published include: *The Development of Service Economy: A General Trend of the Changing Economy in China* (2015) and the edited volume *World City: International Lessons and Shanghai's Development* (2004).